D0830702

I am the Light of the world. So if you follow me, you won't be stumbling through the darkness, for living light will flood your path.

—John 8:12

> *I am bringing all my energies to bear on this one thing: forgetting the past . . . I strain to reach the end of the race and receive the prize for which God is calling us up to heaven.*

Father, I want them with me – these you've given me – so that they can see my glory. You gave me the glory because you loved me before the world began. / I know the one in whom I trust, and I am sure that he is able to guard safely all that I have given him until the day of his return. / God who began the good work within you will keep right on helping you grow in his grace until his task within you is finally finished on that day when Jesus Christ returns.

In a race, everyone runs but only one person gets first prize. So run your race to win. To win the contest you must deny yourselves many things that would keep you from doing your best. An athlete goes to all this trouble just to win a ribbon or a silver cup, but we do it for a heavenly reward that never disappears. / Let us strip off anything that slows us down or holds us back, and especially those sins that wrap themselves so tightly around our feet and trip us up; and let us run with patience the particular race that God has set before us. Keep your eyes on Jesus, our leader and instructor.

Phil. 3:13, 14. Jn. 17:24. 2 Tim. 1:12. Phil. 1:6. 1 Cor. 9:24, 25. Hebr. 12:1, 2.

*Don't be afraid, for the Lord will go before you
and will be with you; he will not fail nor forsake
you.*

If you aren't going with us, don't let us move a step
from this place. / O Lord, I know it is not within the
power of man to map his life and plan his course.

The steps of good men are directed by the Lord. He
delights in each step they take. If they fall it isn't fatal,
for the Lord holds them with his hand.

You love me! You are holding my right hand! You
will keep on guiding me all my life with your wisdom
and counsel; and afterwards receive me into the glories
of heaven! / For I am convinced that nothing can ever
separate us from his love. Death can't, and life can't.
The angels won't, and all the powers of hell itself cannot
keep God's love away. Our fears for today, our worries
about tomorrow, or where we are – high above the
sky, or in the deepest ocean – nothing will ever be able
to separate us from the love of God demonstrated by
our Lord Jesus Christ when he died for us.

*Deut. 31:8. Ex. 33:15. Jer. 10:23. Ps. 37:23, 24. Ps. 73:23, 24.
Rom. 8:38, 39.*

Sing a new song to the Lord.

The Lord makes us strong! Sing praises! Sing to Israel's God! Sing, accompanied by drums; pluck the sweet lyre and harp. / He has given me a new song to sing, of praises to our God. Now many will hear of the glorious things he did for me, and stand in awe before the Lord, and put their trust in him.

Be bold and strong! Banish fear and doubt! For remember, the Lord your God is with you wherever you go. / The joy of the Lord is your strength. / Paul . . . thanked God and took courage.

The night is far gone, the day of his return will soon be here. So discard the evil deeds of darkness and put on the armour of right living, as we who live in the daylight should. Be decent and true in everything you do so that all can approve your behaviour. Don't spend your time in wild parties and getting drunk or in adultery and lust, or fighting, or jealousy. But ask the Lord Jesus Christ to help you live as you should, and don't make plans to enjoy evil.

Is. 42:10. Ps. 81:1, 2. Ps. 40:3. Josh. 1:9. Neh. 8:10. Acts 28:15. Rom. 13:12–14.

Regard my prayer as my evening sacrifice and as incense wafting up to you.

Make a small altar for burning incense. It shall be made from acacia wood. Place the altar just outside the veil, near the place of mercy that is above the Ark containing the Ten Commandments. I will meet with you there. Every morning when Aaron trims the lamps, he shall burn sweet spices on the altar, and each evening when he lights the lamps he shall burn the incense before the Lord, and this shall go on from generation to generation.

(Jesus) is able to save completely all who come to God through him. Since he will live forever, he will always be there to remind God that he has paid for their sins with his blood. / The perfume of the incense mixed with prayers ascended up to God from the altar where the angel had poured them out.

You have become living building-stones for God's use in building his house. What's more, you are his holy priests; so come to him (you are acceptable to him because of Jesus Christ) and offer to God those things that please him.

Always keep on praying.

Ps. 141:2. Ex. 30:1, 6–8. Heb. 7:25. Rev. 8:4. 1 Pet. 2:5. 1 Thess. 5:17.

He led them straight to safety and a place to live.

God protected (Israel) in the howling wilderness as though they were the apple of his eye. He spreads his wings over them, even as an eagle covers her young. She carries them upon her wings – as does the Lord his people. The Lord alone was leading them. / I will be your God through all your lifetime, yes, even when your hair is white with age. I made you and I will care for you. I will carry you along and be your Saviour.

He restores my failing health. He helps me do what honours him the most. Even when walking through the dark valley of death I will not be afraid, for you are close beside me, guarding, guiding all the way.

The Lord will guide you continually, and satisfy you with all good things, and keep you healthy too; and you will be like a well-watered garden, like an ever-flowing spring. / For this great God is our God forever and ever. He will be our guide until we die. / Who is a teacher like him?

Ps. 107:7. Deut. 32:10–12. Is. 46:4. Ps. 23:3, 4. Is. 58:11. Ps. 48:14. Job 36:22.

Jesus asked the man, 'What do you want?'
'Lord,' he pleaded, 'I want to have my sight.'

Open my eyes to see wonderful things in your Word. Then he opened their minds to understand at last these many Scriptures. / But when the Father sends the Comforter to represent me – and by the Comforter I mean the Holy Spirit – he will teach you much, as well as remind you of everything I myself have told you. / But whatever is good and perfect comes to us from God, the creator of all light, and he shines for ever without change or shadow.

God, the glorious Father of our Lord Jesus Christ . . . give you wisdom to see clearly and really understand who Christ is and all that he has done for you. I pray that your hearts will be flooded with light so that you can see something of the future he has called you to share. I want you to realize that God has been made rich because we who are Christ's have been given to him! I pray that you will begin to understand how incredibly great his power is to help those who believe him. It is that same mighty power that raised Christ from the dead and seated him in the place of honour at God's right hand in heaven.

Lk. 18:41. Ps. 119:18. Lk. 24:45. Jn. 14:26. Jas. 1:17. Eph. 1:17–20.

Until you arrive in the place of rest the Lord will give to you.

This is no more your land and home. / There is a full, complete rest still waiting for the people of God. / Behind the sacred curtains of heaven, where Christ has gone ahead to plead for us.

There are many homes up there where my Father lives, and I am going to prepare them for your coming. When everything is ready, then I will come and get you, so that you can always be with me where I am. / To go and be with Christ. How much happier for me than being here!

He will wipe away all tears from their eyes, and there shall be no more death, or sorrow, or crying, or pain. All of that has gone for ever. / In death the wicked cease from troubling, and there the weary are at rest.

Store your profits . . . in heaven where they will never lose their value, and are safe from thieves. If your profits are in heaven your heart will be there too. / Let heaven fill your thoughts; don't spend your time worrying about things down here.

Deut. 12:9. Mic. 2:10. Hebr. 4:9. Hebr. 6:19, 20. Jn. 14:2, 3. Phil. 1:23. Rev. 21:4. Job 3:17. Mt. 6:19–21. Col. 3:2.

O death, where then your victory? Where then your sting?

Sin – the sting that causes death. / He came once for all, at the end of the age, to put away the power of sin for ever by dying for us. And just as it is destined that men die only once, and after that comes judgment, so also Christ died only once as an offering for the sins of many people; and he will come again, but not to deal again with our sins. This time he will come bringing salvation to all those who are eagerly and patiently waiting for him.

Since we, God's children, are human beings – made of flesh and blood – he became flesh and blood too by being born in human form; for only as a human being could he die and in dying break the power of the devil who had the power of death. Only in that way could he deliver those who through fear of death have been living all their lives as slaves to constant dread.

My time has almost run out. Very soon now I will be on my way to heaven. I have fought long and hard for my Lord. . . . Now the time has come for me to stop fighting and rest. In heaven a crown is waiting for me.

1 Cor. 15:55. 1 Cor. 15:56. Heb. 9:26–28. Heb. 2:14, 15. 2 Tim. 4:6–8.

Only we who believe God can enter into his place of rest.

They wear themselves out with all their sinning. / There is something else deep within me, in my lower nature, that is at war with my mind and wins the fight and makes me a slave to the sin that is still within me. In my mind I want to be God's willing servant but instead I find myself still enslaved to sin. So you see how it is: my new life tells me to do right, but the old nature that is still inside me loves to sin. Oh, what a terrible predicament I'm in! Who will free me from my slavery to this deadly lower nature?

Come to me and I will give you rest – all of you who work so hard beneath a heavy yoke. / Since we have been made right in God's sight by faith in his promises, we can have real peace with him because of what Jesus Christ our Lord has done for us. . . . We confidently and joyfully look forward actually to becoming all that God has had in mind for us to be. / No longer counting on being saved by being good enough or by obeying God's laws, but by trusting Christ to save me; for God's way of making us right with himself depends on faith – counting on Christ alone.

They could have rest . . . if they would obey.

Hebr. 4:3. Jer. 9:5. Rom. 7:23, 24. Mt. 11:28. Rom. 5:1, 2. Phil. 3:9. Is. 28:12.

Help me, Lord, to keep my mouth shut and my lips sealed.

Lord, if you keep in mind our sins then who can ever get an answer to his prayers?

You aren't made unholy by eating non-kosher food! It is what you *say* and *think* that makes you unclean.

Gossip separates the best of friends. / Some people like to make cutting remarks, but the words of the wise soothe and heal. Truth stands the test of time; lies are soon exposed. / No human being can tame the tongue. It is always ready to pour out its deadly poison. And so blessing and cursing come pouring out of the same mouth. Dear brothers, surely this is not right!

Now is the time to cast off and throw away all these rotten garments of anger, hatred, cursing, and dirty language. Don't tell lies to each other; it was your old life with all its wickedness that did that sort of thing; now it is dead and gone. / God wants you to be holy and pure.

Gentle words cause life and health.

Ps. 141:3. Ps. 130:3. Mt. 15:11. Prov. 16:28. Prov. 12:18, 19. Jas. 3:8, 10. Col. 3:8, 9. 1 Thess. 4:3. Prov. 15:4.

Let the Lord our God favour us and give us success.

Your reputation was great among the nations for your beauty; it was perfect because of all the gifts I gave you, says the Lord God. / We Christians have no veil over our faces; we can be mirrors that brightly reflect the glory of the Lord. / And as the Spirit of the Lord works within us, we become more and more like him.

Blessings on all who reverence and trust the Lord – on all who obey him! Their reward shall be prosperity and happiness. / Commit your work to the Lord, then it will succeed.

Do the good things that result from being saved, obeying God with deep reverence, shrinking back from all that might displease him. For God is at work within you, helping you want to obey him, and then helping you do what he wants. / May our Lord Jesus Christ himself and God our Father, who has loved us and given us everlasting comfort and hope which we don't deserve, comfort your hearts with all comfort, and help you in every good thing you say and do.

Ps. 90:17. Ezk. 16:14. 2 Cor. 3:18. Ps. 128:1, 2. Prov. 16:3. Phil. 2:12, 13. 2 Thess. 2:16, 17.

The apostles now returned to Jesus . . . and told him all they had done.

The Lord spoke to Moses face to face, as a man speaks to his friend. / And you are my friends if you obey me. I no longer call you slaves, for a master doesn't confide in his slaves; now you are my friends, proved by the fact that I have told you everything the Father told me.

If you merely obey me, you should not consider yourselves worthy of praise. For you have simply done your duty!

We should not be like cringing, fearful slaves, but we should behave like God's very own children, adopted into the bosom of his family, and calling to him, 'Father, Father.' / And because we are his sons God has sent the Spirit of his Son into our hearts, so now we can rightly speak of God as our dear Father. Now we are no longer slaves, but God's own sons. And since we are his sons, everything he has belongs to us, for that is the way God planned.

Don't worry about anything; instead, pray about everything; tell God your needs and don't forget to thank him for his answers. / The Lord . . . delights in the prayers of his people.

Mk. 6:30. Ex. 33:11. Jn. 15:14, 15. Lk. 17:10. Rom. 8:15. Gal. 4:6, 7. Phil. 4:6. Prov. 15:8.

O my God, please keep in mind all that I've done.

The Lord says, I remember how eager you were to please me as a young bride long ago and how you loved me and followed me even through the barren deserts. / I will keep the pledge I made to you when you were young. I will establish an everlasting covenant with you forever. / I will come and do for you all the good things I have promised, and bring you home again. For I know the plans I have for you, says the Lord. They are plans for good and not for evil, to give you a future and a hope. In those days when you pray, I will listen. You will find me when you seek me, if you look for me in earnest.

For just as the heavens are higher than the earth, so are my ways higher than yours, and my thoughts than yours. / Go to God and confess your sins to him. For he does wonderful miracles, marvels without number. / O Lord my God, many and many a time you have done great miracles for us, and we are ever in your thoughts. Who else can do such glorious things? No one else can be compared with you. There isn't time to tell of all your wonderful deeds.

Neh. 5:19. Jer. 2:2. Ezk. 16:60. Jer. 29:10–13. Is. 55:9. Job 5:8, 9. Ps. 40:5.

I will not abandon you or fail to help you.

Every good thing the Lord had promised them came true.

God is not a man, that he should lie; he doesn't change his mind like humans do. Has he ever promised, without doing what he said?

Understand, therefore, that the Lord your God is the faithful God who for a thousand generations keeps his promises and constantly loves those who love him and who obey his commands. / He never forgets his promises. / So don't be anxious about tomorrow. God will take care of your tomorrow too. Live one day at a time.

Can a mother forget her little child and not have love for her own son? Yet even if that should be, I will not forget you. See, I have tattooed your name upon my palm.

For the Lord your God has arrived to live among you. He is a mighty Saviour. He will give you victory. He will rejoice over you in great gladness; he will love you and not accuse you. Is that a joyous choir I hear? No, it is the Lord himself exulting over you in happy song.

Josh. 1:5. Josh. 21:45. Num. 23:19. Deut. 7:9. Ps. 111:5. Mt. 6:34. Is. 49:15, 16. Zeph. 3:17.

All those who know your mercy, Lord, will count on you for help. For you have never yet forsaken those who trust in you.

The Lord is a strong fortress. The good men run to him and are safe. / I will trust and not be afraid, for the Lord is my strength and song; he is my salvation.

I have been young and now I am old. And in all my years I have never seen the Lord forsake a man who loves him; nor have I seen the children of the godly go hungry. / For the Lord loves justice and fairness; he will never abandon his people. They will be kept safe forever; but all who love wickedness shall perish. / The Lord will not abandon his chosen people, for that would dishonour his great name. He made you a special nation for himself – just because he wanted to! / And he did help us, and saved us from a terrible death; yes, and we expect him to do it again and again.

Be satisfied with what you have. For God has said, I will never, *never* fail you nor forsake you. That is why we can say without any doubt or fear, 'The Lord is my helper and I am not afraid of anything that mere man can do to me.'

Ps. 9:10. Prov. 18:10. Is. 12:2. Ps. 37:25. Ps. 37:28. 1 Sam. 12:22. 2 Cor. 1:10. Hebr. 13:5, 6.

No falsehood can be charged against them; they are blameless.

No sin shall be found in Israel or in Judah, for I will pardon the remnant I preserve. / Where is another God like you, who pardons the sins of the survivors among his people? You cannot stay angry with your people, for you love to be merciful. Once again you will have compassion on us. You will tread our sins beneath your feet; you will throw them into the depths of the ocean!

We belong to his dearly loved Son. / Christ has brought you into the very presence of God, and you are standing there before him with nothing left against you – nothing left that he could even chide you for. The only condition is that you fully believe the truth, standing in it steadfast and firm, strong in the Lord, convinced of the Good News that Jesus died for you, and never shifting from trusting him to save you.

And now – all glory to him who alone is God, who saves us through Jesus Christ our Lord; yes, splendour and majesty, all power and authority are his from the beginning; his they are and his they evermore shall be. And he is able to keep you from slipping and falling away, and to bring you, sinless and perfect, into his glorious presence with mighty shouts of everlasting joy. Amen.

Rev. 14:5. Jer. 50:20. Mic. 7:18, 19. Eph. 1:6. Col. 1:22, 23. Jude 24, 25.

You have given us a banner to rally to; all who love
truth will rally to it.

Jehovah-nissi (meaning Jehovah is my flag). / They
will reverence and glorify the name of God from west
to east. For he will come like a flood-tide driven by
Jehovah's breath.

May there be shouts of joy when we hear the news of
your victory, flags flying with praise to God for all
that he has done for you. / The Lord has vindicated us.
Come, let us declare in Jerusalem all the Lord our God
has done. / Overwhelming victory is ours through
Christ who loved us enough to die for us. / How we
thank God for all of this! It is he who makes us victorious
through Jesus Christ our Lord! / Jesus, a perfect leader.

I want to remind you that your strength must come
from the Lord's mighty power within you. / Prove
yourself to be a real soldier by fighting the Lord's
battles. / 'Take courage and work, for I am with you,'
says the Lord of the armies of heaven. 'Don't be
afraid.' / Look around you! Vast fields are ripening
all around us, and are ready now for reaping. / His
coming will not be delayed much longer.

Ps. 60:4. Ex. 17:15. Is. 59:19. Ps. 20:5. Jer. 51:10. Rom. 8:37. 1 Cor.
15:57. Hebr. 2:10. Eph. 6:10. 1 Sam. 18:17. Hag. 2:4, 5. Jn. 4:35.
Heb. 10:37.

Only one thing worth being concerned about.

Many say that God will never help us. Prove them wrong, O Lord, by letting the light of your face shine down upon us. Yes, the gladness you have given me is far greater than their joys at harvest time as they gaze at their bountiful crops.

As the deer pants for water, so I long for you, O God. I thirst for God, the living God. / O God, my God! How I search for you! How I thirst for you in this parched and weary land where there is no water.

'I am the Bread of Life. No one coming to me will ever be hungry again. Those believing in me will never thirst.' 'Sir, give us that bread every day of our lives!' / Mary sat on the floor, listening to Jesus as he talked. / The one thing I want from God, the thing I seek most of all, is the privilege of meditating in his Temple, living in his presence every day of my life, delighting in his incomparable perfections and glory. / Your goodness and unfailing kindness shall be with me all of my life, and afterwards I will live with you for ever in your home.

Lk. 10:42. Ps. 4:6, 7. Ps. 42:1, 2. Ps. 63:1. Jn. 6:35, 34. Lk. 10:39. Ps. 27:4. Ps. 23:6.

May the God of peace himself make you entirely clean; and may your spirit and soul and body be kept strong and blameless until that day when our Lord Jesus Christ comes back again.

Christ showed (love) to the church when he died for her . . . so that he could give her to himself as a glorious church without a single spot or wrinkle or any other blemish, being holy and without a single fault. / So everywhere we go we talk about Christ to all who will listen, warning them and teaching them as well as we know how. We want to be able to present each one to God, perfect because of what Christ has done for each of them.

God's peace . . . far more wonderful than the human mind can understand. His peace will keep your thoughts and your hearts quiet and at rest as you trust in Christ Jesus. / Let the peace of heart which comes from Christ be always present in your hearts and lives, for this is your responsibility and privilege as members of his body.

Our Lord Jesus Christ himself and God our Father, who has loved us and given us everlasting comfort and hope which we don't deserve, comfort your hearts with all comfort, and help you in every good thing you say and do. / And he guarantees right up to the end that you will be counted free from all sin and guilt on that day when he returns.

1 Thess. 5:23. Eph. 5:25, 27. Col. 1:28. Phil. 4:7. Col. 3:15. 2 Thess. 2:16, 17. 1 Cor. 1:8.

Will God really live upon the earth with men?

I want the people of Israel to make me a sacred Temple where I can live among them. / I will meet with the people of Israel there, and the Tabernacle shall be sanctified by my glory. And I will live among the people of Israel and be their God. / I will bring them home again to live safely in Jerusalem, and they will be my people, and I will be their God, just and true and yet forgiving them their sins!

He ascends the heights, leading many captives in his train. He receives gifts for men, even those who once were rebels. God will live among us here. / We Christians are God's house – he lives in us! – if we keep up our courage firm to the end, and our joy and our trust in the Lord.

You are God's temple, the home of the living God, and God has said of you, 'I will live in them and walk among them, and I will be their God and they shall be my people.' / Your body is the home of the Holy Spirit God gave you. / You also are joined with him and with each other by the Spirit, and are part of this dwelling place of God.

Emmanuel . . . God is with us.

2 Chron. 6:18. Ex. 25:8. Ex. 29:43, 45. Zech. 8:8. Ps. 68:18. Hebr. 3:6.
2 Cor. 6:16. 1 Cor. 6:19. Eph. 2:22. Mt. 1:23.

O God in Zion, we wait before you in silent praise.

We know that there is only one God, the Father, who created all things and made us to be his own; and one Lord Jesus Christ, who made everything and gives us life. / So that everyone will honour the Son, just as they honour the Father. But if you refuse to honour God's Son, whom he sent to you, then you are certainly not honouring the Father. / With Jesus' help we will continually offer our sacrifice of praise to God by telling others of the glory of his name. / True praise is a worthy sacrifice; this really honours me. Those who walk my paths will receive salvation from the Lord.

I saw a vast crowd, too great to count, from all nations and provinces and languages, standing in front of the throne and before the Lamb, clothed in white, with palm branches in their hands. And they were shouting with a mighty shout, 'Salvation comes from our God upon the throne, and from the Lamb,' 'Amen!' they said. 'Blessing, and glory, and wisdom, and thanksgiving, and honour, and power, and might be to our God for ever and for ever. Amen!'

Ps. 65:1. 1 Cor. 8:6. Jn. 5:23. Hebr. 13:15. Ps. 50:23. Rev. 7:9, 10, 12.

He ransoms me from hell.

Their Redeemer is strong. His name is the Lord of heaven's armies. / Shall I ransom him from hell? Shall I redeem him from Death? O Death, bring forth your terrors for his tasting! O Grave, demonstrate your plagues!

Since we, God's children, are human beings – made of flesh and blood – he became flesh and blood too by being born in human form; for only as a human being could he die and in dying break the power of the devil who had the power of death. Only in that way could he deliver those who through fear of death have been living all their lives as slaves to constant dread.

All who trust him – God's Son – to save them have eternal life; those who don't believe and obey him shall never see heaven, but the wrath of God remains upon them.

You should have as little desire for this world as a dead person does. Your real life is in heaven with Christ and God. / And when Christ who is our real life comes back again, you will shine with him and share in all his glories. / When he comes to receive praise and admiration because of all he has done for his people, his saints.

Ps. 103:4. Jer. 50:34. Hos. 13:14. Hebr. 2:14, 15. Jn. 3:36. Col. 3:3, 4. 2 Thess. 1:10.

God, who saves us through Jesus Christ.

Christ Jesus. He showed us God's plan of salvation;
he was the one who made us acceptable to God; he
made us pure and holy and gave himself to purchase
our salvation. / Do you know the mind and purposes
of God? Will long searching make them known to you?
Are you qualified to judge the Almighty? He is as
faultless as heaven is high – but who are you? His mind
is fathomless – what can you know in comparison?

Our words are wise because they are from God,
telling of God's wise plan to bring us into the glories of
heaven. This plan was hidden in former times, though it
was made for our benefit before the world began.

If you want to know what God wants you to do, ask
him, and he will gladly tell you, for he is always ready
to give a generous supply of wisdom to all who ask
him. / Trust the Lord completely; don't ever trust
yourself. In everything you do, put God first, and he
will direct you and crown your efforts with success. / For
God gives those who please him wisdom, knowledge,
and joy.

*Jude 25. 1 Cor. 1:30. Job 11:7, 8. 1 Cor. 2:7. Jas. 1:5. Prov. 3:5, 6.
Eccl. 2:26.*

*When I go to bed I think, Oh, that it were morning,
and then I toss till dawn.*

Watchman, what of the night? The watchman replies,
Your judgment day is dawning now.

His coming will not be delayed much longer. / He
shall be as the light of the morning; a cloudless sunrise
when the tender grass springs forth upon the earth.

There are many homes up there where my Father
lives, and I am going to prepare them for your coming.
When everything is ready, then I will come and get you,
so that you can always be with me where I am. If this
weren't so, I would tell you plainly. I am leaving you
with a gift – peace of mind and heart. And the peace I
give isn't fragile like the peace the world gives. So don't
be troubled or afraid. Remember what I told you – I
am going away, but I will come back to you again.

Let heaven fill your thoughts; don't spend your time
worrying about things down here. You should have as
little desire for this world as a dead person does. Your
real life is in heaven with Christ and God. And when
Christ who is our real life comes back again, you will
shine with him and share in all his glories.

*Job 7:4. Is. 21:11, 12. Hebr. 10:37. 2 Sam. 23:4. Jn. 14:2, 3, 27, 28.
Col. 3:2–4.*

He will keep in perfect peace all those who trust in him, whose thoughts turn often to the Lord!

Give your burdens to the Lord. He will carry them. He will not permit the godly to slip or fall. / I will trust and not be afraid, for the Lord is my strength and song; he is my salvation.

O you men of little faith! Why are you so frightened? / Don't worry about anything; instead, pray about everything; tell God your needs and don't forget to thank him for his answers. If you do this you will experience God's peace, which is far more wonderful than the human mind can understand. His peace will keep your thoughts and your hearts quiet and at rest as you trust in Christ Jesus. / In quietness and confidence is your strength.

Out of justice . . . quietness and confidence will reign for evermore. / I am leaving you with a gift – peace of mind and heart! And the peace I give isn't fragile like the peace the world gives. So don't be troubled or afraid. / Grace and peace from God who is, and was, and is to come!

Is. 26:3. Ps. 55:22. Is. 12:2. Mt. 8:26. Phil. 4:6, 7. Is. 30:15. Is. 32:17. Jn. 14:27. Rev. 1:4.

Don't let the sun go down with you still angry.

'If a brother sins against you, go to him privately and confront him with his fault. If he listens and confesses it, you have won back a brother. . . .' 'Sir, how often should I forgive a brother who sins against me? Seven times?' 'No,' Jesus replied, 'seventy times seven!'

When you are praying, first forgive anyone you are holding a grudge against, so that your Father in heaven will forgive you your sins too.

Since you have been chosen by God who has given you this new kind of life, and because of his deep love and concern for you, you should practise tender-hearted mercy and kindness to others. Don't worry about making a good impression on them but be ready to suffer quietly and patiently. Be gentle and ready to forgive; never hold grudges. Remember, the Lord forgave you, so you must forgive others. / Be kind to each other, tenderhearted, forgiving one another, just as God has forgiven you because you belong to Christ.

Eph. 4:26. Mt. 18:15, 21, 22. Mk. 11:25. Col. 3:12, 13. Eph. 4:32.

My Father is greater than I am.

This is the prayer he taught them: 'Father, may your name be honoured.' My Father and your Father, my God and your God.

I will freely do what the Father requires of me. / Don't you believe that I am in the Father and the Father is in me? The words I say are not my own but are from my Father who lives in me. And he does his work through me.

The Father loves this man because he is his Son, and God has given him everything there is. / For you have given him authority over every man and woman in all the earth. He gives eternal life to each one you have given him.

'Sir, show us the Father and we will be satisfied.' Jesus replied: 'Don't you even yet know who I am, Philip, even after all this time I have been with you? Anyone who has seen me has seen the Father. So why are you asking to see him? Don't you believe that I am in the Father and the Father is in me?' / I and the Father are one. / I have loved you even as the Father has loved me. Live within my love. When you obey me you are living in my love, just as I obey my Father and live in his love.

Jn. 14:28. Lk. 11:2. Jn. 20:17. Jn. 14:31. Jn. 14:10. Jn. 3:35. Jn. 17:2. Jn. 14:8–10. Jn. 10:30. Jn. 15:9, 10.

*He shall strike you on your head, while you will
strike at his heel.*

My Servant beaten and bloodied, so disfigured one
would scarcely know it was a person standing there. /
He was wounded and bruised for our sins. He was
chastised that we might have peace; he was lashed –
and we were healed!

This is your moment – the time when Satan's power
reigns supreme. / You would have no power at all over
me unless it were given to you from above.

Since we, God's children, are human beings – made
of flesh and blood – he became flesh and blood too
by being born in human form; for only as a human
being could he die and in dying break the power of the
devil who had the power of death. / The Son of God
came to destroy these works of the Devil. / Jesus . . .
ordered many demons to come out of their victims.
(But he refused to allow the demons to speak, because
they knew who he was.)

I have been given all authority in heaven and earth. /
Those who believe shall use my authority to cast out
demons.

The God of peace will soon crush Satan under your
feet.

*Gen. 3:15. Is. 52:14. Is. 53:5. Lk. 22:53. Jn. 19:11. Hebr. 2:14. 1 Jn. 3:8.
Mk. 1:34. Mt. 28:18. Mk. 16:17. Rom. 16:20.*

I am completely discouraged – I lie in the dust.
Revive me by your Word.

Since you became alive again, so to speak, when Christ
arose from the dead, now set your sights on the rich
treasures and joys of heaven. Let heaven fill your
thoughts; don't spend your time worrying about things
down here. Your real life is in heaven with Christ and
God. / Our homeland is in heaven, with our Saviour
the Lord Jesus Christ in heaven and we are looking
forward to his return from there. When he comes back
he will take these dying bodies of ours and change them
into glorious bodies like his own, using the same mighty
power that he will use to conquer all else everywhere.

We naturally love to do evil things that are just the
opposite of the things that the Holy Spirit tells us to
do. / Dear brothers, you have no obligations whatever
to your old sinful nature to do what it begs you do. For
if you keep on following it you are lost and will perish,
but if through the power of the Holy Spirit you crush
it and its evil deeds, you shall live. / You are only
visitors here. Since your real home is in heaven I beg
you to keep away from the evil pleasures of this world;
they are not for you, for they fight against your very
souls.

*Ps. 119:25. Col. 3:1–3. Phil. 3:20, 21. Gal. 5:17. Rom. 8:12, 13. 1 Pet.
2:11.*

The faith God has given you.

His faith is weak. / His faith and trust grew ever stronger, and he praised God.

O man of little faith. Why did you doubt? / Your faith is large, and your request is granted.

'Do you believe I can make you see?' 'Yes, Lord,' they told him, 'we do.' 'Because of your faith it will happen.'

We need more faith. / Build up your lives ever more strongly upon the foundation of our holy faith. / Let your roots grow down into him and draw up nourishment from him. See that you go on growing in the Lord, and become strong and vigorous in the truth. / It is this God who has made you and me into faithful Christians. / After you have suffered a little while, our God, who is full of kindness through Christ, will give you his eternal glory. He personally will come and pick you up, and set you firmly in place, and make you stronger than ever.

We must bear the 'burden' of being considerate of the doubts and fears of others. Let's please the other fellow, not ourselves. / Don't criticise each other . . . Try instead to live in such a way that you will never make your brother stumble by letting him see you doing something he thinks is wrong.

Rom. 12:3. Rom. 14:1. Rom. 4:20. Mt. 14:31. Mt. 15:28. Mt. 9:28, 29. Lk. 17:5. Jude 20. Col. 2:7. 2 Cor. 1:21. 1 Pet. 5:10. Rom. 15:1. Rom. 14:13.

God wanted all of himself to be in his Son.

The Father loves . . . his Son, and God has given him
everything there is. / God raised him up to the heights
of heaven and gave him a name which is above every
other name, that at the name of Jesus every knee shall
bow in heaven and on earth and under the earth, and
every tongue shall confess that Jesus Christ is Lord, to
the glory of God the Father. / Far, far above any other
king or ruler or dictator or leader. Yes, his honour is
far more glorious than that of anyone else either in this
world or in the world to come. / Christ himself is the
Creator who made everything in heaven and earth, the
things we can see and the things we can't; the spirit
world with its kings and kingdoms, its rulers and
authorities: all were made by Christ for his own use
and glory.

Christ died and rose again . . . so that he can be our
Lord both while we live and when we die. / You have
everything when you have Christ, and you are filled
with God through your union with Christ. He is the
highest ruler, with authority over every other power. /
We have all benefited from the rich blessings he brought
to us – blessing upon blessing heaped upon us.

Col. 1:19. Jn. 3:35. Phil. 2:9–11. Eph. 1:21. Col. 1:16. Rom. 14:9.
Col. 2:10. Jn. 1:16.

Write down what you have just seen, and what will soon be shown to you.

It was the Holy Spirit within these godly men who gave them true messages from God. / He told them to write down the events which . . . have happened to Christ: his suffering, and his great glory afterwards. / We are telling you about what we ourselves have actually seen and heard, so that you may share the fellowship and the joys we have with the Father and with Jesus Christ his Son.

'Look at my hands! Look at my feet! You can see that it is I, myself. Touch me and make sure that I am not a ghost. For ghosts don't have bodies, as you see that I do!' As he spoke, he held out his hands for them to see [the marks of the nails], and showed them [the wounds in] his feet. / I saw all this myself and have given an accurate report so that you also can believe.

We have not been telling you fairy tales when we explained to you the power of our Lord Jesus Christ and his coming again. My own eyes have seen his splendour and his glory. / I wanted your faith to stand firmly upon God, not on some man's great ideas.

Rev. 1:19. 2 Pet. 1:21. 1 Pet. 1:11. 1 Jn. 1:3. Lk. 24:39, 40. Jn. 19:35.
2 Pet. 1:16. 1 Cor. 2:5.

*You have lovingly delivered me from death; you
have forgiven all my sins.*

God showed how much he loved us by sending his only
Son into this wicked world to bring to us eternal life
through his death. In this act we see what real love is:
it is not our love for God, but his love for us when he
sent his Son to satisfy God's anger against our sins.

Where is another God like you, who pardons the sins
of the survivors among his people? You cannot stay
angry with your people, for you love to be merciful.
Once again you will have compassion on us. You will
tread our sins beneath your feet; you will throw them
into the depths of the ocean! / O Lord my God, I
pleaded with you, and you gave me my health again.
You brought me back from the brink of the grave, from
death itself, and here I am alive! / When I had lost all
hope, I turned my thoughts once more to the Lord.
And my earnest prayer went to you in your holy
Temple. / I waited patiently for God to help me; then
he listened and heard my cry. He lifted me out of the pit
of despair, out from the bog and the mire, and set my
feet on a hard, firm path and steadied me as I walked
along.

Is. 38:17. 1 Jn. 4:9, 10. Mic. 7:18, 19. Ps. 30:2, 3. Jon. 2:7. Ps. 40:1, 2.

What you have seen.

We can see and understand only a little about God now, as if we were peering at his reflection in a poor mirror; but some day we are going to see him in his completeness, face to face.

We have seen and proved that what the prophets said came true. You will do well to pay close attention to everything they have written, for, like lights shining into dark corners, their words help us to understand many things that otherwise would be dark and difficult. But when you consider the wonderful truth of the prophets' words, then the light will dawn in your souls and Christ the Morning Star will shine in your hearts. / Your words are a flashlight to light the path ahead of me, and keep me from stumbling.

Dear friends, remember what the apostles of our Lord Jesus Christ told you, that in the last times there would come . . . scoffers. / The Holy Spirit tells us clearly that in the last times some in the church will turn away from Christ and become eager followers of teachers with devil-inspired ideas.

Dear children, this world's last hour has come. / The night is far gone, the day of his return will soon be here. Put on the armour of right living.

Rev. 1:19. 1 Cor. 13:12. 2 Pet. 1:19. Ps. 119:105. Jude 17, 18. 1 Tim. 4:1.
1 Jn. 2:18. Rom. 13:12.

Christ . . . yet to come.

Jesus . . . a little lower than the angels – crowned now by God with glory and honour because he suffered death for us. / Christ died for all of us. / Adam caused many to be sinners because he disobeyed God, and Christ caused many to be made acceptable to God because he obeyed.

The first man, Adam, was given a natural, human body but Christ is more than that, for he was life-giving Spirit. / First, then, we have these human bodies and later on God gives us spiritual, heavenly bodies. / God said, Let us make a man – someone like ourselves, to be the master of all life upon the earth and in the skies and in the seas. So God made man like his Maker. Like God did God make man. / In these days he (God) has spoken to us through his Son. . . . All that God's Son is and does marks him as God. / You have given him authority over every man and woman in all the earth.

Adam was made from the dust of the earth, but Christ came from heaven above. Every human being has a body just like Adam's, made of dust, but all who become Christ's will have the same kind of body as his – a body from heaven.

Rom. 5:14. Hebr. 2:9. 2 Cor. 5:14. Rom. 5:19. 1 Cor. 15:45, 46.
Gen. 1:26, 27. Hebr. 1:2, 3. Jn. 17:2. 1 Cor. 15:47, 48.

What will soon be shown to you.

The Scriptures . . . say that no mere man has ever seen, heard or even imagined what wonderful things God has ready for those who love the Lord. But we know about these things because God has sent his Spirit to tell us.

See! He (Christ) is arriving, surrounded by clouds; and every eye shall see him – yes, and those who pierced him. And the nations will weep in sorrow and in terror when he comes. Yes, Amen! Let it be so.

And now, dear brothers, I want you to know what happens to a Christian when he dies, so that when it happens, you will not be full of sorrow, as those who have no hope. For since we believe that Jesus died and then came back to life again, we can also believe that when Jesus returns, God will bring back with him all the Christians who have died. For the Lord himself will come down from heaven with a mighty shout and with the soul-stirring cry of the archangel and the great trumpet-call of God. And the Christians who are dead will be the first to rise to meet the Lord. Then we who are still alive and remain on the earth will be caught up with them in the clouds to meet the Lord in the air and remain with him forever.

Rev. 1:19. 1 Cor. 2:9, 10. Rev. 1:7. 1 Thess. 4:13, 14, 16, 17.

I have done the Lord's work humbly.

Anyone wanting to be a leader among you must be your servant. And if you want to be right at the top, you must serve like a slave. Your attitude must be like my own, for I, the Son of Mankind, did not come to be served, but to serve, and to give my life as a ransom for many.

If anyone thinks he is too great to stoop to this, he is fooling himself. He is really a nobody. / As God's messenger I give each of you God's warning: be honest in your estimate of yourselves, measuring your value by how much faith God has given you. / If you merely obey me, you should not consider yourselves worthy of praise. For you have simply done your duty!

We are so glad that we can say with utter honesty that in all our dealings we have been pure and sincere, quietly depending upon the Lord for his help, and not on our own skills. / This precious treasure – this light and power that now shine within us – is held in a perishable container, that is, in our weak bodies. Everyone can see that the glorious power within must be from God and is not our own.

Acts 20:19. Mt. 20:26–28. Gal. 6:3. Rom. 12:3. Lk. 17:10. 2 Cor. 1:12. 2 Cor. 4:7.

We . . . left God's paths to follow our own.

Noah . . . planted a vineyard, and he made wine. / Abram . . . asked Sarai his wife to tell everyone that she was his sister. 'If you say you are my sister, then the Egyptians will treat me well because of you.' / Isaac: 'The voice is Jacob's, but the hands are Esau's. . . . Are you really Esau?' Jacob (replied), 'Yes, of course.' / Moses . . . became angry and spoke foolishly. / Joshua and the other leaders . . . did not bother to ask the Lord, but went ahead and signed a peace treaty. / David had obeyed God during his entire life except for the affair concerning Uriah the Hittite.

These men . . . trusted God and won his approval. / They could have gone back to the good things of this world. But they didn't want to. / God declares us 'not guilty' of offending him if we trust in Jesus Christ, who in his kindness freely takes away our sins. / God laid on *him* the guilt and sins of every one of us!

But always remember this: It is not for your own sakes that I will do this, but for mine . . . Be utterly ashamed of all that you have done!

Is. 53:6. Gen. 9:20. Gen. 12:11, 13. Gen. 27:22, 24. Ps. 106:32, 33.
Josh. 9:14, 15. 1 Kgs. 15:5. Hebr. 11:39. Hebr. 11:15, 16. Rom. 3:24.
Is. 53:6. Ezk. 36:32.

His royal title: Wonderful.

And Christ took our human nature and lived here on earth among us and was full of loving forgiveness and truth. And some of us have seen his glory – the glory of the only Son of the heavenly Father. / Your promises are backed by all the honour of your name.

He shall be called 'Emmanuel' (meaning 'God is with us'). / Jesus (meaning 'Saviour'), for he will save his people from their sins.

Everyone will honour the Son, just as they honour the Father. / God raised him up to the heights of heaven and gave him a name which is above every other name. / Far, far above any other king or ruler or dictator or leader. Yes, his honour is far more glorious than that of anyone else either in this world or in the world to come. And God has put all things under his feet. / A name was written on his forehead, and only he knew its meaning . . . 'KING OF KINGS AND LORD OF LORDS.'

We cannot imagine the power of the Almighty. / If there is any other, what is his name?

Is. 9:6. Jn. 1:14. Ps. 138:2. Mt. 1:23. Mt. 1:21. Jn. 5:23. Phil. 2:9. Eph. 1:21, 22. Rev. 19:12, 16. Job 37:23. Prov. 30:4.

God's own personal possession.

You belong to Christ, and Christ is God's. / I am my beloved's and I am the one he desires. / I am his. / The Son of God . . . loved me and gave himself for me.

Your own body does not belong to you. For God has bought you with a great price. So use every part of your body to give glory back to God, because he owns it. / The Lord has rescued you from prison . . . to be his special people, his own inheritance: this is what you are today.

You are *God's* garden . . . you are *God's* building. / But Christ, God's faithful Son, in in complete charge of God's house. And we Christians are God's house – he lives in us! – if we keep up our courage firm to the end, and our joy and our trust in the Lord. / Living building-stones . . . his holy priests.

'They shall be mine,' says the Lord of heaven's armies, 'in that day when I make up my jewels.' / And all of them, since they are mine, belong to you; and you have given them back to me with everything else of yours, and so they are my glory.

Deut. 32:9. 1 Cor. 3:23. Song 7:10. Song 2:16. Gal. 2:20. 1 Cor. 6:19, 20.
Deut. 4:20. 1 Cor. 3:9. Hebr. 3:6. 1 Pet. 2:5. Mal. 3:17. Jn. 17:10.

*He prunes those branches that bear fruit for
even larger crops.*

He is like a blazing fire refining precious metal and
he can bleach the dirtiest garments! Like a refiner of
silver he will sit and watch closely as the dross is
burned away.

We can rejoice . . . when we run into problems
and trials, for we know that they are good for us –
they help us learn to be patient. And patience develops
strength of character in us and helps us trust God
more each time we use it until finally our hope and
faith are strong and steady. Then, when that happens,
we are able to hold our heads high no matter what
happens and know that all is well, for we know how
dearly God loves us, and we feel this warm love everywhere within us because God has given us the Holy
Spirit to fill our hearts with his love. / Let God train
you, for he is doing what any loving father does for
his children. Whoever heard of a son who was never
corrected? If God doesn't punish you when you need
it, as other fathers punish their sons, then it means
that you aren't really God's son at all – that you
don't really belong in his family. Being punished isn't
enjoyable while it is happening – it hurts! But afterwards we can see the result, a quiet growth in grace
and character. So take a new grip with your tired
hands, stand firm on your shaky legs.

Jn. 15:2. Mal. 3:2, 3. Rom. 5:3–5. Hebr. 12:7, 8, 11, 12.

*The proud . . . will be burned up like
straw.*

The high and lofty one who inhabits eternity, the
Holy One, says this: I live in that high and holy place
where those with contrite, humble spirits dwell: and I
refresh the humble and give new courage to those with
repentant hearts.

Better poor and humble than proud and rich. /
Humble men are very fortunate . . . for the Kingdom
of Heaven is given to them.

There are six things the Lord hates – no, seven:
haughtiness, etc. / Pride disgusts the Lord.

Search me, O God, and know my heart; test my
thoughts. Point out anything you find in me that makes
you sad, and lead me along the path of everlasting life.

May God bless you all. Yes, I pray that God our
Father and the Lord Jesus Christ will give each of you
his fullest blessings, and his peace in your hearts and
your lives. All my prayers for you are full of praise to
God! / The meek and lowly are fortunate! For the
whole wide world belongs to them.

*Mal. 4:1. Is. 57:15. Prov. 16:19. Mt. 5:3. Prov. 6:16, 17. Prov. 16:5.
Ps. 139:23, 24. Phil. 1:2, 3. Mt. 5:5.*

For this great God is our God forever and ever.
He will be our guide until we die.

O Lord, I will honour and praise your name, for you
are my God: you do such wonderful things! You planned them long ago, and now you have accomplished
them just as you said! / The Lord himself is my
inheritance, my prize. He is my food and drink, my
highest joy!

He helps me do what honours him the most. Even
when walking through the dark valley of death I will
not be afraid, for you are close beside me, guarding,
guiding all the way. / You are holding my right hand!
You will keep on guiding me all my life with your
wisdom and counsel; and afterwards receive me into
the glories of heaven! Whom have I in heaven but
you? And I desire no one on earth as much as you!
My health fails; my spirits droop, yet God remains!
He is the strength of my heart; he is mine forever! / No
wonder we are happy in the Lord! For we are trusting him. We trust his holy name. / The Lord will
work out his plans for my life – for your lovingkindness, Lord, continues forever. Don't abandon me – for
you made me.

Ps. 48:14. Is. 25:1. Ps. 16:5. Ps. 23:3, 4. Ps. 73:23–26. Ps. 33:21.
Ps. 138:8.

*Lord, when doubts fill my mind, when my heart is
in turmoil, quiet me and give me renewed hope
and cheer.*

When my heart is faint and overwhelmed, lead me to
the mighty, towering Rock of safety.

'O God,' I cried, 'I am in trouble – help me.' / Give
your burdens to the Lord. He will carry them. He will
not permit the godly to slip or fall.

I am as a little child who doesn't know his way
around. / If you want to know what God wants you
to do, ask him, and he will gladly tell you.

Who is adequate for such a task? / I am rotten
through and through so far as my old sinful nature is
concerned. / I am with you· that is all you need. My
power shows up best in weak people.

Cheer up, son. I have forgiven your sins! Daughter…
all is well! Your faith has healed you.

I shall be fully satisfied; I will praise you with great
joy . . . I lie awake at night thinking of you – of how
much you have helped me – and how I rejoice through
the night beneath the protecting shadow of your wings.
I follow close behind you, protected by your strong
right arm.

*Ps. 94:19. Ps. 61:2. Is. 38:14. Ps. 55:22. 1 Kgs. 3:7. Jas. 1:5. 2 Cor.
2:16. Rom. 7:18. 2 Cor. 12:9. Mt. 9:2, 22. Ps. 63:5–8.*

Our hope and faith . . . strong and steady.

I am the Lord. Those who wait for me shall never be ashamed. / Blessed is the man who trusts in the Lord and has made the Lord his hope and confidence. / He will keep in perfect peace all those who trust in him, whose thoughts turn often to the Lord! Trust in the Lord God always, for in the Lord Jehovah is your everlasting strength. / I stand silently before the Lord, waiting for him to rescue me. For salvation comes from him alone. Yes, he alone is my Rock, my rescuer, defence and fortress – why then should I be tense with fear when troubles come? / I am . . . not ashamed . . . I know the one in whom I trust.

God also bound himself with an oath, so that those he promised to help would be perfectly sure and never need to wonder whether he might change his plans. He has given us both his promise and his oath, two things we can completely count on, for it is impossible for God to tell a lie. Now all those who flee to him to save them can take new courage when they hear such assurances from God; now they can know without doubt that he will give them the salvation he has promised them.

Rom. 5:4. Is. 49:23. Jer. 17:7. Is. 26:3, 4. Ps. 62:5, 6. 2 Tim. 1:12. Hebr. 6:17, 18.

> *Persecuted . . . preaching salvation through faith
> in the cross of Christ alone.*

If anyone wants to be a follower of mine, let him
deny himself and take up his cross and follow me.

Don't you realize that making friends with God's
enemies – the evil pleasures of this world – makes you
an enemy of God? I say it again, that if your aim is to
enjoy the evil pleasure of the godless world, you cannot also be a friend of God. / (We) must enter into
the Kingdom of God through many hardships.

Those who believe in him will never be disap-
pointed. / He is very precious to you who believe.

God forbid that I should boast about anything
except the cross of our Lord Jesus Christ. Because of
that cross my interest in all the attractive things of the
world was killed long ago, and the world's interest in
me is also long dead. / I have been crucified with
Christ. / Those who belong to Christ have nailed their
natural evil desires to his cross and crucified them
there.

If we thank that our present service for him is hard,
just remember that some day we are going to sit with
him and rule with him. But if we give up when we
suffer, and turn against Christ, then he must turn
against us.

*Gal. 5:11. Mt. 16:24. Jas. 4:4. Acts 14:22. Rom. 9:33. 1 Pet. 2:7.
Gal. 6:14. Gal. 2:20. Gal. 5:24. 2 Tim. 2:12.*

The Lord is coming soon.

The Lord himself will come down from heaven with a mighty shout and with the soul-stirring cry of the archangel and the great trumpet-call of God. And the Christians who are dead will be the first to rise to meet the Lord. Then we who are still alive and remain on the earth will be caught up with them in the clouds to meet the Lord in the air and remain with him forever. So comfort and encourage each other with this news. / He who has said all these things declares: 'Yes, I am coming soon!' Amen! Come, Lord Jesus!

Dear friends, while you are waiting for these things to happen and for him to come, try hard to live without sinning; and be at peace with everyone so that he will be pleased with you when he returns. / Keep away from every kind of evil. May the God of peace himself make you entirely clean; and may your spirit and soul and body be kept strong and blameless until that day when our Lord Jesus Christ comes back again. God, who called you to become his child, will do all this for you, just as he promised.

Be patient. And take courage, for the coming of the Lord is near.

Phil. 4:5. 1 Thess. 4:16–18. Rev. 22:20. 2 Pet. 3:14. 1 Thess. 5:22–24. Jas. 5:8.

The choicest vine.

My Beloved has a vineyard on a very fertile hill. He ploughed it and took out all the rocks and planted his vineyard with the choicest vines. . . . He waited for the harvest, but the grapes that grew were wild and sour and not at all the sweet ones he expected. / How could this happen? How could this be? For when I planted you, I chose my seed so carefully – the very best. Why have you become this degenerate race of evil men?

When you follow your own wrong inclinations your lives will produce these evil results: impure thoughts, eagerness for lustful pleasure . . . envy, murder, drunkenness, wild parties, and all that sort of thing. But when the Holy Spirit controls our lives he will produce this kind of fruit in us: love, joy, peace, patience, kindness, goodness, faithfulness, gentleness and self-control.

I am the true Vine and my Father is the Gardener. He lops off every branch that doesn't produce. And he prunes those branches that bear fruit for even larger crops. Take care to live in me, and let me live in you. My true disciples produce bountiful harvests. This brings great glory to my Father.

Gen. 49:11. Is. 5:1, 2. Jer. 2:21. Gal. 5:19, 21–23. Jn. 15:1, 2, 4, 8.

*God says he will accept and acquit us . . . if we
trust Jesus Christ to take away our sins.*

God took the sinless Christ and poured into him our
sins. Then, in exchange, he poured God's goodness
into us! / Christ . . . taking the curse for our wrongdoing upon himself. / It is from God alone that you
have your life through Christ Jesus. He showed us
God's plan of salvation; he was the one who made us
acceptable to God: he made us pure and holy and
gave himself to purchase our salvation. / He saved us –
not because we were good enough to be saved, but
because of his kindness and pity – by washing away
our sins and giving us the new joy of the indwelling
Holy Spirit. He poured him out upon us with wonderful fullness – and all because of what Jesus Christ our
Saviour did.

Everything else is worthless when compared with the
priceless gain of knowing Christ Jesus my Lord. I
have put aside all else, counting it worth less than
nothing, in order that I can have Christ, and become
one with him, no longer counting on being saved by
being good enough or by obeying God's laws, but by
trusting Christ to save me; for God's way of making
us right with himself depends on faith – counting on
Christ alone.

Rom. 3:22. 2 Cor. 5:21. Gal. 3:13. 1 Cor. 1:30. Tit. 3:5, 6. Phil. 3:8, 9.

*Adopted into the bosom of his family, and calling
to him, 'Father, Father.'*

Jesus . . . looked up to heaven and said, 'Father . . .
Holy Father . . . O righteous Father.' / Because we are
his sons God has sent the Spirit of his Son into our
hearts, so now we can rightly speak of God as our
dear Father. / All of us, whether Jews or Gentiles,
may come to God the Father with the Holy Spirit's
help because of what Christ has done for us. Now you
are no longer strangers to God and foreigners to
heaven, but you are members of God's very own family,
citizens of God's country,` and you belong in God's
household with every other Christian.

Surely you are still our Father! Our Redeemer from
ages past.

I will go home to my father and say, 'Father, I
have sinned against both heaven and you, and am no
longer worthy of being called your son. Please take me
on as a hired man.' So he returned home to his
father. And while he was still a long distance away,
his father saw him coming, and was filled with loving
pity and ran and embraced him and kissed him.

*Rom. 8:15. Jn. 17:1, 11, 25. Gal. 4:6. Eph. 2:18, 19. Is. 63:16.
Lk. 15:18–20.*

So let us go out to him beyond the city walls [that is, outside the interests of this world, being willing to be despised] to suffer with him there, bearing his shame.

Dear friends, don't be bewildered or surprised when you go through the fiery trials ahead, for this is no strange, unusual thing that is going to happen to you. Instead, be really glad – because these trials will make you partners with Christ in his suffering, and afterwards you will have the wonderful joy of sharing his glory in that coming day when it will be displayed. / God will tenderly comfort you when you undergo these same sufferings. He will give you the strength to endure.

Be happy if you are cursed and insulted for being a Christian, for when that happens the Spirit of God will come upon you with great glory.

They left the Council Chamber rejoicing that God had counted them worthy to suffer dishonour for his name. / Moses . . . chose to share ill-treatment with God's people instead of enjoying the fleeting pleasures of sin. He thought that it was better to suffer for the promised Christ than to own all the treasures of Egypt, for he was looking forward to the great reward that God would give him.

Hebr. 13:13, 14. 1 Pet. 4:12, 13. 2 Cor. 1:7. 1 Pet. 4:14. Acts 5:41. Hebr. 11:25, 26.

The Lord Jesus Christ . . . will take these dying bodies of ours and change them into glorious bodies like his own.

High in the sky . . . was what looked like a throne made of beautiful blue sapphire stones, and upon it sat someone who appeared to be a Man. From his waist up, he seemed to be all glowing bronze, dazzling like fire; and from his waist down he seemed to be entirely flame, and there was a glowing halo like a rainbow all around him. That was the way the glory of the Lord appeared to me.

We Christians have no veil over our faces; we can be mirrors that brightly reflect the glory of the Lord. And as the Spirit of the Lord works within us, we become more and more like him. / We can't even imagine what it is going to be like later on. But we do know this, that when he comes we will be like him, as a result of seeing him as he really is.

They will never be hungry again, nor thirsty. / They were singing the song of Moses, the servant of God, and the song of the Lamb: 'Great and marvellous are your doings, Lord God Almighty.'

Phil. 3:20, 21. Ezk. 1:26–28. 2 Cor. 3:18. 1 Jn. 3:2. Rev. 7:16. Rev. 15:3.

*You know that he became a man so that he could
take away our sins, and that there is no sin in him,
no missing of God's will at any time in any way.*

God . . . now in these days has spoken to us through
his Son. God's Son shines out with God's glory, and
all that God's Son is and does marks him as God.
He regulates the universe by the mighty power of his
command. He is the one who died to cleanse us and
clear our record of all sin, and then sat down in
highest honour beside the great God of heaven. / God
took the sinless Christ and poured into him our sins.
Act in reverent fear of him from now until you get
to heaven. God paid a ransom to save you from the
impossible road to heaven which your fathers tried to
take, and the ransom he paid was not mere gold or
silver, as you very well know; but he paid for you
with the precious lifeblood of Christ, the sinless,
spotless Lamb of God. / Whatever we do, it is certainly not for our own profit, but because Christ's
love controls us now. Since we believe that Christ died
for all of us, we should also believe that we have
died to the old life we used to live. He died for all so
that all who live – having received eternal life from
him – might live no longer for themselves, to please
themselves, but to spend their lives pleasing Christ
who died and rose again for them.

1 Jn. 3:5. Hebr. 1:1–3. 2 Cor. 5:21. 1 Pet. 1:17, 19. 2 Cor. 5:14, 15.

I have set before you life or death, blessing or curse. Oh, that you would choose life; that you and your children might live!

'I do not enjoy seeing you die,' the Lord God says. 'Turn, turn and live!'

They would not be guilty if I had not come and spoken to them. But now they have no excuse for their sin. / For the truth about God is known to them instinctively; God has put this knowledge in their hearts. Since earliest times men have seen the earth and sky and all God made, and have known of his existence and great eternal power.

The wages of sin is death, but the free gift of God is eternal life through Jesus Christ our Lord. / And all who trust him – God's Son – to save them have eternal life; those who don't believe and obey him shall never see heaven, but the wrath of God remains upon them. / Don't you realize that you can choose your own master? You can choose sin (with death) or else obedience (with acquittal). The one to whom you offer yourself – he will take you and be your master and you will be his slave.

Come and follow me, for my servants must be where I am. And if they follow me, the Father will honour them.

Deut. 30:19. Ezk. 18:32. Jn. 15:22. Rom. 1:19, 20. Rom. 6:23. Jn. 3:36. Rom. 6:16. Jn. 12:26.

May your strength match the length of your days.

When you are arrested and stand trial, don't worry about what to say in your defence. Just say what God tells you to. Then you will not be speaking, but the Holy Spirit will. / So don't be anxious about tomorrow. God will take care of your tomorrow too. Live one day at a time.

The God of Israel gives strength and mighty power to his people. Blessed be God! / He gives power to the tired and worn out, and strength to the weak.

I am with you; that is all you need. My power shows up best in weak people. Now I am glad to boast about how weak I am; I am glad to be a living demonstration of Christ's power, instead of showing off my own power and abilities. Since I know it is all for Christ's good, I am quite happy about 'the thorn' and about insults and hardships, persecutions and difficulties; for when I am weak, then I am strong – the less I have, the more I depend on him. / I can do everything God asks me to with the help of Christ who gives me the strength and power. / March on, my soul, with strength!

Deut. 33:25. Mk. 13:11. Mt. 6:34. Ps. 68:35. Is. 40:29. 2 Cor. 12:9, 10. Phil. 4:13. Judg. 5:21.

*Come, north wind, awake . . . south wind, blow
upon my garden and waft its lovely perfume.*

Being punished isn't enjoyable while it is happening –
it hurts! But afterwards we can see the result, a quiet
growth in grace and character. / The Holy Spirit . . .
will produce this kind of fruit.

He is like a father to us, tender and sympathetic to
those who reverence him.

Though our bodies are dying, our inner strength in
the Lord is growing every day. These troubles and
sufferings of ours are, after all, quite small and won't
last very long. Yet this short time of distress will result
in God's richest blessing upon us for ever and ever! So
we do not look at what we can see at this moment,
the troubles all around us, but we look forward to the
joys in heaven which we have not yet seen. The troubles
will soon be over, but the joys to come will last forever.

Even though Jesus was God's Son, he had to learn
from experience what it was like to obey, when obeying
meant suffering. / He had the same temptations we
have, though he never once gave way to them and
sinned.

*Song 4:16. Hebr. 12:11. Gal. 5:22. Ps. 103:13. 2 Cor. 4:16–18. Hebr. 5:8.
Hebr. 4:15.*

The God who looked upon me.

O Lord, you have examined my heart and know everything about me. You know when I sit or stand. When far away you know my every thought. You chart the path ahead of me, and tell me where to stop and rest. Every moment, you know where I am. This is too glorious, too wonderful to believe! I can *never* be lost to your Spirit! I can *never* get away from my God!

The Lord is watching everywhere and keeps his eye on both the evil and the good. / *For God is closely watching you* and he weighs carefully everything you do. / God knows your evil hearts. Your pretence brings you honour from the people, but it is an abomination in the sight of God. / The eyes of the Lord search back and forth across the whole earth, looking for people whose hearts are perfect towards him, so that he can show his great power in helping them.

Jesus . . . knew mankind to the core. No one needed to tell him how changeable human nature is. / Lord, you know my heart. / You know I am your friend.

Gen. 16:13. Ps. 139:1–4, 6, 7. Prov. 15:3. Prov. 5:21. Lk. 16:15. 2 Chron. 16:9. Jn. 2:24, 25. Jn. 21:17. Jn. 21:16.

With all my heart I will praise you. I will give glory to your name forever.

True praise is a worthy sacrifice; this really honours me. / It is good to say, 'Thank you' to the Lord, to sing praises to the God who is above all gods. Every morning tell him, 'Thank you for your kindness,' and every evening rejoice in all his faithfulness.

Let everything alive give praises to the Lord!

Dear brothers, I plead with you to give your bodies to God. Let them be a living sacrifice, holy – the kind he can accept. When you think of what he has done for you, is this too much to ask? / As a sacrifice for sin . . . Jesus suffered and died outside the city, where his blood washed our sins away. With Jesus' help we will continually offer our sacrifice of praise to God by telling others of the glory of his name. / Always give thanks for everything to our God and Father in the name of our Lord Jesus Christ.

The Lamb is worthy . . . the Lamb who was slain. He is worthy to receive the power, and the riches, and the wisdom, and the strength, and the honour, and the glory, and the blessing.

Ps. 86:12. Ps. 50:23. Ps. 92:1, 2. Ps. 150:6. Rom. 12:1. Hebr. 13:11, 12, 15. Eph. 5:20. Rev. 5:12.

Let us run with patience the particular race that God has set before us. Keep your eyes on Jesus, our leader and instructor.

Anyone who wants to follow me must put aside his own desires and conveniences and carry his cross with him every day and keep close to me! / No one can become my disciple unless he first sits down and counts his blessings – and then renounces them all for me! / Discard the evil deeds of darkness.

To win the contest you must deny yourselves many things that would keep you from doing your best. I run straight to the goal with purpose in every step. I fight to win. I'm not just shadow-boxing or playing around. Like an athlete I punish my body, treating it roughly, training it to do what it should, not what it wants to. / I am still not all I should be but I am bringing all my energies to bear on this one thing: forgetting the past and looking forward to what lies ahead, I strain to reach the end of the race and receive the prize for which God is calling us up to heaven because of what Christ Jesus did for us. / Oh, that we might know the Lord! Let us press on to know him, and he will respond to us as surely as the coming of dawn or the rain of early spring.

Hebr. 12:1, 2. Lk. 9:23. Lk. 14:33. Rom. 13:12. 1 Cor. 9:25, 27. Phil. 3:13, 14. Hos. 6:3.

It is good for a young man to be under discipline.

Teach a child to choose the right path, and when he is older he will remain upon it.

Since we respect our fathers here on earth, though they punish us, should we not all the more cheerfully submit to God's training so that we can begin to really live? Our earthly fathers trained us for a few brief years, doing the best for us that they knew how, but God's correction is always right and for our best good, that we may share his holiness.

Lord, in their distress they sought for you. When your punishment was on them, they poured forth a whispered prayer. / I used to wander off until you punished me; now I closely follow all you say. The punishment you gave me was the best thing that could have happened to me, for it taught me to pay attention to your laws.

I know the plans I have for you, says the Lord. They are plans for good and not for evil, to give you a future and a hope. / If you will humble yourselves under the mighty hand of God, in his good time he will lift you up.

Lam. 3:27. Prov. 22:6. Hebr. 12:9, 10. Is. 26:16. Ps. 119:67, 71. Jer. 29:11. 1 Pet. 5:6.

If you refuse to drive out the people living there,
those who remain will be as cinders in your eyes
and thorns in your sides.

Fight on for God. / I use God's mighty weapons, not
those made by men, to knock down the devil's strongholds. With these weapons I can capture rebels and
bring them back to God, and change them into men
whose hearts' desire is obedience to Christ.

Dear brothers, you have no obligations whatever to
your old sinful nature to do what it begs you to do. For
if you keep on following it you are lost and will perish,
but if through the power of the Holy Spirit you crush
it and its evil deeds, you shall live.

For we naturally love to do evil things that are just
the opposite of the things that the Holy Spirit tells us
to do; and the good things we want to do when the Spirit
has his way with us are just the opposite of our natural
desires. These two forces within us are constantly
fighting each other to win control over us, and our
wishes are never free from their pressures. / There is
something else deep within me, in my lower nature,
that is at war with my mind. / Overwhelming victory
is ours through Christ who loved us enough to die for
us.

Num. 33:55. 1 Tim. 6:12. 2 Cor. 10:4, 5. Rom. 8:12, 13. Gal. 5:17.
Rom. 7:23. Rom. 8:37.

Ordinary sin receives heavy punishment, but how much more this sin of yours which has been committed against the Lord?

If you sin, there is someone to plead for you before the Father. His name is Jesus Christ, the one who is all that is good and who pleases God completely. He is the one who took God's wrath against our sins upon himself, and brought us into fellowship with God. / For God sent Christ Jesus to take the punishment for our sins and to end all God's anger against us. He used Christ's blood and our faith as the means of saving us from his wrath. And now in these days also he can receive sinners in this same way, because Jesus took away their sins. But isn't this unfair for God to let criminals go free, and say that they are innocent? No, for he does it on the basis of their trust in Jesus who took away their sins.

What can we ever say to such wonderful things as these? If God is on our side, who can ever be against us? Who dares accuse us whom God has chosen for his own? Will God? No! He is the one who has forgiven us and given us right standing with himself. Who then will condemn us? Will Christ? No! For he is the one who died for us and came back to life again for us and is sitting at the place of highest honour next to God, pleading for us there in heaven.

1 Sam. 2:25. 1 Jn. 2:1, 2. Rom. 3:25, 26. Rom. 8:31, 33, 34.

You love him even though you have never seen him.

We know these things are true by believing, not by seeing. / Our love for him comes as a result of his loving us first. / We know how much God loves us because we have felt his love and because we believe him when he tells us that he loves us dearly. God is love, and anyone who lives in love is living with God and God is living in him. / And because of what Christ did . . . you . . . who heard the Good News about how to be saved, and trusted Christ, were marked as belonging to Christ by the Holy Spirit, who long ago had been promised to all of us Christians. / The riches and glory of his plan are for you. . . . And this is the secret: *that Christ in your hearts is your only hope of glory.*

If anyone says, 'I love God,' but keeps on hating his brother, he is a liar; for if he doesn't love his brother who is right there in front of him, how can he love God whom he has never seen?

Jesus told him, "You believe because you have seen me. But blessed are those who haven't seen me and believe anyway.' / Oh, the joys of those who put their trust in him!

1 Pet. 1:8. 2 Cor. 5:7. 1 Jn. 4:19. 1 Jn. 4:16. Eph. 1:13. Col. 1:27.
1 Jn. 4:20. Jn. 20:29. Ps. 2:12.

The Lord our righteousness.

We are all infected and impure with sin. When we put on our prized robes of righteousness we find they are but filthy rags.

I walk in the strength of the Lord God. I tell everyone that you alone are just and good. / How happy God has made me! For he has clothed me with garments of salvation and draped about me the robe of righteousness. I am like a bridegroom in his wedding suit or a bride with her jewels.

Bring the finest robe in the house and put it on. / Wear the cleanest and whitest and finest of linens. (Fine linen represents the good deeds done by the people of God.)

Everything else is worthless when compared with the priceless gain of knowing Christ Jesus my Lord. I have put aside all else, counting it worth less than nothing, in order that I can have Christ, and become one with him, no longer counting on being saved by being good enough or by obeying God's laws, but by trusting Christ to save me; for God's way of making us right with himself depends on faith – counting on Christ alone.

Jer. 23:6. Is. 64:6. Ps. 71:16. Is. 61:10. Lk. 15:22. Rev. 19:8. Phil. 3:8, 9.

Keep me from all evil and disaster.

Asleep! . . . Get up! Pray God that you will not fall when you are tempted. / The spirit indeed is willing, but how weak the body is.

O God, I beg two favours from you before I die: First, help me never to tell a lie. Second, give me neither poverty nor riches! Give me just enough to satisfy my needs. For if I grow rich, I may become content without God. And if I am too poor, I may steal, and thus insult God's holy name.

He keeps you from all evil, and preserves your life. / I will certainly deliver you from . . . wicked men and rescue you from their ruthless hands. / No one who has become part of God's family makes a practice of sinning, for Christ, God's Son, holds him securely and the Devil cannot get his hands on him.

Because you have patiently obeyed me despite the persecution, therefore I will protect you from the time of great tribulation and temptation, which will come upon the world to test everyone alive. / The Lord can rescue you and me from the temptations that surround us.

1 Chron. 4:10. Lk. 22:46. Mt. 26:41. Prov. 30:7–9. Ps. 121:7. Jer. 15:21.
1 Jn. 5:18. Rev. 3:10. 2 Pet. 2:9.

The stars differ from each other in their beauty and brightness.

They had been arguing about which of them was the greatest. He sat down and called them around him and said, 'Anyone wanting to be the greatest must be the least – the servant of all!' / Serve each other with humble spirits, for God gives special blessings to those who are humble, but sets himself against those who are proud. If you will humble yourselves under the mighty hand of God, in his good time he will lift you up.

Your attitude should be the kind that was shown us by Jesus Christ, who . . . laid aside his mighty power and glory, taking the disguise of a slave and becoming like men. It was because of this that God raised him up to the heights of heaven and gave him a name which is above every other name, that at the name of Jesus every knee shall bow in heaven and on earth and under the earth.

Those who are wise – the people of God – shall shine as brightly as the sun's brilliance, and those who turn many to righteousness will glitter like stars forever.

1 Cor. 15:41. Mk. 9:34, 35. 1 Pet. 5:5, 6. Phil. 2:5–7, 9, 10. Dan. 12:3.

'Take courage and work, for I am with you,' says the Lord of the armies of heaven.

I am the Vine; you are the branches. Whoever lives in me and I in him shall produce a large crop of fruit. For apart from me you can't do a thing. / I can do everything God asks me to with the help of Christ who gives me the strength and power. / Your strength must come from the Lord's mighty power within you. / The joy of the Lord is your strength.

The Lord of heaven's armies says, 'Get on with the job and finish it! You have been listening long enough!' / Bring cheer to all discouraged ones. Encourage those who are afraid. Tell them, 'Be strong, fear not, for your God is coming to destroy your enemies. He is coming to save you.' / The Lord . . . said, 'I will make you strong.'

If God is on our side, who can ever be against us? / It is God himself, in his mercy, who has given us this wonderful work [of telling his Good News to others] and so we never give up.

Let us not get tired of doing what is right, for after a while we will reap a harvest of blessing if we don't get discouraged and give up. / We thank God for all of this! It is he who makes us victorious through Jesus Christ our Lord!

Hag. 2:4. Jn. 15:5. Phil. 4:13. Eph. 6:10. Neh. 8:10. Zech. 8:9. Is. 35:3, 4. Judg. 6:14. Rom. 8:31. 2 Cor. 4:1. Gal. 6:9. 1 Cor. 15:57.

Even darkness cannot hide from God.

God carefully watches the goings on of all mankind; he sees them all. No darkness is thick enough to hide evil men from his eyes. / Can anyone hide from me? Am I not everywhere in all of heaven and earth?

You don't need to be afraid of the dark any more, nor fear the dangers of the day; nor dread the plagues of darkness, nor disasters in the morning. For Jehovah is my refuge! I choose the God above all gods to shelter me. How then can evil overtake me or any plague come near? / He will never let me stumble, slip or fall. For he is always watching, never sleeping.

Jehovah himself is caring for you! He is your defender. He protects you day and night. He keeps you from all evil, and preserves your life.

Even when walking through the dark valley of death I will not be afraid, for you are close beside me, guarding, guiding all the way.

Ps. 139:12. Job 34:21, 22. Jer. 23:24. Ps. 91:5, 6, 9, 10. Ps. 121:3–7.
Ps. 23:4.

Never return.

If they had wanted to, they could have gone back to the good things of this world. But they didn't want to. They were living for heaven. Moses . . . . chose to share ill-treatment with God's people instead of enjoying the fleeting pleasures of sin. He thought that it was better to suffer for the promised Christ than to own all the treasures of Egypt. / Those whose faith has made them good in God's sight must live by faith, trusting him in everything. Otherwise, if they shrink back, God will have no pleasure in them. / Anyone who lets himself be distracted from the work I plan for him is not fit for the Kingdom of God.

God forbid that I should boast about anything except the cross of our Lord Jesus Christ. Because of that cross my interest in all the attractive things of the world was killed long ago, and the world's interest in me is also long dead. / The Lord has said, 'Leave them; separate yourselves from them; don't touch what is unclean: and I will welcome you.'

God who began the good work within you will keep right on helping you grow in his grace until his task within you is finally finished on that day when Jesus Christ returns.

Deut. 17:16. Hebr. 11:15, 16, 25, 26. Hebr. 10:38. Lk. 9:62. Gal. 6:14. 2 Cor. 6:17. Phil. 1:6.

They persecute the one you have smitten, and scoff at the pain of the one you have pierced.

I was only a little displeased with my people, but the nations afflicted them far beyond my intentions.

Dear brothers, if a Christian is overcome by some sin, you who are godly should gently and humbly help him back on to the right path, remembering that next time it might be one of you who is in the wrong.

That person who brings him back to God will have saved a wandering soul from death, bringing about the forgiveness of his many sins. / Comfort those who are frightened; take tender care of those who are weak; and be patient with everyone.

Don't criticize each other any more. Try instead to live in such a way that you will never make your brother stumble by letting him see you doing something he thinks is wrong. / We must bear the 'burden' of being considerate of the doubts and fears of others – of those who feel these things are wrong.

Love . . . is never glad about injustice. / Be careful. If you are thinking, 'Oh, I would never behave like that' – let this be a warning to you. For you too may fall into sin.

Ps. 69:26. Zech. 1:15. Gal. 6:1. Jas. 5:20. 1 Thess. 5:14. Rom. 14:13. Rom. 15:1. 1 Cor. 13:4, 6. 1 Cor. 10:12.

My purpose is to give eternal life – abundantly.

The wages of sin is death, but the free gift of God is eternal life through Jesus Christ our Lord. / The sin of this one man, Adam, caused death to be king over all, but all who will take God's gift of forgiveness and acquittal are kings of life because of this one man, Jesus Christ. / Death came into the world because of what one man (Adam) did, and it is because of what this other man (Christ) has done that now there is the resurrection from the dead. Everyone dies because all of us are related to Adam, being members of his sinful race, and wherever there is sin, death results. But all who are related to Christ will rise again. / Our Saviour Jesus Christ . . . broke the power of death and showed us the way of everlasting life through trusting him.

And what is it that God has said? That he has given us eternal life, and that this life is in his Son. So whoever has God's Son has life; whoever does not have his Son, does not have life. / God did not send his Son into the world to condemn it, but to save it.

Jn. 10:10. Rom. 6:23. Rom. 5:17. 1 Cor. 15:21, 22. 2 Tim. 1:10. 1 Jn. 5:11, 12. Jn. 3:17.

We must all stand before Christ to be judged.

We know that God, in justice, will punish anyone. / When I, the Son of Mankind, shall come in my glory, and all the angels with me, then I shall sit upon my throne of glory. And all the nations shall be gathered before me. And I will separate the people as a shepherd separates the sheep from the goats.

Then the godly will shine as the sun in their Father's Kingdom. / Who dares accuse us whom God has chosen for his own? Will God? No! He is the one who has forgiven us and given us a right standing with himself. Who then will condemn us? Will Christ? No! For he is the one who died for us and came back to life again for us and is sitting at the place of highest honour next to God, pleading for us there in heaven. / There is now no condemnation awaiting those who belong to Christ Jesus.

When we are judged and punished by the Lord, it is so that we will not be condemned with the rest of the world. / He calls his own sheep by name and leads them out.

2 Cor. 5:10. Rom. 2:2. Mt. 25:31, 32. Mt. 13:43. Rom. 8:33, 34.
Rom. 8:1. 1 Cor. 11:32. Jn. 10:3.

How kind our Lord was, for he showed me how to trust him and become full of the love of Christ Jesus.

You know how full of love and kindness our Lord Jesus was: though he was so very rich, yet to help you he became so very poor, so that by being poor he could make you rich. / The more we see our sinfulness, the more we see God's abounding grace forgiving us.

Because of his kindness you have been saved through trusting Christ. And even trusting is not of yourselves; it too is a gift from God. Salvation is not a reward for the good we have done, so none of us can take any credit for it. / We Jewish Christians know very well that we cannot become right with God by obeying our Jewish laws, but only by faith in Jesus Christ to take away our sins. And so we, too, have trusted Jesus Christ, that we might be accepted by God because of faith – and not because we have obeyed the Jewish laws. For no one will ever be saved by obeying them. / He saved us – not because we were good enough to be saved, but because of his kindness and pity – by washing away our sins and giving us the new joy of the indwelling Holy Spirit. He poured him out upon us with wonderful fullness – and all because of what Jesus Christ our Saviour did.

1 Tim. 1:14. 2 Cor. 8:9. Rom. 5:20. Eph. 2:8, 9. Gal. 2:16. Tit, 3:5, 6.

I am the bright Morning Star.

There shall come a star from Jacob!

The night is far gone, the day of his return will soon be here. So discard the evil deeds of darkness and put on the armour of right living. / Before the dawn comes and the shadows flee away, come to me, my beloved, and be like a gazelle or a young stag on the mountains of spices.

'Watchman, what of the night?' The watchman replies, 'Your judgment day is dawning now. Turn again to God, so that I can give you better news. Seek for him, then come and ask again!'

I am the Light of the world. / I will give you the morning star!

Since you do not know when it will happen, stay alert. Be on the watch [for my return]. My coming can be compared with that of a man who went on a trip to another country. He laid out his employees' work for them to do while he was gone, and told the gatekeeper to watch for his return. Keep a sharp lookout! For you do not know when I will come, at evening, at midnight, early dawn or late daybreak. Don't let me find you sleeping. *Watch for my return* This is my message to you and to everyone else.

Rev. 22:16. Num. 24:17. Rom. 13:12. Song 2:17. Is. 21:11, 12. Jn. 8:12. Rev. 2:28. Mk. 13:33–37.

When you have eaten your fill, bless the Lord your God for the good land he has given you.

Beware that in your plenty you don't forget the Lord your God. / One of them came back to Jesus, shouting, 'Glory to God, I'm healed!' He fell flat on the ground in front of Jesus, face downward in the dust, thanking him for what he had done. This man was a despised Samaritan. Jesus asked, 'Didn't I heal ten men? Where are the nine? Does only this foreigner return to give glory to God?'

For everything God made is good, and we may eat it gladly if we are thankful for it, and if we ask God to bless it, for it is made good by the Word of God and prayer. / The Lord's blessing is our greatest wealth. All our work adds nothing to it!

I bless the holy name of God with all my heart. Yes, I will bless the Lord and not forget the glorious things he does for me. He forgives all my sins. He heals me. He ransoms me from hell. He surrounds me with loving-kindness and tender mercies. He fills my life with good things! My youth is renewed like the eagle's!

Deut. 8:10. Deut. 8:11. Lk. 17:15–18. 1 Tim. 4:4, 5. Prov. 10:22. Ps. 103:1–5.

Jesus . . . pitied them.

Jesus Christ is the same yesterday, today, and forever. /
Jesus the Son of God is our great High Priest who has
gone to heaven itself to help us; therefore let us never
stop trusting him. This high priest of ours understands
our weaknesses, since he had the same temptations we
have, though he never once gave way to them and
sinned. / Because he is a man he can deal gently with
other men, though they are foolish and ignorant, for
he, too, is surrounded with the same temptations and
understands their problems very well. / Then he returned to the three disciples and found them asleep.
'Simon!' he said. 'Asleep? Couldn't you watch with me
even one hour? Watch with me and pray in case the
Tempter overpower you. For though the spirit is willing
enough, the body is weak.'

He is like a father to us, tender and sympathetic
to those who reverence him. For he knows we are but
dust.

You are merciful and gentle, Lord, slow in getting
angry, full of constant lovingkindness and of truth; so
look down in pity and grant strength to your servant
and save me.

Mt. 14:14. Hebr. 13:8. Hebr. 4:14, 15. Hebr. 5:2. Mk. 14:37, 38.
Ps. 103:13, 14. Ps. 86:15, 16.

I no longer call you slaves, for a master doesn't confide in his slaves; now you are my friends, proved by the fact that I have told you everything the Father told me.

'Should I hide my plan from Abraham?' God asked. / Then he explained to them that only they were permitted to understand about the Kingdom of Heaven. / We know about these things because God has sent his Spirit to tell us, and his Spirit searches out and shows us all of God's deepest secrets. / Hidden in former times, though it was made for our benefit before the world began.

How greatly to be envied are those you have chosen to come and live with you within the holy tabernacle courts! What joys await us among all the good things there. / Friendship with God is reserved for those who reverence him. With them alone he shares the secrets of his promises. / I have passed on to them the commands you gave me; and they accepted them and know of a certainty that I came down to earth from you, and they believe you sent me.

You are my friends if you obey me.

Jn. 15:15. Gen. 18:17. Mt. 13:11. 1 Cor. 2:10. 1 Cor. 2:7. Ps. 65:4. Ps. 25:14. Jn. 17:8. Jn. 15:14.

*Your walls will be 'Salvation' and your gates
'Praise.'*

The walls had twelve foundation stones, and on them
were written the names of the twelve apostles of the
Lamb.

You are no longer strangers to God and foreigners
to heaven, but you are members of God's very own
family, citizens of God's country, and you belong in
God's household with every other Christian. What a
foundation you stand on now: the apostles and the
prophets; and the cornerstone of the building is Jesus
Christ himself. We who believe are carefully joined
together with Christ as parts of a beautiful, constantly
growing temple for God. And you also are joined with
him and with each other by the Spirit, and are part of
this dwelling place of God. / Come to Christ, who is the
living Foundation of Rock upon which God builds;
though men have spurned him, he is very precious to
God who has chosen him above all others. And now
you have become living building-stones for God's use
in building his house.

O God in Zion, we wait before you in silent praise,
and thus fulfil our vow.

Is. 60:18. Rev. 21:14. Eph. 2:19–22. 1 Pet. 2:4, 5. Ps. 65:1.

Now he is . . . comforted.

Your sun shall never set; the moon shall not go down –
for the Lord will be your everlasting light; your days
of mourning all will end. / He will swallow up death
forever. The Lord God will wipe away all tears and take
away forever all insults and mockery against his land
and people. / These are the ones coming out of the
great tribulation . . . they washed their robes and made
them white by the blood of the Lamb. That is why
they are here before the throne of God, serving him
day and night in his temple. The one sitting on the
throne will shelter them; they will never be hungry
again, nor thirsty, and they will be fully protected from
the scorching noontime heat. For the Lamb standing in
front of the throne will feed them and be their shepherd
and lead them to the springs of the water of life. / He
will wipe away all tears from their eyes, and there shall
be no more death, or sorrow, or crying, or pain. All
of that has gone for ever.

Lk. 16:25. Is. 60:20. Is. 25:8. Rev. 7:14–17. Rev. 21:4.

*There is little time left before the night falls and
all work comes to an end.*

They (who die in the faith of Jesus) are blest indeed . . .
they shall rest from all their toils and trials . . . their
good deeds follow them to heaven! / 'Why have you
disturbed me by bringing me back?' Samuel asked
Saul.

Whatever you do, do well, for in death, where you
are going, there is no working or planning, or knowing
or understanding. / The dead cannot sing praises to
Jehovah here on earth.

I won't be around to help you very much longer. My
time has almost run out. Very soon now I will be on my
way to heaven. I have fought long and hard for my
Lord, and through it all I have kept true to him. And
now the time has come for me to stop fighting and
rest. In heaven a crown is waiting for me which the Lord,
the righteous Judge, will give me on that great day of
his return. And not just to me, but to all those whose
lives show that they are eagerly looking forward to his
coming back again.

There is a full, complete rest *still waiting* for the
people of God.

*Jn. 9:4. Rev. 14:13. 1 Sam. 28:15. Eccl. 9:10. Ps. 115:17. 2 Tim. 4:6–8.
Hebr. 4:9.*

*Your eye lights up your inward being. A pure eye
lets sunshine into your soul.*

The man who hasn't the Spirit can't understand and
can't accept these thoughts from God, which the Holy
Spirit teaches us. They sound foolish to him, because
only those who have the Holy Spirit within them can
understand what the Holy Spirit means. Others just
can't take it in. / Open my eyes to see wonderful things
in your Word.

I am the Light of the world. So if you follow me, you
won't be stumbling through the darkness, for living
light will flood your path. / We Christians have no veil
over our faces; we can be mirrors that brightly reflect
the glory of the Lord. And as the Spirit of the Lord
works within us, we become more and more like him. /
For God, who said, 'Let there be light in the darkness,'
has made us understand that it is the brightness of his
glory that is seen in the face of Jesus Christ.

God, the glorious Father of our Lord Jesus Christ . . .
give you wisdom to see clearly and really understand
who Christ is and all that he has done for you . . . So
that you can see something of the future he has called
you to share.

*Lk. 11:34. 1 Cor. 2:14. Ps. 119:18. Jn. 8:12. 2 Cor. 3:18. 2 Cor. 4:6.
Eph. 1:17, 18.*

*He split open the rocks in the wilderness to give
them plenty of water, as though gushing from a
spring.*

God guided them by sending a cloud that moved along
ahead of them; and he brought them all safely through
the waters of the Red Sea. This might be called their
'baptism' – baptized both in sea and cloud! – as
followers of Moses: – their commitment to him as
their leader. And by a miracle God sent them food to
eat and water to drink there in the desert; they drank
the water that Christ gave them. He was there with
them as a mighty Rock of spiritual refreshment. / One
of the soldiers pierced his side with a spear, and blood
and water flowed out. / He was wounded and bruised
for *our* sins. He was chastised that we might have
peace; he was lashed – and we were healed!

Yet you won't come to me so that I can give you this
life eternal. / My people have done two evil things:
They have forsaken me, the Fountain of Live-giving
Water; and they have built for themselves broken
cisterns that can't hold water!

If anyone is thirsty, let him come to me and drink. /
Let the thirsty one come – anyone who wants to; let
him come and drink the water of life without charge.

*Ps. 78:15. 1 Cor. 10:1–4. Jn. 19:34. Is. 53:5. Jn. 5:40. Jer. 2:13.
Jn. 7:37. Rev. 22:17.*

Those who feared and loved the Lord spoke often of him to each other. And he had a Book of Remembrance drawn up in which he recorded the names of those who feared him and loved to think about him.

Suddenly Jesus himself came along and joined them and began walking beside them. / Where two or three gather together because they are mine, I will be there among them.

Remember what Christ taught and let his words enrich your lives and make you wise; teach them to each other and sing them out in psalms and hymns and spiritual songs, singing to the Lord with thankful hearts. / Speak to each other about these things every day while there is still time, so that none of you will become hardened against God, being blinded by the glamour of sin. / Teach them to your children and talk about them when you are at home or out for a walk; at bedtime and the first thing in the morning.

I tell you this, that you must give account on Judgment Day for every idle word you speak. Your words now reflect your fate then: either you will be justified by them or you will be condemned.

I will talk to others all day long about your justice and your goodness.

Mal. 3:16. Lk. 24:15. Mt. 18:20. Col. 3:16. Hebr. 3:13. Deut. 6:7. Mt. 12:36, 37. Ps. 71:24.

The Lord planted the cedars of Lebanon. They are tall and flourishing.

I will refresh Israel like the dew from heaven; she will blossom as the lily and root deeply in the soil like cedars in Lebanon. Her branches will spread out, as beautiful as olive trees, fragrant as the forests of Lebanon. / Blessed is the man who trusts in the Lord and has made the Lord his hope and confidence. He is like a tree planted along a riverbank, with its roots reaching deep into the water – a tree not bothered by the heat nor worried by long months of drought. Its leaves stay green and it goes right on producing all its luscious fruit.

Everyone shall know that it is I, the Lord, who cuts down the high trees and exalts the low, that I make the green tree wither and the dry tree grow. I, the Lord, have said that I would do it, and I will.

The godly shall flourish like palm trees, and grow tall as the cedars of Lebanon. For they are transplanted into the Lord's own garden, and are under his personal care. Even in old age they will still produce fruit and be vital and green.

Ps. 104:16. Hos. 14:5, 6. Jer. 17:7, 8. Ezk. 17:24. Ps. 92:12–14.

*'They shall be mine,' says the Lord of heaven's
armies, 'in that day when I make up my jewels.'*

I have told these men all about you. They were in the
world, but then you gave them to me. Actually, they
were always yours, and you gave them to me; and they
have obeyed you. My plea is not for the world but for
these you have given me because they belong to you.
And all of them, since they are mine, belong to you; and
you have given them back to me with everything else
of yours, and so they are my glory. Father, I want
them with me – these you've given me – so that they
can see my glory. You gave me the glory because you
loved me before the world began.

I will come and get you, so that you can always be
with me where I am. / He comes to receive praise and
admiration because of all he has done for his people,
his saints. / We who are still alive and remain on the
earth will be caught up with them in the clouds to meet
the Lord in the air and remain with him forever. / He
will hold you aloft in his hands for all to see – a splendid
crown for the King of kings.

Amen! Come, Lord Jesus!

*Mal. 3:17. Jn. 17:6, 9, 10, 24. Jn. 14:3. 2 Thess. 1:10. 1 Thess. 4:17.
Is. 62:3. Rev. 22:20.*

Moses asked to see God's glory.

God, who said, 'Let there be light in the darkness,' has made us understand that it is the brightness of his glory that is seen in the face of Jesus Christ. / Christ took our human nature and lived here on earth among us and was full of loving forgiveness and truth. And some of us have seen his glory – the glory of the only Son of the heavenly Father. No one has ever actually seen God, but, of course, his only Son has, for he is the companion of the Father and has told us all about him.

I thirst for God, the living God. Where can I find him to come and stand before him? / My heart has heard you say, 'Come and talk with me, O my people.' And my heart responds, 'Lord, I am coming.'

We Christians have no veil over our faces; we can be mirrors that brightly reflect the glory of the Lord. And as the Spirit of the Lord works within us, we become more and more like him. / Father, I want them with me – these you've given me – so that they can see my glory. You gave me the glory because you loved me before the world began.

Ex. 33:18. 2 Cor. 4:6. Jn. 1:14, 18. Ps. 42:2. Ps. 27:8. 2 Cor. 3:18. Jn. 17:24.

*High in the sky above them was what looked like
a throne made of beautiful blue sapphire stones,
and upon it sat someone who appeared to be a Man.*

Christ Jesus, himself man. / Laid aside his mighty power and glory, taking the disguise of a slave and becoming like men. / Since we, God's children, are human beings – made of flesh and blood – he became flesh and blood too by being born in human form; for only as a human being could he die and in dying break the power of the devil who had the power of death.

I am . . . the living one who died, who is now alive for evermore. / Christ rose from the dead and will never die again. Death no longer has any power over him. He died once for all, to end sin's power, but now he lives forever in unbroken fellowship with God. / What will you think if you see me, the Son of Mankind, return to heaven again? / Raised . . . from the dead and seated . . . in the place of honour at God's right hand in heaven. / In Christ there is the perfection of God in a human body.

His weak, human body died on the cross, but now he lives by the mighty power of God. We, too, are weak in our bodies, as he was, but now we live and are strong, as he is, and have all of God's power to use.

*Ezk. 1:26. 1 Tim. 2:5. Phil. 2:7. Hebr. 2:14. Rev. 1:18. Rom. 6:9.
Jn. 6:62. Eph. 1:20. Col. 2:9. 2 Cor. 13:4.*

Your promises . . . give me strength.

The first man, Adam, was given a natural human body but Christ is more than that, for he was life-giving Spirit.

The Father has life in himself, and has granted his Son to have life in himself. / I am the one who raises the dead and gives them life again. Anyone who believes in me, even though he dies like anyone else, shall live again. He is given eternal life for believing in me and shall never perish.

Eternal life is in him, and this life gives light to all mankind. To all who received him, he gave the right to become children of God. All they needed to do was to trust him to save them. All those who believe this are reborn – not a physical rebirth resulting from human passion or plan, but from the will of God.

Only the Holy Spirit gives eternal life. Those born only once, with physical birth will never receive this gift. But now I have told you how to get this true spiritual life. / Whatever God says to us is full of living power; it is sharper than the sharpest dagger, cutting swift and deep into every aspect of our innermost thoughts and desires, exposing us for what we really are.

Ps. 119:50. 1 Cor. 15:45. Jn. 5:26. Jn. 11:25, 26. Jn. 1:4, 12, 13.
Jn. 6:63. Hebr. 4:12.

I must do all that is right.

I delight to do your will, my God, for your law is written upon my heart!

Don't misunderstand why I have come – it isn't to cancel the laws of Moses and the warnings of the prophets. No, I came to fulfil them, and to make them all come true. With all the earnestness I have I say: Every law in the Book will continue until its purpose is achieved. / The Lord has magnified his law and made it truly glorious. / Unless your goodness is greater than that of the Pharisees and other Jewish leaders, you can't get into the Kingdom of Heaven at all!

We aren't saved from sin's grasp by knowing the commandments of God, because we can't and don't keep them, but God put into effect a different plan to save us. He sent his own Son in a human body like ours – except that ours are sinful – and destroyed sin's control over us by giving himself as a sacrifice for our sins. So now we can obey God's laws if we are led by the Holy Spirit and no longer obey the old evil nature within us. / Christ gives to those who trust in him everything they are trying to get by keeping his laws.

Mt. 3:15. Ps. 40:8. Mt. 5:17, 18. Is. 42:21. Mt. 5:20. Rom. 8:3, 4.
Rom. 10:4.

I am all that you need.

Whom have I in heaven but you? And I desire no one on earth as much as you! My health fails; my spirits droop, yet God remains! He is the strength of my heart; he is mine forever! / The Lord himself is my inheritance, my prize. He is my food and drink, my highest joy! He guards all that is mine. He sees that I am given pleasant brooks and meadows as my share! What a wonderful inheritance!

My soul claims the Lord as my inheritance; therefore I will hope in him.

Your laws are my joyous treasure forever.

O God, my God! How I search for you! How I thirst for you in this parched and weary land where there is no water. How I long to find you! I shall be fully satisfied; I will praise you with great joy. I lie awake at night thinking of you – of how much you have helped me – and how I rejoice through the night beneath the protecting shadow of your wings.

My beloved is mine and I am his.

Num. 18:20. Ps. 73:25, 26. Ps. 16:5, 6. Lam. 3:24. Ps. 119:111. Ps. 63:1, 5–7. Song. 2:16.

Who can ever say, 'I have cleansed my heart; I am sinless?'

The Lord looks down from heaven on all mankind to see if there are any who are wise, who want to please God. But no, all have strayed away; all are rotten with sin. / Those who are . . . bent on following their own evil desires, can never please God.

I know I am rotten through and through so far as my old sinful nature is concerned. No matter which way I turn I can't make myself do right. I want to but I can't. / We are all infected and impure with sin. When we put on our prized robes of righteousness we find they are but filthy rags.

If we could be saved by his laws, then God would not have had to give us a different way to get out of the grip of sin – for the Scriptures insist we are all its prisoners. The only way out is through faith in Jesus Christ; the way of escape is open to all who believe him. / God was in Christ, restoring the world to himself, no longer counting men's sins against them but blotting them out.

If we say that we have no sin, we are only fooling ourselves, and refusing to accept the truth. But if we confess our sins to him, he can be depended on to forgive us and to cleanse us from every wrong.

Prov. 20:9. Ps. 14:2, 3. Rom. 8:8. Rom. 7:18. Is. 64:6. Gal. 3:22. 2 Cor. 5:19. 1 Jn. 1:8, 9.

The mighty oceans thunder your praise.

You are mightier than all the breakers pounding on the seashores of the world! / O Jehovah, Commander of the heavenly armies, where is there any other Mighty One like you? Faithfulness is your very character. You rule the oceans when their waves arise in fearful storms; you speak, and they lie still.

'Have you no respect at all for me?' the Lord God asks. 'How can it be that you don't even tremble in my presence? I set the shorelines of the world by perpetual decrees, so that the oceans, though they toss and roar, can never pass those bounds.'

When you go through deep waters and great trouble, I will be with you. When you go through rivers of difficulty, you will not drown!

Peter went over the side of the boat and walked on the water towards Jesus. But when he looked around at the high waves, he was terrified and began to sink. 'Save me, Lord!' he shouted. Instantly Jesus reached out his hand and rescued him. 'O man of little faith,' Jesus said. 'Why did you doubt?'

When I am afraid, I will put my confidence in you.

Ps. 93:3. Ps. 93:4. Ps. 89:8, 9. Jer. 5:22. Is. 43:2. Mt. 14:29–31.
Ps. 56:3.

How fragrant your cologne, and how great your name!

Christ . . . loved you and gave himself to God as a sacrifice to take away your sins. And God was pleased, for Christ's love for you was like sweet perfume to him. / He is very precious to you who believe. / God raised him up to the heights of heaven and gave him a name which is above every other name, that at the name of Jesus every knee shall bow in heaven and on earth and under the earth. / For in Christ there is the perfection of God in a human body.

If you love me, obey me. / God loves us, and we feel this warm love everywhere within us because God has given us the Holy Spirit to fill our hearts with his love. / As far as God is concerned there is a sweet, wholesome fragrance in our lives. It is the fragrance of Christ within us, an aroma to both the saved and the unsaved all around us.

O Lord our God, the majesty and glory of your name fills all the earth and overflows the heavens. / 'Emmanuel' . . . God is with us. / These will be his royal titles: 'Wonderful,' 'Counsellor,' 'The Mighty God,' 'The Everlasting Father,' 'The Prince of Peace.' / The Lord is a strong fortress. The good men run to him and are safe.

Song 1:3. Eph. 5:2. 1 Pet. 2:7. Phil. 2:9, 10. Col. 2:9. Jn. 14:15. Rom. 5:5. 2 Cor. 2:15. Ps. 8:1. Mt. 1:23. Is. 9:6. Prov. 18:10.

These earthly bodies make us groan and sigh.

Lord, you know how I long for my health once more. You hear my every sigh. My body is sick, my health is broken beneath my sins. They are like a flood, higher than my head; they are a burden too heavy to bear. / The old nature that is still inside me loves to sin. Oh, what a terrible predicament I'm in! Who will free me from my slavery to this deadly lower nature?

Even the things of nature, like animals and plants, suffer in sickness and death. And even we Christians, although we have the Holy Spirit within us as a fore-taste of future glory, also groan to be released from pain and suffering. We, too, wait anxiously for that day when God will give us our full rights as his children, inlcuding the new bodies he has promised us – bodies that will never be sick again and will never die. / There is wonderful joy ahead, even though the going is rough for a while down here.

My days here on earth are numbered, and I am soon to die. / For our earthly bodies, the ones we have now that can die, must be transformed into heavenly bodies that cannot perish but will live forever.

2 Cor. 5:4. Ps. 38:9, 4. Rom. 7:24. Rom. 8:22, 23. 1 Pet. 1:6. 2 Pet. 1:14. 1 Cor. 15:53.

*The young bull . . . shall be carried to a
ceremonially clean place outside the camp . . . and
burned there on a wood fire.*

Pilate gave Jesus to them to be crucified. So they had
him at last, and he was taken out of the city, carrying
his cross to the place known as The 'Skull,' in Hebrew,
'Golgotha.' There they crucified him. / The high priest
brought the blood of the slain animals into the
sanctuary as a sacrifice for sin, and then the bodies of
the animals were burned outside the city. That is why
Jesus suffered and died outside the city, where his blood
washed our sins away. So let us go out to him beyond
the city walls [that is, outside the interests of this world,
being willing to be despised] to suffer with him there,
bearing his shame.

    Don't be bewildered or surprised when you go
through the fiery trials ahead. Instead, be really glad –
because these trials will make you partners with Christ
in his suffering, and afterwards you will have the
wonderful joy of sharing his glory in that coming day
when it will be displayed. / These troubles and sufferings
of ours are, after all, quite small and won't last very
long. Yet this short time of distress will result in God's
richest blessing upon us for ever and ever!

Lev. 4:12. Jn. 19:16–18. Hebr. 13:11–13. 1 Pet. 4:12, 13. 2 Cor. 4:17.

God made man like his Maker.

We are the sons of God. We shouldn't think of God as an idol made by men from gold or silver or chipped from stone.

God is so rich in mercy; he loved us so much that even though we were spiritually dead and doomed by our sins, he gave us back our lives again when he raised Christ from the dead. It is God himself who has made us what we are and given us new lives from Christ Jesus; and long ages ago he planned that we should spend these lives in helping others. / For from the very beginning God decided that those who came to him – and all along he knew who would – should become like his Son.

We do know this, that when he comes we will be like him, as a result of seeing him as he really is. / When I awake in heaven, I will be fully satisfied, for I will see you face to face.

Everyone who conquers will inherit all these blessings, and I will be his God and he will be my son. / And since we are his children, we will share his treasures – for all God gives to his Son Jesus is now ours too.

Gen. 1:27. Acts. 17:28, 29. Eph. 2:4, 5, 10. Rom. 8:29. 1 Jn. 3:2. Ps. 17:15. Rev. 21:7. Rom. 8:17.

Lord, don't desert me now   You alone are my hope.

Many say that God will never help us. Prove them wrong, O Lord, by letting the light of your face shine down upon us. / I will sing each morning about your power and mercy. For you have been my high tower of refuge, a place of safety in the day of my distress.

In my prosperity I said, 'This is forever; nothing can stop me now!' Then, Lord, you turned your face away from me and cut off your river of blessings. Suddenly my courage was gone; I was terrified and panic-stricken. I cried to you, O Lord; oh, how I pleaded: 'What will you gain, O Lord, from killing me? How can I praise you then to all my friends? How can my dust in the grave speak out and tell the world about your faithfulness? Hear me, Lord; oh, have pity and help me.'

For a brief moment I abandoned you. But with great compassion I will gather you. In a moment of anger I turned my face a little while; but with everlasting love I will have pity on you, says the Lord, your Redeemer. / Your weeping shall suddenly be turned to wonderful joy. / Weeping may go on all night, but in the morning there is joy.

Jer. 17:17. Ps. 4:6. Ps. 59:16. Ps. 30:6–10. Is. 54:7, 8. Jn. 16:20. Ps. 30:5.

The Ten Commandments were given so that all could see the extent of their failure.

How can you demand purity in one born impure? / I was born a sinner, yes, from the moment my mother conceived me.

Once you were under God's curse, doomed forever for your sins. We started out bad, being born with evil natures, and were under God's anger just like everyone else. / I don't understand myself at all, for I really want to do what is right, but I can't. I do what I don't want to – what I hate. I know I am rotten through and through so far as my old sinful nature is concerned. No matter which way I turn I can't make myself do right.

When Adam sinned, sin entered the entire human race. His sin spread death throughout all the world. What a contrast between Adam and Christ. For this one man, Jesus Christ, brought forgiveness to many through God's mercy. Adam caused many to be sinners because he disobeyed God, and Christ caused many to be made acceptable to God because he obeyed.

The power of the life-giving Spirit – and this power is mine through Christ Jesus – has freed me from the vicious circle of sin and death.

How we thank God for all of this! It is he who makes us victorious through Jesus Christ our Lord!

Rom. 5:20. Job 14:4. Ps. 51:5. Eph. 2:1, 3. Rom. 7:15, 18. Rom. 5:12, 14, 15, 19. Rom. 8:2. 1 Cor. 15:57.

*The Lord grants wisdom! His every word is a
treasure of knowledge and understanding.*

Trust the Lord completely; don't ever trust yourself. /
If you want to know what God wants you to do, ask
him, and he will gladly tell you, for he is always ready
to give a generous supply of wisdom to all who ask
him. / God is far wiser than . . . the wisest man, and
God in his weakness – Christ dying on the cross – is
far stronger than any man. / God has deliberately
chosen to use ideas the world considers foolish and of
little worth in order to shame those people considered
by the world as wise and great. So that no one anywhere
can ever boast in the presence of God.

As your plan unfolds, even the simple can understand it. / I have thought much about your words, and
stored them in my heart so that they would hold me
back from sin.

All who were there spoke well of him and were
amazed by the beautiful words that fell from his lips. /
"He says such wonderful things' they mumbled.
'We've never heard anything like it.' / It is from God
alone that you have your life through Christ Jesus.

*Prov. 2:6. Prov. 3:5. Jas. 1:5. 1 Cor. 1:25. 1 Cor. 1:27, 29. Ps. 119:130.
Ps. 119:11. Lk. 4:22. Jn. 7:46. 1 Cor. 1:30.*

The time has come for me to avenge my people, to redeem them from the hands of their oppressors.

For the fiftieth year shall be holy, a time to proclaim liberty throughout the land to all enslaved debtors, and a time for the cancelling of all public and private debts. It shall be a year when all the family estates sold to others shall be returned to the original owners or their heirs.

Those who belong to God shall live again. Their bodies shall rise again! Those who dwell in the dust shall awake and sing for joy! For God's light of life will fall like dew upon them.

The Lord himself will come down from heaven with a mighty shout and with the soul-stirring cry of the archangel and the great trumpet-call of God. And the Christians who are dead will be the first to rise to meet the Lord. Then we who are still alive and remain on the earth will be caught up with them in the clouds to meet the Lord in the air and remain with him forever.

Shall I redeem him from Death? O Death, bring forth your terrors for his tasting! O Grave, demonstrate your plagues! For I will not relent!

Their Redeemer is strong. His name is the Lord of heaven's armies.

Is. 63:4. Lev. 25:10. Is. 26:19. 1 Thess. 4:16, 17. Hos. 13:14. Jer. 50:34.

When he sees all that is accomplished by the anguish of his soul, he shall be satisfied.

Jesus . . . said, 'It is finished,' and bowed his head and dismissed his spirit. / God took the sinless Christ and poured into him our sins. Then, in exchange, he poured God's goodness into us!

I have made Israel for myself, and these my people will some day honour me before the world. / His reason? To show to all the powers of heaven how perfectly wise God is when they see all of his family – Jews and Gentiles – joined together in his church, just as he had always planned to do through Jesus Christ our Lord. / Now God can always point to us as examples of how very, very rich his kindness is, as shown in all he has done for us through Jesus Christ.

His presence within us is God's guarantee that he really will give us all that he promised; and the Spirit's seal upon us means that God has already purchased us and that he guarantees to bring us to himself.

You have been chosen by God himself – you are priests of the King, you are holy and pure, you are God's very own – all this so that you may show to others how God called you out of the darkness into his wonderful light.

Is. 53:11. Jn. 19:30. 2 Cor. 5:21. Is. 43:21. Eph. 3:10, 11. Eph. 2:7. Eph. 1:14. 1 Pet. 2:9.

They steeled themselves against his love and complained against him in the desert while he was testing them.

They . . . demanded better food, testing God's patience to the breaking point.

Jesus, full of the Holy Spirit, left the river Jordan, being urged by the Spirit out into the barren wastelands of Judea where Satan tempted Him for forty days. He ate nothing all that time, and was very hungry. Satan said, 'If you are God's Son, tell this stone to become a loaf of bread.' But Jesus replied, '. . . other things in life are much more important than bread.'

When someone wants to do wrong it is never God who is tempting him, for God never wants to do wrong and never tempts anyone else to do it. Temptation is the pull of man's own evil thoughts and wishes. These evil thoughts lead to evil actions and afterwards to the death penalty from God.

Since he himself has now been through suffering and temptation, he knows what it is like when we suffer and are tempted, and he is wonderfully able to help us. / Simon, Simon, Satan has asked to have you, to sift you like wheat, but I have pleaded in prayer for you that your faith should not completely fail.

Hebr. 3:8. Ps. 106:14. Lk. 4:1–4. Jas. 1:13–15. Hebr. 2:18. Lk. 22:31, 32.

Light is sown for the godly and joy for the good.

Those who sow tears shall reap joy. Yes, they go out weeping, carrying seed for sowing, and return singing, carrying their sheaves. / Plant the good seeds of righteousness and you will reap a crop of my love.

All honour to God, the God and Father of our Lord Jesus Christ; for it is his boundless mercy that has given us the privilege of being born again, so that we are now members of God's own family. Now we live in the hope of eternal life because Christ rose again from the dead. So be truly glad! There is wonderful joy ahead, even though the going is rough for a while down here. These trials are only to test your faith, to see whether or not it is strong and pure. It is being tested as fire tests gold and purifies it – and your faith is far more precious to God than mere gold. So if your faith remains strong after being tried in the test tube of fiery trials, it will bring you much praise and glory and honour on the day of his return.

We will reap a harvest of blessing if we don't get discouraged and give up.

Ps. 97:11. Ps. 126:5, 6. Hos. 10:12. 1 Pet. 1:3, 6, 7. Gal. 6:9.

I am the Lord who sanctifies you.

I am the Lord your God who has made a distinction between you and the people of other nations. You shall be holy to me, for I the Lord am holy, and I have set you apart from all other peoples, to be mine. / God the Father has chosen you and Jesus Christ has kept you safe.

Make them pure and holy through teaching them your words of truth. / May the God of peace himself make you entirely clean; and may your spirit and soul and body be kept strong and blameless until that day when our Lord Jesus Christ comes back again.

Jesus suffered and died outside the city, where his blood washed our sins away. / He died under God's judgment against our sins, so that he could rescue us from constant falling into sin and make us his very own people, with cleansed hearts. / We who have been made holy by Jesus, now have the same Father as he has. That is why Jesus is not ashamed to call us his brothers. / And I consecrate myself to meet their need for growth in truth and holiness. / The Holy Spirit . . . cleansing you with the blood of Jesus Christ and enabling you to please him.

Lev. 20:8. Lev. 20:24, 26. Jude 1. Jn. 17:17. 1 Thess. 5:23. Hebr. 13:12. Tit. 2:14. Hebr. 2:11. Jn. 17:19. 1 Pet. 1:2.

*Where is the man who fears the Lord? God will
teach him how to choose the best.*

The Lord guided them by a pillar of cloud during the
daytime, and by a pillar of fire at night.

Your words are a flashlight to light the path ahead of
me, and keep me from stumbling. / If you leave God's
paths and go astray, you will hear a Voice behind you
say, 'No, this is the way: walk here.' / I will instruct
you (says the Lord) and guide you along the best pathway for your life; I will advise you and watch your
progress. Don't be like a senseless horse or mule that
has to have a bit in its mouth to keep it in line! Many
sorrows come to the wicked, but abiding love surrounds
those who trust in the Lord. So rejoice in him, all those
who are his, and shout for joy, all those who try to obey
him. / And when we obey him, every path he guides us
on is fragrant with his lovingkindness and his truth.

O Lord, I know it is not within the power of man
to map his life and plan his course. / Show me the
path where I should go, O Lord; point out the right
road for me to walk.

Ps. 25:12. Ex. 13:21. Ps. 119:105. Is. 30:21. Ps. 32:8–11. Ps. 25:10.
Jer. 10:23. Ps. 25:4.

You can sleep without fear; you need not be afraid of disaster . . . for the Lord is with you; he protects you.

Soon a terrible storm arose. High waves began to break into the boat until it was nearly full of water and about to sink. Jesus was asleep in the stern of the boat with his head on a cushion.

Don't worry about anything; instead, pray about everything; tell God your needs and don't forget to thank him for his answers. If you do this you will experience God's peace, which is far more wonderful than the human mind can understand. His peace will keep your thoughts and your hearts quiet and at rest as you trust in Christ Jesus.

I will lie down in peace and sleep, for though I am alone, O Lord, you will keep me safe. / God wants his loved ones to get their proper rest.

As the murderous stones came hurtling at him, Stephen prayed, 'Lord Jesus, receive my spirit.' And he fell to his knees, shouting, 'Lord, don't charge them with this sin!' and with that, he died. / We are not afraid, but are quite content to die, for then we will be at home with the Lord.

Prov. 3:24. Mk. 4:37, 38. Phil. 4:6, 7. Ps. 4:8. Ps. 127:2. Acts 7:59, 60. 2 Cor. 5:8.

*The sprinkled blood which graciously forgives
instead of crying out for vengeance as the blood
of Abel did.*

Look! There is the Lamb of God who takes away the
world's sin! / It is not possible for the blood of bulls
and goats really to take away sins. That is why Christ
said, as he came into the world, 'O God, the blood of
bulls and goats cannot satisfy you, so you have made
ready this body of mine for me to lay as a sacrifice upon
your altar.' Under this new plan we have been forgiven
and made clean by Christ's dying for us once and for
all.

Abel brought the fatty cuts of meat from his best
lambs, and presented them to the Lord. And the Lord
accepted Abel's offering. / Christ . . . loved you and
gave himself to God as a sacrifice to take away your
sins. And God was pleased, for Christ's love for you
was like sweet perfume to him.

Let us go right in, to God himself, with true hearts
fully trusting him to receive us, because we have been
sprinkled with Christ's blood to make us clean, and
because our bodies have been washed with pure water. /
We may walk right into the very Holy of Holies where
God is, because of the blood of Jesus.

*Hebr. 12:24. Jn. 1:29. Hebr. 10:4, 5, 10. Gen. 4:4. Eph. 5:2. Hebr. 10:22.
Hebr. 10:19.*

Who can realize the terrors of your anger?

That afternoon, the whole earth was covered with darkness for three hours, from noon until three o'clock. At about three o'clock, Jesus shouted, 'Eli, Eli, lama sabachthani,' which means, 'My God, my God, why have you forsaken me?' / God laid on *him* the guilt and sins of every one of us.

There is now no condemnation awaiting those who belong to Christ Jesus. / Since we have been made right in God's sight by faith in his promises, we can have real peace with him because of what Jesus Christ our Lord has done for us. / Christ has brought us out from under the doom of that impossible system by taking the curse for our wrongdoing upon himself.

God showed how much he loved us by sending his only Son into this wicked world to bring to us eternal life through his death. In this act we see what real love is: it is not our love for God, but his love for us when he sent his Son to satisfy God's anger against our sins. / He can receive sinners . . . because Jesus took away their sins . . . He does it on the basis of their trust in Jesus.

Ps. 90:11. Mt. 27:45, 46. Is. 53:6. Rom. 8:1. Rom. 5:1. Gal. 3:13.
1 Jn. 4:9, 10. Rom. 3:26.

The Lord God says: I am ready to hear Israel's prayers for these blessings, and to grant them their requests. Let them but ask.

The reason you don't have what you want is that you don't ask God for it.

Ask, and you will be given what you ask for. Seek, and you will find. Knock, and the door will be opened. For everyone who asks, receives. Anyone who seeks, finds. If only you will knock, the door will open. / And we are sure of this, that he will listen to us whenever we ask him for anything in line with his will. And if we really know he is listening when we talk to him and make our requests, then we can be sure that he will answer us. / If you want to know what God wants you to do, ask him, and he will gladly tell you, for he is always ready to give a generous supply of wisdom to all who ask him.

The eyes of the Lord are intently watching all who live good lives, and he gives attention when they cry to him. Yes, the Lord hears the good man when he calls to him for help.

Present your petitions over my signature. And I won't need to ask the Father to grant you these requests, for the Father himself loves you dearly because you love me.

Ezk. 36:37. Jas. 4:2. Mt. 7:7, 8. 1 Jn. 5:14, 15. Jas. 1:5. Ps. 34:15, 17. Jn. 16:26, 27.

Shall we receive only pleasant things from the hand of God and never anything unpleasant?

I know, O Lord, that your decisions are right and that your punishment was right and did me good. / O Lord, you are our Father. We are the clay and you are the Potter. We are all formed by your hand. / It is the Lord's will . . . let him do what he thinks best.

Like a refiner of silver he will sit and watch closely as the dross is burned away. / When he punishes you, it proves that he loves you. When he whips you it proves you are really his child. / The student shares his teacher's fate. The servant shares his master's. / And even though Jesus was God's Son, he had to learn from experience what it was like to obey, when obeying meant suffering.

Be really glad – because these trials will make you partners with Christ in his suffering, and afterwards you will have the wonderful joy of sharing his glory in that coming day when it will be displayed. / 'These are the ones coming out of the great tribulation,' he said; 'they washed their robes and made them white by the blood of the Lamb.'

Job 2:10. Ps. 119:75. Is. 64:8. 1 Sam. 3:18. Mal. 3:3. Hebr. 12:6. Mt. 10:25. Hebr. 5:8. 1 Pet. 4:13. Rev. 7:14.

Resist the devil and he will flee from you.

'Get out of here, Satan,' Jesus told him. 'The Scriptures say, 'Worship only the Lord God. Obey only him.'' Then Satan went away, and angels came and cared for Jesus.

Your strength must come from the Lord's mighty power within you. Put on all of God's armour so that you will be able to stand safe against all strategies and tricks of Satan. / Take no part in the worthless pleasures of evil and darkness, but instead rebuke and expose them. / Avoid being outwitted by Satan; for we know what he is trying to do. / Be careful – watch out for attacks from Satan, your great enemy. He prowls around like a hungry, roaring lion, looking for some victim to tear apart. Stand firm when he attacks. Trust the Lord. And remember that other Christians all around the world are going through these sufferings, too. / Every child of God can obey him, defeating sin and evil pleasure by trusting Christ to help him.

For I am convinced that nothing can ever separate us from his love. Death can't, and life can't. The angels won't, and all the powers of hell itself cannot keep God's love away.

Jas. 4:7. Mt. 4:10, 11. Eph. 6:10, 11. Eph. 5:11. 2 Cor. 2:11. 1 Pet. 5:8, 9. 1 Jn. 5:4. Rom. 8:38.

Oh, that I knew where to find God.

Who among you fears the Lord and obeys his Servant? If such men walk in darkness, without one ray of light, let them trust the Lord, let them rely upon their God.

You will find me when you seek me, if you look for me in earnest. / Keep on asking and you will keep on getting; keep on looking and you will keep on finding; knock and the door will be opened. Everyone who asks, receives; all who seek, find; and the door is opened to everyone who knocks.

Share the fellowship and the joys we have with the Father and with Jesus Christ his Son. / You belong to Christ Jesus, and though you once were far away from God, now you have been brought very near to him because of what Jesus Christ has done for you with his blood. Now all of us, whether Jews or Gentiles, may come to God the Father with the Holy Spirit's help because of what Christ has done for us.

If we say we are his friends, but go on living in spiritual darkness and sin, we are lying.

I am with you always. / I will never, *never* fail you nor forsake you. / The Comforter . . . lives with you now and some day shall be in you.

Job. 23:3. Is. 50:10. Jer. 29:13. Lk. 11:9, 10. 1 Jn. 1:3. Eph. 2:13, 18.
1 Jn. 1:6. Mt. 28:20. Heb. 13:5. Jn. 14:16, 17.

Let us examine ourselves instead, and repent and turn again to the Lord.

Cross-examine me, O Lord . . . test my motives and affections. / You deserve honesty from the heart; yes, utter sincerity and truthfulness. Oh, give me this wisdom. / I thought about the wrong direction in which I was headed, and turned around and came running back to you. / A man should examine himself carefully.

If we confess our sins to him, he can be depended on to forgive us and to cleanse us from every wrong. / If you sin, there is someone to plead for you before the Father. His name is Jesus Christ, the one who is all that is good and who pleases God completely. / And so, dear brothers, now we may walk right into the very Holy of Holies where God is, because of the blood of Jesus. This is the fresh, new, life-giving way which Christ has opened up for us by tearing the curtain – his human body – to let us into the holy presence of God. And since this great high priest of ours rules over God's household, let us go right in, to God himself, with true hearts fully trusting him to receive us, because we have been sprinkled with Christ's blood to make us clean, and because our bodies have been washed with pure water.

Lam. 3:40. Ps. 26:2. Ps. 51:6. Ps. 119:59, 60. 1 Cor. 11:28. 1 Jn. 1:9. 1 Jn. 2:1. Hebr. 10:19–22.

A rainbow glowing like an emerald encircled his throne.

I seal this promise with this sign: I have placed my rainbow in the clouds as a sign of my promise until the end of time, to you and to all the earth. For I will see the rainbow in the cloud and remember my eternal promise to every living being on the earth. / An everlasting covenant . . . eternal, final, sealed. / He has given us both his promise and his oath, two things we can completely count on, for it is impossible for God to tell a lie. Now all those who flee to him to save them can take new courage when they hear such assurances from God; now they know without doubt that he will give them the salvation he has promised them. This certain hope of being saved is a strong and trustworthy anchor for our souls, connecting us with God himself behind the sacred curtains of heaven, where Christ has gone ahead to plead for us from his position as our high priest, with the honour and rank of Melchizedek. / In this man, Jesus, there is forgiveness for your sins. Everyone who trusts in him is freed from all guilt and declared righteous.

Jesus Christ is the same yesterday, today, and forever.

Rev. 4:3. Gen. 9:12, 13, 16. 2 Sam. 23:5. Hebr. 6:18, 19. Acts 13:38, 39. Hebr. 13:8.

Look upon your old sin nature as dead and
unresponsive to sin, and instead be alive to God,
alert to him, through Jesus Christ our Lord.

Anyone who listens to my message and believes in
God who sent me has eternal life, and will never be
damned for his sins, but has already passed out of death
into life. / It was through reading the Scriptures
that I came to realize that I could never find God's
favour by trying – and failing – to obey the laws. I
came to realize that acceptance with God comes by
believing in Christ. I have been crucified with Christ:
and I myself no longer live, but Christ lives in me. And
the real life I now have within this body is a result of
my trusting in the Son of God, who loved me and gave
himself for me.

I will live again – and you will too. / I give them
eternal life and they shall never perish. No one shall
snatch them away from me, for my Father has given
them to me, and he is more powerful than anyone
else, so no one can kidnap them from me. I and the
Father are one.

Since you became alive again, so to speak, when
Christ arose from the dead, now set your sights on the
rich treasures and joys of heaven where he sits beside
God in the place of honour and power. You should
have as little desire for this world as a dead person
does. Your real life is in heaven with Christ and God.

Rom. 6:11. Jn. 5:24. Gal. 2:19, 20. Jn. 14:19. Jn. 10:28–30. Col. 3:1, 3.

*God . . . will give . . . a generous supply . . . to
all who ask him.*

Jesus . . . said to her, 'Where are your accusers? Didn't
even one of them condemn you?' 'No, sir,' she said.
And Jesus said, 'Neither do I. Go and sin no more.'

What a difference between man's sin and God's forgiveness! For this one man, Adam, brought death to
many through his sin. But this one man, Jesus Christ,
brought forgiveness to many through God's mercy.
Adam's one sin brought the penalty of death to many,
while Christ freely takes away many sins and gives
glorious life instead.

God is so rich in mercy; he loved us so much that
even though we were spiritually dead and doomed by
our sins, he gave us back our lives again when he raised
Christ from the dead – only by his undeserved favour
have we ever been saved – and lifted us up from the
grave into glory along with Christ, where we sit with
him in the heavenly realms – all because of what Christ
Jesus did. And now God can always point to us as
examples of how very, very rich his kindness is, as
shown in all he has done for us through Jesus Christ.

Since he did not spare even his own Son for us but
gave him up for us all, won't he also surely give us
everything else?

Jas. 1:5. Jn. 8:10, 11. Rom. 5:15, 16. Eph. 2:4–7. Rom. 8:32.

*God loved the world so much that he gave his only
Son so that anyone who believes in him shall not
perish but have eternal life.*

God . . . brought us back to himself through what
Christ Jesus did. And God has given us the privilege of
urging everyone to come into his favour and be reconciled to him. For God was in Christ, restoring
the world to himself, no longer counting men's sins
against them but blotting them out. This is the wonderful message he has given us to tell others. We are
Christ's ambassadors. God is using us to speak to you:
we beg you, as though Christ himself were here pleading
with you, receive the love he offers you – be reconciled
to God. For God took the sinless Christ and poured
into him our sins. Then, in exchange, he poured God's
goodness into us!

God is love. God showed how much he loved us by
sending his only Son into this wicked world to bring to
us eternal life through his death. In this act we see what
real love is: it is not our love for God, but his love for
us when he sent his Son to satisfy God's anger against
our sins. Dear friends, since God loved us as much as
that, we surely ought to love each other too.

Jn. 3:16. 2 Cor. 5:18–21. 1 Jn. 4:8–11.

*A man's conscience is the Lord's search-light
exposing his hidden motives.*

'All right, stone her to death – but only a man who
has never sinned may throw the first stone.' And the
Jewish leaders slipped away one by one, beginning
with the eldest.

'Who told you you were naked?' the Lord God
asked. 'Have you eaten fruit from the tree I warned you
about?'

Knowing what is right to do and then not doing it is
sin. / If we have bad consciences and feel that we have
done wrong, the Lord will feel it even more acutely,
for he knows everything we do. But, dearly loved
friends, if our consciences are clear, we can come to
the Lord with perfect assurance and trust.

There is nothing wrong with meat, but it is wrong
to eat it if it makes another stumble. Happy is the
man who does not sin by doing what he knows is right.

Search me, O God, and know my heart; test my
thoughts. Point out anything you find in me that makes
you sad, and lead me along the path of everlasting life.

*Prov. 20:27. Jn. 8:7, 9. Gen. 3:11. Jas. 4:17. 1 Jn. 3:20, 21. Rom. 14:20,
22. Ps. 139:23, 24.*

Don't brag about your plans for tomorrow –
wait and see what happens.

Your cry came to me at a favourable time, when the doors of welcome were wide open. I helped you on a day when salvation was being offered. / My light will shine out for you just a little while longer. Walk in it while you can, and go where you want to go before the darkness falls, for then it will be too late for you to find your way. Make use of the Light while there is still time; then you will become light bearers.

Whatever you do, do well, for in death, where you are going, there is no working or planning, or knowing, or understanding.

Friend, you have enough stored away for years to come. Now take it easy – wine, women and song for you! Fool! Tonight you die. Then who will get it all? Yes, every man is a fool who gets rich on earth but not in heaven.

For the length of your lives is as uncertain as the morning mist – now you see it; soon it is gone. / This world is fading away, and these evil, forbidden things will go with it, but whoever keeps doing the will of God will live forever.

Prov. 27:1. 2 Cor. 6:2. Jn. 12:35, 36. Eccl. 9:10. Lk. 12:19–21. Jas. 4:14.
1 Jn. 2:17.

You are forever, and your years never end.

Before the mountains were created, before the earth was formed, you are God without beginning or end.

I am the Lord – I do not change. That is why you are not already utterly destroyed. / Jesus Christ is the same yesterday, today, and forever.

Whatever is good and perfect comes to us from God, the creator of all light, and he shines for ever without change or shadow. / God's gifts and his call can never be withdrawn; he will never go back on his promises.

God is not a man, that he should lie. He doesn't change his mind like humans do. / *His compassion never ends.* It is only the Lord's mercies that have kept us from complete destruction.

Jesus lives forever and continues to be a priest so that no one else is needed. He is able to save completely all who come to God through him. Since he will live forever, he will always be there to remind God that he has paid for their sins with his blood. / Don't be afraid! I am the First and the Last.

Ps. 102:27. Ps. 90:2. Mal. 3:6. Hebr. 13:8. Jas. 1:17. Rom. 11:29.
Num. 23:19. Lam. 3:22. Hebr. 7:24, 25. Rev. 1:17.

When the Holy Spirit controls our lives he will produce . . . love.

God is love, and anyone who lives in love is living with God and God is living in him. / How dearly God loves us, and we feel this warm love everywhere within us because God has given us the Holy Spirit to fill our hearts with his love. / He is very precious to you who believe. / Our love for him comes as a result of his loving us first. / Whatever we do, it is certainly not for our own profit, but because Christ's love controls us now. Since we believe that Christ died for all of us, we should also believe that we have died to the old life we used to live. He died for all so that all who live – having received eternal life from him – might live no longer for themselves, to please themselves, but to spend their lives pleasing Christ who died and rose again for them.

God himself is teaching you to love one another. / I demand that you love each other as much as I love you. / Most important of all, continue to show deep love for each other, for love makes up for many of your faults. / Be full of love for others, following the example of Christ who loved you and gave himself to God as a sacrifice to take away your sins. And God was pleased, for Christ's love for you was like sweet perfume to him.

Gal. 5:22. 1 Jn. 4:16. Rom. 5:5. 1 Pet. 2:7. 1 Jn. 4:19. 2 Cor. 5:14, 15. 1 Thess. 4:9. Jn. 15:12. 1 Pet. 4:8. Eph. 5:2.

Jehovah-nissi . . . Raise the banner of the Lord.

If God is on our side, who can ever be against us? / He is for me! How can I be afraid? What can mere man do to me?

You have given us a banner to rally to; all who love truth will rally to it.

The Lord is my light and my salvation; whom shall I fear? Yes, though a mighty army marches against me, my heart shall know no fear! I am confident that God will save me.

God is with us; he is our Leader. / The Commander of the armies of heaven is here among us. He, the God of Jacob, has come to rescue us.

They will wage war against the Lamb and the Lamb will conquer them.

What fools the nations are to rage against the Lord! How strange that men should try to outwit God! God in heaven merely laughs! He is amused by all their puny plans. / Call your councils of war, develop your strategies, prepare your plans of attacking us, and perish! For God is with us.

Ex. 17:15. Rom. 8:31. Ps. 118:6. Ps. 60:4. Ps. 27:1, 3. 2 Chron. 13:12. Ps. 46:7. Rev. 17:14. Ps. 2:1, 4. Is. 8:10.

God has made me fruitful in this land of my slavery.

What a wonderful God we have – he is the Father of our Lord Jesus Christ, the source of every mercy and the one who so wonderfully comforts and strengthens us in our hardships and trials. And why does he do this? So that when others are troubled, needing our sympathy and encouragement, we can pass on to them this same help and comfort God has given us. You can be sure that the more we undergo sufferings for Christ, the more he will shower us with his comfort and encouragement.

There is wonderful joy ahead, even though the going is rough for a while down here. These trials are only to test your faith, to see whether or not it is strong and pure. It is being tested as fire tests gold and purifies it – and your faith is far more precious to God than mere gold. So if your faith remains strong after being tried in the test tube of fiery trials, it will bring you much praise and glory and honour on the day of his return.

If you are suffering according to God's will, keep on doing what is right and trust yourself to the God who made you, for he will never fail you.

Gen. 41:52. 2 Cor. 1:3–5. 1 Pet. 1:6, 7. 1 Pet. 4:19.

There is a full, complete rest still waiting *for the people of God.*

They are blest indeed, for now they shall rest from all their toils and trials; for their good deeds follow them to heaven!

These earthly bodies make us groan and sigh. / And even we Christians, although we have the Holy Spirit within us as a foretaste of future glory, also groan to be released from pain and suffering. We, too, wait anxiously for that day when God will give us our full rights as his children, including the new bodies he has promised us – bodies that will never be sick and will never die. / What we suffer now is nothing compared to the glory he will give us later.

Now we look forward with confidence to our heavenly bodies, realizing that every moment we spend in these earthly bodies is time spent away from our eternal home in heaven with Jesus. We know these things are true by believing, not by seeing. And we are not afraid, but are quite content to die, for then we will be at home with the Lord.

I long to go and be with Christ.

Hebr. 4:9. Rev. 14:13. 2 Cor. 5:4. Rom. 8:23. Rom. 8:18. 2 Cor. 5:6–8. Phil. 1:23.

*Trust the Lord completely; don't ever trust
yourself.*

In everything you do, put God first, and he will direct
you and crown your efforts with success. / O my
people, trust him all the time. Pour out your longings
before him, for he can help!

I will instruct you (says the Lord) and guide you
along the best pathway for your life; I will advise you
and watch your progress. Don't be like a senseless
horse or mule that has to have a bit in its mouth to
keep it in line! Many sorrows come to the wicked, but
abiding love surrounds those who trust in the Lord. / If
you leave God's paths and go astray, you will hear a
Voice behind you say, 'No, this is the way: walk
here.' / And the Lord will guide you continually, and
satisfy you with all good things, and keep you healthy
too; and you will be like a well-watered garden, like
an ever-flowing spring.

If you aren't going with us, don't let us move a step
from this place. If you don't go with us, who will ever
know that I and my people have found favour with you,
and that we are different from any other people upon
the face of the earth?

Prov. 3:5, 6. Ps. 62:8. Ps. 32:8–10. Is. 30:21. Is. 58:11. Ex. 33:15, 16.

The prize for which God is calling us up to heaven because of what Christ Jesus did for us.

You will have treasure in heaven . . . come, follow me. / I will give you great blessings.

His master praised him for good work. 'You have been faithful in handling this small amount,' he told him, 'so now I will give you many more responsibilities.' Begin the joyous tasks I have assigned to you. / They shall reign for ever and ever.

Your reward will be a never-ending share in his glory and honour. / The crown of life. / A crown . . . waiting for me. / A heavenly reward that never disappears.

Father, I want them with me – these you've given me – so that they can see my glory. You gave me the glory because you loved me before the world began. / To . . . remain with him forever.

What we suffer now is nothing compared to the glory he will give us later.

No mere man has ever seen, heard or even imagined what wonderful things God has ready for those who love the Lord. But we know about these things because God has sent his Spirit to tell us.

Phil. 3:14. Mt. 19:21. Gen. 15:1. Mt. 25:21. Rev. 22:5. 1 Pet. 5:4. Jas. 1:12. 2 Tim. 4:8. 1 Cor. 9:25. Jn. 17:24. 1 Thess. 4:17. Rom. 8:18. 1 Cor. 2:9, 10.

*Let heaven fill your thoughts; don't spend your
time worrying about things down here.*

Stop loving this evil world and all that it offers you,
for when you love these things you show that you do
not really love God. / Don't store your profits here on
earth where they can erode away or may be stolen.
Store them in heaven where they will never lose their
value, and are safe from thieves. If your profits are in
heaven your heart will be there too.

We know these things are true by believing, not by
seeing. / That is why we never give up. Though our
bodies are dying, our inner strength in the Lord is
growing every day. These troubles and sufferings of
ours are, after all, quite small and won't last very
long. Yet this short time of distress will result in God's
richest blessing upon us for ever and ever. So we do
not look at what we can see at this moment, the
troubles all around us, but we look forward to the joys
in heaven which we have not yet seen. The troubles
will soon be over, but the joys to come will last forever.

The priceless gift of eternal life . . . kept in heaven
for you, pure and undefiled, beyond the reach of
change and decay.

Col. 3:2. 1 Jn. 2:15. Mt. 6:19–21. 2 Cor. 5:7. 2 Cor. 4:16–18. 1 Pet. 1:4.

He willingly bent his shoulder to the task.

For examples of patience in suffering, look at the Lord's prophets. / All these things happened to them as examples – as object lessons to us – to warn us against doing the same things; they were written down so that we could read about them and learn from them in these last days as the world nears its end.

Shall we receive only pleasant things from the hand of God and never anything unpleasant? / Job is an example of a man who continued to trust the Lord in sorrow; from his experiences we can see how the Lord's plan finally ended in good, for he is full of tenderness and mercy. / It is the Lord's will . . . let him do what he thinks best.

Give your burdens to the Lord. He will carry them. He will not permit the godly to slip or fall. / It was *our* grief he bore, *our* sorrows that weighed him down.

Come to me and I will give you rest – all of you who work so hard beneath a heavy yoke. Wear my yoke – for it fits perfectly – and let me teach you; for I am gentle and humble, and you shall find rest for your souls; for I give you only light burdens.

Gen. 49:15. Jas. 5:10. 1 Cor. 10:11. Job. 2:10. Jas. 5:11. 1 Sam. 3:18. Ps. 55:22. Is. 53:4. Mt. 11:28–30.

O God, I cried, I am in trouble – help me.

O God enthroned in heaven, I lift my eyes to you. We look to Jehovah our God for his mercy and kindness just as a servant keeps his eyes upon his master or a slave girl watches her mistress for the slightest signal. / O God, listen to me! Hear my prayer! For wherever I am, though far away at the ends of the earth, I will cry to you for help. When my heart is faint and overwhelmed, lead me to the mighty, towering Rock of safety. For you are my refuge, a high tower where my enemies can never reach me. I shall live forever in your tabernacle; oh, to be safe beneath the shelter of your wings! / To the poor, O Lord, you are a refuge from the storm, a shadow from the heat.

Christ, who suffered for you, is your example. Follow in his steps: he never sinned, never told a lie, never answered back when insulted; when he suffered he did not threaten to get even; he left his case in the hands of God who always judges fairly. / This high priest of ours understands our weaknesses, since he had the same temptations we have, though he never once gave way to them and sinned. So let us come boldly to the very throne of God and stay there to receive his mercy and to find grace to help us in our times of need.

Is. 38:14. Ps. 123:1,2. Ps. 61:1–4. Is. 25:4. 1 Pet. 2:21–23. Hebr. 4:15,16.

Fight on for God.

Trouble was on every hand and all around us; within us, our hearts were full of dread and fear. / Don't be afraid . . . our army is bigger than theirs! / Your strength must come from the Lord's mighty power within you.

You come to me with a sword and a spear, but I come to you in the name of the Lord of the armies of heaven and of Israel – the very God whom you have defied. / God is my strong fortress . . . he gives me skill in war and strength to bend a bow of bronze. / Our . . . power and success comes from God.

The Angel of the Lord guards and rescues all who reverence him. / 'Lord, open his eyes and let him see!' And the Lord opened the young man's eyes so that he could see horses of fire and chariots of fire everywhere upon the mountain!

How much more do I need to say? It would take too long to recount the stories. . . . These people all trusted God and as a result won battles, overthrew kingdoms. . . . Some were made strong again after they had been weak or sick. Others were given great power in battle; they made whole armies turn and run away.

1 Tim. 6:12. 2 Cor. 7:5. 2 Kgs. 6:16. Eph. 6:10. 1 Sam. 17:45. 2 Sam. 22:33, 35. 2 Cor. 3:5. Ps. 34:7. 2 Kgs. 6:17. Hebr. 11:32–34.

*He grants good sense to the godly – his saints.
He is their shield, protecting them and guarding
their pathway.*

The Lord God . . . led them all the way, and had
selected the best places for them to camp, and had
guided them by a pillar of fire at night and a pillar of
cloud during the day. / He spreads his wings over them,
even as an eagle covers her young. She carries them
upon her wings – as does the Lord his people! . . . The
Lord alone was leading them. / The steps of good men
are directed by the Lord. He delights in each step they
take. If they fall it isn't fatal, for the Lord holds
them with his hand. / The good man does not escape
all troubles – he has them too. But the Lord helps
him in each and every one. / For the Lord watches over
all the plans and paths of godly men, but the paths of
the godless lead to doom. / And we know that all that
happens to us is working for our good if we love God
and are fitting into his plans. / We have the Lord our
God to fight our battles for us!

The Lord your God has arrived to live among you.
He is a mighty Saviour. He will give you victory. He
will rejoice over you in great gladness.

*Prov. 2:8. Deut. 1:32, 33. Deut. 32:11, 12. Ps. 37:23, 24. Ps. 34:19.
Ps. 1:6. Rom. 8:28. 2 Chron. 32:8. Zeph. 3:17.*

My God, my God, why have you forsaken me?

He was wounded and bruised for *our* sins. He was chastised that we might have peace; he was lashed – and we were healed! *We* are the ones who strayed away like sheep! Yet God laid on *him* the guilt and sins of every one of us. From prison and trial they led him away to his death. But who among the people of that day realized it was their sins that he was dying for – that he was suffering their punishment?

He died for our sins. / He died once for the sins of all us guilty sinners, although he himself was innocent of any sin at any time, that he might bring us safely home to God. / He personally carried the load of our sins in his own body when he died on the cross, so that we can be finished with sin and live a good life from now on. For his wounds have healed ours!

God took the sinless Christ and poured into him our sins. Then, in exchange, he poured God's goodness into us!

Christ has bought us out from under the doom of that impossible system by taking the curse for our wrongdoing upon himself. For it is written in the Scriptures, 'Anyone who is hanged on a tree is cursed' [as Jesus was hung upon a wooden cross].

Mt. 27:46. Is. 53:5, 6, 8. Rom. 4:25. 1 Pet. 3:18. 1 Pet. 2:24. 2 Cor. 5:21. Gal. 3:13.

*Your Creator will be your 'husband.' The Lord
of heaven's armies is his name.*

I know this is hard to understand, but it is an illustration
of the way we are parts of the body of Christ.

Never again shall you be called 'The God-for-
saken Land' or the 'Land that God Forgot.' Your
new name will be 'The Land of God's Delight' and
'The Bride,' for the Lord delights in you and will claim
you as his own. . . . God will rejoice over you as a
bridegroom with his bride. / The Lord has anointed
me to bring good news to the suffering and afflicted.
He has sent me to comfort the broken-hearted, to
announce liberty to captives and to open the eyes of
the blind. He has sent me to tell those who mourn
that the time of God's favour to them has come, and
the day of his wrath to their enemies. To all who
mourn in Israel he will give: beauty for ashes; joy
instead of mourning; praise instead of heaviness.

Let me tell you how happy God has made me! For
he has clothed me with garments of salvation and
draped about me the robe of righteousness. I am like
a bridegroom in his wedding suit or a bride with her
jewels.

And I will bind you to me forever with chains of
righteousness and justice and love and mercy.

Who then can ever keep Christ's love from us?

*Is. 54:5. Eph. 5:32. Is. 62:4, 5. Is. 61:1–3. Is. 61:10. Hos. 2:19.
Rom. 8:35.*

My times are in your hands.

His holy ones are in his hands. / Then the Lord said to Elijah, 'Go to the east and hide by Cherith Brook at a place east of where it enters the river Jordan. Drink from the brook and eat what the ravens bring you, for I have commanded them to feed you.' Then the Lord said to him, 'Go and live in the village of Zarephath, near the city of Sidon. There is a widow there who will feed you. I have given her my instructions.'

Don't worry about *things* – food, drink, money and clothes. For you already have life and a body – and they are far more important than what to eat and wear. Your heavenly Father already knows perfectly well that you need them. And he will gladly give them to you if you give him first place in your life. So don't be anxious about tomorrow. God will take care of your tomorrow too. Live one day at a time.

Trust the Lord completely; don't ever trust yourself. In everything you do, put God first, and he will direct you and crown your efforts with success. / Let him have all your worries and cares, for he is always thinking about you and watching everything that concerns you.

Ps. 31:15. Deut. 33:3. 1 Kgs. 17:2–4, 8, 9. Mt. 6:25, 32–34. Prov. 3:5, 6. 1 Pet. 5:7.

You have forgiven all my sins.

Where is another God like you, who pardons the sins of the survivors among his people? You cannot stay angry with your people, for you love to be merciful. Once again you will have compassion on us. You will tread our sins beneath your feet; you will throw them into the depths of the ocean!

'For a brief moment I abandoned you. But with great compassion I will gather you. In a moment of anger I turned my face a little while; but with everlasting love I will have pity on you,' says the Lord, your Redeemer. / I will forgive and forget their sins.

What happiness for those whose guilt has been forgiven! What joys when sins are covered over! What relief for those who have confessed their sins and God has cleared their record. / The blood of Jesus his Son cleanses us from every sin. If we say that we have no sin, we are only fooling ourselves, and refusing to accept the truth. But if we confess our sins to him, he can be depended on to forgive us and to cleanse us from every wrong. And it is perfectly proper for God to do this for us because Christ died to wash away our sins.

Is. 38:17. Mic. 7:18, 19. Is. 54:7, 8. Jer. 31:34. Ps. 32:1, 2. 1 Jn. 1:7–9.

*I know the one in whom I trust, and I am sure that
he is able to guard safely all that I have given
him until the day of his return.*

Able to do far more than we would ever dare to ask
or even dream of.

Able to make it up to you by giving you everything
you need and more, so that there will not only be
enough for your own needs, but plenty left over to give
joyfully to others.

Wonderfully able to help us . . . when we suffer and
are tempted.

Able to save completely all who come to God through
him. Since he will live forever, he will always be there
to remind God that he has paid for their sins with his
blood.

Able to keep you from slipping and falling away,
and to bring you, sinless and perfect, into his glorious
presence with mighty shouts of everlasting joy.

Able to guard safely all that I have given him until
the day of his return.

He will take these dying bodies of ours and change
them into glorious bodies like his own, using the same
mighty power that he will use to conquer all else
everywhere.

'Do you believe?' . . . 'Yes, Lord,' they told him,
'we do.' 'Because of your faith it will happen.'

2 Tim. 1:12. Eph. 3:20. 2 Cor. 9:8. Hebr. 2:18. Hebr. 7:25. Jude 24.
2 Tim. 1:12. Phil. 3:21. Mt. 9:28, 29.

*The living God who always richly gives us all we
need for our enjoyment.*

Beware that in your plenty you don't forget the Lord
your God and begin to disobey him. For when you
have become full and prosperous and have built fine
homes to live in . . . that is the time to watch out that
you don't become proud, and forget the Lord your
God. Always remember that it is the Lord your God
who gives you power to become rich.

Unless the Lord builds a house, the builders' work
is useless. Unless the Lord protects a city, sentries do
no good. It is senseless for you to work so hard from
early morning until late at night, fearing you will
starve to death; for God wants his loved ones to get
their proper rest. / They did not conquer by their own
strength and skill, but by your mighty power and
because you smiled upon them and favoured them. /
Many say that God will never help us. Prove them
wrong, O Lord, by letting the light of your face shine
down upon us. Yes, the gladness you have given me is
far greater than their joys at harvest time as they gaze
at their bountiful crops. I will lie down in peace and
sleep. for though I am alone, O Lord, you will keep me
safe.

1 Tim. 6:17. Deut. 8:11, 12, 14, 18. Ps. 127:1, 2. Ps. 44:3. Ps. 4:6–8.

*This tremendous choir . . . sang a wonderful
new song.*

The fresh, new, life-giving way which Christ has
opened up for us. / Then he saved us – not because we
were good enough to be saved, but because of his
kindness and pity – by washing away our sins and
giving us the new joy of the indwelling Holy Spirit.
He poured him out upon us with wonderful fullness –
and all because of what Jesus Christ our Saviour did. /
Because of his kindness you have been saved through
trusting Christ. And even trusting is not of yourselves;
it too is a gift from God. Salvation is not a reward
for the good we have done, so none of us can take any
credit for it.

Glorify your name, not yours, O Lord! Cause
everyone to praise your lovingkindness and your
truth. / All praise to him who always loves us and who
set us free from our sins by pouring out his lifeblood
for us. He has gathered us into his kingdom and made
us priests of God his Father. Give to him everlasting
glory! He rules forever! Amen. / You were slain, and
your blood has bought people from every nation as
gifts for God. / I saw a vast crowd, too great to count . . .
shouting with a mighty shout, 'Salvation comes from
our God upon the throne, and from the Lamb.'

*Rev. 14:3. Hebr. 10:20. Tit. 3:5, 6. Eph. 2:8, 9. Ps. 115:1. Rev. 1:5, 6.
Rev. 5:9. Rev. 7:9, 10.*

Jehovah provides.

Don't fail me, Lord, for I am trusting you. Don't let my enemies succeed.

The Lord isn't too weak to save you. And he isn't getting deaf! He can hear you when you call! / There shall come out of Zion a deliverer.

Happy is the man who has the God of Jacob as his helper, whose hope is in the Lord his God. / The eyes of the Lord are watching over those who fear him, who rely upon his steady love. He will keep them from death even in times of famine!

It is he who will supply all your needs from his riches in glory, because of what Christ Jesus has done for us. / For God has said, I will never, *never* fail you nor forsake you. That is why we can say without any doubt or fear, 'The Lord is my helper and I am not afraid of anything that mere man can do to me.' / He is my strength, my shield from every danger. I trusted in him, and he helped me. Joy rises in my heart until I burst out in songs of praise to him. The Lord protects his people.

Gen. 22:14. Ps. 25:2. Is. 59:1. Rom. 11:26. Ps. 146:5. Ps. 33:18, 19. Phil. 4:19. Hebr. 13:5, 6. Ps. 28:7, 8.

I am my beloved's and my beloved is mine. He pastures his flock among the lilies!

Where two or three gather together because they are mine, I will be there among them. / I will only reveal myself to those who love me and obey me. The Father will love them too, and we will come to them and live with them.

When you obey me you are living in my love, just as I obey my Father and live in his love.

Let him come into his garden and eat its choicest fruits. / I am here in my garden, my darling, my bride! I gather my myrrh with my spices and eat my honeycomb with my honey. / When the Holy Spirit controls our lives he will produce this kind of fruit in us: love, joy, peace, patience, kindness, goodness, faithfulness, gentleness, and self-control.

My true disciples produce bountiful harvests. This brings great glory to my Father. / He lops off every branch that doesn't produce. And he prunes those branches that bear fruit for even larger crops. / May you always be doing those good, kind things which show that you are a child of God, for this will bring much praise and glory to the Lord.

Song 6:3. Mt. 18:20. Jn. 14:23. Jn. 15:10. Song 4:16. Song 5:1. Gal. 5:22, 23. Jn. 15:8. Jn. 15:2. Phil. 1:11.

May the Lord bless and protect you.

The Lord's blessing is our greatest wealth. All our work adds nothing to it! / Make everyone rejoice who puts his trust in you. Keep them shouting for joy because you are defending them. Fill all who love you with your happiness. For you bless the godly man, O Lord; you protect him with your shield of love.

He will never let me stumble, slip or fall. For he is always watching, never sleeping. Jehovah himself is caring for you! He is your defender. He keeps you from all evil, and preserves your life. He keeps his eye upon you as you come and go, and always guards you. / I, the Lord, will tend the fruitful vines; every day I'll water them, and day and night I'll watch to keep all enemies away.

Holy Father, keep them in your own care – all those you have given me – so that they will be united just as we are, with none missing. During my time here I have kept safe within your family all of these you gave to me.

The Lord will always deliver me from all evil and will bring me into his heavenly kingdom. To God be the glory for ever and ever. Amen.

Num. 6:24. Prov. 10:22. Ps. 5:11, 12. Ps. 121:3–5, 7, 8. Is. 27:3. Jn. 17:11, 12. 2 Tim. 4:18.

Tears came to Jesus' eyes.

A man of sorrows, acquainted with bitterest grief. / This high priest of ours understands our weaknesses, since he had the same temptations we have, though he never once gave way to them and sinned. / It was right and proper that God, who made everything for his own glory, should allow Jesus to suffer, for in doing this he was bringing vast multitudes of God's people to heaven; for his suffering made Jesus a perfect leader, one fit to bring them into their salvation. / Even though Jesus was God's Son, he had to learn from experience what it was like to obey, when obeying meant suffering.

I do not rebel nor turn away. I give my back to the whip, and my cheeks to those who pull out the beard. I do not hide from shame – they spit in my face.

How much he loved. / He did not come as an angel but as a human being. And it was necessary for Jesus to be like us, his brothers, so that he could be our merciful and faithful high priest before God, a priest who would be both merciful to us and faithful to God in dealing with the sins of the people.

Jn. 11:35. Is. 53:3. Hebr. 4:15. Hebr. 2:10. Hebr. 5:8. Is. 50:5, 6.
Jn. 11:36. Hebr. 2:16, 17.

*May the Lord's face radiate with joy because of
you; may he be gracious to you, show you his
favour, and give you his peace.*

No one has ever actually seen God, but, of course, his
only Son has, for he is the companion of the Father
and has told us all about him. / God's Son shines out
with God's glory, and all that God's Son is and does
marks him as God. / If the Good News . . . is hidden
from anyone, it is hidden from the one who is on the
road to eternal death. Satan, who is the god of this evil
world, has made him blind, unable to see the glorious
light of the Gospel that is shining upon him, or to understand the amazing message we preach about the glory
of Christ, who is God.

Let your favour shine again upon your servant; save
me just because you are so kind! Don't disgrace me,
Lord, by not replying when I call to you for aid. / The
Lord has shown me his favour. He has made me steady
as a mountain. Then, Lord, you turned your face away
from me and cut off your river of blessings. Suddenly
my courage was gone; I was terrified and panic-
stricken. / Blessed are those who hear the joyful blast
of the trumpet, for they shall walk in the light of your
presence.

He will give his people strength. He will bless them
with peace.

Don't be afraid!

Num. 6:25, 26. Jn. 1:18. Hebr. 1:3. 2 Cor. 4:3, 4. Ps. 31:16, 17.
Ps. 30:7. Ps. 89:15. Ps. 29:11. Mt. 14:27.

The things that please him.

You can never please God without faith, without depending on him. / Those who are still under the control of their old sinful selves, bent on following their old evil desires, can never please God. / Jehovah enjoys his people; he will save the humble. Let his people rejoice in this honour.

Praise the Lord if you are punished for doing right! Of course, you get no credit for being patient if you are beaten for doing wrong; but if you do right and suffer for it, and are patient beneath the blows. God is well pleased. / Be beautiful inside, in your hearts, with the lasting charm of a gentle and quiet spirit which is so precious to God.

True praise is a worthy sacrifice; this really honours me. Those who walk my paths will receive salvation from the Lord. / Then I will praise God with my singing! My thanks will be his praise – that will please him more than sacrificing a bullock or an ox.

Dear brothers, I plead with you to give your bodies to God. Let them be a living sacrifice, holy – the kind he can accept. When you think of what he has done for you, is this too much to ask?

1 Jn. 3:22. Hebr. 11:6. Rom. 8:8. Ps. 149:4. 1 Pet. 2:19, 20. 1 Pet. 3:4. Ps. 50:23. Ps. 69:30, 31. Rom. 12:1.

*God is on one side and all the people on the other
side, and Christ Jesus, himself man, is between
them to bring them together.*

Since we, God's children, are human beings – made of
flesh and blood – he became flesh and blood too by
being born in human form.

Let all the world look to me for salvation! For I am
God; there is no other.

There is someone to plead for you before the Father.
His name is Jesus Christ, the one who is all that is good
and who pleases God completely. / But now you belong
to Christ Jesus, and though you once were far away
from God, now you have been brought very near to him
because of what Jesus Christ has done for you with his
blood. For Christ himself is our way of peace. / He
went into that greater, perfect tabernacle in heaven,
not made by men nor part of this world, and once for
all took blood into that inner room, the Holy of Holies,
and sprinkled it on the mercy seat; but it was not the
blood of goats and calves. No, he took his own
blood, and with it he, by himself, made sure of our
eternal salvation. / He is able to save completely all
who come to God through him. Since he will live
forever, he will always be there to remind God that he
has paid for their sins with his blood.

*1 Tim. 2:5. Hebr. 2:14. Is. 45:22. 1 Jn. 2:1. Eph. 2:13, 14. Hebr. 9:11, 12.
Hebr. 7:25.*

I am standing here depressed and gloomy.

He will keep in perfect peace all those who trust in him, whose thoughts turn often to the Lord! Trust in the Lord God always, for in the Lord Jehovah is your ever-lasting strength.

Give your burdens to the Lord. He will carry them. He will not permit the godly to slip or fall. / He has not despised my cries of deep despair; he has not turned and walked away. When I cried to him, he heard and came. / Is any among you suffering? He should keep on praying about it.

Don't be troubled or afraid. / Don't worry about *things* – food, drink, money and clothes. For you already have life and a body – and they are far more important than what to eat and wear. Look at the birds! They don't worry about what to eat – they don't need to sow or reap or store up food – for your heavenly Father feeds them. And you are far more valuable to him than they are. Will all your worries add a single moment to your life? And why worry about your clothes? Look at the field lilies. They don't worry about theirs. Yet King Solomon in all his glory was not clothed as beautifully as they. And if God cares so wonderfully for flowers that are here today and gone tomorrow, won't he more surely care for you? / Don't be faithless any longer. Believe! / I am with you always.

Ps. 42:6. Is. 26:3, 4. Ps. 55:22. Ps. 22:24. Jas. 5:13. Jn. 14:27.
Mt. 6:25–30. Jn. 20:27. Mt. 28:20.

Make people want to believe in our Saviour and God.

Live as Christians should. / Keep away from every kind of evil. / Be happy if you are cursed and insulted for being a Christian, for when that happens the Spirit of God will come upon you with great glory. Don't let me hear of your suffering for murdering or stealing or making trouble or being a busybody and prying into other people's affairs. / In everything you do, stay away from complaining and arguing, so that no one can speak a word of blame against you. You are to live clean, innocent lives as children of God in a dark world full of people who are crooked and stubborn. Shine out among them like beacon lights. / Don't hide your light! Let it shine for all; let your good deeds glow for all to see, so that they will praise your heavenly Father.

Never forget to be truthful and kind. Hold these virtues tightly. Write them deep within your heart. If you want favour with both God and man, and a reputation for good judgment and common sense, then trust the Lord completely; don't ever trust yourself. / Fix your thoughts on what is true and good and right. Think about things that are pure and lovely, and dwell on the fine, good things in others. Think about all you can praise God for and be glad about.

Tit. 2:10. Phil. 1:27. 1 Thess. 5:22. 1 Pet. 4:14, 15. Phil. 2:14, 15. Mt. 5:15, 16. Prov. 3:3, 4. Phil. 4:8.

I have told you how to get this true spiritual life.

He gave us our new lives, through the truth of his Word, and we became, as it were, the first children in his new family. / The old way, trying to be saved by keeping the Ten Commandments, ends in death; in the new way, the Holy Spirit gives them life.

The same kind of love . . . as Christ showed to the church when he died for her, to make her holy and clean, washed by baptism and God's word; so that he could give her to himself as a glorious church without a single spot or wrinkle or any other blemish, being holy and without a single fault.

How can a young man stay pure? By reading your Word and following its rules. They give me strength in all my troubles; how they refresh and revive me! I have thought much about your words, and stored them in my heart so that they would hold me back from sin. I will delight in them and not forget them. I trust your promises. They are more valuable to me than millions in silver and gold! I will never lay aside your laws, for you have used them to restore my joy and health. Your words are sweeter than honey. And since only your rules can give me wisdom and understanding, no wonder I hate every false teaching.

Jn. 6:63. Jas. 1:18. 2 Cor. 3:6. Eph. 5:25–27. Ps. 119:9, 50, 11, 16, 42, 72, 93, 103, 104.

His suffering made Jesus a perfect leader.

'My soul is crushed with horror and sadness to the point of death . . . stay here . . . stay awake with me.' He went forward a little, and fell face downward on the ground, and prayed, 'My Father! If it is possible, let this cup be taken away from me. But I want your will, not mine.' / He was in such agony of spirit that he broke into a sweat of blood, with great drops falling to the ground as he prayed more and more earnestly.

Death stared me in the face – I was frightened and sad. / Their contempt has broken my heart; my spirit is heavy within me. If even one would show some pity, if even one would comfort me! / No one gives me a passing thought. No one will help me; no one cares a bit what happens to me.

We despised him and rejected him – a man of sorrows, acquainted with bitterest grief. We turned our backs on him and looked the other way when he went by. He was despised and we didn't care. He was wounded and bruised for *our* sins. He was chastised that we might have peace; he was lashed – and we were healed! He was oppressed and he was afflicted, yet he never said a word.

Therefore, I will give him the honours of one who is mighty and great, because he has poured out his soul unto death.

Hebr. 2:10. Mt. 26:38, 39. Lk. 22:24. Ps. 116:3. Ps. 69:20. Ps. 142:4. Is. 53:3, 5, 7, 12.

The Lord made the heaven, earth, and sea, and everything in them.

The heavens are telling the glory of God; they are a marvellous display of his craftsmanship. / He merely spoke, and the heavens were formed, and all the galaxies of stars. He made the oceans, pouring them into his vast reservoirs. When he but spoke, the world began! It appeared at his command. / All the peoples of the world are nothing in comparison with him – they are but a drop in the bucket, dust on the scales. He picks up the islands as though they had no weight at all.

Who else has held the oceans in his hands and measured off the heavens with his ruler? Who else knows the weight of all the earth and weighs the mountains and the hills?

By faith – by believing God – we know that the world and the stars – in fact, all things – were made at God's command; and that they were made from nothing.

When I look up into the night skies and see the work of your fingers – the moon and the stars you have made – I cannot understand how you can bother with mere puny man, to pay any attention to him!

Ex. 20:11. Ps. 19:1. Ps. 33:6, 7, 9. Is. 40:15. Is. 40:12. Hebr. 11:3. Ps. 8:3, 4.

How do you know what is going to happen tomorrow? For the length of your lives is as uncertain as the morning mist – now you see it; soon it is gone.

My life passes swiftly away, filled with tragedy. My years disappear like swift ships, like the eagle that swoops upon its prey. / We glide along the tides of time as swiftly as a racing river, and vanish as quickly as a dream. We are like grass that is green in the morning but mowed down and withered before the evening shadows fall. / He blossoms for a moment like a flower – and withers; as the shadow of a passing cloud, he quickly disappears. / For we are here for but a moment, strangers in the land as our fathers were before us; our days on earth are like a shadow, gone so soon, without a trace. / Lord, help me to realize how brief my time on earth will be. Help me to know that I am here for but a moment more.

This world is fading away . . . but whoever keeps doing the will of God will live for ever. / They shall perish, but you go on forever. They will grow old, like worn-out clothing, and you will change them like a man putting on a new shirt and throwing away the old one! But you yourself never grow old. You are forever, and your years never end. / Jesus Christ is the same yesterday, today, and forever.

Jas. 4:14. Job. 9:25, 26. Ps. 90:5, 6. Job. 14:2. 1 Chron. 29:15. Ps. 39:4. 1 Jn. 2:17. Ps. 102:26, 27. Hebr. 13:8.

*I will sing in unknown tongues and also in
ordinary language, so that I can understand the
praise I am giving.*

Be filled instead with the Holy Spirit, and controlled
by him. Talk with each other much about the Lord,
quoting psalms and hymns and singing sacred songs,
making music in your hearts to the Lord. / Remember
what Christ taught and let his words enrich your lives
and make you wise; teach them to each other and sing
them out in psalms and hymns and spiritual songs,
singing to the Lord with thankful hearts.

I will praise the Lord and call on all men everywhere
to bless his holy name forever and forever.

Praise the Lord! How good it is to sing his praises!
How delightful, and how right! Sing out your thanks
to him; sing praises to our God, accompanied by harps.

And I heard a sound from heaven like the roaring of
a great waterfall or the rolling of mighty thunder.
It was the singing of a choir accompanied by harps. /
And I saw in heaven another mighty pageant . . . all
were holding harps of God, and they were singing the
song of Moses, the servant of God, and the song of the
Lamb: 'Great and marvellous are your doings, Lord
God Almighty. Just and true are your ways, O King
of Ages.'

*1 Cor. 14:15. Eph. 5:18, 19. Col. 3:16. Ps. 145:21. Ps. 147:1, 7.
Rev. 14:2. Rev. 15:1–4.*

*The person bringing it is to lay his hand upon its
head, and it then becomes his substitute: the death
of the animal will be accepted by God instead of
the death of the man who brings it, as the penalty
for his sins.*

God paid a ransom to save you from the impossible
road to heaven which your fathers tried to take, and the
ransom he paid was not mere gold or silver, as you very
well know; but he paid for you with the precious
lifeblood of Christ, the sinless, spotless Lamb of God. /
He personally carried the load of our sins in his own
body when he died on the cross.

You have become living building-stones for God's
use in building his house. What's more, you are his holy
priests; so come to him [you who are acceptable to him
because of Jesus Christ] and offer to God those things
that please him. / I plead with you to give your bodies
to God. Let them be a living sacrifice, holy – the kind
he can accept. When you think of what he has done for
you, is this too much to ask?

And now – all glory to him who alone is God, who
saves us through Jesus Christ our Lord; yes, splendour
and majesty, all power and authority are his from the
beginning; his they are and his they evermore shall be.
And he is able to keep you from slipping and falling
away, and to bring you, sinless and perfect, into his
glorious presence with mighty shouts of everlasting joy.
Lev. 1:4. 1 Pet. 1:18, 19. 1 Pet. 2:24. 1 Pet. 2:5. Rom. 12:1. Jude 24, 25.

*He had the same temptations we have, though he
never once gave way to them and sinned.*

How lovely and fresh looking it was. And it would
make her so wise! So she ate some of the fruit and gave
some to her husband, and he ate it too. / Stop loving
this evil world and all that it offers you, for when you
love these things you show that you do not really love
God.

Then Satan tempted him to get food by changing
stones into loaves of bread. But Jesus told him, 'No!
For the Scriptures tell us that bread won't feed men's
souls: obedience to every word of God is what we
need.' Next Satan took him to the peak of a very high
mountain and showed him the nations of the world and
all their glory. 'I'll give it all to you,' he said, 'if you will
only kneel and worship me.' 'Get out of here, Satan,'
Jesus told him. / Stop loving this evil world and all
that it offers you . . . these are not from God.

For since he himself has now been through suffering
and temptation, he knows what it is like when we suffer
and are tempted, and he is wonderfully able to help us.

Happy is the man who doesn't give in and do wrong
when he is tempted.

*Hebr. 4:15. Gen. 3:6. 1 Jn. 2:15. Mt. 4:3, 4, 8–10. 1 Jn. 2:15, 16.
Hebr. 2:18. Jas. 1:12.*

My eyes grew weary of looking up for help.

Pity me, O Lord, for I am weak. Heal me, for my body is sick, and I am upset and disturbed. My mind is filled with apprehension and with gloom. Oh, restore me soon. Come, O Lord, and make me well. In your kindness save me. / My heart is in anguish within me. Stark fear overpowers me. Trembling and horror overwhelm me. Oh, for wings like a dove, to fly away and rest!

You need to keep on patiently doing God's will. / And let us not get tired of doing what is right, for after a while we will reap a harvest of blessing if we don't get discouraged and give up.

As they were straining their eyes for another glimpse, suddenly two white-robed men were standing there among them, and said, 'Men of Galilee, why are you standing here staring at the sky? Jesus has gone away to heaven, and some day, just as he went, he will return!' / Our homeland is in heaven, with our Saviour the Lord Jesus Christ in heaven; and we are looking forward to his return from there. / Looking forward to that time when his glory shall be seen – the glory of our great God and Saviour Jesus Christ.

Is. 38:14. Ps. 6:2–4. Ps. 55:4–6. Hebr. 10:36. Gal. 6:9. Acts 1:10, 11. Phil. 3:20. Tit. 2:13.

His name shall be written on their foreheads.

I am the Good Shepherd and know my own sheep. /
God's truth stands firm like a great rock, and nothing
can shake it. It is a foundation stone with these words
written on it: 'The Lord knows those who are really his.'

The Lord is good. When trouble comes, he is the
place to go! And he knows everyone who trusts in
him!

You . . . who heard the Good News about how to be
saved, and trusted Christ, were marked as belonging to
Christ by the Holy Spirit, who long ago had been
promised to all of us Christians. His presence within
us is God's guarantee that he really will give us all that
he promised. / It is this God who has made you and
me into faithful Christians and commissioned us
apostles to preach the Good News. He has put his
brand upon us – his mark of ownership – and given us
his Holy Spirit in our hearts as guarantee that we belong
to him, and as the first instalment of all that he is
going to give us.

I will write my God's name on him, and he will be a
citizen in the city of my God – the new Jerusalem,
coming down from heaven from my God; and he will
have my new name inscribed upon him. / Their motto
will be, 'The Lord is our righteousness!'

*Rev. 22:4. Jn. 10:14. 2 Tim. 2:19. Nah. 1:7. Eph. 1:13,14. 2 Cor. 1:21,22.
Rev. 3:12. Jer. 33:16.*

*As soon as God had brought his servant to life
again, he sent him . . . to bless you by turning
you back from your sins.*

All honour to God, the God and Father of our Lord
Jesus Christ; for it is his boundless mercy that has
given us the privilege of being born again, so that we
are now members of God's own family. Now we live in
the hope of eternal life because Christ rose again
from the dead.

Our . . . Saviour Jesus Christ . . . died under God's
judgment against our sins, so that he could rescue us
from constant falling into sin and make us his very own
people, with cleansed hearts and real enthusiasm for
doing kind things for others. / Be holy now in everything you do, just as the Lord is holy, who invited you
to be his child. He himself has said, 'You must be holy,
for I am holy.'

God, the Father of our Lord Jesus Christ . . . has
blessed us with every blessing in heaven because we
belong to Christ. / For in Christ there is the perfection
of God in a human body; so you have everything when
you have Christ. / We have all benefited from the rich
blessings he brought to us – blessing upon blessing
heaped upon us.

Since he did not spare even his own Son for us but
gave him up for us all, won't he also surely give us
everything else?

*Acts 3:26. 1 Pet. 1:3. Tit. 2:13, 14. 1 Pet. 1:15, 16. Eph. 1:3. Col. 2:9, 10.
Jn. 1:16. Rom. 8:32.*

Encourage and cheer me with your words.

Never forget your promises to me your servant, for they are my only hope. / 'O God,' I cried, 'I am in trouble – help me.'

All heaven and earth shall pass away, yet my words remain forever true. / You know very well that God's promises to you have all come true.

Fear not, for I am with you. Do not be dismayed. I am your God. I will strengthen you; I will help you; I will uphold you with my victorious right hand. / 'Take courage and work, for I am with you,' says the Lord of the armies of heaven. / 'Not by might, nor by power, but by my Spirit,' says the Lord of heaven's armies – 'you will succeed because of my Spirit, though you are few and weak.' / Constantly remind the people about these laws, and you yourself must think about them every day and every night so that you will be sure to obey all of them. For only then will you succeed. Yes, be bold and strong! Banish fear and doubt! For remember, the Lord your God is with you wherever you go.

Your strength must come from the Lord's mighty power within you.

Ps. 119:28. Ps. 119:49. Is. 38:14. Lk. 21:33. Josh. 23:14. Is. 41:10.
Hag. 2:4. Zech. 4:6. Josh. 1:8, 9. Eph. 6:10.

As your plan unfolds, even the simple can understand it.

This is the message God has given us to pass on to you: that God is Light and in him is no darkness at all. / For God, who said, 'Let there be light in the darkness,' has made us understand that it is the brightness of his glory that is seen in the face of Jesus Christ. / Before anything else existed, there was Christ with God. Eternal life is in him, and this life gives light to all mankind. / If we are living in the light of God's presence, just as Christ does, then we have wonderful fellowship and joy with each other, and the blood of Jesus his Son cleanses us from every sin.

I have thought much about your words, and stored them in my heart so that they would hold me back from sin. / He has already tended you by pruning you back for greater strength and usefulness by means of the commands I gave you.

For though once your heart was full of darkness, now it is full of light from the Lord, and your behaviour should show it. / You are priests of the King, you are holy and pure, you are God's very own – all this so that you may show to others how God called you out of the darkness into his wonderful light.

Ps. 119:130. 1 Jn. 1:5. 2 Cor. 4:6. Jn. 1:1, 4. 1 Jn. 1:7. Ps. 119:11. Jn. 15:3. Eph. 5:8. 1 Pet. 2:9.

> *Noah . . . was the only truly righteous man*
> *living on the earth at that time.*

God has said that the only way we can be right in his sight is by faith. / Noah built an altar and sacrificed on it some of the animals and birds God had designated for that purpose. And Jehovah was pleased with the sacrifice.

Now do you see it? No one can ever be made right in God's sight by doing what the law commands. For the more we know of God's laws, the clearer it becomes that we aren't obeying them; his laws serve only to make us see that we are sinners. But now God has shown us a different way to heaven. Now God says he will accept and acquit us – declare us 'not guilty' – if we trust Jesus Christ to take away our sins. And we all can be saved in this same way, by coming to Christ, no matter who we are or what we have been like.

We rejoice in our wonderful new relationship with God – all because of what our Lord Jesus Christ has done in dying for our sins – making us friends of God. / He called us to come to him; and when we came, he declared us 'not guilty,' filled us with Christ's goodness, gave us a right standing with himself, and promised us his glory.

Gen. 6:8, 9. Gal. 3:11. Gen. 8:20, 21. Rom. 3:20–22. Rom. 5:11.
Rom. 8:30.

Wake up! Strengthen what little remains – for even what is left is at the point of death.

The end of the world is coming soon. Therefore be earnest, thoughtful men of prayer. / Be careful – watch out for attacks from Satan, your great enemy. He prowls around like a hungry, roaring lion, looking for some victim to tear apart. / Watch out! Be very careful never to forget what you have seen God doing for you. May his miracles have a deep and permanent effect upon your lives. / And those whose faith has made them good in God's sight must live by faith, trusting him in everything. Otherwise, if they shrink back, God will have no pleasure in them. . . . Our faith in him assures our souls' salvation.

Keep a sharp lookout! For you do not know when I will come, at evening, at midnight, early dawn or late daybreak. Don't let me find you sleeping. *Watch for my return!*

Fear not, for I am with you. Do not be dismayed. I am your God. I will strengthen you; I will help you; I will uphold you with my victorious right hand. I am holding you by your right hand – I, the Lord your God – and I say to you, 'Don't be afraid; I am here to help you.'

Rev. 3:2. 1 Pet. 4:7. 1 Pet. 5:8. Deut. 4:9. Hebr. 10:38, 39. Mk. 13:35–37. Is. 41:10, 13.

Is his lovingkindness gone forever?

He remembered our utter weakness, for his loving-kindness continues forever. / Show the great power [of your patience] by forgiving our sins and showing us your steadfast love. / Where is another God like you, who pardons the sins of the survivors among his people? You cannot stay angry with your people, for you love to be merciful. Once again you will have compassion on us. You will tread our sins beneath your feet; you will throw them into the depths of the ocean! / He saved us – not because we were good enough to be saved, but because of his kindness and pity – by washing away our sins and giving us the new joy of the indwelling Holy Spirit.

What a wonderful God we have – he is the Father of our Lord Jesus Christ, the source of every mercy, and the one who so wonderfully comforts and strengthens us in our hardships and trials.

Our merciful and faithful high priest before God, a priest . . . both merciful to us and faithful to God in dealing with the sins of the people. For since he himself has now been through suffering and temptation, he knows what it is like when we suffer and are tempted, and he is wonderfully able to help us.

Ps. 77:8. Ps. 136:23. Num. 14:18. Mic. 7:18, 19. Tit. 3:5. 2 Cor. 1:3, 4. Hebr. 2:17, 18.

Lot took a long look at the fertile plains of the river Jordan, well watered everywhere (this was before Jehovah destroyed Sodom and Gomorrah); the whole section was like the Garden of Eden. So that is what Lot chose – the Jordan valley to the east of them.

Lot . . . was a good man.

Don't be misled; remember that you can't ignore God and get away with it: a man will always reap just the kind of crop he sows! / Remember what happened to Lot's wife!

Don't enter into partnership with those who do not love the Lord, for what do the people of God have in common with the people of sin? How can light live with darkness? The Lord has said, 'Leave them; separate yourselves from them; don't touch what is unclean: and I will welcome you, and be a Father to you, and you will be my sons and daughters.' / Don't even associate with such people. For though once your heart was full of darkness, now it is full of light from the Lord, and your behaviour should show it! Learn as you go along what pleases the Lord. Take no part in the worthless pleasures of evil and darkness, but instead rebuke and expose them. / Learn to put aside your own desires so that you will become patient and godly, gladly letting God have his way with you. The more you go on in this way, the more you will grow strong spiritually and become fruitful and useful to our Lord Jesus Christ.

Gen. 13:10, 11. 2 Pet. 2:7, 8. Gal. 6:7. Lk. 17:32. 2 Cor. 6:14, 17. Eph. 5:7, 8, 10, 11. 2 Pet. 1:6, 8.

If the Lord is with me I shall drive them out of the land.

God has said, 'I will never, *never* fail you nor forsake you.' That is why we can say without any doubt or fear, 'The Lord is my helper and I am not afraid of anything that mere man can do to me.' / I walk in the strength of the Lord God. I tell everyone that you alone are just and good.

Out of justice, peace. Quietness and confidence will reign for evermore.

You will need the strong belt of truth and the breast-plate of God's approval. You will need faith as your shield to stop the fiery arrows aimed at you by Satan. And you will need the helmet of salvation and the sword of the Spirit – which is the Word of God. For we are not fighting against people made of flesh and blood, but against persons without bodies – the evil rulers of the unseen world, those mighty satanic beings and great evil princes of darkness who rule this world; and against huge numbers of wicked spirits in the spirit world. So use every piece of God's armour to resist the enemy whenever he attacks, and when it is all over, you will still be standing up. / The Lord is with you! I will make you strong. Go . . . I am sending you!

Josh. 14:12. Hebr. 13:5, 6. Ps. 71:16. Is. 32:17. Eph. 6:14, 16, 17, 12, 13. Judg. 6:12, 14.

Holy, holy, holy, Lord God Almighty.

The praises of our fathers surrounded your throne. /
'Don't come any closer,' God told him. 'Take off your
shoes, for you are standing on holy ground. I am the
God of your fathers – the God of Abraham, Isaac,
and Jacob.' (Moses covered his face with his hands, for
he was afraid to look at God.) / 'With whom will
you compare me? Who is my equal?' asks the Holy
One. / I am the Lord your God, your Saviour, the Holy
One of Israel. I am the Lord, and there is no other
Saviour.

Be holy now in everything you do, just as the Lord is
holy, who invited you to be his child. He himself has
said, 'You must be holy, for I am holy.' / Haven't you
yet learned that your body is the home of the Holy
Spirit God gave you, and that he lives within you?
Your own body does not belong to you.

And so . . . I plead with you to give your bodies to
God. Let them be a living sacrifice, holy – the kind he
can accept. When you think of what he has done for
you, is this too much to ask?

Rev. 4:8. Ps. 22:3. Ex. 3:5, 6. Is. 40:25. Is. 43:3, 11. 1 Pet. 1:15, 16.
1 Cor. 6:19. Rom. 12:1.

Do not hide yourself when I am trying to find you.

I have been standing at the door and I am constantly knocking. If anyone hears me calling him and opens the door, I will come in and enjoy fellowship with him and he with me. / Tell me, O one I love, where are you leading your flock today? Where will you be at noon? For I will come and join you there instead of wandering like a vagabond among the flocks of your companions. / I found him and held him and would not let him go.

Let him come into his garden and eat its choicest fruits. / I am here in my garden. / I didn't tell Israel to ask me for what I didn't plan to give! No, for I, Jehovah, speak only truth and righteousness.

I am with you always, even to the end of the world. / I will never, *never* fail you nor forsake you. / For where two or three gather together because they are mine, I will be right there among them. / I will be gone from the world, but I will still be present with you. / You have everything when you have Christ, and you are filled with God through your union with Christ.

Ps. 27:9. Rev. 3:20. Song 1:7. Song 3:4. Song 4:16. Song 5:1. Is. 45:19. Mt. 28:20. Hebr. 13:5. Mt. 18:20. Jn. 14:19. Col. 2:10.

Abraham believed God; then God considered him righteous on account of his faith.

Abraham never doubted. He believed God, for his faith and trust grew ever stronger. He was completely sure that God was well able to do anything he promised. And because of Abraham's faith God forgave his sins and declared him 'not guilty.' Now this wonderful statement – that he was accepted and approved through his faith – wasn't just for Abraham's benefit. It was for us, too, assuring us that God will accept us in the same way as he accepted Abraham – when we believe the promises of God who brought back Jesus our Lord from the dead.

It is clear, then, that God's promise to give the whole earth to Abraham and his descendents was not because Abraham obeyed God's laws but because he trusted God to keep his promise.

God makes us ready for heaven – makes us right in God's sight – when we put our faith and trust in Christ to save us. / We can look forward to the salvation God has promised us. There is no longer any room for doubt, and we can tell others that salvation is ours. / For he is in the heavens, and does as he wishes. / Every promise from God will surely come true. You believed that God would do what he said; that is why he has given you this wonderful blessing.

Gen. 15:6. Rom. 4:20–24. Rom. 4:13. Rom. 1:17. Hebr. 10:23.
Ps. 115:3. Lk. 1:37, 45.

God . . . invited you into his kingdom to share his glory.

Jesus answered, 'I am not an earthly king. If I were, my followers would have fought when I was arrested by the Jewish leaders. But my Kingdom is not of the world.'

The kingdom of this world now belongs to our Lord, and to his Christ; and he shall reign forever and ever. / You have gathered them into a kingdom and made them priests of our God; they shall reign upon the earth. / I saw thrones, and sitting on them were those who had been given the right to judge. They reigned with Christ for a thousand years.

Father, I want them with me – these you've given me – so that they can see my glory. You gave me the glory because you loved me before the world began. / Then the godly shall shine as the sun in their Father's Kingdom. / Don't be afraid, little flock. For it gives your Father great happiness to give you the Kingdom.

The glory of God and of the Lamb illuminate it. Its light will light the nations of the earth. And the glory and honour of all the nations shall be brought into it.

We ask that your kingdom will come.

1 Thess. 2:12. Jn. 18:36. Rev. 11:15. Rev. 5:10. Rev. 20:4. Jn. 17:24. Mt. 13:43. Lk. 12:32. Rev. 21:23, 24, 26. Mt. 6:10.

I will never, never *fail you nor forsake you.*

That is why we can say without any doubt or fear, 'The Lord is my Helper and I am not afraid of anything that mere man can do to me.'

I am with you, and will protect you wherever you go, and will bring you back safely to this land; I will be with you constantly until I have finished giving you all I am promising. / Be strong! Be courageous! Do not be afraid of them. For the Lord your God will be with you. He will neither fail you nor forsake you.

Demas has left me. He loved the good things of this life. The first time I was brought before the judge no one was here to help me. Everyone had run away. I hope that they will not be blamed for it. But the Lord stood with me and gave me the opportunity boldly to preach a whole sermon for all the world to hear. / If my father and mother should abandon me, you would welcome and comfort me.

I am with you always, even to the end of the world. / I am the First and Last, the living one who died, who is now alive for evermore. / I will not abandon you or leave you as orphans – I will come to you. / I am leaving you with a gift – peace of mind and heart.

Hebr. 13:5. Hebr. 13:6. Gen. 28:15. Deut. 31:6. 2 Tim. 4:10, 16, 17. Ps. 27:10. Mt. 28:20. Rev. 1:18. Jn. 14:18. Jn. 14:27.

Sir, we worked hard all last night and didn't catch a thing. But if you say so, we'll try again.

I have been given all authority in heaven and earth. Therefore go and make disciples in all the nations, baptizing them into the name of the Father and of the Son and of the Holy Spirit. . . . I am with you always, even to the end of the world.

The Kingdom of Heaven can be illustrated by a fisherman – he casts a net into the water.

Just preaching the Gospel isn't any special credit to me – I couldn't stop preaching it if I wanted to. I would be utterly miserable. Woe unto me if I don't. Whatever a person is like, I try to find common ground with him so that he will let me tell him about Christ and let Christ save him.

Let us not get tired of doing what is right, for after a while we will reap a harvest of blessing if we don't get discouraged and give up. / My Word . . . always produces fruit. It shall accomplish all I want it to, and prosper everywhere I send it. / The person who does the planting or watering isn't very important, but God is important because he is the one who makes things grow. / We're just God's servants, each of us with certain special abilities.

I appointed you to go and produce good fruit always.

Lk. 5:5. Mt. 28:18–20. Mt. 13:47. 1 Cor. 9:16, 22. Gal. 6:9. Is. 55:11.
1 Cor. 3:7. 1 Cor. 3:5. Jn. 15:16.

*The Kingdom of Heaven can be illustrated by the
story of a man going into another country, who
called together his servants and loaned them
money to invest for him . . . dividing it in
proportion to their abilities.*

Don't you realize that you can choose your own
master? You can choose sin (with death) or else
obedience (with acquittal). The one to whom you offer
yourself – he will take you and be your master and you
will be his slave.

It is the same and only Holy Spirit who gives all these
gifts and powers, deciding which each one of us should
have. The Holy Spirit displays God's power through
each of us as a means of helping the entire church. /
God has given each of you some special abilities; be
sure to use them to help each other, passing on to others
God's many kinds of blessings. / The most important
thing about a servant is that he does just what his master
tells him to. / Much is required from those to whom
much is given, for their responsibility is greater.

Who is adequate for such a task as this? / I can do
everything God asks me to with the help of Christ who
gives me the strength and power.

*Mt. 25:14, 15. Rom. 6:16. 1 Cor. 12:11, 7. 1 Pet. 4:10. 1 Cor. 4:2.
Lk. 12:48. 2 Cor. 2:16. Phil. 4:13.*

> *When God's children are in need, you should be*
> *the one to help them out.*

One day David began wondering if any of Saul's family was still living, for he wanted to be kind to them, as he had promised Prince Jonathan.

Come, blessed of my Father, into the Kingdom prepared for you from the founding of the world. For I was hungry and you fed me; I was thirsty and you gave me water; I was a stranger and you invited me into your homes; naked and you clothed me; sick and in prison, and you visited me. When you did it to these my brothers you were doing it to me! / And if, as my representatives, you give even a cup of cold water to a little child, you will surely be rewarded.

Don't forget to do good and to share what you have with those in need, for such sacrifices are very pleasing to him. / For God is not unfair. How can he forget your hard work for him, or forget the way you used to show your love for him – and still do – by helping his children? And we are anxious that you keep on loving others as long as life lasts, so that you will get your full reward.

Rom. 12:13. 2 Sam. 9:1. Mt. 25:34–36, 40. Mt. 10:42. Hebr. 13:16.
Hebr. 6:10, 11.

The good man's reward lasts forever.

After a long time their master returned from his trip
and called them to him to account for his money. The
man to whom he had entrusted the £500 brought him
£1,000. His master praised him for good work. 'You
have been faithful in handling this small amount,' he
told him, 'so now I will give you many more responsibilities. Begin the joyous tasks I have assigned to you.'

We must all stand before Christ to be judged and
have our lives laid bare before him. Each of us will
receive whatever he deserves for the good or bad things
he has done in his earthly body.

I have fought long and hard for my Lord, and
through it all I have kept true to him. And now the
time has come for me to stop fighting and rest. In heaven
a crown is waiting for me which the Lord, the righteous
Judge, will give me on that great day of his return.
And not just to me, but to all those whose lives show
that they are eagerly looking forward to his coming
back again.

I am coming soon! Hold tightly to the little strength
you have – so that no one will take away your crown.

Prov. 11:18. Mt. 25:19–21. 2 Cor. 5:10. 2 Tim. 4:7, 8. Rev. 3:11.

God . . . will do what he says.

God is not a man, that he should lie; he doesn't change his mind like humans do. Has he ever promised, without doing what he said? / The Lord has sworn and will never change his mind.

God also bound himself with an oath, so that those he promised to help would be perfectly sure and never need to wonder whether he might change his plans. He has given us both his promise and his oath, two things we can completely count on, for it is impossible for God to tell a lie. Now all those who flee to him to save them can take new courage when they hear such assurances from God; now they can know without doubt that he will give them the salvation he has promised them. / So if you are suffering according to God's will, keep on doing what is right and trust yourself to the God who made you, for he will never fail you.

I know the one in whom I trust, and I am sure that he is able to guard safely all that I have given him until the day of his return. / God, who called you to become his child, will do all this for you, just as he promised. / He carries out and fulfils all of God's promises, no matter how many of them there are; and we have told everyone how faithful he is, giving glory to his name.

1 Cor. 10:13. Num. 23:19. Hebr. 7:21. Hebr. 6:17, 18. 1 Pet. 4:19.
2 Tim. 1:12. 1 Thess. 5:24. 2 Cor. 1:20.

Lead on with courage and strength!

The Lord is my light and my salvation; whom shall I fear? / He gives power to the tired and worn out, and strength to the weak. Even the youths shall be exhausted, and the young men will all give up. But they that wait upon the Lord shall renew their strength. They shall mount up with wings like eagles; they shall run and not be weary; they shall walk and not faint. / My health fails; my spirits droop, yet God remains! He is the strength of my heart; he is mine forever!

What can we ever say to such wonderful things as these? If God is on our side, who can ever be against us? Since he did not spare even his own Son for us but gave him up for us all, won't he also surely give us everything else? / He is for me! How can I be afraid? What can mere man do to me? / It is only by your power and through your name that we tread down our enemies. / Overwhelming victory is ours through Christ who loved us enough to die for us.

So now, my son, may the Lord be with you and prosper you. Be strong and courageous, fearless and enthusiastic!

Josh. 1:18. Ps. 27:1. Is. 40:29–31. Ps. 73:26. Rom. 8:31, 32. Ps. 118:6. Ps. 44:5. Rom. 8:37. 1 Chron. 22:11, 13.

Our friend Lazarus has gone to sleep.

I want you to know what happens to a Christian when he dies, so that when it happens, you will not be full of sorrow, as those are who have no hope. For since we believe that Jesus died and then came back to life again, we can also believe that when Jesus returns, God will bring back with him all the Christians who have died.

If they don't, then Christ is still dead, and you are very foolish to keep on trusting God to save you, and you are still under condemnation for your sins. In that case all Christians who have died are lost. But the fact is that Christ did actually rise from the dead, and has become the first of millions who will come back to life again some day.

When all the people were safely across, the Lord said to Joshua, 'Tell the twelve men chosen for a special task, one from each tribe, each to take a stone from where the priests are standing in the middle of the Jordan, and to carry them out and pile them up as a monument . . . the monument will be a permanent reminder to the people of Israel.' / We all are witnesses that Jesus rose from the dead. / Witnesses God had selected beforehand . . . who ate and drank with him after he rose from the dead.

Jn. 11:11. 1 Thess. 4:13, 14. 1 Cor. 15:16–18, 20. Josh. 4:1–3, 7. Acts 2:32. Acts 10:41.

*Come, blessed of my Father, into the Kingdom
prepared for you from the founding of the world.*

Don't be afraid, little flock. For it gives your Father
great happiness to give you the Kingdom. / God has
chosen poor people to be rich in faith, and the kingdom
of heaven is theirs, for that is the gift God has promised
to all those who love him. / Since we are his children,
we will share his treasures – for all God gives to his
Son Jesus is now ours too. But if we are to share his
glory, we must also share his suffering.

The Father himself loves you dearly because you
love me and believe that I came from the Father. / God
is not ashamed to be called their God, for he has made
a heavenly city for them.

Everyone who conquers will inherit all these
blessings, and I will be his God and he will be my son. /
In heaven a crown is waiting for me which the Lord,
the righteous Judge, will give me on that great day
of his return. And not just to me, but to all those whose
lives show that they are eagerly looking forward to
his coming back again. / God who began the good
work within you will keep right on helping you grow in
his grace until his task within you is finally finished
on that day when Jesus Christ returns.

*Mt. 25:34. Lk. 12:32. Jas. 2:5. Rom. 8:17. Jn. 16:27. Hebr. 11:16.
Rev. 21:7. 2 Tim. 4:8. Phil. 1:6.*

Riches can disappear fast. And the king's crown doesn't stay in his family forever.

Proud man! Frail as breath! A shadow! And all his busy rushing ends in nothing. He heaps up riches for someone else to spend. / Let heaven fill your thoughts; don't spend your time worrying about things down here. / Don't store your profits here on earth where they can erode away or may be stolen. Store them in heaven where they will never lose their value, and are safe from thieves. If your profits are in heaven your heart will be there too.

Deny yourselves many things that would keep you from doing your best. An athlete goes to all this trouble just to win a ribbon or a silver cup, but we do it for a heavenly reward that never disappears. / We do not look at what we can see at this moment, the troubles all around us, but we look forward to the joys in heaven which we have not yet seen. / The good man's reward lasts forever. / In heaven a crown is waiting for me which the Lord, the righteous Judge, will give me on that great day of his return. And not just to me, but to all those whose lives show that they are eagerly looking forward to his coming back again. / Your reward will be a never-ending share in his glory and honour.

Prov. 27:23, 24. Ps. 39:6. Col. 3:2. Mt. 6:19–21. 1 Cor. 9:25. 2 Cor. 4:18. Prov. 11:18. 2 Tim. 4:8. 1 Pet. 5:4.

Isaac . . . was taking a walk out in the fields, meditating.

May my spoken words and unspoken thoughts be pleasing even to you, O Lord my Rock and my Redeemer.

When I look up into the night skies and see the work of your fingers – the moon and the stars you have made – I cannot understand how you can bother with mere puny man, to pay any attention to him! / I want to express publicly before his people my heartfelt thanks to God for his mighty miracles. All who are thankful should ponder them with me.

Oh, the joys of those who do not follow evil men's advice, who do not hang around with sinners, scoffing at the things of God: but they delight in doing everything God wants them to, and day and night are always meditating on his laws and thinking about ways to follow him more closely. / Constantly remind the people about these laws, and you yourself must think about them every day and every night. / I will praise you with great joy. I lie awake at night thinking of you – of how much you have helped me – and how I rejoice through the night beneath the protecting shadow of your wings. I follow close behind you, protected by your strong right arm.

Gen. 24:62, 63. Ps. 19:14. Ps. 8:3, 4. Ps. 111:1, 2. Ps. 1:1, 2. Josh. 1:8. Ps. 63:5–8.

How long will you forget me, Lord? Forever?
How long will you look the other way when I am
in need?

Whatever is good and perfect comes to us from God, the creator of all light, and he shines for ever without change or shadow. / Yet they say, 'My Lord deserted us; he has forgotten us.' Never! Can a mother forget her little child and not have love for her own son? Yet even if that should be, I will not forget you.

I will not forget to help you. I've blotted out your sins; they are gone like morning mist at noon!

Although Jesus was very fond of Martha, Mary, and Lazarus, he stayed where he was for the next two days and made no move to go to them. / A woman . . . came to him, pleading, 'Have mercy on me, O Lord.' But Jesus gave her no reply – not even a word.

These trials are only to test your faith, to see whether or not it is strong and pure. It is being tested as fire tests gold and purifies it – and your faith is far more precious to God than mere gold. So if your faith remains strong after being tried in the test tube of fiery trials, it will bring you much praise and glory and honour on the day of his return.

Ps. 13:1. Jas. 1:17. Is. 49:14, 15. Is. 44:21, 22. Jn. 11:5, 6. Mt. 15:22, 23.
1 Pet. 1:7.

He will supply all your needs from his riches in glory, because of what Christ Jesus has done for us.

Your heavenly Father already knows perfectly well that you need them. And he will gladly give them to you if you give him first place in your life. / Since he did not spare even his own Son for us but gave him up for us all, won't he also surely give us everything else? / God has already given you everything you need. He has given you the whole world to use, and life and even death are your servants. He has given you all of the present and all of the future. All are yours, and you belong to Christ, and Christ is God's. / We own nothing, and yet we enjoy everything.

Because the Lord is my Shepherd, I have everything I need! / For Jehovah God is our Light and our Protector. He gives us grace and glory. No good thing will he withhold from those who walk along his paths. / The living God . . . richly gives us all we need for our enjoyment. / God is able to make it up to you by giving you everything you need and more, so that there will not only be enough for your own needs, but plenty left over to give joyfully to others.

Phil. 4:19. Mt. 6:32, 33. Rom. 8:32. 1 Cor. 3:21–23. 2 Cor. 6:10.
Ps. 23:1. Ps. 84:11. 1 Tim. 6:17. 2 Cor. 9:8.

*What do the people of God have in common with
the people of sin?*

They loved the darkness more than the Light, for their
deeds were evil. / You are all children of the light and
the day, and do not belong to darkness and night.

Darkness has made him blind. / Your words are a
flashlight to light the path ahead of me.

The land is full of darkness and cruel men. / Love
comes from God and those who are loving and kind
show that they are the children of God, and that they
are getting to know him better. But if a person isn't
loving and kind, it shows that he doesn't know God –
for God is love.

The evil man gropes and stumbles in the dark. But
the good man walks along in the ever-brightening
light of God's favour; the dawn gives way to morning
splendour.

I have come as a Light to shine in this dark world,
so that all who put their trust in me will no longer
wander in the darkness. / Though once your heart
was full of darkness, now it is full of light from the
Lord, and your behaviour should show it! Because of
this light within you, you should do only what is good
and right and true. Learn as you go along what pleases
the Lord.

2 Cor. 6:14. Jn. 3:19. 1 Thess. 5:5. 1 Jn. 2:11. Ps. 119:105. Ps. 74:20.
1 Jn. 4:7, 8. Prov. 4:19, 18. Jn. 12:46. Eph. 5:8–10.

*When the Holy Spirit controls our lives he will
produce . . . joy.*

Joy from the Holy Spirit. / Inexpressible joy that
comes from heaven itself.

Our hearts ache, but at the same time we have the
joy of the Lord. / Happy in spite of all my suffering. /
We . . . rejoice . . . when we run into problems and
trials.

Jesus, our leader and instructor . . . willing to die a
shameful death on the cross because of the joy he knew
would be his afterwards. / I have told you this so that
you will be filled with my joy. Yes, your cup of joy
will overflow! / The more we undergo sufferings for
Christ, the more he will shower us with his comfort
and encouragement.

Always be full of joy in the Lord; I say it again,
rejoice! / The joy of the Lord is your strength.

You have let me experience the joys of life and the
exquisite pleasures of your own eternal presence. /
For the Lamb standing in front of the throne will feed
them and be their shepherd and lead them to the springs
of the water of life. And God will wipe their tears
away. / For them all sorrow and all sighing will be
gone forever; only joy and gladness will be there.

*Gal. 5:22. Rom. 14:17. 1 Pet. 1:8. 2 Cor. 6:10. 2 Cor. 7:4. Rom. 5:3.
Hebr. 12:2. Jn. 15:11. 2 Cor. 1:5. Phil. 4:4. Neh. 8:10. Ps. 16:11.
Rev. 7:17. Is. 35:10.*

The Altar of Peace with Jehovah.

'But I will give you a son,' he told me, 'who will be a man of peace, for I will give him peace with his enemies in the surrounding lands. His name shall be Solomon (meaning 'Peaceful'), and I will give peace and quietness to Israel during his reign.'

Now a greater than Solomon is here. / For unto us a Child is born; unto us a Son is given; and the government shall be upon his shoulder. These will be his royal titles: 'Wonderful,' 'Counsellor,' 'The Mighty God,' 'The Everlasting Father,' 'The Prince of Peace.' / My people will live in safety, quietly at home, but the Assyrians will be destroyed and their cities laid low.

Christ himself is our way of peace. / He will be our Peace . . . when the Assyrian invades our land and marches across our hills. / He will keep in perfect peace all those who trust in him, whose thoughts turn often to the Lord!

Together they will wage war against the Lamb, and the Lamb will conquer them; for he is Lord over all lords, and King of kings.

I am leaving you with a gift – peace of mind and heart. And the peace I give isn't fragile like the peace the world gives. / His peace will keep your thoughts and your hearts quiet and at rest as you trust in Christ Jesus.

Judg. 6:24. 1 Chron. 22:9. Mt. 12:42. Is. 9:6. Is. 32:18, 19. Eph. 2:14. Mic. 5:5. Is. 26:3. Rev. 17:14. Jn. 14:27. Phil. 4:7.

*If you are really serious about wanting to return
to the Lord, get rid of your foreign gods and
your Ashtaroth idols. Determine to obey only the
Lord.*

Dear children, keep away from anything that might
take God's place in your hearts. / The Lord has said,
'Leave them; separate yourselves from them; don't
touch what is unclean: and I will welcome you, and be
a Father to you, and you will be my sons and
daughters.' / You cannot serve two masters: God and
money.

You must worship no other gods, but only Jehovah,
for he is a God who claims absolute loyalty and
exclusive devotion. / Worship and serve him with a
clean heart and a willing mind, for the Lord sees every
heart and understands and knows every thought.

You deserve honesty from the heart; yes, utter
sincerity and truthfulness. Oh, give me this wisdom. /
Men judge by outward appearance, but I look at a
man's thoughts and intentions. / Dearly loved friends,
if our consciences are clear, we can come to the Lord
with perfect assurance and trust. / Cling tightly to
your faith in Christ and always keep your conscience
clear, doing what you know is right.

*1 Sam. 7:3. 1 Jn. 5:21. 2 Cor. 6:17, 18. Mt. 6:24. Ex. 34:14. 1 Chron. 28:9.
Ps. 51:6. 1 Sam. 16:7. 1 Jn. 3:21. 1 Tim. 1:19.*

*When I, the Son of Mankind, return, how many
will I find who have faith?*

In his own land and among his own people . . . he
was not accepted. / The Holy Spirit tells us clearly that
in the last times some in the church will turn away
from Christ.

Preach the Word of God urgently at all times,
whenever you get the chance, in season and out, when
it is convenient and when it is not. Correct and rebuke
your people when they need it, encourage them to do
right, and all the time be feeding them patiently with
God's word. For there is going to come a time when
people won't listen to the truth, but will go around
looking for teachers who will tell them just what they
want to hear. They won't listen to what the Bible says
but will blithely follow their own misguided ideas.

No one, not even the angels in heaven, nor I myself,
knows the day or hour when these things will happen;
only the Father knows. And since you do not know
when it will happen, stay alert. Be on the watch [for
my return]. / There will be great joy for those who are
ready and waiting for his return. / Looking forward to
that time when his glory shall be seen – the glory of
our great God and Saviour Jesus Christ.

*Lk. 18:8. Jn. 1:11. 1 Tim. 4:1. 2 Tim. 4:2–4. Mk. 13:32, 33. Lk. 12:37.
Tit. 2:13.*

*Don't forget this, dear friends, that a day or a
thousand years from now is like tomorrow to the
Lord.*

This plan of mine is not what you would work out,
neither are my thoughts the same as yours! For just as
the heavens are higher than the earth, so are my ways
higher than yours, and my thoughts than yours. As the
rain and snow come down from heaven and stay upon
the ground to water the earth . . . so also is my Word.
I sent it out and it always produces fruit. It shall
accomplish all I want it to, and prosper everywhere
I send it.

For God has given them all up to sin so that he could
have mercy upon all alike. Oh, what a wonderful God
we have! How great are his wisdom and knowledge
and riches! How impossible it is for us to understand
his decisions and his methods! For who among us can
know the mind of the Lord? Who knows enough to be
his counsellor and guide? And who could ever offer to
the Lord enough to induce him to act? For everything
comes from God alone. Everything lives by his power,
and everything is for his glory. To him be glory evermore.

So be on your guard, not asleep like the others.
Watch for his return. Always be thankful no matter
what happens, for that is God's will for you who
belong to Christ Jesus.

2 Pet. 3:8. Is. 55:8–11. Rom. 11:32–36. 1 Thess. 5:6, 18.

*I destroyed some of your cities . . . those left
are like half-burned firebrands snatched away
from fire.*

The sinners among my people shake with fear. 'Which
one of us,' they cry, 'can live here in the presence of
this all-consuming, Everlasting Fire?' / We felt we
were doomed to die and saw how powerless we were
to help ourselves; but that was good, for then we put
everything into the hands of God, who alone could
save us, for he can even raise the dead. And he did
help us, and saved us from a terrible death; yes, and
we expect him to do it again and again. / The wages
of sin is death, but the free gift of God is eternal life
through Jesus Christ our Lord.

It is a fearful thing to fall into the hands of the living
God. / It is because of this solemn fear of the Lord,
which is ever present in our minds, that we work so
hard to win others.

Preach the Word of God urgently at all times, whenever you get the chance, in season and out, when it is
convenient and when it is not. / Save some by snatching
them as from the very flames of hell itself.

Not by might, nor by power, but by my Spirit, says
the Lord of heaven's armies. / For he longs for all to
be saved and to understand this truth.

*Amos 4:11. Is. 33:14. 2 Cor. 1:9, 10. Rom. 6:23. Hebr. 10:31. 2 Cor. 5:11.
2 Tim. 4:2. Jude 23. Zech. 4:6. 1 Tim. 2:4.*

Don't be afraid . . . I am the First and Last.

You have not had to stand face to face with terror,
flaming fire, gloom, darkness and a terrible storm . . .
but you have come right up into Mount Zion . . . to
God who is Judge of all; and to the spirits of the redeemed in heaven, already made perfect; and to Jesus
himself, who has brought us his wonderful new
agreement. / Jesus, our leader and instructor. / This
high priest of ours understands our weaknesses, since
he had the same temptations we have, though he never
once gave way to them and sinned. So let us come
boldly to the very throne of God and stay there to
receive his mercy and to find grace to help us in our
times of need.

The Lord, the King of Israel, says – yes, it is Israel's
Redeemer, the Lord of the armies of heaven, who says
it – 'I am the First and Last; there is no other God.
Haven't I proclaimed from ages past [that I would save
you]?' . . . There is no other Rock! / 'The Mighty
God,' 'The Everlasting Father,' 'The Prince of Peace.'

O Lord my God, my Holy One, you who are eternal. /
Our Lord alone is God; we have no other Saviour.

*Rev. 1:17. Hebr. 12:18, 22–24. Hebr. 12:2. Hebr. 4:15, 16. Is. 44:6, 8.
Is. 9:6. Hab. 1:12. 2 Sam. 22:32.*

Lead me to the mighty, towering Rock of safety.

Dont't worry about anything; instead, pray about everything; tell God your needs and don't forget to thank him for his answers. If you do this you will experience God's peace, which is far more wonderful than the human mind can understand. His peace will keep your thoughts and your hearts quiet and at rest as you trust in Christ Jesus.

I am overwhelmed and desperate, and you alone know which way I ought to turn. / He knows every detail of what is happening to me; and when he has examined me, he will pronounce me completely innocent – as pure as solid gold! / Lord, through all the generations you have been our home! / To the poor, O Lord, you are a refuge from the storm, a shadow from the heat.

For who is God except our Lord? / Who but he is as a rock? / They shall never perish. No one shall snatch them away from me. / Lord, you promised to let me live! Never let it be said that God failed me. / This certain hope of being saved is a strong and trustworthy anchor for our souls, connecting us with God himself behind the sacred curtains of heaven.

Ps. 61:2. Phil. 4:6, 7. Ps. 142:3. Job 23:10. Ps. 90:1. Is. 25:4. Ps. 18:31. Jn. 10:28. Ps. 119:116. Hebr. 6:19.

I will not let you go until you bless me.

I will burn them up, unless these enemies of mine surrender and beg for peace and my protection.

'Woman,' Jesus told her. 'Your faith is large, and your request is granted.' / Because of your faith it will happen. / When you ask him, be sure that you really expect him to tell you, for a doubtful mind will be as unsettled as a wave of the sea that is driven and tossed by the wind; and every decision you then make will be uncertain, as you turn first this way, and then that. If you don't ask with faith, don't expect the Lord to give you any solid answer.

By this time they were nearing Emmaus and the end of their journey. Jesus would have gone on, but they begged him to stay the night with them, as it was getting late. When suddenly . . . he disappeared. They began telling each other how their hearts had warmed as he talked with them and explained the Scriptures during the walk down the road. / 'Guide me clearly along the way you want me to travel so that I will understand you and walk acceptably before you.' And the Lord replied, 'I myself will go with you and give you success.'

Gen. 32:26. Is. 27:5. Mt. 15:28. Mt. 9:29. Jas. 1:6, 7. Lk. 24:28, 29, 31, 32. Ex. 33:13, 14.

Jesus, our leader and instructor.

'I am the A and the Z, the beginning and the ending of all things,' says God, who is the Lord, the all powerful one who is, and was, and is coming again! / Who has done such mighty deeds, directing the affairs of generations of mankind as they march by? It is I, the Lord, the First and Last; I alone am he.

Take care to live in me, and let me live in you. / May the God of peace himself make you entirely clean; and may your spirit and soul and body be kept strong and blameless until that day when our Lord Jesus Christ comes back again. / God who began the good work within you will keep right on helping you grow in his grace until his task within you is finally finished on that day when Jesus Christ returns. / If trying to obey the Jewish laws never gave you spiritual life in the first place, why do you think that trying to obey them now will make you stronger Christians? / The Lord will work out his plans for my life.

God is at work within you, helping you want to obey him, and then helping you do what he wants.

Hebr. 12:2. Rev. 1:8. Is. 41:4. Jn. 15:4. 1 Thess. 5:23. Phil. 1:6. Gal. 3:3. Ps. 138:8. Phil. 2:13.

*Since he will live forever, he will always be there
to remind God that he has paid for their sins
with his blood.*

Who then will condemn us? Will Christ? No! For he
is the one who died for us ... and is sitting at the
place of highest honour next to God, pleading for us
there in heaven. / Christ has entered into heaven itself,
to appear now before God as our Friend.

If you sin, there is someone to plead for you before
the Father. His name is Jesus Christ, the one who is all
that is good and who pleases God completely. / God
is on one side and all the people on the other side, and
Christ Jesus, himself man, is between them to bring
them together.

Jesus the Son of God is our great high priest who
has gone to heaven itself to help us; therefore let us
never stop trusting him. This high priest of ours understands our weaknesses, since he had the same temptations we have, though he never once gave way to
them and sinned. So let us come boldly to the very
throne of God and stay there to receive his mercy and
to find grace to help us in our times of need.

All of us ... may come to God the Father with the
Holy Spirit's help because of what Christ has done for
us.

*Hebr. 7:25. Rom. 8:34. Hebr. 9:24. 1 Jn. 2:1. 1 Tim. 2:5. Hebr. 4:14–16.
Eph. 2:18.*

All those who know your mercy, Lord, will count on you for help.

This is his name: *The Lord Our Righteousness.* / I walk in the strength of the Lord God. I tell everyone that you alone are just and good.

His royal titles: 'Wonderful,' 'Counsellor.' / O Lord, I know it is not within the power of man to map his life and plan his course.

'The Mighty God,' 'The Everlasting Father.' / I know the one in whom I trust, and I am sure that he is able to guard safely all that I have given him until the day of his return.

'The Prince of Peace.' / Christ himself is our way of peace. / Since we have been made right in God's sight by faith in his promises, we can have real peace with him because of what Jesus Christ our Lord has done for us.

The Lord is a strong fortress. The good men run to him and are safe. / Woe to those who run to Egypt for help, trusting their mighty cavalry and chariots instead of looking to the Holy One of Israel and consulting him. / There is none like the God of Jerusalem – he descends from the heavens in majestic splendour to help you. The eternal God is your Refuge, and underneath are the everlasting arms.

Ps. 9:10. Jer. 23:6. Ps. 71:16. Is. 9:6. Jer. 10:23. Is. 9:6. 2 Tim. 1:12. Is. 9:6. Eph. 2:14. Rom. 5:1. Prov. 18:10. Is. 31:1. Deut. 33:26, 27.

Our hearts ache, but at the same time we have the joy of the Lord. We are poor, but we give rich spiritual gifts to others. We own nothing, and yet we enjoy everything.

We confidently and joyfully look forward actually to becoming all that God has had in mind for us to be. We . . . rejoice, too, when we run into problems and trials. / Trust him; and even now you are happy with the inexpressible joy that comes from heaven itself.

Though they have been going through much trouble and hard times, they have mixed their wonderful joy with their deep poverty, and the result has been an overflow of giving to others. / Though I did nothing to deserve it, and though I am the most useless Christian there is, yet I was the one chosen for this special joy of telling the Gentiles the Glad News of the endless treasures available to them in Christ.

God has chosen poor people to be rich in faith, and the kingdom of heaven is theirs, for that is the gift God has promised to all those who love him. / God is able to make it up to you by giving you everything you need and more, so that there will not only be enough for your own needs, but plenty left over to give joyfully to others.

2 Cor. 6:10. Rom. 5:2, 3. 1 Pet. 1:8. 2 Cor. 8:2. Eph. 3:8. Jas. 2:5. 2 Cor. 9:8.

He nurses them when they are sick, and soothes their pains and worries.

In all their affliction he was afflicted, and he personally saved them. In his love and pity he redeemed them and lifted them up and carried them through all the years. / Sir, your good friend is very, very ill. / I am with you; that is all you need. My power shows up best in weak people.

I am glad to boast about how weak I am; I am glad to be a living demonstration of Christ's power, instead of showing off my own power and abilities. / I can do everything God asks me to with the help of Christ who gives me the strength and power.

Though our bodies are dying, our inner strength in the Lord is growing every day.

For in him we live and move and exist. / He gives power to the tired and worn out, and strength to the weak. Even the youths shall be exhausted, and the young men will all give up. But they that wait upon the Lord shall renew their strength. They shall mount up with wings like eagles; they shall run and not be weary; they shall walk and not faint. / The eternal God is your Refuge and underneath are the everlasting arms.

*Ps. 41:3. Is. 63:9. Jn. 11:3. 2 Cor. 12:9. Phil. 4:13. 2 Cor. 4:16.
Acts 17:28. Is. 40:29–31. Deut. 33:27.*

He has enriched your whole life.

When we were utterly helpless with no way of escape,
Christ came at just the right time and died for us sinners
who had no use for him. / Since he did not spare even
his own Son for us but gave him up for us all, won't
he also surely give us everything else?

For in Christ there is the perfection of God in a
human body; so you have everything when you have
Christ, and you are filled with God through your
union with Christ. He is the highest ruler, with authority
over every other power.

Take care to live in me, and let me live in you. For a
branch can't produce fruit when severed from the vine.
Nor can you be fruitful apart from me. Yes, I am the
Vine; you are the branches. Whoever lives in me and
I in him shall produce a large crop of fruit. For apart
from me you can't do a thing. / Christ has given each
of us special abilities -- whatever he wants us to have out
of his rich storehouse of gifts.

If you stay in me and obey my commands, you may
ask any request you like, and it will be granted. / Let
his words enrich your lives and make you wise.

1 Cor. 1:5. Rom. 5:6. Rom. 8:32. Col. 2:9, 10. Jn. 15:4, 5. Eph. 4:7.
Jn. 15:7. Col. 3:16.

They shall see his face.

Moses asked to see God's glory. 'You may not see the glory of my face, for man may not see me and live.' / No one has ever actually seen God, but, of course, his only Son has, for he is the companion of the Father and has told us all about him.

Every eye will see him – yes, and those who pierced him. And the nations will weep in sorrow and in terror when he comes. / We can see and understand only a little about God now, as if we were peering at his reflection in a poor mirror.

I know that my Redeemer lives, and that he will stand upon the earth at last. And I know that after this body has decayed, this body shall see God! / My contentment is not in wealth but in seeing you and knowing all is well between us. And when I awake in heaven, I will be fully satisfied, for I will see you face to face. / We will be like him, as a result of seeing him as he really is. / For the Lord himself will come down from heaven . . . the Christians who are dead will be the first to rise to meet the Lord. Then we who are still alive and remain on the earth will be caught up with them in the clouds to meet the Lord in the air and remain with him forever.

Rev. 22:4. Ex. 33:18, 20. Jn. 1:18. Rev. 1:7. 1 Cor. 13:12. Job 19:25, 26. Ps. 17:15. 1 Jn. 3:2. 1 Thess. 4:16, 17.

Don't be afraid, for I have ransomed you.

Fear not; you will no longer live in shame. The shame of your youth and the sorrows of widowhood will be remembered no more, for your Creator will be your 'husband.' The Lord of heaven's armies is his name; he is your Redeemer, the Holy One of Israel, the God of all the earth. / I've blotted out your sins; they are gone like morning mist at noon! Oh, return to me, for I have paid the price to set you free. / He paid for you with the precious lifeblood of Christ, the sinless, spotless Lamb of God. / He will feed his flock like a shepherd; he will carry the lambs in his arms and gently lead the ewes with young. / In all their affliction he was afflicted, and he personally saved them. In his love and pity he redeemed them and lifted them up and carried them through all the years.

Their Redeemer is strong. His name is the Lord of heaven's armies. He will plead for them. / My Father has given them to me, and he is more powerful than anyone else, so no one can kidnap them from me.

May peace and blessing be yours from God the Father and from the Lord Jesus Christ, who died for our sins just as God our Father planned, and rescued us from this evil world in which we live. All glory to God through all the ages of eternity. Amen.

Is. 43:1. Is. 54:4, 5. Is. 44:22. 1 Pet. 1:19. Is. 40:11. Is. 63:9. Jer. 50:34. Jn. 10:29. Gal. 1:3–5.

*I will tell of the lovingkindness of God. I will
praise him for all he has done; I will rejoice in his
great goodness.*

He lifted me out of the pit of despair, out from the bog
and the mire, and set my feet on a hard, firm path and
steadied me as I walked along. / The Son of God . . .
loved me and gave himself for me. / Since he did not
spare even his own Son for us but gave him up for us all,
won't he also surely give us everything else? / God
showed his great love for us by sending Christ to die
for us while we were still sinners.

He has put his brand upon us – his mark of ownership – and given us his Holy Spirit in our hearts as
guarantee that we belong to him. / His presence within
us is God's guarantee that he really will give us all that
he promised; and the Spirit's seal upon us means that
God has already purchased us and that he guarantees
to bring us to himself.

God is so rich in mercy; he loved us so much that
even though we were spiritually dead and doomed by
our sins, he gave us back our lives again when he raised
Christ from the dead – only by his undeserved favour
have we ever been saved – and lifted us up from the
grave into glory along with Christ, where we sit with
him in the heavenly realms – all because of what Christ
Jesus did.

*Is. 63:7. Ps. 40:2. Gal. 2:20. Rom. 8:32. Rom. 5:8. 2 Cor. 1:22. Eph. 1:14.
Eph. 2:4–6.*

I am dark but beautiful.

I was born a sinner, yes, from the moment my mother conceived me. / Your reputation was great among the nations for your beauty; it was perfect because of all the gifts I gave you, says the Lord God.

I'm too much of a sinner to be near you. / How beautiful you are, my love, how beautiful!

I loathe myself and repent in dust and ashes. / You are so beautiful, my love.

When I want to do what is right, I inevitably do what is wrong. / Cheer up, son. I have forgiven your sins!

I know I am rotten through and through so far as my old sinful nature is concerned. / You have everything when you have Christ. / Perfect because of what Christ has done.

Your sins are washed away . . . you are set apart for God . . . he has accepted you because of what the Lord Jesus Christ and the Spirit of our God have done for you. / You have been chosen by God himself – you are priests of the King, you are holy and pure, you are God's very own – all this so that you may show to others how God called you out of the darkness into his wonderful light.

Song 1:5. Ps. 51:5. Ezk. 16:14. Lk. 5:8. Song 4:1. Job 42:6. Song 4:7. Rom. 7:21. Mt. 9:2. Rom. 7:18. Col. 2:10. Col. 1:28. 1 Cor. 6:11. 1 Pet. 2:9.

Suffering will come to all who decide to live godly lives to please Christ Jesus, from those who hate him.

I have come to set a man against his father, and a daughter against her mother, and a daughter-in-law against her mother-in-law – a man's worst enemies will be right in his own home! / If your aim is to enjoy the evil pleasure of the godless world, you cannot also be a friend of God. / Stop loving this evil world and all that it offers you, for when you love these things you show that you do not really love God. For all these worldly things, these evil desires – the craze for sex, the ambition to buy everything that appeals to you, and the pride that comes from wealth and importance – these are not from God. They are from this evil world itself.

For you get enough hate from the world. But then, it hated me before it hated you. The world would love you if you belonged to it; but you don't – for I chose you to come out of the world, and so it hates you. Do you remember what I told you? A slave isn't greater than his master!

I have given them your commands. And the world hates them because they don't fit in with it, just as I don't. / This world is fading away . . . but whoever keeps doing the will of God will live forever.

2 Tim. 3:12. Mt. 10:35, 36. Jas. 4:4. 1 Jn. 2:15, 16. Jn. 15:18–20.
Jn. 17:14. 1 Jn. 2:17.

Don't talk so much. Every time you open your mouth you put your foot in it. Be sensible and turn off the flow!

Dear brothers, don't ever forget that it is best to listen much, speak little, and not become angry. / It is better to be slow-tempered than famous; it is better to have self-control than to control an army. / If anyone can control his tongue, it proves that he has perfect control over himself in every other way. / Your words . . . reflect your fate: either you will be justified by them or you will be condemned. / Help me, Lord, to keep my mouth shut and my lips sealed.

Christ, who suffered for you, is your example. Follow in his steps: he never sinned, never told a lie, never answered back when insulted; when he suffered he did not threaten to get even; he left his case in the hands of God who always judges fairly. / If you want to keep from becoming fainthearted and weary, think about his patience as sinful men did such terrible things to him. / Gentle words cause life and health.

No falsehood can be charged against them; they are blameless.

Prov. 10:19. Jas. 1:19. Prov. 16:32. Jas. 3:2. Mt. 12:37. Ps. 141:3. 1 Pet. 2:21–23. Hebr. 12:3. Prov. 15:4. Rev. 14:5.

Tell me what to do, O Lord.

I will instruct you (says the Lord) and guide you along the best pathway for your life; I will advise you and watch your progress. / The Lord is good and glad to teach the proper path to all who go astray; he will teach the ways that are right and best to those who humbly turn to him.

Yes, I am the Gate. Those who came in by way of the Gate will be saved and will go in and out and find green pastures.

Jesus told him, 'I am the Way – yes, and the Truth and the Life. No one can get to the Father except by means of me.' / Now we may walk right into the very Holy of Holies where God is, because of the blood of Jesus. This is the fresh, new, life-giving way which Christ has opened up for us by tearing the curtain – his human body – to let us into the holy presence of God. And since this great high priest of ours rules over God's household, let us go right in, to God himself, with true hearts fully trusting him to receive us.

Oh, that we might know the Lord! Let us press on to know him. / And when we obey him, every path he guides us on is fragrant with his lovingkindness and his truth.

Ps. 27:11. Ps. 32:8. Ps. 25:8, 9. Jn. 10:9. Jn. 14:6. Hebr. 10:19–22. Hos. 6:3. Ps. 25:10.

We aren't saved from sin's grasp by knowing the commandments of God, because we can't and don't keep them, but God put into effect a different plan to save us. He sent his own Son in a human body like ours – except that ours are sinful – and destroyed sin's control over us by giving himself as a sacrifice for our sins.

The old system of Jewish laws gave only a dim fore-taste of the good things Christ would do for us. The sacrifices under the old system were repeated again and again, year after year, but even so they could never save those who lived under their rules. If they could have, one offering would have been enough. / Everyone who trusts in him is freed from all guilt and declared righteous – something the Jewish law could never do.

Since we, God's children, are human beings – made of flesh and blood – he became flesh and blood too by being born in human form; for only as a human being could he die and in dying break the power of the devil who had the power of death. Only in that way could he deliver those who through fear of death have been living all their lives as slaves to constant dread. We all know he did not come as an angel but as a human being – yes, a Jew. And it was necessary for Jesus to be like us . . . so that he could be our merciful and faithful high priest before God.

Rom. 8:3. Hebr. 10:1, 2. Acts 13:39. Hebr. 2:14–17.

All have sinned; all fall short of God's glorious ideal.

No one is good – no one in all the world is innocent. No one anywhere has kept on doing what is right; not one. / There is not a single man in all the earth who is always good and never sins. / How can mere man stand before God and claim to be righteous? Who in all the world can boast that he is clean?

Although God's promise still stands – his promise that all may enter his place of rest – we ought to tremble with fear because some of you may be on the verge of failing to get there after all.

For I admit my shameful deed – it haunts me day and night. I was born a sinner, yes, from the moment my mother conceived me.

The Lord has forgiven you, and you won't die for this sin. / He . . . gave us a right standing with himself, and promised us his glory. / We Christians have no veil over our faces; we can be mirrors that brightly reflect the glory of the Lord. And as the Spirit of the Lord works within us, we become more and more like him. / The only condition is that you fully believe the truth, standing in it steadfast and firm, strong in the Lord, convinced of the Good News that Jesus died for you, and never shifting from trusting him to save you.

Rom. 3:23. Rom. 3:10, 12. Eccl. 7:20. Job 25:4. Hebr. 4:1. Ps. 51:3, 5.
2 Sam. 12:13. Rom. 8:30. 2 Cor. 3:18. Col. 1:23.

*Honour the Lord by giving him the first part of all
your income.*

If you give little, you will get little. A farmer who
plants just a few seeds will get only a small crop, but
if he plants much, he will reap much. / God will give
you much so that you can give away much. / Every
Sunday each of you should put aside something from
what you have earned during the week.

God is not unfair. How can he forget your hard work
for him, or forget the way you used to show your love
for him – and still do – by helping his children?

I plead with you to give your bodies to God. Let
them be a living sacrifice, holy – the kind he can accept.
When you think of what he has done for you, is this
too much to ask?

Christ's love controls us now. Since we believe that
Christ died for all of us, we should also believe that we
have died to the old life we used to live. He died for all
so that all who live – having received eternal life from
him – might live no longer for themselves, to please
themselves, but to spend their lives pleasing Christ who
died and rose again for them. / You must do everything
for the glory of God.

*Prov. 3:9. 2 Cor. 9:6. 2 Cor. 9:11. 1 Cor. 16:2. Hebr. 6:10. Rom. 12:1.
2 Cor. 5:14, 15. 1 Cor. 10:31.*

There is no night.

The Lord will be your everlasting light; your days of mourning all will end. / The city has no need of sun or moon to light it, for the glory of God and of the Lamb illuminate it. / There will be no night there – no need for lamps or sun – for the Lord God will be their light.

You have been chosen by God himself – you are priests of the King, you are holy and pure, you are God's very own – all this so that you may show to others how God called you out of the darkness into his wonderful light. / Always thankful to the Father who has made us fit to share all the wonderful things that belong to those who live in the kingdom of light. For he has rescued us out of the darkness and gloom of Satan's kingdom and brought us into the kingdom of his dear Son. / Though once your heart was full of darkness, now it is full of light from the Lord, and your behaviour should show it!

You . . . do not belong to darkness and night.

The good man walks along in the ever-brightening light of God's favour; the dawn gives way to morning splendour, while the evil man gropes and stumbles in the dark.

Rev. 21:25. Is. 60:20. Rev. 21:23. Rev. 22:5. 1 Pet. 2:9. Col. 1:12, 13. Eph. 5:8. 1 Thess. 5:5. Prov. 4:18, 19.

I will praise you with great joy. I lie awake at night thinking of you.

How precious it is, Lord, to realize that you are thinking about me constantly! I can't even count how many times a day your thoughts turn towards me. And when I wake in the morning, you are still thinking of me! / Your words are sweeter than honey. / Your love is sweeter than wine.

Your steadfast love, O Lord, is as great as all the heavens. Your faithfulness reaches beyond the clouds. Your justice is as solid as God's mountains. Your decisions are as full of wisdom as the oceans are with water. You are concerned for men and animals alike. How precious is your constant love, O God! All humanity takes refuge in the shadow of your wings. You feed them with blessings from your own table and let them drink from your rivers of delight. / Whom have I in heaven but you? And I desire no one on earth as much as you! / You have let me experience the joys of life and the exquisite pleasures of your own eternal presence.

Oh, what a wonderful God we have! How great are his wisdom and knowledge and riches! For everything comes from God alone. Everything lives by his power, and everything is for his glory. To him be glory ever-more.

Ps. 63:5, 6. Ps. 139:17, 18. Ps. 119:103. Song 1:2. Ps. 36:5–8. Ps. 73:25. Ps. 16:11. Rom. 11:33, 36.

Restore to me again the joy of your salvation.

I have seen what they do, but I will heal them anyway!
I will lead them and comfort them, helping them to
mourn and to confess their sins.

'Come, let's talk this over!' says the Lord. 'No
matter how deep the stain of your sins, I can take it out
and make you as clean as freshly fallen snow. Even if
you are stained as red as crimson, I can make you white
as wool!' / 'O my rebellious children, come back to me
again and I will heal you from your sins.' And they
reply, 'Yes, we will come, for you are the Lord our
God.' / I am listening carefully to all the Lord is saying –
for he speaks peace to his people, his saints, if they will
only stop their sinning.

I will bless the Lord and not forget the glorious
things he does for me. He forgives all my sins. He
heals me. / He restores my failing health. / Praise the
Lord! He was angry with me, but now he comforts me.

Hold me safe above the heads of all my enemies.

I, yes, I alone am he who blots away your sins for
my own sake and will never think of them again.

*Ps. 51:12. Is. 57:18. Is. 1:18. Jer. 3:22. Ps. 85:8. Ps. 103:2, 3. Ps. 23:3.
Is. 12:1. Ps. 119:117. Is. 43:25.*

Their Redeemer is strong.

Many and great are your sins. I know them all so well. /
I, the Lord, am your Saviour and Redeemer, the
Mighty One of Israel. / Mighty to save! / Able to keep
you from slipping and falling away. / The more we see
our sinfulness, the more we see God's abounding grace
forgiving us.

There is no eternal doom awaiting those who trust
him to save them. But those who don't trust him have
already been tried and condemned for not believing in
the only Son of God. / He is able to save completely
all who come to God through him.

Was I too weak to save you? . . . Have I no longer
power to deliver?

Who then can ever keep Christ's love from us? I am
convinced that nothing can ever separate us from his
love. Death can't, and life can't. The angels won't, and
all the powers of hell itself cannot keep God's love
away. Our fears for today, our worries about tomorrow, or where we are – high above the sky, or in
the deepest ocean – nothing will ever be able to separate
us from the love of God demonstrated by our Lord
Jesus Christ when he died for us.

*Jer. 50:34. Amos. 5:12. Is. 49:26. Is. 63:1. Jude 24. Rom. 5:20. Jn. 3:18.
Hebr. 7:25. Is. 50:2. Rom. 8:35, 38, 39.*

Are you seeking great things for yourself? Don't do it!

Wear my yoke – for it fits perfectly – and let me teach you; for I am gentle and humble, and you shall find rest for your souls. / Your attitude should be the kind that was shown us by Jesus Christ, who, though he was God, did not demand and cling to his rights as God, but laid aside his mighty power and glory, taking the disguise of a slave and becoming like men. And he humbled himself even further, going so far as actually to die a criminal's death on a cross.

If you refuse to take up your cross and follow me, you are not worthy of being mine. / Christ, who suffered for you, is your example. Follow in his steps. / Many who are first now will be last . . . and some who are last now will be first.

Do you want to be truly rich? You already are if you are happy and good. After all, we didn't bring any money with us when we came into the world, and we can't carry away a single penny when we die. So we should be well satisfied without money if we have enough food and clothing. / I have learned how to get along happily whether I have much or little.

Jer. 45:5. Mt. 11:29. Phil. 2:5–8. Mt. 10:38. 1 Pet. 2:21. Mt. 19:30. 1 Tim. 6:6–8. Phil. 4:11.

I spoke too hastily when I said, 'The Lord has deserted me,' for you listened to my plea and answered me.

Save me, O my God. The floods have risen. Deeper and deeper I sink in the mire; the waters rise around me. I have wept until I am exhausted; my throat is dry and hoarse; my eyes are swollen with weeping, waiting for my God to act.

Has the Lord rejected me forever? Will he never again be favourable? Is his lovingkindness gone forever? Has his promise failed? Has he forgotten to be kind to one so undeserving?

Listen to my pleading, Lord! Be merciful and send the help I need. Oh, do not hide yourself when I am trying to find you. Do not angrily reject your servant. You have been my help in all my trials before; don't leave me now. Don't forsake me, O God of my salvation. I am expecting the Lord to rescue me again, so that once again I will see his goodness to me here in the land of the living.

O Lord my God, I pleaded with you, and you gave me my health again. You brought me back from the brink of the grave, from death itself, and here I am alive! Oh, sing to him you saints of his; give thanks to his holy name. His anger lasts a moment; his favour lasts for life! Weeping may go on all night, but in the morning there is joy.

Ps. 31:22. Ps. 69:1–3. Ps. 77:7–9. Ps. 27:7, 9, 13. Ps. 30:2–5.

*When he calls on me I will answer; I will be with
him in trouble, and rescue him and honour him.*

Jabez . . . prayed to the God of Israel, 'Oh, that you
would wonderfully bless me and help me in my work;
please be with me in all that I do, and keep me from all
evil and disaster!' And God granted him his request. /
God appeared to Solomon and told him, 'Ask me for
anything, and I will give it to you!' Solomon replied,
'O God . . . give me wisdom and knowledge to rule . . .
properly, for who is able to govern by himself such a
great nation as this one of yours?' / God gave Solomon
great wisdom and understanding. His wisdom excelled
that of any of the wise men of the East.

King Asa sent his troops to meet them there. 'O
Lord,' he cried out to God, 'no one else can help us!
Here we are, powerless against this mighty army. Oh,
help us, Lord our God! For we trust in you alone to
rescue us, and in your name we attack this vast horde.
Don't let mere men defeat you!' Then the Lord defeated
the Ethiopians, and Asa and the army of Judah
triumphed as the Ethiopians fled.

Because you answer prayer, all mankind will come to
you with their requests.

*Ps. 91:15. 1 Chron. 4:9, 10. 2 Chron. 1:7, 8, 10. 1 Kgs. 4:29, 30.
2 Chron. 14:10–12. Ps. 65:2.*

*True praise is a worthy sacrifice; this really
honours me.*

Remember what Christ taught and let his words enrich
your lives and make you wise; teach them to each other
and sing them out in psalms and hymns and spiritual
songs, singing to the Lord with thankful hearts. And
whatever you do or say, let it be as a representative of
the Lord Jesus, and come with him into the presence of
God the Father to give him your thanks.

For God has bought you with a great price. So use
every part of your body to give glory back to God,
because he owns it.

You are priests of the King . . . that you may show to
others how God called you out of the darkness into his
wonderful light. / You have become living building-
stones for God's use in building his house. What's
more, you are his holy priests; so come to him [you
are acceptable to him because of Jesus Christ] and
offer to God those things that please him. / With Jesus'
help we will continually offer our sacrifice of praise
to God by telling others of the glory of his name.

I will praise the Lord no matter what happens. I will
constantly speak of his glories and grace. I will boast of
all his kindness to me. Let all who are discouraged take
heart. Let us praise the Lord together, and exalt his
name.

*Ps. 50:23. Col. 3:16, 17. 1 Cor. 6:20. 1 Pet. 2:9. 1 Pet. 2:5. Hebr. 13:15.
Ps. 34:1–3.*

Take me with you; come, let's run!

For long ago the Lord had said to Israel: 'I have loved you, O my people, with an everlasting love; with lovingkindness I have drawn you to me.' / I led Israel with my ropes of love. / When I am lifted up [on the cross], I will draw everyone to me. / The Lamb of God. / As Moses in the wilderness lifted up the bronze image of a serpent on a pole, even so I must be lifted up upon a pole, so that anyone who believes in me will have eternal life.

Whom have I in heaven but you? And I desire no one on earth as much as you! / Our love for him comes as a result of his loving us first.

My beloved said to me, 'Rise up, my love, my fair one, and come away. For the winter is past, the rain is over and gone. The flowers are springing up and the time of the singing of birds has come. Yes, spring is here. The leaves are coming out and the grape vines are in blossom. How delicious they smell! Arise, my love, my fair one, and come away.'

Stay always within the boundaries where God's love can reach and bless you.

Song 1:4. Jer. 31:3. Hos. 11:4. Jn. 12:32. Jn. 1:36. Jn. 3:14, 15. Ps. 73:25. 1 Jn. 4:19. Song 2:10–13. Jude 21.

*I will raise up from among them a Prophet, an
Israeli like you.*

I [Moses] stood as an intermediary between you and
Jehovah, for you were afraid. . . . He spoke to me and
I passed on his laws to you. / God is on one side and
all the people on the other side, and Christ Jesus, himself
man, is between them to bring them together.

Moses was the humblest man on earth. / Wear my
yoke – for it fits perfectly – and let me teach you; for I
am gentle and humble, and you shall find rest for your
souls. / Your attitude should be the kind that was shown
us by Jesus Christ, who, though he was God, did not
demand and cling to his rights as God, but laid aside
his mighty power and glory, taking the disguise of a slave
and becoming like men.

Moses did a fine job working in God's house, but he
was only a servant; and his work was mostly to illustrate
and suggest those things that would happen later on.
But Christ, God's faithful Son, is in complete charge of
God's house. And we Christians are God's house – he
lives in us! – if we keep up our courage firm to the end,
and our joy and our trust in the Lord. And since
Christ is so much superior, the Holy Spirit warns us to
listen to him, to be careful to hear his voice today and
not let our hearts become set against him.

*Deut. 18:18. Deut. 5:5. 1 Tim. 2:5. Num. 12:3. Mt. 11:29. Phil. 2:5–7.
Hebr. 3:5–7.*

Everlasting comfort.

I will keep the pledge I made to you when you were young. I will establish an everlasting covenant with you forever.

By . . . one offering he made for ever perfect in the sight of God all those whom he is making holy. / He is able to save completely all who come to God through him. Since he will live forever, he will always be there to remind God that he has paid for their sins with his blood. / I know the one in whom I trust, and I am sure that he is able to guard safely all that I have given him until the day of his return.

God's gifts and his call can never be withdrawn; he will never go back on his promises. / Who then can ever keep Christ's love from us? / The Lamb standing in front of the throne will feed them and be their shepherd and lead them to the springs of the water of life. And God will wipe their tears away. / To meet the Lord . . . and remain with him forever. So comfort and encourage each other with this news.

I long to go and be with Christ. How much happier for *me* than being here! / This world is not our home; we are looking forward to our everlasting home in heaven.

2 Thess. 2:16. Ezk. 16:60. Hebr. 10:14. Hebr. 7:25. 2 Tim. 1:12. Rom. 11:29. Rom. 8:35. Rev. 7:17. 1 Thess. 4:17, 18. Phil. 1:23. Hebr. 13:14.

'I am the Gate for the sheep,' he said.

The curtain separating the Holiest Place in the Temple
was split apart from top to bottom. / Christ . . .
suffered. He died once for the sins of all us guilty
sinners, although he himself was innocent of any sin at
any time, that he might bring us safely home to God. /
Under the old system the common people could not go
into the Holy of Holies.

I am the Gate. Those who come in by way of the
Gate will be saved and will go in and out and find
green pastures.

No one can get to the Father except by means of
me. / Now all of us . . . may come to God the Father
with the Holy Spirit's help because of what Christ has
done for us. Now you are no longer strangers to God
and foreigners to heaven, but you are members of God's
very own family, citizens of God's country. / We may
walk right into the very Holy of Holies where God is,
because of the blood of Jesus. This is the fresh, new
life-giving way which Christ has opened up for us by
tearing the curtain – his human body – to let us into the
holy presence of God. / Since we have been made right
in God's sight by faith in his promises, we can have
real peace with him because of what Jesus Christ our
Lord has done for us.

*Jn. 10:7. Mt. 27:51. 1 Pet. 3:18. Hebr. 9:8. Jn. 10:9. Jn. 14:6.
Eph. 2:18, 19. Hebr. 10:19, 20. Rom. 5:1.*

His word in my heart is like fire that burns in my bones, and I can't hold it in any longer.

Preaching the Gospel isn't any special credit to me – I couldn't stop preaching it if I wanted to. I would be utterly miserable. If I were volunteering my services of my own free will, then the Lord would give me a special reward; but that is not the situation, for God has picked me out and given me this sacred trust and I have no choice. . . . What is my pay? It is the special joy I get from preaching the Good News. / They . . . told them never again to speak about Jesus. But Peter and John replied, 'We cannot stop telling about the wonderful things we saw Jesus do and heard him say.'

'I was afraid you would rob me of what I earned, so I hid your money in the earth and here it is!' 'You lazy rogue! . . . You should at least have put my money into the bank so I could have some interest. The man who uses well what he is given shall be given more, and he will have abundance. But from the man who is unfaithful, even what little responsibility he has will be taken from him.'

Go home to your friends . . . tell them what wonderful things God has done for you. / Woe unto me if I don't.

Jer. 20:9. 1 Cor. 9:16–18. Acts 4:18–20. Mt. 25:25–27, 29. Mk. 5:19. 1 Cor. 9:16.

Keep none of the booty!

Leave them; separate yourselves from them; don't touch what is unclean. / Dear brothers, you are only visitors here. Since your real home is in heaven I beg you to keep away from the evil pleasures of this world; they are not for you, for they fight against your very souls. / Hate every trace of their sin.

We are already God's children, right now, and we can't even imagine what it is going to be like later on. But we do know this, that when he comes we will be like him, as a result of seeing him as he really is. And everyone who really believes this will try to stay pure because Christ is pure. / For the free gift of eternal salvation is now being offered to everyone; and along with this gift comes the realization that God wants us to turn from godless living and sinful pleasures and to live good, God-fearing lives day after day, looking forward to that time when his glory shall be seen – the glory of our great God and Saviour Jesus Christ, who died under God's judgment against our sins, so that he could rescue us from constant falling into sin and make us his very own people, with cleansed hearts and real enthusiasm for doing kind things to others.

Deut. 13:17. 2 Cor. 6:17. 1 Pet. 2:11. Jude 23. 1 Jn. 3:2, 3. Tit. 2:11–14.

Who are you, sir? I am Jesus.

Don't be afraid! / When you go through deep waters and great trouble, I will be with you. When you go through rivers of difficulty, you will not drown! When you walk through the fire of oppression, you will not be burned up – the flames will not consume you. For I am the Lord your God, your Saviour.

Even when walking through the dark valley of death I will not be afraid, for you are close beside me, guarding, guiding all the way. / 'Emmanuel' . . . 'God is with us.'

You shall name him Jesus (meaning 'Saviour'), for he will save his people from their sins. / If you sin, there is someone to plead for you before the Father. His name is Jesus Christ, the one who is all that is good and who pleases God completely. / Who then will condemn us? Will Christ? No! For he is the one who died for us and came back to life again for us and is sitting at the place of highest honour next to God, pleading for us there in heaven. Who then can ever keep Christ's love from us? When we have trouble or calamity, when we are hunted down or destroyed, is it because he doesn't love us any more? And if we are hungry, or penniless, or in danger, or threatened with death, has God deserted us?

Acts 26:15. Mt. 14:27. Is. 43:2, 3. Ps. 23:4. Mt. 1:23. Mt. 1:21. 1 Jn. 2:1. Rom. 8:34, 35.

Stay true to the Lord.

I have stayed in God's paths, following his steps. I have not turned aside. / The Lord loves justice and fairness; he will never abandon his people. They will be kept safe forever. / He keeps you from all evil, and preserves your life.

Those whose faith has made them good in God's sight must live by faith, trusting him in everything. Otherwise, if they shrink back, God will have no pleasure in them. But we have never turned our backs on God and sealed our fate. No, our faith in him assures our souls' salvation. / These 'against-Christ' people used to be members of our churches, but they never really belonged to us or else they would have stayed. When they left us it proved that they were not of us at all.

You are truly my disciples if you live as I tell you to. / Those enduring to the end shall be saved. / Keep your eyes open for spiritual danger; stand true to the Lord; act like men; be strong. / Hold tightly to the little strength you have – so that no one will take away your crown. / Everyone who conquers will be clothed in white, and I will not erase his name from the book of life, but I will announce before my Father and his angels that he is mine.

Phil. 4:1. Job 23:11. Ps. 37:28. Ps. 121:7. Hebr. 10:38, 39. 1 Jn. 2:19. Jn. 8:31. Mt. 24:13. 1 Cor. 16:13. Rev. 3:11. Rev. 3:5.

He lived . . . in fellowship with God.

How can we walk together with your sins between us?

Christ's death on the cross has made peace with God for all by his blood. This includes you who were once so far away from God. You were his enemies and hated him and were separated from him by your evil thoughts and actions, yet now he has brought you back as his friends. . . . As a result Christ has brought you into the very presence of God, and you are standing there before him with nothing left against you – nothing left that he could even chide you for. / You have been brought very near to him because of what Jesus Christ has done for you with his blood.

And since, when we were his enemies, we were brought back to God by the death of his Son, what blessings he must have for us now that we are his friends, and he is living within us! Now we rejoice in our wonderful new relationship with God – all because of what our Lord Jesus Christ has done.

Fellowship and joys . . . with the Father and with Jesus Christ his Son.

The grace of our Lord Jesus Christ be with you all. May God's love and the Holy Spirit's friendship be yours.

Gen. 5:22. Amos 3:3. Col. 1:20–22. Eph. 2:13. Rom. 5:10, 11. 1 Jn. 1:3. 2 Cor. 13:14.

*If your sacrifice is to be an ox given as a burnt
offering, use only a bull with no physical defects.
Bring the animal to the entrance of the Tabernacle
where the priests will accept your gift for the
Lord. The person bringing it is to lay his hand upon
its head, and it then becomes his substitute: the
death of the animal will be accepted by God
instead of the death of the man who brings it, as
the penalty for his sins.*

'Where is the lamb for the sacrifice?' 'God will see to
it, my son.' Then Abraham noticed a ram caught by
its horns in a bush. So he took the ram and sacrificed
it. Abraham named the place 'Jehovah provides.' /
Look. There is the Lamb of God who takes away the
world's sin! / We have been forgiven and made clean
by Christ's dying for us once and for all. / A ransom
for many.

No one can kill me without my consent – I lay down
my life voluntarily. For I have the right and power to
lay it down when I want to and also the right and
power to take it again.

My love will know no bounds. / The Son of God . . .
loved me and gave himself for me.

God took the sinless Christ and poured into him our
sins. Then, in exchange, he poured God's goodness into
us! / We belong to his dearly loved Son.

*Lev. 1:3, 4. Gen. 22:7, 8, 13, 14. Jn. 1:29. Hebr. 10:10. Mt. 20:28.
Jn. 10:18. Hos. 14:4. Gal. 2:20. 2 Cor. 5:21. Eph. 1:6.*

*You love me so much! You are constantly so
kind! You have rescued me from deepest hell.*

Don't be afraid, for I have ransomed you; I have
called you by name; you are mine. I am the Lord, and
there is no other Saviour. I, yes, I alone am he who
blots away your sins for my own sake and will never
think of them again. / They trust in their wealth and
boast about how rich they are, yet not one of them,
though rich as kings, can ransom his own brother
from the penalty of sin! For God's forgiveness does
not come that way. For a soul is far too precious to be
ransomed by mere earthly wealth. / I have found a substitute. / God is so rich in mercy; he loved us so much
that even though we were spiritually dead and doomed
by our sins, he gave us back our lives again when he
raised Christ from the dead.

There is salvation in no one else! Under all heaven
there is no other name for men to call upon to save
them. / God our Saviour . . . longs for all to be saved
and to understand this truth: that God is on one side
and all the people on the other side, and Christ Jesus,
himself man, is between them to bring them together,
by giving his life for all mankind.

Your love and kindness are forever; your truth is as
enduring as the heavens.

*Ps. 86:13. Is. 43:1, 11, 25. Ps. 49:6–8. Job 33:24. Eph. 2:4, 5. Acts 4:12.
1 Tim. 2:3–6. Ps. 89:2.*

The Lord held me steady.

We are weary of worshipping idols on the hills and of having orgies on the mountains. It is all a farce. Only in the Lord our God can Israel ever find her help and her salvation. / The Lord is my fort where I can enter and be safe; no one can follow me in and slay me. He is a rugged mountain where I hide; he is my Saviour, a rock where none can reach me, and a tower of safety. He is my shield. He is like the strong horn of a mighty fighting bull.

Let all the people of Jerusalem shout his praise with joy. For great and mighty is the Holy One of Israel, who lives among you.

The Angel of the Lord guards and rescues all who reverence him. The Lord hears the good man when he calls to him for help, and saves him out of all his troubles. / The eternal God is your Refuge, and underneath are the everlasting arms. / We can say without any doubt or fear, 'The Lord is my helper and I am not afraid of anything that mere man can do to me.' / For who is God except our Lord? Who but he is as a rock? He fills me with strength and protects me wherever I go.

Whatever I am now it is all because God poured out such kindness and grace upon me.

Ps. 18:18. Jer. 3:23. Ps. 18:2. Is. 12:6. Ps. 34:7, 17. Deut. 33:27. Hebr. 13:6. Ps. 18:31, 32. 1 Cor. 15:10.

We *are the ones who strayed away like sheep!*

If we say that we have no sin, we are only fooling our-selves, and refusing to accept the truth. / No one is good – no one in all the world is innocent. No one has ever really followed God's paths, or even truly wanted to. Every one has turned away; all have gone wrong. No one anywhere has kept on doing what is right; not one.

Like sheep you wandered away from God, but now you have returned to your Shepherd, the Guardian of your souls. / I have wandered away like a lost sheep; come and find me for I have not turned away from your commandments.

He restores my failing health. He helps me do what honours him the most.

My sheep recognize my voice, and I know them, and they follow me. I give them eternal life and they shall never perish. No one shall snatch them away from me.

If you had a hundred sheep and one of them strayed away and was lost in the wilderness, wouldn't you leave the ninety-nine others to go and search for the lost one until you found it?

Is. 53:6. 1 Jn. 1:8. Rom. 3:10–12. 1 Pet. 2:25. Ps. 119:176. Ps. 23:3.
Jn. 10:27, 28. Lk. 15:4.

God did as he had promised, and Sarah became pregnant and gave Abraham a baby son.

Trust him all the time. Pour out your longings before him, for he can help! / David took strength from the Lord. / God will surely come and get you, and bring you out of this land of Egypt and take you back to the land he promised to the descendants of Abraham, Isaac and Jacob. / I have seen the anguish of my people in Egypt and have heard their cries. I have come down to deliver them. Come, I will send you to Egypt. And by means of many remarkable miracles he led them out of Egypt and through the Red Sea, and back and forth through the wilderness for forty years. / Every good thing the Lord had promised them came true.

There is no question that he will do what he says. / God is not a man, that he should lie; he doesn't change his mind like humans do. Has he ever promised, without doing what he said? / God also bound himself with an oath, so that those he promised to help would be perfectly sure and never need to wonder whether he might change his plans. / Heaven and earth will disappear, but my words remain forever. / The grass withers, the flowers fade, but the Word of our God shall stand forever.

Gen. 21:1. Ps. 62:8. 1 Sam. 30:6. Gen. 50:24. Acts 7:34, 36. Josh. 21:45. Hebr. 10:23. Num. 23:19. Hebr. 6:17. Mt. 24:35. Is. 40:8.

The eyes of all mankind look up to you for help.

He himself gives life and breath to everything, and satisfies every need there is. / He is good to everyone, and his compassion is intertwined with everything he does. / Look at the birds! They don't worry about what to eat – they don't need to sow or reap or store up food – for your heavenly Father feeds them.

The same Lord . . . generously gives his riches to all those who ask him for them.

My help is from Jehovah who made the mountains! And the heavens too! / We look to Jehovah our God for his mercy and kindness just as a servant keeps his eyes upon his master or a slave girl watches her mistress for the slightest signal.

The Lord is faithful to his promises. Blessed are all those who wait for him to help them. / In that day the people will proclaim, 'This is our God, in whom we trust, for whom we waited. Now at last he is here.' What a day of rejoicing! / If we must keep trusting God for something that hasn't happened yet, it teaches us to wait patiently and confidently. And in the same way – by our faith – the Holy Spirit helps us with our daily problems and in our praying.

Ps. 145:15. Acts 17:25. Ps. 145:9. Mt. 6:26. Rom. 10:12. Ps. 121:2. Ps. 123:2. Is. 30:18. Is. 25:9. Rom. 8:25, 26.

*You shall name him Jesus (meaning 'Saviour'),
for he will save his people from their sins.*

You know that he became a man so that he could take
away our sins. / That we can be finished with sin and
live a good life. / He is able to save completely all who
come to God through him.

He was wounded and bruised for *our* sins. He was
chastised that we might have peace; he was lashed –
and we were healed! *We* are the ones who strayed
away like sheep! We, who left God's paths to follow
our own. Yet God laid on *him* the guilt and sins of every
one of us! He was oppressed and he was afflicted, yet
he never said a word. From prison and trial they led
him away to his death. / It was written long ago that
the Messiah must suffer . . . that this message of salvation should be taken from Jerusalem to all the
nations: *There is forgiveness of sins for all who turn to
me.* / He came . . . to put away the power of sin forever
by dying for us.

With mighty power, God exalted him to be a Prince
and Saviour . . . for repentance. / In this man, Jesus,
there is forgiveness for your sins. Everyone who trusts
in him is freed from all guilt and declared righteous –
something the Jewish law could never do. / Your sins
have been forgiven in the name of Jesus our Saviour.

*Mt. 1:21. 1 Jn. 3:5. 1 Pet. 2:24. Hebr. 7:25. Is. 53:5–8. Lk. 24:46, 47.
Hebr. 9:26. Acts 5:31. Acts 13:38, 39. 1 Jn. 2:12.*

*Our Lord Jesus . . . though he was so very rich,
yet to help you . . . became so very poor, so that
by being poor he could make you rich.*

God wanted all of himself to be in his Son. / God's Son
shines out with God's glory, and all that God's Son is
and does marks him as God. He regulates the universe
by the mighty power of his command. He is the one who
died to cleanse us and clear our record of all sin, and
then sat down in highest honour beside the great God
of heaven. Thus he became far greater than the angels,
as proved by the fact that his name 'Son of God,' which
was passed on to him from his Father, is far greater
than the names and titles of the angels. / Who, though
he was God, did not demand and cling to his rights as
God, but laid aside his mighty power and glory, taking
the disguise of a slave and becoming like men.

Foxes have dens and birds have nests, but I, the Son
of Mankind, have no home of my own – no place to
lay my head.

God has already given you everything you need. . . .
He has given you the whole world to use, and life and
even death are your servants. He has given you all of
the present and all of the future. All are yours, and you
belong to Christ, and Christ is God's.

2 Cor. 8:9. Col. 1:19. Hebr. 1:3, 4. Phil. 2:6, 7. Mt. 8:20. 1 Cor. 3:21–23.

*His left hand is under my head and with his right
hand he embraces me.*

Underneath are the everlasting arms. / When [Peter]
looked around at the high waves, he was terrified and
began to sink. 'Save me, Lord!' he shouted. Instantly
Jesus reached out his hand and rescued him. 'O man of
little faith,' Jesus said 'Why did you doubt?'

The steps of good men are directed by the Lord. He
delights in each step they take. If they fall it isn't fatal,
for the Lord holds them with his hand. I have been
young and now I am old. And in all my years I have
never seen the Lord forsake a man who loves him.

He is beloved of God and lives in safety beside him.
God surrounds him with his loving care, and preserves
him from every harm. / Let him have all your worries
and cares, for he is always thinking about you and
watching everything that concerns you. / He who harms
you sticks his finger in Jehovah's eye!

They shall never perish. No one shall snatch them
away from me, for my Father has given them to me, and
he is more powerful than anyone else, so no one can
kidnap them from me.

*Song 2:6. Deut. 33:27. Mt. 14:30, 31. Ps. 37:23–25. Deut. 33:12.
1 Pet. 5:7. Zech. 2:8. Jn. 10:28, 29.*

*Who is this . . . arising as the dawn, fair as the
moon, pure as the sun, so utterly captivating?*

His church, purchased with his blood.

The . . . love . . . Christ showed to the church when
he died for her, to make her holy and clean, washed
by baptism and God's Word; so that he could give her
to himself as a glorious church without a single spot or
wrinkle or any other blemish, being holy and without a
single fault.

A great pageant appeared in heaven . . . a woman
clothed with the sun, with the moon beneath her feet,
and a crown of twelve stars on her head. / Let us be
glad and rejoice and honour him; for the time has come
for the wedding banquet of the Lamb, and his bride
has prepared herself. She is permitted to wear the
cleanest and whitest and finest of linens. (Fine linen
represents the good deeds done by the people of God). /
God . . . will accept . . . us if we trust Jesus Christ to
take away our sins. And we all can be saved in this same
way, by coming to Christ, no matter who we are or
what we have been like.

I have given them the glory you gave me – the
glorious unity of being one.

*Song 6:10. Acts 20:28. Eph. 5:25–27. Rev. 12:1. Rev. 19:7, 8. Rom. 3:22.
Jn. 17:22.*

Our remaining time is very short.

How frail is man, how few his days, how full of trouble! He blossoms for a moment like a flower – and withers; as the shadow of a passing cloud, he quickly disappears. / This world is fading away, and these evil, forbidden things will go with it, but whoever keeps doing the will of God will live forever. / Everyone dies because all of us are related to Adam, being members of his sinful race, and wherever there is sin, death results. But all who are related to Christ will rise again. Death is swallowed up in victory. / Living or dying we follow the Lord. Either way we are his.

Living means opportunities for Christ, and dying – well, that's even better!

Do not let this happy trust in the Lord die away, no matter what happens. Remember your reward! You need to keep on patiently doing God's will if you want him to do for you all that he has promised. His coming will not be delayed much longer. / The night is far gone, the day of his return will soon be here. So discard the evil deeds of darkness and put on the armour of right living. / The end of the world is coming soon. Therefore be earnest, thoughtful men of prayer.

1 Cor. 7:29. Job 14:1, 2. 1 Jn. 2:17. 1 Cor. 15:22, 54. Rom. 14:8. Phil. 1:21. Hebr. 10:35–37. Rom. 13:12. 1 Pet. 4:7.

A new name.

At Antioch . . . the believers were first called 'Christians.' / A person who calls himself a Christian should not be doing things that are wrong. / Those who belong to Christ have nailed their natural evil desires to his cross and crucified them there. / God has bought you with a great price. So use every part of your body to give glory back to God, because he owns it.

God forbid that I should boast about anything except the cross of our Lord Jesus Christ. Because of that cross my interest in all the attractive things of the world was killed long ago, and the world's interest in me is also long dead. It doesn't make any difference now whether we have been circumcised or not; what counts is whether we really have been changed into new and different people.

Follow God's example in everything you do just as a much loved child imitates his father. Be full of love for others, following the example of Christ who loved you and gave himself to God as a sacrifice to take away your sins. And God was pleased, for Christ's love for you was like sweet perfume to him. Though once your heart was full of darkness, now it is full of light from the Lord, and your behaviour should show it!

Rev. 2:17. Acts 11:26. 2 Tim. 2:19. Gal. 5:24. 1 Cor. 6:20. Gal. 6:14, 15.
Eph. 5:1, 2, 8.

There is the Lamb of God.

It is not possible for the blood of bulls and goats really to take away sins. That is why Christ said, as he came into the world, 'O God, the blood of bulls and goats cannot satisfy you, so you have made ready this body of mine for me to lay as a sacrifice upon your altar. You were not satisfied with the animal sacrifices, slain and burnt before you as offerings for sin. Then I said, 'See, I have come to do your will, to lay down my life, just as the Scriptures said that I would.' / He was oppressed and he was afflicted, yet he never said a word. He was brought as a lamb to the slaughter; and as a sheep before her shearers is dumb, so he stood silent before the ones condemning him.

God paid a ransom to save you . . . and the ransom he paid was not mere gold or silver, as you very well know; but he paid for you with the precious lifeblood of Christ, the sinless, spotless Lamb of God. Now your faith and hope can rest in him alone.

The Lamb is worthy – the Lamb who was slain. He is worthy to receive the power, and the riches, and the wisdom, and the strength, and the honour, and the glory, and the blessing.

Jn. 1:29. Hebr. 10:4–7. Is. 53:7. 1 Pet. 1:18, 19, 21. Rev. 5:12.

I will keep on expecting you to help me.

I don't mean to say I am perfect. I haven't learned all I should. / Let us stop going over the same old ground again and again, always teaching those first lessons about Christ. Let us go on instead to other things and become mature in our understanding, as strong Christians ought to be. Surely we don't need to speak further about the foolishness of trying to be saved by being good, or about the necessity of faith in God. / The good man walks along in the ever-brightening light of God's favour; the dawn gives way to morning splendour.

I love the Lord because he hears my prayers and answers them. Because he bends down and listens, I will pray as long as I breathe! / I will praise the Lord no matter what happens. I will constantly speak of his glories and grace.

O God in Zion, we wait before you in silent praise. / Day after day and night after night they kept on saying, 'Holy, holy, holy, Lord God Almighty.' / True praise is a worthy sacrifice; this really honours me. / Always be joyful. Always keep on praying. Always be thankful no matter what happens, for that is God's will for you who belong to Christ Jesus. / Always be full of joy in the Lord; I say it again, rejoice!

Ps. 71:14. Phil. 3:12. Hebr. 6:1. Prov. 4:18. Ps. 116:1, 2. Ps. 34:1.
Ps. 65:1. Rev. 4:8. Ps. 50:23. 1 Thess. 5:16–18. Phil. 4:4.

*Think of all the tremendous things he has done
for you.*

Do you remember how the Lord led you through the
wilderness for all those forty years, humbling you and
testing you to find out how you would respond, and
whether or not you would really obey him? So you
should realize that, as a man punishes his son, the Lord
punishes you to help you.

I know, O Lord, that your decisions are right and that
your punishment was right and did me good. The
punishment you gave me was the best thing that could
have happened to me, for it taught me to pay attention
to your laws. I used to wander off until you punished
me; now I closely follow all you say. / The Lord has
punished me, but not handed me over to death.

He has not punished us as we deserve for all our sins,
for his mercy toward those who fear and honour him is
as great as the height of the heavens above the earth.
He has removed our sins as far away from us as the
east is from the west. He is like a father to us, tender
and sympathetic to those who reverence him. For he
knows we are but dust, and that our days are few and
brief, like grass, like flowers, blown by the wind and
gone forever.

1 Sam. 12:24. Deut. 8:2, 5. Ps. 119:75, 71, 67. Ps. 118:18. Ps. 103:10–16.

That time when his glory shall be seen – the glory of our great God and Saviour Jesus Christ.

This certain hope of being saved is a strong and trustworthy anchor for our souls, connecting us with God himself behind the sacred curtains of heaven, where Christ has gone ahead to plead for us. / For he must remain in heaven until the final recovery of all things from sin. / When he comes to receive praise and admiration because of all he has done for his people, his saints.

Even the things of nature, like animals and plants, suffer in sickness and death . . . as they await this great event. And even we Christians . . . groan to be released from pain and suffering. We, too, wait anxiously for that day when God will give us our full rights as his children, including the new bodies he has promised us – bodies that will never be sick and will never die. / Dear friends, we are already God's children, right now, and we can't even imagine what it is going to be like later on. But we do know this, that when he comes we will be like him, as a result of seeing him as he really is. / When Christ who is our real life comes back again, you will shine with him and share in all his glories.

'I am coming soon!' Amen! Come, Lord Jesus!

Tit. 2:13. Hebr. 6:19, 20. Acts 3:21. 2 Thess. 1:10. Rom. 8:22, 23.
1 Jn. 3:2. Col. 3:4. Rev. 22:20.

*Those who do what Christ tells them to will learn
to love God more and more.*

May the God of peace who brought again from the
dead our Lord Jesus, the great Shepherd of the sheep,
equip you with all you need for doing his will, through
the blood of the everlasting agreement between God
and you. And may he produce in you through the
power of Christ all that is pleasing to him, to whom be
glory forever and ever. Amen.

How can we be sure that we belong to him? By
looking within ourselves: are we really trying to do
what he wants us to? / I will only reveal myself to
those who love me and obey me. The Father will love
them too, and we will come to them and live with
them. / If we stay close to him, obedient to him, we
won't be sinning either; but as for those who keep on
sinning, they should realize this: they sin because they
have never really known him or become his. Oh, dear
children, don't let anyone deceive you about this: if you
are constantly doing what is good, it is because you
are good, even as he is.

As we live with Christ, our love grows more perfect
and complete; so we will not be ashamed and embarrassed at the day of judgment, but can face him
with confidence and joy, because he loves us and we
love him too.

1 Jn. 2:5. Hebr. 13:20, 21. 1 Jn. 2:3. Jn. 14:23. 1 Jn. 3:6, 7. 1 Jn. 4:17.

A wise man controls his temper.

The Lord descended in the form of a pillar of cloud and stood there with him, and passed in front of him and announced the meaning of his name. 'I am Jehovah, the merciful and gracious God,' he said, 'slow to anger and rich in steadfast love and truth.'

Follow God's example in everything you do just as a much loved child imitates his father. / When the Holy Spirit controls our lives he will produce this kind of fruit in us: love, joy, peace, patience, kindness, goodness, faithfulness, gentleness and self-control. / Praise the Lord if you are punished for doing right! Of course, you get no credit for being patient if you are beaten for doing wrong; but if you do right and suffer for it, and are patient beneath the blows, God is well pleased. This suffering is all part of the work God has given you. Christ, who suffered for you, is your example. Follow in his steps: he never sinned, never told a lie, never answered back when insulted; when he suffered he did not threaten to get even; he left his case in the hands of God who always judges fairly.

Don't let the sun go down with you still angry – get over it quickly; for when you are angry you give a mighty foothold to the devil.

Prov. 14:29. Ex. 34:6. Eph. 5:1. Gal. 5:22, 23. 1 Pet. 2:19–23. Eph. 4:26.

*When the Holy Spirit controls our lives he will
produce . . . peace.*

Following after the Holy Spirit leads to life and peace.
    God wants his children to live in peace. / I am leaving
you with a gift – peace of mind and heart. And the
peace I give isn't fragile like the peace the world gives.
So don't be troubled or afraid. / I pray . . . that God
who gives you hope will keep you happy and full of
peace as you believe in him through the Holy Spirit's
power within you.
    I know the one in whom I trust, and I am sure that
he is able to guard safely all that I have given him until
the day of his return. / Christ himself is our way of
peace. / He will keep in perfect peace all those who trust
in him, whose thoughts turn often to the Lord!
    Out of justice, peace. Quietness and confidence will
reign for evermore. My people will live in safety,
quietly at home. / All who listen to me shall live in
peace and safety, unafraid.
    Those who love your laws have great peace of heart
and mind. / Peace flowing like a gentle river, and great
waves of righteousness.

*Gal. 5:22. Rom. 8:6. 1 Cor. 7:15. Jn. 14:27. Rom. 15:13. 2 Tim. 1:12.
Eph. 2:14. Is. 26:3. Is. 32:17, 18. Prov. 1:33. Ps. 119:165. Is. 48:18.*

The name of the city will be, 'The City of God.'

The home of God is now among men, and he will live with them and they will be his people; yes, God himself will be among them.

No temple could be seen in the city, for the Lord God Almighty and the Lamb are worshipped in it everywhere. And the city has no need of sun or moon to light it, for the glory of God and of the Lamb illuminate it. / Its light will light the nations of the earth, and the rulers of the world will come and bring their glory to it.

When I awake in heaven, I will be fully satisfied, for I will see you face to face. / Whom have I in heaven but you? And I desire no one on earth as much as you!

Israel will prosper forever, and Jerusalem will thrive as generations pass. For I will avenge the blood of my people; I will not clear their oppressors of guilt. For my home is in Jerusalem with my people. / 'Sing, Jerusalem, and rejoice! For I have come to live among you,' says the Lord. / There shall be nothing in the city which is evil; for the throne of God and of the Lamb will be there, and his servants will worship him.

Ezk. 48:35. Rev. 21:3. Rev. 21:22–24. Ps. 17:15. Ps. 73:25. Joel 3:20, 21. Zech. 2:10. Rev. 22:3.

*God lives here. I've stumbled into his home. This
is the awesome entrance to heaven!*

Where two or three gather together because they are
mine, I will be there among them. / I am with you
always, even to the end of the world. / I myself will go
with you and give you success.

I can *never* be lost to your Spirit! I can *never* get
away from my God! If I go up to heaven, you are
there; if I go down to the place of the dead, you are
there. If I ride the morning winds to the farthest oceans,
even there your hand will guide me, your strength will
support me. If I try to hide in the darkness, the night
becomes light around me. For even darkness cannot
hide from God; to you the night shines as bright as day. /
Am I a God who is only in one place and cannot see
what they are doing? Can anyone hide from me? Am I
not everywhere in all of heaven and earth?

Is it possible that God would really live on earth?
Why, even the skies and the highest heavens cannot
contain you, much less this Temple. / The high and
lofty one who inhabits eternity, the Holy One, says this:
I live in that high and holy place where those with
contrite, humble spirits dwell; and I refresh the humble
and give new courage to those with repentant hearts.

Gen. 28:16. Mt. 18:20. Mt. 28:20. Ex. 33:14. Ps. 139:7–12. Jer. 23:23,
24. 1 Kgs. 8:27. Is. 57:15.

Keep away from anything that might take God's place in your hearts.

O my son, trust my advice. / Let heaven fill your thoughts; don't spend your time worrying about things down here.

Son of dust, these men worship idols in their hearts – should I let them ask me anything? / Away . . . with sinful, earthly things; deaden the evil desires lurking within you; have nothing to do with sexual sin, impurity, lust and shameful desires; don't worship the good things of this life, for that is idolatry. / People who long to be rich soon begin to do all kinds of wrong things to get money, things that hurt them and make them evil-minded and finally send them to hell itself. For the love of money is the first step toward all kinds of sin. Some people have even turned away from God because of their love for it, and as a result have pierced themselves with many sorrows. . . . You are God's man. Run from all these evil things and work instead at what is right and good, learning to trust him and love others, and to be patient and gentle. / Don't become rich by extortion and robbery. / My gifts are better than the purest gold or sterling silver!

If your profits are in heaven your heart will be there too. / I [the Lord] look at a man's thoughts and intentions.

1 Jn. 5:21. Prov. 23:26. Col. 3:2. Ezk. 14:3. Col. 3:5. 1 Tim. 6:9–11.
Ps. 62:10. Prov. 8:19. Mt. 6:21. 1 Sam. 16:7.

You are to be perfect, even as your Father in heaven is perfect.

I am the Almighty; obey me and live as you should. / You shall be holy to me, for I the Lord am holy, and I have set you apart from all other peoples, to be mine.

God has bought you with a great price. So use every part of your body to give glory back to God, because he owns it.

So you have everything when you have Christ, and you are filled with God through your union with Christ. He is the highest ruler, with authority over every other power. / He died under God's judgment against our sins, so that he could rescue us from constant falling into sin. / Try hard to live without sinning; and be at peace with everyone so that he will be pleased with you when he returns.

Happy are all who perfectly follow the laws of God. / If anyone keeps looking steadily into God's law for free men, he will not only remember it but he will do what it says, and God will greatly bless him in everything he does. / Search me, O God, and know my heart; test my thoughts. Point out anything you find in me that makes you sad, and lead me along the path of everlasting life.

Mt. 5:48. Gen. 17:1. Lev. 20:26. 1 Cor. 6:20. Col. 2:10. Tit. 2:14. 2 Pet. 3:14. Ps. 119:1. Jas. 1:25. Ps. 139:23, 24.

*Let us . . . purify ourselves, living in the
wholesome fear of God.*

Let us turn away from everything wrong, whether
of body or spirit.

You deserve honesty from the heart; yes, utter
sincerity and truthfulness. Oh, give me this wisdom. /
God wants us to turn from godless living and sinful
pleasures and to live good, God-fearing lives day after
day. / Don't hide your light! Let it shine for all; let
your good deeds glow for all to see, so that they will
praise your heavenly Father. / I don't mean to say I am
perfect. I haven't learned all I should even yet.

When he comes we will be like him, as a result of
seeing him as he really is. And everyone who really
believes this will try to stay pure because Christ is
pure.

This is what God has prepared for us and, as a
guarantee, he has given us his Holy Spirit. / Why is it
that he gives . . . special abilities to do certain things
best? It is that God's people will be equipped to do
better work for him, building up the church, the body
of Christ, to a position of strength and maturity; until
finally we all believe alike about our salvation and about
our Saviour, God's Son, and all become full-grown in
the Lord – yes, to the point of being filled full with
Christ.

*2 Cor. 7:1. Ps. 51:6. Tit. 2:12. Mt. 5:15, 16. Phil. 3:12. 1 Jn. 3:2, 3.
2 Cor. 5:5. Eph. 4:12, 13.*

The Lord isn't too weak to save you. And he isn't getting deaf!

When I pray, you answer me, and encourage me by giving me the strength I need. / Though I am surrounded by troubles, you will bring me safely through them. You will clench your fist against my angry enemies! Your power will save me.

Do not hide yourself when I am trying to find you. Do not angrily reject your servant. You have been my help in all my trials before; don't leave me now. Don't forsake me, O God of my salvation. / O Lord, don't stay away. O God my Strength, hurry to my aid. / I have been young and now I am old. And in all my years I have never seen the Lord forsake a man who loves him; nor have I seen the children of the godly go hungry.

O Lord God! You have made the heavens and earth by your great power; nothing is too hard for you! / He did help us, and saved us from a terrible death; yes, and we expect him to do it again and again. / Don't you think that God will surely give justice to his people who plead with him day and night? Yes, he will answer them quickly! / Keep travelling steadily along his pathway and in due season he will honour you with every blessing.

Is. 59:1. Ps. 138:3. Ps. 138:7. Ps. 27:9. Ps. 22:19. Ps. 37:25. Jer. 32:17. 2 Cor. 1:10. Lk. 18:7, 8. Ps. 37:34.

I brought glory to you here on earth.

My nourishment comes from doing the will of God who sent me, and from finishing his work. / All of us must quickly carry out the tasks assigned to us by the one who sent me, for there is little time left before the night falls and all work comes to an end.

'Didn't you realize that I would be here at the Temple, in my Father's house?' But they didn't understand what he meant. / 'The purpose of his illness is not death, but for the glory of God. I, the Son of God, will receive glory from this situation. Didn't I tell you that you will see a wonderful miracle from God if you believe?" Jesus asked [Martha].

Jesus grew both tall and wise, and was loved by God and man. / You are my much loved Son, yes, my delight. / All who were there spoke well of him and were amazed by the beautiful words that fell from his lips.

You are worthy . . . for you were slain, and your blood has bought people from every nation as gifts for God. And you have gathered them into a kingdom and made them priests of our God; they shall reign upon the earth.

Jn. 17:4. Jn. 4:34. Jn. 9:4. Lk. 2:49, 50. Jn. 11:4, 40. Lk. 2:52.
Lk. 3:22. Lk. 4:22. Rev. 5:9, 10.

Don't worry at all about having enough food and clothing.

Why be like the heathen? For they take pride in all these things and are deeply concerned about them. But your heavenly Father already knows perfectly well that you need them.

If you belong to the Lord, reverence him; for everyone who does this has everything he needs. Even strong young lions sometimes go hungry, but those of us who reverence the Lord will never lack any good thing. / No good thing will he withhold from those who walk along his paths. O Lord of the armies of heaven, blessed are those who trust in you.

I want you to be free from worry. / Don't worry about anything; instead, pray about everything; tell God your needs and don't forget to thank him for his answers. If you do this you will experience God's peace, which is far more wonderful than the human mind can understand.

Not one sparrow – what do they cost – two for a penny? – can fall to the ground without your Father knowing it. And the very hairs of your head are all numbered. So don't worry! You are more valuable to him than many sparrows. / Why were you so fearful? Don't you even yet have confidence in me? / Have faith in God.

Mt. 6:31, 32. Ps. 34:9, 10. Ps. 84:11, 12, 1 Cor. 7:32. Phil. 4:6, 7. Mt. 10:29–31. Mk. 4:40. Mk. 11:22.

He spread out a cloud above them to shield them from the burning sun, and gave them a pillar of flame at night to give them light.

He is like a father to us, tender and sympathetic to those who reverence him. For he knows we are but dust.

He protects you day and night. / Protecting . . . from daytime heat and from rains and storms.

Jehovah himself is caring for you! He is your defender. He keeps his eye upon you as you come and go, and always guards you. / God protected them in the howling wilderness as though they were the apple of his eye. / In your great mercy you didn't abandon them to die in the wilderness! The pillar of cloud led them forward day by day, and the pillar of fire showed them the way through the night. You sent your good Spirit to instruct them, and you did not stop giving them bread from heaven or water for their thirst. For forty years you sustained them in the wilderness; they lacked nothing in all that time. Their clothes didn't wear out and their feet didn't swell! / You have led the people you redeemed. But in your lovingkindness you have guided them wonderfully.

Jesus Christ is the same yesterday, today and forever.

Ps. 105:39. Ps. 103:13, 14. Ps. 121:6. Is. 4:6. Ps. 121:5, 8. Deut. 32:10. Neh. 9:19–21. Ex. 15:13. Hebr. 13:8.

Mercy and truth have met together. Grim justice and peace have kissed!

A just God and a Saviour.

The Lord has magnified his law and made it truly glorious. Through it he had planned to show the world that he is righteous.

God was in Christ, restoring the world to himself, no longer counting men's sins against them but blotting them out. / For God sent Christ Jesus to take the punishment for our sins and to end all God's anger against us. He used Christ's blood and our faith as the means of saving us from his wrath. In this way he was being entirely fair, even though he did not punish those who sinned in former times. For he was looking forward to the time when Christ would come and take away those sins. And now in these days also he can receive sinners in this same way, because Jesus took away their sins. But isn't this unfair for God to let criminals go free, and say that they are innocent? No, for he does it on the basis of their trust in Jesus who took away their sins. / He was wounded and bruised for *our* sins. He was chastised that we might have peace; he was lashed – and we were healed! / God declares sinners to be good in his sight if they have faith in Christ to save them from God's wrath.

Ps. 85:10. Is. 45:21. Is. 42:21. 2 Cor. 5:19. Rom. 3:25, 26. Is. 53:5. Rom. 4:5.

How will the dead be brought back to life again?
What kind of bodies will they have?

Dear friends, we can't even imagine what it is going to be like later on. But we do know this, that when he comes we will be like him, as a result of seeing him as he really is. / Just as each of us now has a body like Adam's, so we shall some day have a body like Christ's.

Our homeland is in heaven, with our Saviour the Lord Jesus Christ in heaven; and we are looking forward to his return from there. When he comes back he will take these dying bodies of ours and change them into glorious bodies like his own, using the same mighty power that he will use to conquer all else everywhere.

Jesus himself was suddenly standing there among them, and greeting them. But the whole group was terribly frightened, thinking they were seeing a ghost. / He was seen by Peter and later by the rest of 'the Twelve.' After that he was seen by more than five hundred Christian brothers at one time.

If the Spirit of God, who raised up Jesus from the dead, lives in you, he will make your dying bodies live again after you die, by means of this same Holy Spirit living within you.

1 Cor. 15:35. 1 Jn. 3:2. 1 Cor. 15:49. Phil. 3:20, 21. Lk. 24:36, 37.
1 Cor. 15:5, 6. Rom. 8:11.

*When you hear of wars beginning, this does not
signal my return; these must come, but the end is
not yet.*

God is our refuge and strength, a tested help in times
of trouble. And so we need not fear even if the world
blows up, and the mountains crumble into the sea. Let
the oceans roar and foam; let the mountains tremble! /
Go home, my people, and lock the doors! Hide for a
little while until the Lord's wrath against your enemies
has passed. Look! The Lord is coming from the
heavens to punish the people of the earth for their
sins. / I will hide beneath the shadow of your wings
until this storm is past. / Your real life is in heaven
with Christ and God.

All who fear God and trust in him are blessed
beyond expression. Such a man will not be overthrown
by evil circumstances. God's constant care of him will
make a deep impression on all who see it. He does not
fear bad news, nor live in dread of what may happen.
For he is settled in his mind that Jehovah will take care
of him.

I have told you all this so that you will have peace
of heart and mind. Here on earth you will have many
trials and sorrows; but take courage, I have overcome
the world.

Mt. 24:6. Ps. 46:1–3. Is. 26:20, 21. Ps. 57:1. Col. 3:3. Ps. 112:1, 6, 7.
Jn. 16:33.

They persecute the one you have smitten.

'There will always be temptations to sin,' Jesus said one day to his disciples, 'but woe to the man who does the tempting.' / God, following his pre-arranged plan, let you use the Roman government to nail him to the cross and murder him. / They spat in his face and struck him and some slapped him, saying, 'Prophesy to us, you Messiah! Who struck you that time?' / And the chief priests, and Jewish leaders also mocked him. 'He saved others,' they scoffed, 'but he can't save himself! So you are the King of Israel, are you? Come down from the cross and we'll believe you!' / Herod the king, and Pontius Pilate the governor, and all the Romans – as well as the people of Israel – are united against Jesus, your anointed Son, your holy servant. They won't stop at anything that you in your wise power will let them do. The kings of the earth unite to fight against him.

It was *our* grief he bore, *our* sorrows that weighed him down. And we thought his troubles were a punishment from God, for his *own* sins! But he was wounded and bruised for *our* sins. He was chastised that we might have peace; he was lashed – and we were healed!

Ps. 69:26. Lk. 17:1. Acts 2:23. Mt. 26:67, 68. Mt. 27:41, 42. Acts 4:27, 28, 26. Is. 53:4, 5.

*It was the Lord's good plan to bruise him and
fill him with grief.*

Now my soul is deeply troubled. Shall I pray, 'Father,
save me from what lies ahead'? But that is the very
reason why I came. Father, bring glory and honour to
your name.' Then a voice spoke from heaven saying, 'I
have already done this, and I will do it again.' / 'Father,
if you are willing, please take away this cup of horror
from me. But I want your will, not mine.' Then an
angel from heaven appeared and strengthened him, for
he was in such agony of spirit that he broke into a
sweat of blood, with great drops falling to the ground
as he prayed more and more earnestly.

He humbled himself even further, going so far as
actually to die a criminal's death on a cross. / The
Father loves me because I lay down my life that I may
have it back again. / I have come here from heaven
to do the will of God who sent me, not to have my
own way. / Shall I not drink from the cup the Father
has given me?

And he who sent me is with me – he has not deserted
me – for I always do those things that are pleasing to
him. / This is my beloved Son . . . I am wonderfully
pleased with him. / My Chosen One, in whom I delight.

*Is. 53:10. Jn. 12:27, 28. Lk. 22:42–44. Phil. 2:8. Jn. 10:17. Jn. 6:38.
Jn. 18:11. Jn. 8:29. Mt. 3:17. Is. 42:1.*

I have set intercessors on your walls who shall cry to God all day and all night for the fulfilment of his promises.

You have gathered them into a kingdom and made them priests of our God. / Only the priests are permitted to blow the trumpets. This is a permanent instruction to be followed from generation to generation. When you arrive in the Promised Land and go to war against your enemies, God will hear you and save you from your enemies when you sound the alarm with these trumpets.

I didn't tell Israel to ask me for what I didn't plan to give! / The Lord heard their prayers from his holy temple in heaven.

The eyes of the Lord are intently watching all who live good lives, and he gives attention when they cry to him. / Pray for each other so that you may be healed. The earnest prayer of a righteous man has great power and wonderful results. / Come, Lord Jesus. / You are my Saviour.

The day of the Lord is surely coming, as unexpectedly as a thief. You should look forward to that day and hurry it along. We are looking forward to God's promise of new heavens and a new earth afterwards, where there will be only goodness.

Is. 62:6. Rev. 5:10. Num. 10:8, 9. Is. 45:19. 2 Chron. 30:27. Ps. 34:15. Jas. 5:16. Rev. 22:20. Ps. 40:17. 2 Pet. 3:10, 12, 13.

*What is faith? It is the confident assurance that
something we want is going to happen. It is the
certainty that what we hope for is waiting for us,
even though we cannot see it ahead.*

If being a Christian is only of value to us now in this
life, we are the most miserable of creatures.

No mere man has ever seen, heard or even imagined
what wonderful things God has ready for those who
love the Lord. But we know about these things because
God has sent his Spirit to tell us, and his Spirit searches
out and shows us all of God's deepest secrets. / His
presence within us is God's guarantee that he really will
give us all that he promised.

Jesus told him [Thomas], 'You believe because you
have seen me. But blessed are those who haven't seen
me and believe anyway.' / You love him even though
you have never seen him; though not seeing him, you
trust him; and even now you are happy with the inexpressible joy that comes from heaven itself. And your
further reward for trusting him will be the salvation of
your souls.

We know these things are true by believing, not by
seeing. / Do not let this happy trust in the Lord die
away, no matter what happens. Remember your reward!

*Hebr. 11:1. 1 Cor. 15:19. 1 Cor. 2:9, 10. Eph. 1:14. Jn. 20:29. 1 Pet. 1:8, 9.
2 Cor. 5:7. Hebr. 10:35.*

He . . . told them not to be afraid.

When I saw him, I fell at his feet as dead; but he laid his right hand on me and said, 'Don't be afraid! Though I am the First and Last, the living one who died, who is now alive for evermore, who has the keys of hell and death – don't be afraid!' / I, yes, I alone am he who blots away your sins for my own sake and will never think of them again.

My doom is sealed, for I am a foul-mouthed sinner. . . . I have looked upon the King, the Lord of heaven's armies. Then one of the seraphs flew over to the altar and with a pair of tongs picked out a burning coal. He touched my lips with it and said, 'Now you are pronounced "Not guilty" because this coal has touched your lips. Your sins are all forgiven,' / I've blotted out your sins; they are gone like morning mist at noon! Oh, return to me, for I have paid the price to set you free.

If you sin, there is someone to plead for you before the Father. His name is Jesus Christ, the one who is all that is good and who pleases God completely. He is the one who took God's wrath against our sins upon himself, and brought us into fellowship with God.

Jn. 6:20. Rev. 1:17, 18. Is. 43:25. Is. 6:5–7. Is. 44:22. 1 Jn. 2:1, 2.

The Son of God came to destroy these works of the Devil.

We are not fighting against people made of flesh and blood, but against persons without bodies – the evil rulers of the unseen world, those mighty satanic beings and great evil princes of darkness who rule this world; and against huge numbers of wicked spirits in the spirit world. / Since we, God's children, are human beings – made of flesh and blood – he became flesh and blood too by being born in human form; for only as a human being could he die and in dying break the power of the devil who had the power of death. / In this way God took away Satan's power to accuse you of sin, and God openly displayed to the whole world Christ's triumph at the cross where your sins were all taken away. / I heard a loud voice shouting across the heavens, 'It has happened at last! God's salvation and the power and the rule, and the authority of his Christ are finally here; for the Accuser of our brothers has been thrown down from heaven on to earth – he accused them day and night before our God. They defeated him by the blood of the Lamb, and by their testimony; for they did not love their lives but laid them down for him.'

How we thank God for all of this! It is he who makes us victorious through Jesus Christ our Lord!

1 Jn. 3:8. Eph. 6:12. Hebr. 2:14. Col. 2:15. Rev. 12:10, 11. 1 Cor. 15:57.

Nothing is worthwhile; everything is futile.

All our days are filled with sighing. Seventy years are given us! And some may even live to eighty. But even the best of these years are often emptiness and pain; soon they disappear, and we are gone.

If being a Christian is only of value to us now in this life, we are the most miserable of creatures. / This world is not our home; we are looking forward to our everlasting home in heaven. / I am the Lord – I do not change. / Our homeland is in heaven, with our Saviour the Lord Jesus Christ in heaven; and we are looking forward to his return from there. When he comes back he will take these dying bodies of ours and change them into glorious bodies like his own, using the same mighty power that he will use to conquer all else everywhere. / You should look forward to that day and hurry it along. There will be only goodness. / For on that day thorns and thistles, sin, death, and decay – the things that overcame the world against its will at God's command – will all disappear.

Jesus Christ is the same yesterday, today, and forever. / Holy, holy, holy, Lord God Almighty – the one who was, and is, and is to come.

Eccl. 1:2. Ps. 90:9, 10. 1 Cor. 15:19. Hebr. 13:14. Mal. 3:6. Phil. 3:20, 21. 2 Pet. 3:12, 13. Rom. 8:20. Hebr. 13:8. Rev. 4:8.

Get some sense and stop sinning.

You are all children of the light and the day, and do not belong to darkness and night. So be on your guard, not asleep like the others. Watch for his return and stay sober.

Another reason for right living is this: you know how late it is; time is running out. Wake up, for the coming of the Lord is nearer now than when we first believed. The night is far gone, the day of his return will soon be here. So discard the evil deeds of darkness and put on the armour of right living, as we who live in the daylight should. / Use every piece of God's armour to resist the enemy whenever he attacks, and when it is all over, you will still be standing up. / Turn from your sins . . . put them behind you and receive a new heart and a new spirit. / Get rid of all that is wrong in your life, both inside and outside, and humbly be glad for the wonderful message we have received, for it is able to save our souls as it takes hold of our hearts.

My little children, stay in happy fellowship with the Lord so that when he comes you will be sure that all is well, and will not have to be ashamed and shrink back from meeting him.

1 Cor. 15:34. 1 Thess. 5:5, 6. Rom. 13:11, 12. Eph. 6:13. Ezk. 18:30, 31. Jas. 1:21. 1 Jn. 2:28.

My sheep recognize my voice.

I have been standing at the door and I am constantly knocking. If anyone hears me calling him and opens the door, I will come in and fellowship with him and he with me.

One night as I was sleeping, my heart awakened in a dream. I heard the voice of my beloved; he was knocking at my bedroom door. 'Open to me, my darling, my lover, my lovely dove,' he said, 'for I have been out in the night and am covered with dew.' I opened to my beloved, but he was gone. My heart stopped. I searched for him but couldn't find him anywhere. I called to him, but there was no reply.

I will reveal my name to my people and they shall know the power in that name. Then at last they will recognize that it is I, yes, I, who speaks to them.

When Jesus came by he looked up at Zacchaeus and called him by name. 'Zacchaeus,' he said, 'Quick! Come down! For I am going to be a guest in your home today.' Zacchaeus hurriedly climbed down and took Jesus to his house in great excitement and joy. / I am listening carefully to all the Lord is saying – for he speaks peace to his people, his saints.

Jn. 10:27. Rev. 3:20. Song 5:2, 6. Is. 52:6. Lk. 19:5, 6. Ps. 85:8.

Dear friends, let us practise loving each other,
for love comes from God and those who are
loving and kind show that they are the children of
God, and that they are getting to know him better.

God loves us, and we feel this warm love everywhere within us because God has given us the Holy Spirit to fill our hearts with his love. / And so we should not be like cringing, fearful slaves, but we should behave like God's very own children, adopted into the bosom of his family, and calling to him, 'Father, Father.' For his Holy Spirit speaks to us deep in our hearts, and tells us that we really are God's children. / All who believe this know in their hearts that it is true.

God showed how much he loved us by sending his only Son into this wicked world to bring to us eternal life through his death. / So overflowing is his kindness towards us that he took away all our sins through the blood of his Son, by whom we are saved. / And now God can always point to us as examples of how very, very rich his kindness is, as shown in all he has done for us through Jesus Christ.

Dear friends, since God loved us as much as that, we surely ought to love each other.

1 Jn. 4:7. Rom. 5:5. Rom. 8:15, 16. 1 Jn. 5:10. 1 Jn. 4:9. Eph. 1:7.
Eph. 2:7. 1 Jn. 4:11. .

Contempt has broken my heart.

He's just a carpenter's son. / Nazareth! Can anything
good come from there? / The reason he can cast out
demons is that he is demon-possessed himself – possessed by Satan, the demon king! / We know Jesus is
an evil person. / He's fooling the public. / Blasphemy!
This man is saying he is God! / I, the Son of Mankind
feast and drink, and you complain that I am 'a
glutton and a drinking man, and hang around with
the worst sort of sinners!'

The student shares his teacher's fate. The servant
his master's.

Praise the Lord if you are punished for doing
right! Of course, you get no credit for being patient
if you are beaten for doing wrong; but if you do right
and suffer for it, and are patient beneath the blows,
God is well pleased. This suffering is all part of the
work God has given you. Christ, who suffered for you,
is your example. Follow in his steps: he never sinned,
never told a lie, never answered back when insulted;
when he suffered he did not threaten to get even; he
left his case in the hands of God who always judges
fairly. / Be happy if you are cursed and insulted
for being a Christian.

*Ps. 69:20. Mt. 13:55. Jn. 1:46. Mt. 9:34. Jn. 9:24. Jn. 7:12. Mt. 9:3.
Mt. 11:19. Mt. 10:25. 1 Pet. 2:19–23. 1 Pet. 4:14.*

*I want men everywhere to pray with holy hands
lifted up to God, free from sin and anger and
resentment.*

It's not *where* we worship that counts, but *how* we
worship—is our worship spiritual and real? For God
is Spirit and we must have his help to worship as
we should. The Father wants this kind of worship
from us. / When you call, the Lord will answer,
'Yes, I am here.' / When you are praying, first forgive anyone you are holding a grudge against.

You can never please God without faith, without
depending on him. Anyone who wants to come to
God must believe that there is a God and that he
rewards those who sincerely look for him. / When you
ask him, be sure that you really expect him to tell you,
for a doubtful mind will be as unsettled as a wave of
the sea that is driven and tossed by the wind. . . . If
you don't ask with faith, don't expect the Lord to give
you any solid answer.

He would not have listened if I had not confessed
my sins. / My little children, I am telling you this
so that you will stay away from sin. But if you sin,
there is someone to plead for you before the Father.
His name is Jesus Christ, the one who is all that is
good and who pleases God completely.

*1 Tim. 2:8. Jn. 4:23, 24. Is. 58:9. Mk. 11:25. Hebr. 11:6. Jas. 1:6, 7.
Ps. 66:18. 1 Jn. 2:1, 2.*

My heart beats wildly, my strength fails.

O God, listen to me! Hear my prayer! For wherever I am, though far away at the ends of the earth, I will cry to you for help. When my heart is faint and overwhelmed, lead me to the mighty, towering Rock of safety.

I am with you; that is all you need. My power shows up best in weak people. Now I am glad to boast about how weak I am; I am glad to be a living demonstration of Christ's power, instead of showing off my own power and abilities. When I am weak, then I am strong – the less I have, the more I depend on him.

When he [Peter] looked at the high waves, he was terrified and began to sink. 'Save me, Lord!' he shouted. Instantly Jesus reached out his hand and rescued him. 'O man of little faith,' Jesus said, 'Why did you doubt?' / You are a poor specimen if you can't stand the pressure of adversity. / He gives power to the tired and worn out, and strength to the weak. / The eternal God is your Refuge, and underneath are the everlasting arms. / Filled with his mighty, glorious strength so that you can keep going no matter what happens.

Ps. 38:10. Ps. 61:1, 2. 2 Cor. 12:9, 10. Mt. 14:30, 31. Prov. 24:10. Is. 40:29. Deut. 33:27. Col. 1:11.

To suffer and to die with him.

The student shares his teacher's fate. The servant shares his master's.

We despised him and rejected him – a man of sorrows, acquainted with bitterest grief. We turned our backs on him and looked the other way when he went by. He was despised and we didn't care. / Here on earth you will have many trials and sorrows. / The world would love you if you belonged to it; but you don't – for I chose you to come out of the world, and so it hates you.

If even one would show some pity, if even one would comfort me! / The first time I was brought before the judge no one was here to help me. Everyone had run away.

Foxes have dens and birds have nests, but I, the Son of Mankind, have no home of my own – no place to lay my head. / This world is not our home; we are looking forward to our everlasting home in heaven.

Let us strip off anything that slows us down or holds us back . . . run with patience the particular race that God has set before us. Keep your eyes on Jesus, our leader and instructor. He was willing to die a shameful death on the cross because of the joy he knew would be his afterwards; and now he sits in the place of honour by the throne of God.

Phil. 3:10. Mt. 10:25. Is. 53:3. Jn. 16:33. Jn. 15:19. Ps. 69:20. 2 Tim. 4:16. Mt. 8:20. Hebr. 13:14. Hebr. 12:1, 2.

We thank God. It is he who makes us victorious through Jesus Christ our Lord!

Who dares accuse us whom God has chosen for his own? Will God? No! He is the one who has forgiven us and given us right standing with himself. Who then will condemn us? Will Christ? No! For he is the one who died for us. / It is the blood that makes atonement, because it is the life. / I am Jehovah. The blood you have placed on the doorposts will be proof that you obey me, and when I see the blood I will pass over you.

There is . . . no condemnation awaiting those who belong to Christ Jesus.

Do you know who these are, who are clothed in white, and where they come from? These are the ones coming out of the great tribulation . . . they washed their robes and made them white by the blood of the Lamb. That is why they are here before the throne of God, serving him day and night in his temple. They will never he hungry again, not thirsty.

All praise to him who always loves us and who set us free from our sins by pouring out his lifeblood for us. He has gathered us into the kingdom and made us priests of God his Father. Give to him everlasting glory! He rules for ever! Amen.

1 Cor. 15:57. Rom. 8:33, 34. Lev. 17:11. Ex. 12:12, 13. Rom. 8:1.
Rev. 7:13–16. Rev. 1/5, 6.

He will wipe away all tears from their eyes.

There shall be no more death, or sorrow, or crying, or pain. All of that has gone forever. / He will swallow up death forever. The Lord God will wipe away all tears and take away forever all insults and mockery against his land and people. The Lord has spoken – he will surely do it! / Your sun shall never set; the moon shall not go down – for the Lord will be your everlasting light; your days of mourning all will end. / The people of Israel will no longer say, 'We are sick and helpless,' for the Lord will forgive them their sins and bless them. / The voice of weeping and crying shall not be heard there any more. / All sorrow and all sighing will be gone forever.

Shall I ransom him from hell? Shall I redeem him from Death? O Death, bring forth your terrors for his tasting! O Grave, demonstrate your plagues! For I will not relent! / Christ will be King until he has defeated all his enemies, including the last enemy – death. This too must be defeated and ended. When this happens, then at last this Scripture will come true – 'Death is swallowed up in victory.'

The joys to come will last for ever.

Rev. 21:4. Is. 25:8. Is. 60:20. Is. 33:24. Is. 65:19. Is. 35:10. Hos. 13:14. 1 Cor. 15:25, 26, 54. 2 Cor. 4:18.

Lifted . . . into glory along with Christ.

Don't be afraid . . . I am . . . the living one who died. /
Father, I want them with me – these you've given
me – so that they can see my glory.

Christ cares for his body the church, of which we
are parts. / He is the head of the body made up of
his people – that is, his church – which he began; and
he is the leader of all who arise from the dead. / You
have everything when you have Christ, and you are
filled with God through your union with Christ. He
is the highest ruler.

Since we, God's children, are human beings – made
of flesh and blood – he became flesh and blood too
by being born in human form; for only as a human
being could he die and in dying break the power of
the devil who had the power of death. Only in that
way could he deliver those who through fear of death
have been living all their lives as slaves to constant
dread.

For our earthly bodies, the ones we have now that
can die, must be transformed into heavenly bodies
that cannot perish but will live forever. When this
happens, then at last this Scripture will come true –
'Death is swallowed up in victory.' So, my dear
brothers, since future victory is sure, be strong and
steady, always abounding in the Lord's work.

Eph. 2:6. Rev. 1:17, 18. Jn. 17:24. Eph. 5:30. Col. 1:18. Col. 2:10.
Hebr. 2:14, 15. 1 Cor. 15:53, 54, 58.

You belong in God's household.

You call me 'Master' and 'Lord' and you do well to say it, for it is true. / If these Greeks want to be my disciples, tell them to come and follow me, for my servants must be where I am. And if they follow me, the Father will honour them. / Wear my yoke – for it fits perfectly – and let me teach you; for I am gentle and humble, and you shall find rest for your souls; for I give you only light burdens.

All these things that I once thought very worth-while – now I've thrown them all away so that I can put my trust and hope in Christ alone. / You are free from the power of sin and are slaves of God, and his benefits to you include holiness and everlasting life.

I no longer call you slaves, for a master doesn't con-fide in his slaves; now you are my friends, proved by the fact that I have told you everything the Father told me. / No longer slaves, but God's own sons.

Christ has made us free. Now make sure that you stay free and don't get all tied up again in the chains of slavery to Jewish laws and ceremonies. For, dear brothers, you have been given freedom: not freedom to do wrong, but freedom to love and serve each other.

Eph. 2:19. Jn. 13:13. Jn. 12:26. Mt. 11:29, 30. Phil. 3:7. Rom. 6:22. Jn. 15:15. Gal. 4:7. Gal. 5:1, 13.

Evening

I will bless the Lord who counsels me.

His royal titles: 'Wonderful', Counsellor'. / I, Wisdom, give good advice and common sense. / Your words are a flashlight to light the path ahead of me, and keep me from stumbling. / Trust the Lord completely; don't ever trust yourself. In everything you do, put God first, and he will direct you and crown your efforts with success.

O Lord, I know it is not within the power of man to map his life and plan his course. / If you leave God's paths and go astray, you will hear a Voice behind you say, 'No, this is the way; walk here.' / Commit your work to the Lord, then it will succeed. / Since the Lord is directing our steps, why try to understand everything that happens long the way?

You will keep on guiding me all my life with your wisdom and counsel; and afterwards receive me into the glories of heaven! / Even when walking through the dark valley of death I will not be afraid, for you are close beside me, guarding, guiding all the way. / For this great God is our God forever and ever. He will be our guide until we die.

Ps. 16:7. Is. 9:6. Prov. 8:14. Ps. 119:105. Prov. 3:5, 6. Jer. 10:23. Is. 30:21. Prov. 16:3. Prov. 20:24. Ps. 73:24. Ps. 23:4. Ps. 48:14.

I am the Lord your God. Follow my laws;
keep my ordinances.

Be holy now in everything you do, just as the Lord is holy, who invited you to be his child. / Anyone who says he is a Christian should live as Christ did.

Not because we think we can do anything of lasting value by ourselves. Our only power and success comes from God. / Take care to live in me, and let me live in you. For a branch can't produce fruit when severed from the vine. Nor can you be fruitful apart from me.

Do the good things that result from being saved, obeying God with deep reverence, shrinking back from all that might displease him. For God is at work within you, helping you want to obey him, and then helping you do what he wants. / The God of peace, who brought again from the dead our Lord Jesus, the great Shephered of the sheep, equip you with all you need for doing his will, through the blood of the ever-lasting agreement between God and you. And may he produce in you through the power of Christ all that is pleasing to him.

Ezk. 20:19. 1 Pet. 1:15. 1 Jn. 2:6. 2 Cor. 3:5. Jn. 15:4. Phil. 2:12, 13.
Hebr. 13:20, 21.

He gave his only Son.

We all know he did not come as an angel but as a human being – yes, a Jew. And it was necessary for Jesus to be like us. / High in the sky above them was what looked like a throne made of beautiful blue sapphire stones, and upon it sat someone who appeared to be a Man. / I, the Man of Heaven, have come to earth and will return to heaven again. / Look at my hands! Look at my feet! You can see that it is I, myself. Touch me and make sure that I am not a ghost. For ghosts don't have bodies, as you see that I do!

Jesus Christ, who, though he was God, did not demand and cling to his rights as God, but laid aside his mighty power and glory, taking the disguise of a slave and becoming like men. And he humbled himself even further, going so far as actually to die a criminal's death on a cross. Yet it was because of this that God raised him up to the heights of heaven and gave him a name which is above every other name, that at the name of Jesus every knee shall bow in heaven and on earth and under the earth, and every tongue shall confess that Jesus Christ is Lord, to the glory of God the Father.

Jn. 3:16. Hebr. 2:16, 17. Ezk. 1:26. Jn. 3:13. Lk. 24:39. Phil. 2:5–11.

*The Father has life in himself, and has granted
his Son to have life in himself.*

Our Saviour Jesus Christ . . . broke the power of death
and showed us the way of everlasting life through
trusting him. / I am the one who raises the dead and
gives them life again. / I will live again – and you will
too. / We will share in all that belongs to Christ. / The
first man, Adam, was given a natural human body but
Christ is more than that, for he was life-giving Spirit.
I am telling you this strange and wonderful secret: we
shall not all die, but we shall all be given new bodies!
It will all happen in a moment, in the twinkling of an
eye, when the last trumpet is blown. For there will be a
trumpet blast from the sky and all the Christians who
have died will suddenly become alive, with new bodies
that will never, never die; and then we who are still alive
shall suddenly have new bodies too.

Holy, holy, holy, Lord God Almighty – the one who
was, and is, and is to come. Who lives for ever and
ever. / The blessed and only Almighty God, the King
of Kings, and Lord of Lords. / Glory and honour to
God for ever and ever. He is the King of the ages, the
unseen one who never dies; he alone is God, and full
of wisdom. Amen.

*Jn. 5:26. 2 Tim. 1:10. Jn. 11:25. Jn. 14:19. Hebr. 3:14. 1 Cor. 15:45, 51, 52.
Rev. 4:8, 9. 1 Tim. 6:15. 1 Tim. 1:17.*

We won't need to look for honours.

Gideon replied . . . 'I have one request. Give me all the earrings collected from your fallen foes,' – for the troops of Midian, being Ishmaelites, all wore golden earrings. 'Gladly!' they replied, and spread out a sheet for everyone to throw in the gold earrings he had gathered. Gideon made an ephod from the gold and put it in Ophrah, his home town. But all Israel soon began worshipping it, so it became an evil deed that Gideon and his family did.

Are you seeking great things for yourself? Don't do it! / Because these experiences I had were so tremendous, God was afraid I might be puffed up by them; so I was given a sickness which has been a thorn in my flesh, a messenger from Satan to hurt and bother me, and prick my pride. How weak I am; I am glad to be a living demonstration of Christ's power, instead of showing off my own power and abilities.

Don't be selfish; don't live to make a good impression on others. Be humble, thinking of others as better than yourself. / Love is very patient and kind, never jealous or envious, never boastful or proud, never haughty or selfish or rude. Love does not demand its own way.

Wear my yoke – for it fits perfectly – and let me teach you.

Gal. 5:26. Judg. 8:24, 25, 27. Jer. 45:5. 2 Cor. 12:7, 9. Phil. 2:3. 1 Cor. 13:4, 5. Mt. 11:29.

Wash me, cleanse me from this guilt.

I will cleanse away all their sins against me, and pardon them. / Then it will be as though I had sprinkled clean water on you, for you will be clean – your filthiness will be washed away, your idol worship gone.

Unless one is born of water and the Spirit, he cannot enter the Kingdom of God. / And if under the old system the blood of bulls and goats and the ashes of young cows could cleanse men's bodies from sin, just think how much more surely the blood of Christ will transform our lives and hearts. His sacrifice frees us from the worry of having to obey the old rules, and makes us want to serve the living God. For by the help of the eternal Holy Spirit, Christ willingly gave himself to God to die for our sins – he being perfect, without a single sin or fault. Christ came with this new agreement so that all who are invited may come and have forever all the wonders God has promised them. For Christ died to rescue them.

You saved them – to defend the honour of your name and demonstrate your power to all the world. / Glorify your name, not ours, O Lord! Cause everyone to praise your lovingkindness and your truth.

Ps. 51:2. Jer. 33:8. Ezk. 36:25. Jn. 3:5. Hebr. 9:13–15. Ps. 106:8.
Ps. 115:1.

*Your wonderful help in making known the Good
News about Christ.*

Our bodies have many parts, but the many parts make
up only one body when they are all put together. So it
is with the 'body' of Christ. Each of us is a part of the
one body of Christ. Some of us are Jews, some are
Gentiles, some are slaves and some are free. But the
Holy Spirit has fitted us all together into one body. We
have been baptized into Christ's body by the one Spirit.

God will surely do this for you, for he always does
just what he says, and he is the one who invited you
into this wonderful friendship with his Son, even Christ
our Lord. / We are telling you about what we ourselves
have actually seen and heard, so that you may share the
fellowship and the joys we have with the Father and
with Jesus Christ his Son.

If we are living in the light of God's presence, just
as Christ does, then we have wonderful fellowship and
joy with each other, and the blood of Jesus his Son
cleanses us from every sin. / He looked up to heaven
and said . . . 'I am not praying for these alone but also
for the future believers. . . . My prayer for all of them is
that they will be of one heart and mind, just as you
and I are, Father – that just as you are in me and I am in
you, so they will be in us.'

Phil. 1:5. 1 Cor. 12:12, 13. 1 Cor. 1:9. 1 Jn. 1:3. 1 Jn. 1:7. Jn. 17:1, 20, 21.

Keep a close watch on all you do and think.

To win the contest you must deny yourselves many things that would keep you from doing your best. An athlete goes to all this trouble just to win a ribbon or a silver cup, but we do it for a heavenly reward that never disappears. So I run straight to the goal with purpose in every step. I fight to win. I'm not just shadow-boxing or playing around. Like an athlete I punish my body, treating it roughly, training it to do what it should, not what it wants to. Otherwise I fear that after enlisting others for the race, I myself might be declared unfit and ordered to stand aside.

Put on all of God's armour so that you will be able to stand safe against all strategies and tricks of Satan. For we are not fighting against people made of flesh and blood, but against persons without bodies – the evil rulers of the unseen world, those mighty satanic beings and great evil princes of darkness who rule this world; and against huge numbers of wicked spirits in the spirit world.

Those who belong to Christ have nailed their natural evil desires to his cross and crucified them there. If we are living now by the Holy Spirit's power let us follow the Holy Spirit's leading in every part of our lives.

1 Tim. 4:16. 1 Cor. 9:25–27. Eph. 6:11, 12. Gal. 5:24, 25.

I, the Lord, the God of Israel, the one who calls you by your name.

'Mary!' Jesus said. / Don't be afraid, for I have ransomed you; I have called you by name; you are mine. / The sheep hear his voice and come to him; and he calls his own sheep by name . . . and they follow him, for they recognize his voice.

Yet they say, 'My Lord deserted us; he has forgotten us,' Never! Can a mother forget her little child and not have love for her own son? Yet even if that should be, I will not forget you. See, I have tattooed your name upon my palm.

God's truth stands firm like a great rock, and nothing can shake it. It is a foundation stone with these words written on it: 'The Lord knows those who are really his.' / Jesus the Son of God is our great high priest who has gone to heaven itself to help us; therefore let us never stop trusting him. This high priest of ours understands our weaknesses, since he had the same temptations we have, though he never once gave way to them and sinned. So let us come boldly to the very throne of God and stay there to receive his mercy and to find grace to help us in our times of need.

Everyone who conquers will be clothed in white, and I will not erase his name from the book of life.

Is. 45:3. Jn. 20:16. Is. 43:1. Jn. 10:3, 4. Is. 49:14–16. 2 Tim. 2:19. Hebr. 4:14–16. Rev. 3:5.

*I want to remind you that your strength must come
from the Lord's mighty power within you.*

'I am with you; that is all you need. My power shows
up best in weak people.' Now I am glad to boast about
how weak I am; I am glad to be a living demonstration
of Christ's power, instead of showing off my own
power and abilities. Since I know it is all for Christ's
good, I am quite happy about 'the thorn,' and about
insults and hardships, persecutions and difficulties; for
when I am weak, then I am strong – the less I have, the
more I depend on him. / I walk in the strength of the
Lord God. I tell everyone that you alone are just and
good. / This Good News about Christ . . . is God's
powerful method of bringing all who believe it to
heaven.

I can do everything God asks me to with the help of
Christ who gives me the strength and power. / This is
my work, and I can do it only because Christ's
mighty energy is at work within me. / This precious
treasure – this light and power that now shine within
us – is held in a perishable container, that is, in our weak
bodies. Everyone can see that the glorious power within
must be from God and is not our own.

The joy of the Lord is your strength.

*Eph. 6:10. 2 Cor. 12:9, 10. Ps. 71:16. Rom. 1:16. Phil. 4:13. Col. 1:29.
2 Cor. 4:7. Neh. 8:10.*

Christ our Lord.

You shall name him Jesus (meaning 'Saviour'), for he will save his people from their sins. / He humbled himself . . . going so far as actually to die a criminal's death on a cross. Yet it was because of this that God raised him up to the heights of heaven and gave him a name which is above every other name, that at the name of Jesus every knee shall bow in heaven and on earth and under the earth.

The Messiah . . . the one they call Christ. / The Spirit of the Lord God is upon me, because the Lord has anointed me to bring good news to the suffering and afflicted. He has sent me to comfort the broken-hearted, to announce liberty to captives and to open the eyes of the blind. He has sent me to tell those who mourn that the time of God's favour to them has come.

Christ . . . was life-giving Spirit. Christ came from heaven above. / My Lord and my God! / You call me 'Master' and 'Lord,' and you do well to say it, for it is true. And since I, the Lord and Teacher, have washed your feet, you ought to wash each other's feet. I have given you an example to follow: do as I have done to you.

1 Cor. 1:9. Mt. 1:21. Phil. 2:8–10. Jn. 4:25. Is. 61:1, 2. 1 Cor. 15:45, 47. Jn. 20:28. Jn. 13:13–15.

*I am leaving you with a gift – peace of mind and
heart. And the peace I give isn't fragile like the
peace the world gives.*

This world is fading away, and these evil, forbidden
things will go with it. / Proud man! Frail as breath!
A shadow! And all his busy rushing ends in nothing.
He heaps up riches for someone else to spend. / What
was the result? Evidently not good, since you are
ashamed now even to think about those things you used
to do, for all of them end in eternal doom.

Martha, dear friend, you are so upset over all these
details! There is really only one thing worth being
concerned about. Mary has discovered it – and I won't
take it away from her. / In all you do, I want you to
be free from worry.

I have told you all this so that you will have peace of
heart and mind. Here on earth you will have many
trials and sorrows; but take courage, I have overcome
the world. / May the Lord of peace himself give you
his peace no matter what happens. / May the Lord bless
and protect you; may the Lord's face radiate with joy
because of you; may he be gracious to you, show
you his favour, and give you his peace.

*Jn. 14:27. 1 Jn. 2:17. Ps. 39:6. Rom. 6:21. Lk. 10:41, 42. 1 Cor. 7:32.
Jn. 16:33. 2 Thess. 3:16. Num. 6:24–26.*

The Holy Spirit helps us with our daily problems.

The Comforter . . . the Holy Spirit. / Haven't you yet learned that your body is the home of the Holy Spirit God gave you, and that he lives within you? / God is at work within you.

The Holy Spirit helps us with our daily problems and in our praying. For we don't even know what we should pray for, nor how to pray as we should; but the Holy Spirit prays for us with such feeling that it cannot be expressed in words. And the Father who knows all hearts knows, of course, what the Spirit is saying as he pleads for us in harmony with God's own will.

He knows we are but dust. / He will not break the bruised reed, nor quench the dimly burning flame.

The spirit indeed is willing, but how weak the body is!

Because the Lord is my Shepherd, I have everything I need! He lets me rest in the meadow grass and leads me beside the quiet streams. He restores my failing health. He helps me do what honours him the most. Even when walking through the dark valley of death I will not be afraid, for you are close beside me, guarding, guiding all the way.

Rom. 8:26. Jn. 14:26. 1 Cor. 6:19. Phil. 2:13. Rom. 8:26, 27. Ps. 103:14. Is. 42:3. Mt. 26:41. Ps. 23:1–4.

Fasten the two stones upon the shoulders of the ephod, as memorial stones for the people of Israel: Aaron will carry their names before the Lord as a constant reminder.

Jesus lives forever and continues to be a priest so that no one else is needed. He is able to save completely all who come to God through him. Since he will live forever, he will always be there to remind God that he has paid for their sins with his blood. / All glory to him who alone is God, who saves us through Jesus Christ our Lord; yes, splendour and majesty, all power and authority are his from the beginning; his they are and his they evermore shall be. And he is able to keep you from slipping and falling away, and to bring you, sinless and perfect, into his glorious presence.

Jesus the Son of God is our great high priest who has gone to heaven itself to help us; therefore let us never stop trusting him. This high priest of ours understands our weaknesses, since he had the same temptations we have, though he never once gave way to them and sinned. So let us come boldly to the very throne of God and stay there to receive his mercy and to find grace to help us in our times of need.

He is beloved of God and lives in safety beside him. God surrounds him with his loving care, and preserves him from every harm.

Ex. 28:12. Hebr. 7:24, 25. Jude 24, 25. Hebr. 4:14–16. Deut. 33:12.

That night the king had trouble sleeping.

I cannot sleep until you act. / Who can be compared with God enthroned on high? Far below him are the heavens and the earth; he stoops to look.

All the people of the earth are nothing when compared with him; he does whatever he thinks best among the hosts of heaven, as well as here among the inhabitants of earth. / All the peoples of the world are nothing in comparison with him – they are but a drop in the bucket, dust on the scales. / Your road led by a pathway through the sea – a pathway no one knew was there! / Man's futile wrath will bring you glory. You will use it as an ornament!

The eyes of the Lord search back and forth across the whole earth, looking for people whose hearts are perfect towards him, so that he can show his great power in helping them. / We know that all that happens to us is working for our good if we love God.

Not one sparrow – what do they cost – two for a penny? – can fall to the ground without your Father knowing it. And the very hairs of your head are all numbered.

Esther 6:1. Ps. 77:4. Ps. 113:5, 6. Dan. 4:35. Is. 40:15. Ps. 77:19. Ps. 76:10. 2 Chron. 16:9. Rom. 8:28. Mt. 10:29, 30.

Don't cause the Holy Spirit sorrow by the way you live.

Love . . . given to you by the Holy Spirit. / The Comforter . . . the Holy Spirit. / In all their affliction he was afflicted, and he personally saved them. In his love and pity he redeemed them and lifted them up and carried them through all the years.

He has put his own Holy Spirit into our hearts as a proof to us that we are living with him and he with us. / Marked as belonging to Christ by the Holy Spirit, who long ago had been promised to all of us Christians. His presence within us is God's guarantee that he really will give us all that he promised; and the Spirit's seal upon us means that God has already purchased us and that he guarantees to bring us to himself. / I advise you to obey only the Holy Spirit's instructions. He will tell you where to go and what to do, and then you won't always be doing the wrong things your evil nature wants you to. For we naturally love to do evil things that are just the opposite of the things that the Holy Spirit tells us to do; and the good things we want to do when the Spirit has his way with us are just the opposite of our natural desires.

The Holy Spirit helps us with our daily problems.

Eph. 4:30. Rom. 15:30. Jn. 14:26. Is. 63:9. 1 Jn. 4:13. Eph. 1:13, 14. Gal. 5:16, 17. Rom. 8:26.

I will abandon them and return to my home until they admit their guilt and look to me for help.

Your sins have cut you off from God. Because of sin he has turned his face away from you and will not listen any more. / I opened to my beloved, but he was gone. I searched for him but couldn't find him anywhere. I called to him, but there was no reply. / I was angry and smote these greedy men. But they went right on sinning, doing everything their evil hearts desired. I have seen what they do. / You have brought this on yourselves by rebelling against the Lord your God when he wanted to lead you and show you the way!

He returned home to his father. And while he was still a long distance away, his father saw him coming, and was filled with loving pity and ran and embraced him and kissed him. / I will cure you of idolatry and faithlessness, and my love will know no bounds, for my anger will be forever gone!

If we confess our sins to him, he can be depended on to forgive us and to cleanse us from every wrong. And it is perfectly proper for God to do this for us because Christ died to wash away our sins.

Hos. 5:15. Is. 59:2. Song 5:6. Is. 57:17, 18. Jer. 2:17. Lk. 15:20. Hos. 14:4. 1 Jn. 1:9.

*How great is your goodness . . . you have stored
up great blessings for those who trust and reverence
you.*

Since the world began no one has seen or heard of such
a God as ours, who works for those who wait for him! /
No mere man has even seen, heard or even imagined
what wonderful things God has ready for those who
love the Lord. But we know about these things because
God has sent his Spirit to tell us, and his Spirit searches
out and shows us all of God's deepest secrets. / You
have let me experience the joys of life and the exquisite
pleasures of your own eternal presence.

How precious is your constant love, O God! All
humanity takes refuge in the shadow of your wings.
You feed them with blessings from your own table and
let them drink from your rivers of delight.

Spend your time and energy in the exercise of keeping
spiritually fit. Bodily exercise is all right, but spiritual
exercise is much more important and is a tonic for all
you do. So exercise yourself spiritually and practise
being a better Christian, because that will help you not
only now in this life, but in the next life too.

Ps. 31:19. Is. 64:4. 1 Cor. 2:9, 10. Ps. 16:11. Ps. 36:7, 8. 1 Tim. 4:7, 8.

The Son of God, whose eyes penetrate like flames of fire.

The heart is the most deceitful thing there is, and desperately wicked. No one can really know how bad it is! Only the Lord knows! He searches all hearts and examines deepest motives so he can give to each person his right reward, according to his deeds – how he has lived. / You spread out our sins before you – our secret sins – and see them all. / Jesus turned and looked at Peter. And Peter walked out of the courtyard, weeping bitterly.

Jesus didn't trust them, for he knew mankind to the core. No one needed to tell him how changeable human nature is. / He knows we are but dust. / He will not break the bruised reed, nor quench the dimly burning flame.

The Lord knows those who are really his. / I am the Good Shepherd and know my own sheep, and they know me. My sheep recognize my voice, and I know them, and they follow me. I give them eternal life and they shall never perish. No one shall snatch them away from me, for my Father has given them to me, and he is more powerful than anyone else, so no one can kidnap them from me.

Rev. 2:18. Jer. 17:9, 10. Ps. 90:8. Lk. 22:61, 62. Jn. 2:24, 25. Ps. 103:14. Is. 42:3. 2 Tim. 2:19. Jn. 10:14, 27–29.

Our Lord Jesus, the great Shepherd of the sheep.

The Head Shepherd. / I am the Good Shepherd and know my own sheep, and they know me. My sheep recognize my voice, and I know them, and they follow me. I give them eternal life and they shall never perish. No one shall snatch them away from me. I have other sheep, too, in another fold. I must bring them also, and they will heed my voice.

Because the Lord is my Shepherd, I have everything I need! He lets me rest in the meadow grass and leads me beside the quiet streams. He restores my failing health. He helps me do what honours him the most.

We are the ones who strayed away like sheep! *We*, who left God's paths to follow our own. Yet God laid on *him* the guilt and sins of every one of us. / I am the Good Shepherd. The Good Shepherd lays down his life for the sheep. / I will seek my lost ones, those who strayed away, and bring them safely home again. I will put splints and bandages upon their broken limbs and heal the sick. / Like sheep you wandered away from God, but now you have returned to your Shepherd, the Guardian of your souls who keeps you safe from all attacks.

Hebr. 13:20. 1 Pet. 5:4. Jn. 10:14, 27, 28, 16. Ps. 23:1–3. Is. 53:6. Jn. 10:11. Ezk. 34:16. 1 Pet. 2:25.

The city has no need of sun or moon to light it, for the glory of God and of the Lamb illuminate it.

A light from heaven brighter than the sun shone down on me and my companions. 'Who are you, sir?' I asked. And the Lord replied, 'I am Jesus, the one you are persecuting.' / Jesus took Peter, James, and his brother John to the top of a high and lonely hill. And as they watched, his appearance changed so that his face shone like the sun and his clothing became dazzling white. / No longer will you need the sun or moon to give you light, for the Lord your God will be your everlasting light, and he will be your glory. Your sun shall never set; the moon shall not go down – for the Lord will be your everlasting light; your days of mourning all will end.

After you have suffered a little while, our God, who is full of kindness through Christ, will give you his eternal glory. He personally will come and pick you up, and set you firmly in place, and make you stronger than ever. To him be all power over all things, for ever and ever. / So be truly glad! There is wonderful joy ahead, even though the going is rough for a while down here.

Rev. 21:23. Acts 26:13. 15. Mt. 17:1, 2. Is. 60:19, 20. 1 Pet. 5:10. 1 Pet. 1:6.

The Lord is good. When trouble comes, he is the place to go! And he knows everyone who trusts in him!

Praise the Lord! For he is good and his mercy endures forever! / God is our refuge and strength, a tested help in times of trouble. / This I declare, that he alone is my refuge, my place of safety; he is my God, and I am trusting him. / What blessings are yours, O Israel! Who else has been saved by the Lord? He is your shield and your helper. He is your excellent sword. / As for God, his way is perfect; the word of the Lord is true. He shields all who hide behind him. Our Lord alone is God; we have no other Saviour.

The person who truly loves God is the one who is open to God's knowledge. / God's truth stands firm like a great rock, and nothing can shake it. It is a foundation stone with these words written on it: 'The Lord knows those who are really his,' and 'A person who calls himself a Christian should not be doing things that are wrong.' / The Lord watches over all the plans and paths of godly men, but the paths of the godless lead to doom. / You have certainly found favour with me, and you are my friend.

Nah. 1:7. Jer. 33:11. Ps. 46:1. Ps. 91:2. Deut. 33:29. 2 Sam. 22:31, 32. 1 Cor. 8:3. 2 Tim. 2:19. Ps. 1:6. Ex. 33:17.

I want you to be free from worry.

He is always thinking about you and watching everything that concerns you. / The eyes of the Lord search back and forth across the whole earth, looking for people whose hearts are perfect towards him, so that he can show his great power in helping them.

Put God to the test and see how kind he is! See for yourself the way his mercies shower down on all who trust in him. Even strong young lions sometimes go hungry, but those of us who reverence the Lord will never lack any good thing. / So my counsel is: don't worry about *things* – food, drink, money, and clothes. For you already have life and a body – and they are far more important than what to eat and wear. Look at the birds! They don't worry about what to eat – they don't need to sow or reap or store up food – for your heavenly Father feeds them. And you are far more valuable to him than they are. / Don't worry about anything; instead, pray about everything; tell God your needs and don't forget to thank him for his answers. If you do this you will experience God's peace, which is far more wonderful than the human mind can understand. His peace will keep your thoughts and your hearts quiet and at rest as you trust in Christ Jesus.

1 Cor. 7:32. 1 Pet. 5:7. 2 Chron. 16:9. Ps. 34:8, 10. Mt. 6:25, 26. Phil. 4:6, 7.

We are looking forward to his return.

The free gift of eternal salvation is now being offered to everyone; and along with this gift comes the realization that God wants us to turn from godless living and sinful pleasures and to live good, God-fearing lives day after day, looking forward to that time when his glory shall be seen – the glory of our great God and Saviour Jesus Christ. He died under God's judgment against our sins, so that he could rescue us from constant falling into sin and make us his very own people, with cleansed hearts and real enthusiasm for doing kind things for others. / We are looking forward to God's promise of new heavens and a new earth afterwards, where there will be only goodness. Dear friends, while you are waiting for these things to happen and for him to come, try hard to live without sinning; and be at peace with everyone so that he will be pleased with you when he returns.

So also Christ died only once as an offering for the sins of many people; and he will come again, but not to deal again with our sins. This time he will come bringing salvation to all those who are eagerly and patiently waiting for him. / What a day of rejoicing!

Phil. 3:20. Tit. 2:11–14. 2 Pet. 3:13, 14. Hebr. 9:28. Is. 25:9.

Run your race to win.

Let us strip off anything that slows us down or holds us back, and especially those sins that wrap themselves so tightly around our feet and trip us up; and let us run with patience the particular race that God has set before us. Keep your eyes on Jesus, our leader and instructor.

Let us turn away from everything wrong, whether of body or spirit, and purify ourselves, living in the wholesome fear of God, giving ourselves to him alone.

I strain to reach the end of the race. / I run straight to the goal with purpose in every step. I fight to win. I'm not just shadow-boxing or playing around. Like an athlete I punish my body, treating it roughly, training it to do what it should, not what it wants to.

The world in its present form will soon be gone. / But we are looking forward to God's promise of new heavens and a new earth afterwards, where there will be only goodness. Dear friends, while you are waiting for these things to happen and for him to come, try hard to live without sinning. / So . . . you can look forward soberly and intelligently to more of God's kindness to you when Jesus Christ returns.

1 Cor. 9:24. Hebr. 12:1, 2. 2 Cor. 7:1. Phil. 3:14. 1 Cor. 9:26, 27.
1 Cor. 7:31. 2 Pet. 3:13, 14. 1 Pet. 1:13.

*The life of the flesh is in the blood, and I have
given you the blood to sprinkle upon the altar as
an atonement for your souls; it is the blood that
makes atonement, because it is the life.*

The Lamb of God who takes away the world's sin! /
The blood of the Lamb. / The precious lifeblood of
Christ, the sinless, spotless Lamb of God.

Without the shedding of blood there is no forgiveness
of sins. / The blood of Jesus his Son cleanses us
from every sin.

He took his own blood, and with it he, by himself,
made sure of our eternal salvation. / When sins have
been forgiven once and for all and forgotten, there is
no need to offer more sacrifices to get rid of them. And
so, dear brothers, now we may walk right into the very
Holy of Holies where God is, because of the blood of
Jesus. This is the fresh, new, life-giving way which
Christ has opened up for us by tearing the curtain – his
human body – to let us into the holy presence of God.
Let us go right in, to God himself, with true hearts
fully trusting him to receive us, because we have been
sprinkled with Christ's blood to make us clean.

God has bought you with a great price. So use every
part of your body to give glory back to God, because
he owns it.

Lev. 17:11. Jn. 1:29. Rev. 7:14. 1 Pet. 1:19. Hebr. 9:22. 1 Jn. 1:7.
Hebr. 9:12. Hebr. 10:18–20, 22. 1 Cor. 6:20.

Oh, for wings like a dove, to fly away and rest!

When the sun was hot, God ordered a scorching east wind to blow on Jonah, and the sun beat down upon his head until he grew faint and wished to die. For he said, 'Death is better than this!'

Job spoke. 'Oh, why should light and life be given to those in misery and bitterness, who long for death, and it won't come; who search for death as others search for food or money?' / The Lord is close to those whose hearts are breaking; he rescues those who are humbly sorry for their sins. The good man does not escape all troubles – he has them too. But the Lord helps him in each and every one.

Now my soul is deeply troubled. Shall I pray, 'Father, save me from what lies ahead?' But that is the very reason why I came. / It was necessary for Jesus to be like us, his brothers, so that he could be our merciful and faithful high priest before God, a priest who would be both merciful to us and faithful to God in dealing with the sins of the people. For since he himself has now been through suffering and temptation, he knows what it is like when we suffer and are tempted, and he is wonderfully able to help us.

Ps. 55:6. Jon. 4:8. Job 3:1, 20, 21. Ps. 34:18, 19. Jn. 12:27. Hebr. 2:17, 18.

Let us do our best to go into that place of rest.

Heaven can be entered only through the narrow gate. The highway to hell is broad, and its gate is wide enough for all the multitudes who choose its easy way. But the Gateway to Life is small, and the road is narrow, and only a few ever find it. / You shouldn't be so concerned about perishable things like food. No, spend your energy seeking the eternal life that I the Man from heaven can give you. For God the Father has sent me for this very purpose.

Work hard to prove that you really are among those God has called and chosen . . . and God will open wide the gates of heaven for you to enter into the eternal kingdom for our Lord and Saviour Jesus Christ. / Run your race to win. To win the contest you must deny yourselves many things that would keep you from doing your best. An athlete goes to all this trouble just to win a ribbon or a silver cup, but we do it for a heavenly reward that never disappears.

Christ has already entered there. He is resting from his work, just as God did after the creation. / The Lord your God will be your everlasting light, and he will be your glory.

Hebr. 4:11. Mt. 7:13, 14. Jn. 6:27. 2 Pet. 1:10, 11. 1 Cor. 9:24, 25.
Hebr. 4:10. Is. 60:19.

You always hear me.

Jesus looked up to heaven and said, 'Father, thank you for hearing me.' / 'Father, bring glory and honour to your name,' Then a voice spoke from heaven saying, 'I have already done this, and I will do it again.' / I have come to do your will. / I want your will, not mine.

As we live with Christ, our love grows more perfect and complete; so we . . . can face him with confidence and joy, because he loves us and we love him too. / We are sure of this, that he will listen to us whenever we ask him for anything in line with his will.

We . . . get whatever we ask for because we are obeying him and doing the things that please him.

You can never please God without faith, without depending on him. Anyone who wants to come to God must believe that there is a God and that he rewards those who sincerely look for him.

Since he will live forever, he will always be there to remind God that he has paid for their sins with his blood. / If you sin, there is someone to plead for you before the Father. His name is Jesus Christ, the one who is all that is good and who pleases God completely.

Jn. 11:42. Jn. 11:41. Jn. 12:28. Hebr. 10:7. Lk. 22:42. 1 Jn. 4:17. 1 Jn. 5:14. 1 Jn. 3:22. Hebr. 11:6. Hebr. 7:25. 1 Jn. 2:1.

> *Because you have been strong with God, you*
> *shall prevail with men.*

When he became a man, he even fought with God. Yes, he wrestled with the Angel and prevailed. He wept and pleaded for a blessing from him. / Abraham never doubted. He believed God, for his faith and trust grew ever stronger, and he praised God for this blessing even before it happened.

Jesus said to the disciples, 'If you only have faith in God – this is the absolute truth – you can say to this Mount of Olives, 'Rise up and fall into the Mediterranean,' and your command will be obeyed. All that's required is that you really believe and have no doubt! Listen to me! You can pray for *anything,* and *if you believe, you have it;* it's yours!' / *Anything* is possible if you have faith. / 'Woman,' Jesus told her, 'your faith is large, and your request is granted.' And her daughter was healed immediately. / You believed that God would do what he said; that is why he has given you this wonderful blessing.

We need more faith.

Gen. 32:28. Hos. 12:3, 4. Rom. 4:20. Mk. 11:22–24. Mk. 9:23. Mt. 15:28. Lk. 1:45. Lk. 17:5.

Little children, stay in happy fellowship with the Lord.

A doubtful mind will be as unsettled as a wave of the sea that is driven and tossed by the wind; and every decision you then make will be uncertain, as you turn first this way, and then that.

I am amazed that you are turning away so soon from God who, in his love and mercy, invited you to share the eternal life he gives through Christ; you are already following a different 'way to heaven,' which really doesn't go to heaven at all.

Christ is useless to you if you are counting on clearing your debt to God by keeping those laws; you are lost from God's grace. You were getting along so well. Who has interfered with you to hold you back from following the truth?

Take care to live in me, and let me live in you. For a branch can't produce fruit when severed from the vine. Nor can you be fruitful apart from me. But if you stay in me and obey my commands, you may ask any request you like, and it will be granted. / He carries out and fulfils all of God's promises, no matter how many of them there are; and we have told everyone how faithful he is, giving glory to his name.

1 Jn. 2:28. Jas. 1:6, 7. Gal. 1:6. Gal. 5:4, 7. Jn. 15:4, 7. 2 Cor. 1:20.

When the Holy Spirit controls our lives he will produce . . . faithfulness, gentleness.

I am Jehovah, the merciful and gracious God, slow to anger and rich in steadfast love and truth.

Live and act in a way worthy of those who have been chosen for such wonderful blessings as these. Be humble and gentle. Be patient with each other, making allowance for each other's faults because of your love. / Be kind to each other, tender-hearted, forgiving one another, just as God has forgiven you because you belong to Christ. / The wisdom that comes from heaven is first of all pure and full of quiet gentleness. Then it is peace-loving and courteous. It allows discussion and is willing to yield to others; it is full of mercy and good deeds. It is wholehearted and straightforward and sincere. / Love is very patient and kind.

Let us not get tired of doing what is right, for after a while we will reap a harvest of blessing if we don't get discouraged and give up. / Now as for you, dear brothers who are waiting for the Lord's return, be patient, like a farmer who waits until the autumn for his precious harvest to ripen. Yes, be patient. And take courage, for the coming of the Lord is near.

Gal. 5:22. Ex. 34:6. Eph. 4:1, 2. Eph. 4:32. Jas. 3:17. 1 Cor. 13:4.
Gal. 6:9. Jas. 5:7, 8.

'Emmanuel' . . . 'God is with us.'

Will God really live upon the earth with men? Why, even the heaven and the heaven of heavens cannot contain you. / Christ took our human nature and lived here on earth among us and was full of loving forgiveness and truth. / Christ . . . came to earth as a man.

God . . . has spoken to us through his Son to whom he has given everything, and through whom he made the world and everything there is.

That evening the disciples were meeting behind locked doors . . . when suddenly Jesus was standing there among them. After greeting them, he showed them his hands and side. And how wonderful was their joy as they saw their Lord! Eight days later the disciples were together again, and this time Thomas was with them. The doors were locked; but suddenly, as before, Jesus was standing among them and greeting them. Then he said to Thomas, 'Put your finger into my hands. Put your hand into my side. Don't be faithless any longer. Believe!' 'My Lord and my God!' Thomas said. / Unto us a Son is given: . . . 'The Mighty God.'

Mt. 1:23. 2 Chron. 6:18. Jn. 1:14. 1 Tim. 3:16. Hebr. 1:2. Jn. 20:19, 20, 26–28, Is. 9:6.

*Eat it with your travelling clothes on . . . eat
it hurriedly. This observance shall be called the
Lord's Passover.*

Up! Go away! This is no more your land and home. /
This world is not our home; we are looking forward to
our everlasting home in heaven. / There is a full complete rest *still waiting* for the people of God. / There
are many homes up there where my Father lives, and I
am going to prepare them for your coming. When everything is ready, then I will come and get you.

Be prepared – all dressed and ready – for your
Lord's return from the wedding feast. Then you will be
ready to open the door and let him in the moment he
arrives and knocks. There will be great joy for those
who are ready and waiting for his return.

Now you have every grace and blessing; every
spiritual gift and power for doing his will are yours
during this time of waiting for the return of our Lord
Jesus Christ. / Look forward soberly and intelligently
to more of God's kindness to you when Jesus Christ
returns. / I am bringing all my energies to bear on this
one thing: forgetting the past and looking forward to
what lies ahead, I strain to reach the end of the race
and receive the prize for which God is calling us up to
heaven because of what Christ Jesus did for us.

*Ex. 12:11. Mic. 2:10. Hebr. 13:14. Hebr. 4:9. Jn. 14:2. Lk. 12:35–37.
1 Cor. 1:7. 1 Pet. 1:13. Phil. 3:13–15.*

The Lord himself is my inheritance, my prize.

We are his children, we will share his treasures. / God has already given you everything you need. / My beloved is mine. / The Son of God . . . loved me and gave himself for me.

You priests may own no property, nor have any other income, for I am all that you need.

Whom have I in heaven but you? And I desire no one on earth as much as you! My health fails; my spirits droop, yet God remains! He is the strength of my heart; he is mine forever!

Even when walking through the dark valley of death I will not be afraid, for you are close beside me, guarding, guiding all the way. / I know the one in whom I trust, and I am sure that he is able to guard safely all that I have given him until the day of his return.

O God, my God! How I search for you! How I thirst for you in this parched and weary land where there is no water. How I long to find you! / In those days when you pray, I will listen. You will find me when you seek me, if you look for me in earnest. Yes, says the Lord, I will be found by you.

Ps. 16:5. Rom. 8:17. 1 Cor. 3:21. Song 2:16. Gal. 2:20. Num. 18:20.
Ps. 73:25, 26. Ps. 23:4. 2 Tim. 1:12. Ps. 63:1. Jer. 29:12–14.

*Stay awake and be prepared, for you do not know
the date or moment of my return.*

Watch out! Don't let my sudden coming catch you
unawares; don't let me find you living in careless ease,
carousing and drinking, and occupied with the
problems of this life, like all the rest of the world.
Keep a constant watch. And pray that if possible you
may arrive in my presence without having to experience
these horrors. Before all this occurs, there will be a time
of special persecution, and you will be dragged into
synagogues and prisons and before kings and governors
for my name's sake.

That day of the Lord will come unexpectedly like a
thief in the night. When people are saying, 'All is well,
everything is quiet and peaceful' – then, all of a sudden,
disaster will fall upon them as suddenly as a woman's
birth pains begin when her child is born. And these
people will not be able to get away anywhere – there
will be no place to hide. But, dear brothers, you are
not in the dark about these things, and you won't be
surprised as by a thief when that day of the Lord comes.
For you are all children of the light and of the day, and
do not belong to darkness and night. So be on your
guard, not asleep like the others. Watch for his return
and stay sober.

Mt. 25:13. Lk. 21/34, 36, 12. 1 Thess. 5:2–6.

I am the Almighty; obey me and live as you should.

I [Paul] don't mean to say I am perfect. I haven't learned all I should even yet, but I keep working towards that day when I will finally be all that Christ saved me for and wants me to be. No, dear brothers, I am still not all I should be but I am bringing all my energies to bear on this one thing: forgetting the past and looking forward to what lies ahead, I strain to reach the end of the race and receive the prize for which God is calling us up to heaven because of what Christ Jesus did for us.

Grow in spiritual strength and become better acquainted with our Lord and Saviour Jesus Christ. / Christians have no veil over our faces; we can be mirrors that brightly reflect the glory of the Lord. And as the Spirit of the Lord works within us, we become more and more like him. / The good man walks along in the ever-brightening light of God's favour; the dawn gives way to morning splendour.

Jesus . . . looked up to heaven and said . . . 'I'm not asking you to take them out of the world, but to keep them safe from Satan's power. I in them and you in me, all being perfected into one.'

Gen. 17:1. Phil. 3:12–14. 2 Pet. 3:18. 2 Cor. 3:18. Prov. 4:18. Jn. 17:1, 15, 23.

*The future splendour of this Temple will be
greater than the splendour of the first one! And
here I will give peace.*

The Temple of the Lord must be a marvellous structure,
famous and glorious throughout the world. / The glory
of the Lord filled the Temple.

'Destroy this sanctuary and in three days I will raise
it up!' By 'this sanctuary' he meant his body. / That
first glory as it shone from Moses' face is worth nothing
at all in comparison with the overwhelming glory of the
new agreement. / And Christ took our human nature
and lived here on earth among us and was full of loving
forgiveness and truth. And some of us have seen his
glory – the glory of the only Son of the heavenly
Father. / God . . . has spoken to us through his Son to
whom he has given everything, and through whom he
made the world and everything there is.

Glory to God in the highest heaven . . . and peace on
earth for all those pleasing him. / The Prince of
Peace. / Christ himself is our way of peace. / God's
peace . . . far more wonderful than the human mind can
understand. His peace will keep your thoughts and
your hearts quiet and at rest as you trust in Christ Jesus.

*Hag. 2:9. 1 Chron. 22:5. 2 Chron. 7:2. Jn. 2:19, 21. 2 Cor. 3:10.
Jn. 1:14. Hebr. 1:1, 2. Lk. 2:14. Is. 9:6. Eph. 2:14. Phil. 4:7.*

Put on the armour of right living.

Ask the Lord Jesus Christ to help you live as you should. / I have put aside all else, counting it worth less than nothing, in order that I can have Christ, and become one with him, no longer counting on being saved by being good enough or by obeying God's laws, but by trusting Christ to save me; for God's way of making us right with himself depends on faith – counting on Christ alone. / He will accept and acquit us – declare us 'not guilty' – if we trust Jesus Christ to take away our sins. And we all can be saved in this same way, by coming to Christ, no matter who we are or what we have been like.

He has clothed me with garments of salvation and draped about me the robe of righteousness. / I walk in the strength of the Lord God. I tell everyone that you alone are just and good.

For though once your heart was full of darkness, now it is full of light from the Lord, and your behaviour should show it! Take no part in the worthless pleasures of evil and darkness, but instead, rebuke and expose them. But when you expose them, the light shines in upon their sin and shows it up, and when they see how wrong they really are, some of them may even become children of light.

Rom. 13:12, 14. Phil. 3:8, 9. Rom. 3:22. Is. 61:10. Ps. 71:16. Eph. 5:8, 11, 13–15.

*If you merely obey me, you should not consider
yourselves worthy of praise. For you have simply
done your duty!*

Then what can we boast about doing, to earn our
salvation? Nothing at all. Why? Because our acquittal
is not based on our good deeds; it is based on what
Christ has done and our faith in him. / What are you
so puffed up about? What do you have that God hasn't
given you? And if all you have is from God, why act
as though you are so great, and as though you have
accomplished something on your own? / Because of his
kindness you have been saved through trusting Christ.
And even trusting is not of yourselves; it too is a gift
from God. Salvation is not a reward for the good we
have done, so none of us can take any credit for it. It
is God himself who has made us what we are and given
us new lives from Christ Jesus; and long ages ago he
planned that we should spend these lives in helping
others.

But whatever I am now it is all because God poured
out such kindness and grace upon me. / For everything
comes from God alone. Everything lives by his power,
and everything is for his glory. / Everything we have
has come from you, and we only give you what is yours
already!

Lk. 17:10. Rom. 3:27. 1 Cor. 4:7. Eph. 2:8–10. 1 Cor. 15:10. Rom. 11:36.
1 Chron. 29:14.

He knows we are but dust.

The Lord God formed a man's body from the dust of the ground and breathed into it the breath of life. And man became a living person.

Thank you for making me so wonderfully complex! It is amazing to think about. Your workmanship is marvellous – and how well I know it. You were there while I was being formed in utter seclusion! You saw me before I was born and scheduled each day of my life before I began to breathe. You made all the delicate, inner parts of my body, and knit them together in my mother's womb.

We are children of the same father, Abraham, all created by the same God. / For in him we live and move and exist. / He is like a father to us, tender and sympathetic to those who reverence him. For he knows we are but dust, and that our days are few and brief, like grass, like flowers, blown by the wind and gone forever.

He was merciful and forgave their sins and didn't destroy them all. Many and many a time he held back his anger. For he remembered that they were merely mortal men, gone in a moment like a breath of wind.

Ps. 103:14. Gen. 2:7. Ps. 139:14–16, 13. Mal. 2:10. Acts 17:28.
Ps. 103:13–16. Ps. 78:38, 39.

He will love you.

He didn't choose you and pour out his love upon you
because you were a larger nation than any other, for
you were the smallest of all! It was just because he
loves you. / Our love for him comes as a result of his
loving us first. / He has brought you back as his
friends . . . through the death on the cross of his own
human body, and now as a result Christ has brought
you into the very presence of God, and you are standing
there before him with nothing left against you —
nothing left that he could even chide you for.

In this act we see what real love is: it is not our love
for God, but his love for us when he sent his Son to
satisfy God's anger against our sins. / God showed his
great love for us by sending Christ to die for us while
we were still sinners.

A voice from heaven said, 'This is my beloved Son,
and I am wonderfully pleased with him.' / The Father
loves me because I lay down my life that I may have it
back again. / God's Son shines out with God's glory,
and all that God's Son is and does marks him as God.
He regulates the universe by the mighty power of his
command. He is the one who died to cleanse us and
clear our record of all sin, and then sat down in highest
honour beside the great God of heaven.

*Zeph. 3:17. Deut. 7:7, 8. 1 Jn. 4:19. Col. 1:21, 22. 1 Jn. 4:10. Rom. 5:8.
Mt. 3:17. Jn. 10:17. Hebr. 1:3.*

The fresh, new, life-giving way.

Cain went out from the presence of the Lord. / Your sins have cut you off from God. Because of sin he has turned his face away from you and will not listen any more. / One who is not holy will not see the Lord.

I am the Way – yes, and the Truth and the Life. No one can get to the Father except by means of me. / Our Saviour Jesus Christ . . . broke the power of death and showed us the way of everlasting life through trusting him.

Under the old system the common people could not go into the Holy of Holies as long as the outer room and the entire system it represents were still in use. / Christ himself is our way of peace. He has made peace between us Jews and you Gentiles by making us all one family, breaking down the wall of contempt that used to separate us. / The curtain separating the Holiest Place in the Temple was split apart from top to bottom.

The Gateway to Life is small, and the road is narrow, and only a few ever find it. / You have let me experience the joys of life and the exquisite pleasures of your own eternal presence.

Hebr. 10:20. Gen. 4:16. Is. 59:2. Hebr. 12:14. Jn. 14:6. 2 Tim. 1:10.
Hebr. 9:8. Eph. 2:14. Mt. 27:51. Mt. 7:14. Ps. 16:11.

Keep praying until the answer comes.

Then, teaching them more about prayer, he said,
'Suppose you went to a friend's house at midnight,
wanting to borrow three loaves of bread. You would
shout up to him, 'A friend of mine has just arrived for
a visit and I've nothing to give him to eat.' He would
call down from his bedroom, 'Please don't ask me to
get up. The door is locked for the night and we are all
in bed. I just can't help you this time.' But I'll tell you
this – though he won't do it as a friend, if you keep
knocking long enough he will get up and give you everything you want – just because of your persistence.' /
Pray all the time. Ask God for anything in line with the
Holy Spirit's wishes. Plead with him, reminding him of
your needs, and keep praying earnestly for all Christians
everywhere.

I will not let you go until you bless me. Because you
have been strong with God, you shall prevail with men. /
Don't be weary in prayer; keep at it; watch for God's
answers and remember to be thankful when they come.

[Jesus] went out into the mountains to pray, and
prayed all night.

Lk. 18:1. Lk. 11:5–8. Eph. 6:18. Gen. 32:26, 28. Col. 4:2. Lk. 6:12.

Forgive my sins.

'Come, let's talk this over!' says the Lord; 'no matter how deep the stain of your sins, I can take it out and make you as clean as freshly fallen snow. Even if you are stained as red as crimson, I can make you white as wool!'

Cheer up, son. I have forgiven your sins! / I, yes, I alone am he who blots away your sins for my own sake and will never think of them again.

So overflowing is his kindness towards us that he took away all our sins through the blood of his Son, by whom we are saved. / He saved us – not because we were good enough to be saved, but because of his kindness and pity – by washing away our sins and giving us the new joy of the indwelling Holy Spirit. He poured him out upon us with wonderful fullness – and all because of what Jesus Christ our Saviour did. / He forgave all your sins, and blotted out the charges proved against you, the list of his commandments which you had not obeyed. He took this list of sins and destroyed it by nailing it to Christ's cross.

Yes, I will bless the Lord. . . . He forgives all my sins.

Ps. 25:18. Is. 1:18. Mt. 9:2. Is. 43:25. Eph. 1:7. Tit. 3:5,6. Col. 2:13, 14. Ps. 103:2, 3.

The Lord was with Joseph in a very special way.

Blessings on all who reverence and trust the Lord – on all who obey him! Their reward shall be prosperity and happiness. / Trust in the Lord instead. Be kind and good to others; then you will live safely here in the land and prosper, feeding in safety. Be delighted with the Lord. Then he will give you all your heart's desires. / Be bold and strong! Banish fear and doubt! For remember, the Lord your God is with you wherever you go.

Don't worry at all about having enough food and clothing . . . your heavenly Father already knows perfectly well that you need them, and he will gladly give them to you if you give him first place in your life.

As long as the king followed the paths of God, he prospered, for God blessed him. / Beware that in your plenty you don't forget the Lord your God and begin to disobey him. Never feel that it was your own power and might that made you wealthy.

The Lord your God is with you. He has given you peace with the surrounding nations. Now try with every fibre of your being to obey the Lord your God.

Gen. 39:3. Ps. 128:1, 2. Ps. 37:3, 4. Josh. 1:9. Mt. 6:31–33. 2 Chron. 26:5. Deut. 8:11, 17. 1 Chron. 22:18, 19.

Why does this bother you?

Because his faith was strong, he didn't worry about the fact that he was too old to be a father, at the age of one hundred, and that Sarah his wife, at ninety, was also much too old to have a baby. But Abraham never doubted. He believed God, for his faith and trust grew ever stronger, and he praised God for this blessing even before it happened.

'So, to prove that I, the Man from Heaven, have forgiven his sins' – turning to the paralysed man – he said, 'You are healed. Pick up your stretcher and go home!' / *Anything* is possible if you have faith.

I have been given all authority in heaven and earth. / Why were you so fearful? Don't you even yet have confidence in me?/ Look at the birds . . . your heavenly Father feeds them. And you are far more valuable to him than they are. / Why are you so worried about having no food? Don't you remember at all the five thousand I fed with five loaves, and the basketfuls left over?

He will supply all your needs from his riches in glory, because of what Christ Jesus has done for us.

Mk. 2:8. Rom. 4:19, 20. Mk. 2:9–11. Mk. 9:23. Mt. 28:18. Mk. 4:40.
Mt. 6:26. Mt. 16:8, 9. Phil. 4:19.

'He says such wonderful things!' they mumbled.
'We've never heard anything like it.'

You are the fairest of all; your words are filled with
grace; God himself is blessing you forever. / The Lord
God has given me his words of wisdom so that I may
know what I should say to all these weary ones.

All who were there spoke well of him and were
amazed by the beautiful words that fell from his lips. /
For he taught as one who had great authority, and not
as their Jewish leaders.

Remember what Christ taught and let his words
enrich your lives and make you wise. / The sword of
the Spirit – which is the Word of God. / Whatever
God says to us is full of living power: it is sharper
than the sharpest dagger, cutting swift and deep into
every aspect of our innermost thoughts and desires,
exposing us for what we really are. / I use God's mighty
weapons, not those made by men, to knock down the
devil's strongholds. These weapons can break down
every proud argument against God and every wall that
can be built to keep men from finding him. With these
weapons I can capture rebels and bring them back to
God, and change them into men whose hearts' desire
is obedience to Christ.

Jn. 7:46. Ps. 45:2. Is. 50:4. Lk. 4:22. Mt. 7:29. Col. 3:16. Eph. 6:17.
Hebr. 4:12. 2 Cor. 10:4, 5.

The triumph of the wicked has been short-lived,
and the joy of the godless but for a moment.

You will strike at his heel. / This is your moment –
the time when Satan's power reigns supreme. / Since
we, God's children, are human beings – made of flesh
and blood – he became flesh and blood too by being
born in human form; for only as a human being could
he die and in dying break the power of the devil who
had the power of death. / In this way God took away
Satan's power to accuse you of sin, and God openly
displayed to the whole world Christ's triumph at the
cross where your sins were all taken away.

Be careful – watch out for attacks from Satan, your
great enemy. He prowls around like a hungry, roaring
lion, looking for some victim to tear apart. Stand firm
when he attacks. Trust the Lord. And remember that
other Christians all around the world are going through
these sufferings too. / Resist the devil and he will flee
from you.

The Lord is laughing at those who plot against the
godly, for he knows their judgment day is coming. / The
God of peace will soon crush Satan under your feet. /
The devil . . . will again be thrown into the lake of
fire . . . tormented day and night for ever and ever.

Job 20:5. Gen. 3:15. Lk. 22:53. Hebr. 2:14. Col 2:15. 1 Pet. 5:8,, 9.
Jas. 4:7. Ps. 37:12, 13. Rom. 16:20. Rev. 20:10.

*This younger son packed all his belongings and
took a trip to a distant land, and there wasted all
his money.*

There was a time when some of you were just like that,
but now your sins are washed away, and you are set
apart for God, and he has accepted you because of
what the Lord Jesus Christ and the Spirit of our God
have done for you. / All of us used to be just as they
are, our lives expressing the evil within us. But God is
so rich in mercy; he loved us so much that even though
we were spiritually dead and doomed by our sins, he
gave us back our lives again when he raised Christ from
the dead – only by his undeserved favour have we ever
been saved – and lifted us up from the grave into glory
along with Christ, where we sit with him in the heavenly
realms – all because of what Christ Jesus did.

In this act we see what real love is: it is not our love
for God, but his love for us when he sent his Son to
satisfy God's anger against our sins. / God showed his
great love for us by sending Christ to die for us while
we were still sinners. And since, when we were his
enemies, we were brought back to God by the death of
his Son, what blessings he must have for us now that we
are his friends, and he is living within us!

Lk. 15:13. 1 Cor. 6:11. Eph. 2:3–6. 1 Jn. 4:10. Rom. 5:8, 10.

---

*Remember, the Lord forgave you, so you must
forgive others.*

Then Jesus told him this story: A man loaned money
to two people – £500 to one and £50 to the other. But
neither of them could pay him back, so he kindly forgave them both, letting them keep the money. / I
forgave you all that tremendous debt, just because you
asked me to – shouldn't you have mercy on others, just
as I had mercy on you?

But when you are praying, first forgive anyone you
are holding a grudge against, so that your Father in
heaven will forgive you your sins too. / Since you have
been chosen by God who has given you this new kind
of life, and because of his deep love and concern for
you, you should practise tenderhearted mercy and
kindness to others. Don't worry about making a good
impression on them but be ready to suffer quietly and
patiently. Be gentle and ready to forgive; never hold
grudges.

'Sir, how often should I forgive a brother who sins
against me? Seven times?' 'No,' Jesus replied, 'seventy
times seven!'

Let love guide your life. / Trust him and become
full of the love of Christ Jesus.

*Col. 3:13. Lk. 7:41, 42. Mt. 18:32, 33. Mk. 11:25. Col. 3:12, 13.
Mt. 18:21, 22. Col. 3:14. 1 Tim. 1:14.*

*He returned home to his father. And while he was
still a long distance away, his father saw him
coming, and was filled with loving pity and ran
and embraced him and kissed him.*

He is merciful and tender toward those who don't
deserve it; he is slow to get angry and full of kindness
and love. He never bears a grudge, nor remains angry
forever. He has not punished us as we deserve for all our
sins, for his mercy toward those who fear and honour
him is as great as the height of the heavens above
the earth. He has removed our sins as far away from us
as the east is from the west. He is like a father to us,
tender and sympathetic to those who reverence him.

And so we should not be like cringing, fearful slaves,
but we should behave like God's very own children,
adopted into the bosom of his family, and calling to him,
'Father, Father.' For his Holy Spirit speaks to us deep
in our hearts, and tells us that we really are God's
children. / Though you once were far away from God,
now you have been brought very near to him because
of what Jesus Christ has done for you with his blood.
Now you are no longer strangers to God and foreigners
to heaven, but you are members of God's very own
family, citizens of God's country, and you belong in
God's household with every other Christian.

Lk. 15:20. Ps. 103:8–13. Rom. 8:15, 16. Eph. 2:13, 19.

Evening

I am making all things new!

Unless you are born again, you can never get into the Kingdom of God. / When someone becomes a Christian he becomes a brand new person inside. He is not the same any more. A new life has begun!

It will be as though I had sprinkled clean water on you, for you will be clean – your filthiness will be washed away. And I will give you a new heart – I will give you new and right desires – and put a new spirit within you. I will take out your stony hearts of sin and give you new hearts of love. And I will put my Spirit within you so that you will obey my laws and do whatever I command. / Yes, you must be a new and different person, holy and good. Clothe yourself with this new nature.

God will confer on you a new name. He will hold you aloft in his hands for all to see – a splendid crown for the King of kings.

I am creating new heavens and a new earth – so wonderful that no one will even think about the old ones any more. / And so since everything around us is going to melt away, what holy, godly lives we should be living.

Rev. 21:5. Jn. 3:3. 2 Cor. 5:17. Ezk. 36:25–27. Eph. 4:24. Is. 62:2, 3.
Is. 65:17. 2 Pet. 3:11.

*Anything that will stand heat . . . shall be passed
through fire in order to be made ceremonially
pure.*

The Lord is testing you to find out whether or not you
really love him with all your heart and soul. / Like a
refiner of silver he will sit and closely watch as the dross
is burned away. He will purify the Levites, the ministers
of God, refining them like gold or silver, so that they
will do their work for God with pure hearts. / There
is going to come a time of testing at Christ's
Judgment Day to see what kind of material each builder
has used. Everyone's work will be put through the
fire so that all can see whether or not it's of lasting
value, and what was really accomplished.

I myself will melt you in a smelting pot, and skim
off your slag. / I will melt them in a crucible of
affliction. I will refine them and test them like metal.

You have purified us with fire, O Lord, like silver in
a crucible. You sent troops to ride across our broken
bodies. We went through fire and flood. But in the end,
you brought us into wealth and great abundance.

When you walk through the fire of oppression, you
will not be burned up – the flames will not consume
you.

Num. 31:22, 23. Deut. 13:3. Mal. 3:3. 1 Cor. 3:13. Is. 1:25. Jer. 9:7.
Ps. 66:10, 12. Is. 43:2.

We can be finished with sin and live a good life.

Throw off your old evil nature – the old you that was a partner in your evil ways – rotten through and through, full of lust and sham. Now your attitudes and thoughts must all be constantly changing for the better. Yes, you must be a new and different person, holy and good. Clothe yourself with this new nature.

You should have as little desire for this world as a dead person does. Your real life is in heaven with Christ and God. / Your old sin-loving nature was buried with him by baptism when he died, and when God the Father, with glorious power, brought him back to life again, you were given his wonderful new life to enjoy. Your old evil desires were nailed to the cross with him; that part of you that loves to sin was crushed and fatally wounded, so that your sin-loving body is no longer under sin's control, no longer needs to be a slave to sin; for when you are deadened to sin you are freed from all its allure and its power over you. So look upon your old sin nature as dead and unresponsive to sin, and instead be alive to God, alert to him, through Jesus Christ our Lord. Give yourselves completely to God – every part of you – for you are back from death and you want to be tools in the hands of God, to be used for his good purposes.

1 Pet. 2:24. Eph. 4:22–24. Col. 3:3. Rom. 6:4, 6, 7, 11, 13.

Take care to live in me, and let me live in you.

I have been crucified with Christ: and I myself no longer live, but Christ lives in me. And the real life I now have within this body is a result of my trusting in the Son of God, who loved me and gave himself for me.

I know I am rotten through and through so far as my old sinful nature is concerned. No matter which way I turn I can't make myself do right. I want to but I can't. Oh, what a terrible predicament I'm in! Who will free me from my slavery to this deadly lower nature? Thank God! It has been done by Jesus Christ our Lord. He has set me free. / Yet, even though Christ lives within you, your body will die because of sin; but your spirit will live, for Christ has pardoned it. / The only condition is that you fully believe the truth, standing in it steadfast and firm, strong in the Lord, convinced of the Good News that Jesus died for you, and never shifting from trusting him to save you.

And now, my little children, stay in happy fellowship with the Lord so that when he comes you will be sure that all is well, and will not have to be ashamed and shrink back from meeting him. / Anyone who says he is a Christian should live as Christ did.

Jn. 15:4. Gal. 2:20. Rom. 7:18, 24, 25. Rom. 8:10. Col. 1:23. 1 Jn. 2:28. 1 Jn. 2:6.

Do you believe in the Messiah?

Who is he, sir?

God's Son shines out with God's glory, and all that God's Son is and does marks him as God. / The blessed and only Almighty God, the King of Kings and Lord of Lords, who alone can never die, who lives in light so terrible that no human being can approach him. No mere man has ever seen him, nor ever will. Unto him be honour and everlasting power and dominion forever and ever. Amen. / 'I am the A and Z, the beginning and the ending of all things,' says God, who is the Lord, the all powerful one who is, and was, and is coming again!

Yes, Lord, I believe! / I know the one in whom I trust, and I am sure that he is able to guard safely all that I have given him until the day of his return. / We believe because we have heard him ourselves, not just because of what you told us. He is indeed the Saviour of the world.

I am sending Christ to be the carefully chosen, precious cornerstone of my church, and I will never disappoint those who trust in him. Yes, he is very precious to you who believe.

Jesus Christ is the same yesterday, today, and forever.

Jn. 9:35. Jn. 9:36. Hebr. 1:3. 1 Tim. 6:15,16. Rev. 1:8. Jn. 9:38.
2 Tim. 1:12. Jn. 4:42. 1 Pet. 2:6, 7. Hebr. 13:8.

> *The more we undergo sufferings for Christ, the more he will shower us with his comfort and encouragement.*

To suffer and to die with him. / Don't be bewildered or surprised when you go through the fiery trials. Instead, be really glad – because these trials will make you partners with Christ in his suffering, and afterwards you will have the wonderful joy of sharing his glory in that coming day when it will be displayed. / When we suffer and die for Christ it only means that we will begin living with him in heaven. / Since we are his children, we will share his treasures – for all God gives to his Son Jesus is now ours too. But if we are to share his glory, we must also share his suffering.

God also bound himself with an oath, so that those he promised to help would be perfectly sure and never need to wonder whether he might change his plans. He has given us both his promise and his oath, two things we can completely count on, for it is impossible for God to tell a lie. Now all those who flee to him to save them can take new courage when they hear such assurances from God. / May our Lord Jesus Christ himself and God our Father, who has loved us and given us everlasting comfort and hope which we don't deserve, comfort your hearts with all comfort, and help you in every good thing you say and do.

2 Cor. 1:5. Phil. 3:10. 1 Pet. 4:12, 13. 2 Tim. 2:11. Rom. 8:17. Hebr. 6:17, 18. 2 Thess. 2:16, 17.

*Martha, dear friend, you are so upset over all
these details!*

Look at the ravens – they don't plant or harvest or have
barns to store away their food, and yet they get by all
right – for God feeds them. And you are far more
valuable to him than any birds! Look at the lilies. They
don't toil and spin. And don't worry about food –
what to eat and drink; don't let it cause you anxiety.
All mankind scratches for its daily bread, but your
heavenly Father knows your needs.

We should be well satisfied without money if we have
enough food and clothing. People who long to be rich
soon begin to do all kinds of wrong things to get money,
things that hurt them and make them evil-minded and
finally send them to hell itself. For the love of money
is the first step towards all kinds of sin. Some people
have even turned away from God because of their love
for it, and as a result have pierced themselves with
many sorrows.

The attractions of this world, and the delights of
wealth, and the search for success and the lure of
attractive things come in and crowd out God's message
from their hearts.

Let us strip off anything that slows us down or holds
us back . . . and let us run with patience the particular
race that God has set before us.

Lk. 10:41. Lk. 12:24, 27, 29, 30. 1 Tim. 6:8–10. Mk. 4:19. Hebr. 12:1.

There are secrets the Lord your God has not revealed to us, but these words which he has revealed are for us.

Lord, I am not proud and haughty. I don't think myself better than others. I don't pretend to 'know it all.' I am quiet now before the Lord, just as a child who is weaned from the breast. Yes, my begging has been stilled.

Friendship with God is reserved for those who reverence him. With them alone he shares the secrets of his promises. / There is a God in heaven who reveals secrets. / I will only reveal myself to those who love me and obey me.

I no longer call you slaves, for a master doesn't confide in his slaves; now you are my friends, proved by the fact that I have told you everything the Father told me. / There is so much more I want to tell you, but you can't understand it now. / If you love me, obey me; and I will ask the Father and he will give you another Comforter, and he will never leave you. He is the Holy Spirit, the Spirit who leads into all truth. The world at large cannot receive him, for it isn't looking for him and doesn't recognize him. But you do, for he lives with you now and some day shall be in you.

Deut. 29:29. Ps. 131:1, 2. Ps. 25:14. Dan. 2:28. Jn. 14:23. Jn. 15:15. Jn. 16:12. Jn. 14:15–17.

*The Spirit . . . pleads for us in harmony with
God's own will.*

At that time you won't need to ask me for anything,
for you can go directly to the Father and ask him, and
he will give you what you ask for because you use my
name. You haven't tried this before, [but begin now].
Ask, using my name, and you will receive, and your cup
of joy will overflow. / Pray all the time. Ask God for
anything in line with the Holy Spirit's wishes. Plead
with him, reminding him of your needs.

We are sure of this, that he will listen to us whenever
we ask him for anything in line with his will. And if
we really know he is listening when we talk to him and
make our requests, then we can be sure that he will
answer us. / God wants you to be holy and pure. / Be
holy now in everything you do, just as the Lord is holy,
who invited you to be his child. He himself has said,
'You must be holy, for I am holy.'

Always be joyful. Always keep on praying. Always
be thankful no matter what happens, for that is God's
will for you who belong to Christ Jesus. Do not
smother the Holy Spirit.

*Rom. 8:27. Jn. 16:23, 24. Eph. 6:18. 1 Jn. 5:14, 15. 1 Thess. 4:3.
1 Pet. 1:15, 16. 1 Thess. 5:16–19.*

Be careful how you act; these are difficult days.
Don't be fools; be wise: make the most of every
opportunity you have for doing good.

Be sure to continue to obey all of the commandments. . . . Love the Lord and follow his plan for your lives. Cling to him and serve him enthusiastically. / Make the most of your chances to tell others the Good News. Be wise in all your contacts with them. Let your conversation be gracious as well as sensible, for then you will have the right answer for everyone. / Keep away from every kind of evil.

When the bridegroom was delayed, they lay down to rest until midnight, when they were roused by the shout, 'The bridegroom is coming! Come out and welcome him!' Stay awake and be prepared, for you do not know the date or moment of my return.

Work hard to prove that you really are among those God has called and chosen, and then you will never stumble or fall away. And God will open wide the gates of heaven for you to enter into the eternal kingdom of our Lord and Saviour Jesus Christ. / There will be great joy for those who are ready and waiting for his return. So be ready all the time. For I, the Man of glory, will come when least expected.

Eph. 5:15, 16. Josh. 22:5. Col. 4:5, 6. 1 Thess. 5:22. Mt. 25:5, 6, 13.
2 Pet. 1:10, 11. Lk. 12:37, 40.

*Hold tightly to the little strength you have – so
that no one will take away your crown.*

If I only touch him, I will be healed. / 'Sir, if you want
to, you can heal me.' 'I want to; be healed.' / Faith
even as small as a tiny mustard seed.

Do not let this happy trust in the Lord die away, no
matter what happens. Remember your reward! / Do
the good things that result from being saved, obeying
God with deep reverence, shrinking back from all that
might displease him. For God is at work within you,
helping you want to obey him, and then helping you to
do what he wants.

May the God of peace . . . equip you with all you
need for doing his will. May he . . . produce in you
through the power of Christ all that is pleasing to him. /
Press on to know him. / Run your race to win.

I have fought long and hard for my Lord, and
through it all I have kept true to him. And now the
time has come for me to stop fighting and rest. In
heaven a crown is waiting for me which the Lord, the
righteous Judge, will give me on that great day of his
return.

*Rev. 3:11. Mt. 9:21. Mt. 8:2, 3. Mt. 17:20. Hebr. 10:35. Phil. 2:12, 13.
Hebr. 13:20, 21. Hos. 6:3. 1 Cor. 9:24. 2 Tim. 4:7, 8.*

*Don't worry about anything; instead, pray about
everything; tell God your needs and don't forget
to thank him for his answers.*

I love the Lord because he hears my prayers and
answers them. Because he bends down and listens, I will
pray as long as I breathe! / I know you will answer
me, O God! Yes, listen as I pray.

Don't recite the same prayer over and over as the
heathen do, who think prayers are answered if they are
repeated again and again. / The Holy Spirit helps us
with our daily problems and in our praying. For we
don't even know what we should pray for, nor how to
pray as we should; but the Holy Spirit prays for us
with such feeling that it cannot be expressed in words.
And the Father who knows all hearts knows, of course,
what the Spirit is saying as he pleads for us in harmony
with God's own will.

I want men everywhere to pray with holy hands lifted
up to God, free from sin and anger and resentment. /
Pray all the time. Ask God for anything in line with
the Holy Spirit's wishes. Plead with him, reminding
him of your needs, and keep praying earnestly for all
Christians everywhere.

If two of you agree down here on earth concerning
anything you ask for, my Father in heaven will do it
for you.

*Phil. 4:6. Ps. 116:1, 2. Ps. 17:6. Mt. 6:7. Rom. 8:26, 27. 1 Tim. 2:8.
Eph. 6:18. Mt. 18:19.*

*All living things shall thank you, Lord, and your
people will bless you.*

I bless the holy name of God with all my heart. Yes, I
will bless the Lord and not forget the glorious things
he does for me. / I will praise the Lord no matter
what happens. I will constantly speak of his glories
and grace. I will boast of all his kindness to me. / I
will praise you, my God and King, and bless your
name each day and forever. Great is Jehovah! Greatly
praise him! His greatness is beyond discovery! Let
each generation tell its children what glorious things
he does. I will meditate about your glory, splendour,
majesty and miracles. Your awe-inspiring deeds shall
be on every tongue; I will proclaim your greatness.

Your love and kindness are better to me than life
itself. How I praise you! I will bless you as long as I
live, lifting up my hands to you in prayer. At last I shall
be fully satisfied; I will praise you with great joy.

Oh, how I praise the Lord. How I rejoice in God
my Saviour!

O Lord, you are worthy to receive the glory and the
honour and the power, for you have created all things.
They were created and called into being by your act of
will.

*Ps. 145:10. Ps. 103:1, 2. Ps. 34:1, 2. Ps. 145:1–6. Ps. 63:3–5. Lk. 1:46, 47.
Rev. 4:11.*

I will meet with you there.

Common people could not go into the Holy of Holies
as long as the outer room and the entire system it
represents were still in use. / Jesus shouted out again,
dismissed his spirit, and died. And look – the curtain
separating the Holiest Place in the Temple was split
apart from top to bottom.

Now we may walk right into the very Holy of Holies
where God is, because of the blood of Jesus. This is
the fresh, new. life-giving way which Christ has opened
up for us by tearing the curtain – his human body – to
let us into the holy presence of God. Let us go right
in, to God himself, with true hearts fully trusting him
to receive us, because we have been sprinkled with
Christ's blood to make us clean, and because our bodies
have been washed with pure water. / So let us come
boldly to the very throne of God and stay there to
receive his mercy and to find grace to help us in our
times of need.

Jesus Christ . . . freely takes away our sins. For God
sent Christ Jesus to take the punishment for our sins
and to end all God's anger against us. / All of us . . .
may come to God the Father with the Holy Spirit's help
because of what Christ has done for us.

*Ex. 25:22. Hebr. 9:8. Mt. 27:50, 51. Hebr. 10:19, 20, 22. Hebr. 4:16.
Rom. 3:24, 25. Eph. 2:18.*

Faith even as small as a tiny mustard seed.

'The Lord God of Israel has commanded you to
mobilize ten thousand men. Lead them to Mount
Tabor, to fight King Jabin's mighty army.' 'I'll go,
but only if you go with me!' Barak told [Deborah].
That day the Lord used Israel to subdue King Jabin
of Canaan. / Gideon . . . did as the Lord had commanded. But he did it at night for fear of the other
members of his father's household, and for fear of the
men of the city. Then Gideon said to God, 'If you are
really going to use me to save Israel as you promised . . .
let me make one more test. . . .' So the Lord did as
he asked.

   You aren't strong, but you have tried to obey and
have not denied my name. / Do not despise this small
beginning.

   Dear brothers, giving thanks to God for you is not
only the right thing to do, but it is our duty to God,
because of the really wonderful way your faith has
grown. / We need more faith. / I will refresh Israel
like the dew from heaven; she will blossom as the lily
and root deeply in the soil like cedars in Lebanon.
Her branches will spread out, as beautiful as olive trees,
fragrant as the forests of Lebanon.

*Mt. 17:20. Judg. 4:6–8, 23. Judg. 6:27, 36, 39, 40. Rev. 3:8. Zech. 4:10.
2 Thess. 1:3. Lk. 17:5. Hos. 14:5, 6.*

*Seek to live a clean and holy life, for one who
is not holy will not see the Lord.*

Unless you are born again, you can never get into the
Kingdom of God. / Nothing evil will be permitted in
it – no one immoral or dishonest.

You must be holy because I, the Lord your God,
am holy. / Obey God because you are his children;
don't slip back into your old ways – doing evil because
you knew no better. But be holy now in everything
you do, just as the Lord is holy, who invited you to
be his child. He himself has said, 'You must be holy,
for I am holy.' And remember that your heavenly
Father to whom you pray has no favourites when he
judges. He will judge you with perfect justice for
everying you do; so act in reverent fear of him from
now on until you get to heaven. / Throw off your old
evil nature. Now your attitudes and thoughts must all
be constantly changing for the better. Yes, you must be
a new and different person, holy and good. Clothe
yourself with this new nature. / Long ago, even before
he made the world, God chose us to be his very own,
through what Christ would do for us; he decided then
to make us holy in his eyes, without a single fault –
we who stand before him covered with his love.

*Hebr. 12:14. Jn. 3:3. Rev. 21:27. Lev. 19:2. 1 Pet. 1:14–17. Eph. 4:22–24.
Eph. 1:4.*

Gold purified by fire.

Let me assure you that no one has ever given up anything – home, brothers, sisters, mother, father, children, or property – for love of me and to tell others the Good News, who won't be given back, a hundred times over, homes, brothers, sisters, mothers, children, and land – with persecutions! All these will be his here on earth, and in the world to come he shall have eternal life.

Don't be bewildered or surprised when you go through the fiery trials ahead, for this is no strange, unusual thing that is going to happen to you. / Be truly glad! There is wonderful joy ahead, even though the going is rough for a while down here. These trials are only to test your faith, to see whether or not it is strong and pure. If your faith remains strong after being tried in the test tube of fiery trials, it will bring you much praise and glory and honour on the day of his return.

After you have suffered a little while, our God, who is full of kindness through Christ, will give you his eternal glory. He personally will come and pick you up, and set you firmly in place, and make you stronger than ever. / Here on earth you will have many trials and sorrows; but take courage, I have overcome the world.

Rev. 3:18. Mk. 10:29, 30. 1 Pet. 4:12. 1 Pet. 1:6, 7. 1 Pet. 5:10. Jn. 16:33.

*Take this child home and nurse him for me, and I
will pay you well.*

He sent them also into his fields, telling them he would
pay them whatever was right at the end of the day. / If
anyone so much as gives you a cup of water because
you are Christ's – I say this solemnly – he won't lose
his reward. / The liberal man shall be rich! By watering
others, he waters himself. / God is not unfair. How can
he forget your hard work for him, or forget the way
you used to show your love for him – and still do – by
helping his children?

Each of us will be rewarded for his own hard work.

'Sir, when did we ever see you hungry and feed you?
Or thirsty and give you anything to drink? Or a stranger,
and help you? Or naked, and clothe you? When did
we ever see you sick or in prison, and visit you?' And
I, the King, will tell them, 'When you did it to these
my brothers you were doing it to me! Come, blessed of
my Father, into the Kingdom prepared for you from the
founding of the world. For I was hungry and you fed
me; I was thirsty and you gave me water.'

*Ex. 2:9. Mt. 20:4. Mk. 9:41. Prov. 11:25. Hebr. 6:10. 1 Cor. 3:8.
Mt. 25:37–40, 34, 35.*

You chart the path ahead of me, and tell me where to stop and rest.

Jacob . . . found a stone for a headrest and lay down to sleep, and dreamed that a staircase reached from earth to heaven, and he saw the angels of God going up and down upon it. At the top of the stairs stood the Lord. 'I am Jehovah,' he said . . . 'I will be with you constantly until I have finished giving you all I am promising.' Then Jacob woke up. 'God lives here!' he exclaimed in terror. 'I've stumbled into his home. This is the awesome entrance to heaven!'

For the eyes of the Lord search back and forth across the whole earth, looking for people whose hearts are perfect towards him, so that he can show his great power in helping them.

I will lie down in peace and sleep, for though I am alone, O Lord, you will keep me safe.

For Jehovah is my refuge! I choose the God above all gods to shelter me. How then can evil overtake me or any plague come near? For he orders his angels to protect you wherever you go. / With them on guard you can sleep without fear. / God wants his loved ones to get their proper rest.

Ps. 139:3. Gen. 28:11–13, 15–17. 2 Chron. 16:9. Ps. 4:8. Ps. 91:9–11. Prov. 3:24. Ps. 127:2.

This suffering is all part of the work God has given you. Christ, who suffered for you, is your example. Follow in his steps.

For even I, the Man from Heaven, am not here to be served, but to help others. / And whoever wants to be greatest of all must be the slave of all. / Jesus Christ . . . laid aside his mighty power and glory, taking the disguise of a slave.

Jesus of Nazareth . . . went around doing good. / Share each other's troubles and problems, and so obey our Lord's command.

Gently, as Christ himself would do. / Be humble, thinking of others as better than yourself.

Father, forgive these people, for they don't know what they are doing. / Be kind to each other, tenderhearted, forgiving one another, just as God has forgiven you because you belong to Christ.

Anyone who says he is a Christian should live as Christ did. / Keep your eyes on Jesus, our leader and instructor. He was willing to die a shameful death on the cross because of the joy he knew would be his afterwards; and now he sits in the place of honour by the throne of God.

1 Pet. 2:21. Mk. 10:45. Mk. 10:44. Phil. 2:5–7. Acts 10:38. Gal. 6:2. 2 Cor. 10:1. Phil. 2:3. Lk. 23:34. Eph. 4:32. 1 Jn. 2:6. Hebr. 12:2.

I searched for him but couldn't find him anywhere.
I called to him, but there was no reply.

'O Lord, what am I to do now that Israel has fled from her enemies!' But the Lord said to Joshua, 'Get up off your face! Israel has sinned and disobeyed my commandment and has taken loot when I said it was not to be taken; and they have not only taken it, they have lied about it and have hidden it among their belongings. That is why the people of Israel are being defeated. That is why your men are running from their enemies – for they are cursed. I will not stay with you any longer unless you completely rid yourselves of this sin.'

Listen now! The Lord isn't too weak to save you. And he isn't getting deaf! He can hear you when you call! But the trouble is that your sins have cut you off from God. Because of sin he has turned his face away from you and will not listen any more.

He would not have listened if I had not confessed my sins.

But, dearly loved friends, if our consciences are clear, we can come to the Lord with perfect assurance and trust, and get whatever we ask for because we are obeying him and doing the things that please him.

Song 5:6. Josh. 7:8, 10–12. Is. 59:1, 2. Ps. 66:18. 1 Jn. 3:21, 22.

You should have as little desire for this world as a dead person does. Your real life is in heaven with Christ and God.

Should we keep on sinning when we don't have to? / I have been crucified with Christ: and I myself no longer live, but Christ lives in me. And the real life I now have within this body is a result of my trusting in the Son of God, who loved me and gave himself for me. / He died for all so that all who live – having received eternal life from him – might live no longer for themselves, to please themselves, but to spend their lives pleasing Christ who died and rose again for them. / When someone becomes a Christian he becomes a brand new person inside. He is not the same any more. A new life has begun!

We are in God because we are in Jesus Christ his Son, who is the only true God; and he is eternal life. / All of you together are the one body of Christ and each one of you is a separate and necessary part of it. / I will live again – and you will too.

Every one who is victorious shall eat of the hidden manna, the secret nourishment from heaven; and I will give to each a white stone, and on the stone will be engraved a new name that no one else knows except the one receiving it.

Col. 3:3. Rom. 6:2. Gal. 2:20. 2 Cor. 5:15. 2 Cor. 5:17. 1 Jn. 5:20. 1 Cor. 12:27. Jn. 14:19. Rev. 2:17.

See how much he loved him.

He died for all. / The greatest love is shown when a person lays down his life for his friends.

He will always be there to remind God that he has paid for their sins with his blood. / There are many homes up there where my Father lives, and I am going to prepare them for your coming.

When everything is ready, then I will come and get you, so that you can always be with me where I am. / Father, I want them with me – these you've given me. / How he loved his disciples!

Our love for him comes as a result of his loving us first. / Christ's love controls us now. Since we believe that Christ died for all of us, we should also believe that we have died to the old life we used to live. He died for all so that all who live – having received eternal life from him – might live no longer for themselves, to please themselves, but to spend their lives pleasing Christ who died and rose again for them.

When you obey me you are living in my love, just as I obey my Father and live in his love.

Jn. 11:36. 2 Cor. 5:15. Jn. 15:13. Hebr. 7:25. Jn. 14:2. Jn. 14:3.
Jn. 17:24. Jn. 13:3. 1 Jn. 4:19. 2 Cor. 5:14, 15. Jn. 15:10.

*I will ask the Father and he will give you another
Comforter, and he will never leave you. He is the
Holy Spirit, the Spirit who leads into all truth.*

It is best for you that I go away, for if I don't, the
Comforter won't come. If I do, he will – for I will
send him to you.

His Holy Spirit speaks to us deep in our hearts, and
tells us that we really are God's children. / And so we
should not be like cringing, fearful slaves, but we should
behave like God's very own children, adopted into the
bosom of his family, and calling to him, 'Father,
Father.' / The Holy Spirit helps us with our daily
problems and in our praying. For we don't even know
what we should pray for, nor how to pray as we should;
but the Holy Spirit prays for us with such feeling that
it cannot be expressed in words.

I pray . . . that God who gives you hope will keep
you happy and full of peace as you believe in him
through the Holy Spirit's power within you. / We are
able to hold our heads high no matter what happens
and know that all is well, for we know how dearly
God loves us, and we feel this warm love everywhere
within us because God has given us the Holy Spirit
to fill our hearts with his love.

*Jn. 14:16, 17. Jn. 16:7. Rom. 8:16. Rom. 8:15. Rom. 8:26. Rom. 15:13.
Rom 5:5.*

Rest in the Lord; wait patiently for him.

There is a full complete rest *still waiting* for the people of God. / My people will live in safety, quietly at home. / They shall rest from all their toils and trials.

Christ has gone ahead to plead for us from his position as our high priest, with the honour and rank of Melchizedek.

Come to me and I will give you rest – all of you who work so hard beneath a heavy yoke. Wear my yoke – for it fits perfectly – and let me teach you; for I am gentle and humble, and you shall find rest for your souls; for I give you only light burdens. / Only in returning to me and waiting for me will you be saved; in quietness and confidence is your strength. / Ask where the good road is, the godly paths you used to walk in, in the days of long ago. Travel there, and you will find rest for your souls.

Because the Lord is my Shepherd, I have everything I need! He lets me rest in the meadow grass and leads me beside the quiet streams. / Now I can relax. For the Lord has done this wonderful miracle for me.

Ps. 37:7. Hebr. 4:9. Is. 32:18. Rev. 14:13. Hebr. 6:20. Mt. 11:28–30. Is. 30:15. Jer. 6:16. Ps. 23:1, 2. Ps. 116:7.

*Don't be anxious about tomorrow. Live one day
at a time.*

My times are in your hands. / He subdues the nations
before us, and will personally select his choicest
blessings . . . the very best for those he loves. / Lord,
lead me as you promised me you would. Tell me clearly
what to do, which way to turn.

Commit everything you do to the Lord. Trust him to
help you do it and he will. / In everything you do,
put God first, and he will direct you and crown your
efforts with success. / If you leave God's paths and go
astray, you will hear a Voice behind you say, 'No, this
is the way: walk here.'

Because the Lord is my Shepherd, I have everything
I need! He lets me rest in the meadow grass and leads
me beside the quiet streams. / He is like a father to us,
tender and sympathetic to those who reverence him.
For he knows we are but dust. / Don't worry at all
about having enough food and clothing. Your heavenly
Father already knows perfectly well that you need
them. / Let him have all your worries and cares, for he
is always thinking about you and watching everything
that concerns you.

*Mt. 6:34. Ps. 31:15. Ps. 47:3, 4. Ps. 5:8. Ps. 37:5. Prov. 3:6. Is. 30:21.
Ps. 23:1, 2. Ps. 103:13, 14. Mt. 6:31, 32. 1 Pet. 5:7.*

'Sir, where do you live?' 'Come and see,' he said.

Let not your heart be troubled. You are trusting God, now trust in me. There are many homes up there where my Father lives, and I am going to prepare them for your coming. When everything is ready, then I will come and get you, so that you can always be with me where I am. If this weren't so, I would tell you plainly. / I will let every one who conquers sit beside me on my throne.

The high and lofty one who inhabits eternity, the Holy One, says this: 'I live in that high and holy place where those with contrite, humble spirits dwell; and I refresh the humble and give new courage to those with repentant hearts.'

Look! I have been standing at the door and I am constantly knocking. If anyone hears me calling him and opens the door, I will come in and fellowship with him and he with me.

I am with you always, even to the end of the world. / How precious is your constant love, O God! All humanity takes refuge in the shadow of your wings. You feed them with blessings from your own table and let them drink from your rivers of delight.

Jn. 1:38, 39. Jn. 14:1–3. Rev. 3:21. Is. 57:15. Rev. 3:20. Mt. 28:20. Ps. 36:7, 8.

*When he comes we will be like him, as a result of
seeing him as he really is.*

To all who received him, he gave the right to become
children of God. All they needed to do was to trust
him to save them. / And by that same mighty power
he has given us all the other rich and wonderful
blessings he promised; for instance, the promise to . . .
give us his own character.

For since the world began no one has seen or heard
of such a God as ours, who works for those who wait
for him!

We can see and understand only a little about God
now, as if we were peering at his reflection in a poor
mirror; but someday we are going to see him in his
completeness, face to face. Now all that I know is
hazy and blurred, but then I will see everything clearly,
just as clearly as God sees into my heart right now. /
Christ . . . will take these dying bodies of ours and
change them into glorious bodies like his own, using
the same mighty power that he will use to conquer all
else everywhere. / But as for me, my contentment is
not in wealth but in seeing you and knowing all is well
between us. And when I awake in heaven, I will be fully
satisfied, for I will see you face to face.

*1 Jn. 3:2. Jn. 1:12. 2 Pet. 1:4. Is. 64:4. 1 Cor. 13:12. Phil. 3:20, 21.
Ps. 17:15.*

*'My associate and equal,' says the Lord of
heaven's armies.*

In Christ there is the perfection of God in a human
body. / He humbled himself even further, going so far
as actually to die a criminal's death on a cross. Yet it
was because of this that God raised him up to the
heights of heaven and gave him a name which is above
every other name.

It is quite true that the way to live a godly life is not
an easy matter. But the answer lies in Christ, who came
to earth as a man. / For unto us a Child is born: unto
us a Son is given; and the government shall be upon
his shoulder. These will be his royal titles: 'Wonderful,' 'Counsellor,' 'The Mighty God,' 'The Everlasting
Father,' 'the Prince of Peace.'

God's Son shines out with God's glory, and all that
God's Son is and does marks him as God. He regulates
the universe by the mighty power of his command. He
is the one who died to cleanse us and clear our record
of all sin, and then sat down in highest honour beside
the great God of heaven. Your kingdom, O God, will
last for ever and ever.

Let all the angels of God worship him. / KING OF
KINGS AND LORD OF LORDS.

*Zech. 13:7. Col. 2:9. Phil. 2:8, 9. 1 Tim. 3:16. Is. 9:6. Hebr. 1:3, 8, 6.
Rev. 19:16.*

*'Oh, that you would wonderfully bless me and
help me in my work; please be with me in all that I
do, and keep me from all evil and disaster!' And
God granted him his request.*

The Lord's blessing is our greatest wealth. All our
work adds nothing to it! / Yet when he chooses not
to speak, who can criticize? Again, he may prevent a
vile man from ruling, thus saving a nation from ruin.

Salvation comes from God. What joys he gives to all
his people. / Oh, how great is your goodness to those
who publicly declare that you will rescue them. For you
have stored up great blessings for those who trust and
reverence you. / I'm not asking you to take them out of
the world, but to keep them safe from Satan's power.

Ask, and you will be given what you ask for. Seek, and
you will find. Knock, and the door will be opened. For
everyone who asks, receives. Anyone who seeks, finds.
If only you will knock, the door will open. / But as for
those who serve the Lord, he will redeem them; everyone who takes refuge in him will be freely pardoned.

*1 Chron. 4:10. Prov. 10:22. Job 34:29. Ps. 3:8. Ps. 31:19. Jn. 17:15.
Mt. 7:7, 8. Ps. 34:22.*

This night was selected by the Lord to bring his people out from the land of Egypt; so the same night was selected as the date of the annual celebration of God's deliverance.

On the night when Judas betrayed him, the Lord Jesus took bread, and when he had given thanks to God for it, he broke it and gave it to his disciples and said, 'Take this and eat it. This is my body, which is given for you. Do this in memory of me.' In the same way, he took the cup of wine after supper, saying. 'This cup is the new agreement between God and you that has been established and set in motion by my blood. Do this in remembrance of me whenever you drink it.'

He walked away, perhaps a stone's throw, and knelt down and prayed this prayer: 'Father, if you are willing, please take away this cup of horror from me. But I want your will, not mine.' He was in such agony of spirit that he broke into a sweat of blood, with great drops falling to the ground as he prayed more and more earnestly.

It was now about noon of the day before Passover. He was taken . . . to the place known as . . . 'Golgotha.' There they crucified him.

Christ, God's Lamb, has been slain for us. So let us feast upon him and grow strong in the Christian life.

Ex. 12:42. 1 Cor. 11:23–25. Lk. 22:41, 42, 44. Jn. 19:14, 17, 18. 1 Cor. 5:7, 8.

Who can survive?

Who can endure his coming? For he is like a blazing fire refining precious metal and he can bleach the dirtiest garments!

I saw a vast crowd, too great to count, from all nations and provinces and languages, standing in front of the throne and before the Lamb, clothed in white, with palm branches in their hands. 'These are the ones coming out of the great tribulation,' he said; 'they washed their robes and made them white by the blood of the Lamb. That is why they are here before the throne of God, serving him day and night in his temple. The one sitting on the throne will shelter them; they will never be hungry again, nor thirsty, and they will be fully protected from the scorching noontime heat. For the Lamb standing in front of the throne will feed them and be their shepherd and lead them to the springs of the water of life. And God will wipe their tears away.'

There is now no condemnation awaiting those who belong to Christ Jesus. / So Christ has made us free. Now make sure that you stay free and don't get tied up again in the chains of slavery.

Rev. 6:17. Mal. 3:2. Rev. 7:9, 14–17. Rom. 8:1. Gal. 5:1.

Don't bring me to trial! For compared with you,
no one is perfect.

'Come, let's talk this over!' says the Lord; 'no matter how deep the stain of your sins, I can take it out and make you as clean as freshly fallen snow. Even if you are stained as red as crimson, I can make you white as wool!'

If I find thorns and briars bothering her, I will burn them up, unless these enemies of mine surrender and beg for peace and my protection. / Stop quarrelling with God! Agree with him and you will have peace at last!

Since we have been made right in God's sight by faith in his promises, we can have real peace with him because of what Jesus Christ our Lord has done for us. / So we, too, have trusted Jesus Christ, that we might be accepted by God. / The more we know of God's laws, the clearer it becomes that we aren't obeying them; his laws serve only to make us see that we are sinners. No one can ever be made right in God's sight by doing what the law commands.

Everyone who trusts in him is freed from all guilt and declared righteous. / How we thank God for all of this! It is he who makes us victorious through Jesus Christ our Lord!

Ps. 143:2. Is. 1:18. Is. 27:5. Job 22:21. Rom. 5:1. Gal. 2:16. Rom. 3:20.
Acts 13:39. 1 Cor. 15:57.

I know that my Redeemer lives.

And since, when we were his enemies, we were brought
back to God by the death of his Son, what blessings
he must have for us now that we are his friends, and
he is living within us! / But Jesus lives forever and
continues to be a priest so that no one else is needed.
He is able to save completely all who come to God
through him. Since he will live forever, he will always
be there to remind God that he has paid for their sins
with his blood.

I will live again – and you will too. / And if being a
Christian is only of value to us now in this life, we are
the most miserable of creatures. But the fact is that
Christ actually did rise from the dead, and has become
the first of millions who will come back to life again
some day.

He will come as a Redeemer to those in Zion who
have turned away from me. / So overflowing is his
kindness towards us that he took away all our sins
through the blood of his Son, by whom we are saved. /
God paid a ransom to save you from the impossible
road to heaven which your fathers tried to take, and
the ransom he paid was not mere gold or silver, as you
very well know; but he paid for you with the precious
lifeblood of Christ, the sinless, spotless Lamb of God.

Job 19:25. Rom. 5:10. Hebr. 7:24, 25. Jn. 14:19. 1 Cor. 15:19, 20.
Is. 59:20. Eph. 1:7. 1 Pet. 1:18, 19.

*The Holy Spirit tells us clearly that in the last
times some in the church will turn away from
Christ and become eager followers of teachers
with devil-inspired ideas.*

Be careful how you listen. / Remember what Christ
taught and let his words enrich your lives and make
you wise. / In every battle you will need faith as your
shield to stop the fiery arrows aimed at you by Satan.

Those who love your laws have great peace of heart
and mind and do not stumble. Your words are sweeter
than honey. And since only your rules can give me
wisdom and understanding, no wonder I hate every
false teaching.

Your words are a flashlight to light the path ahead
of me, and keep me from stumbling. They make me
wiser than my enemies, because they are my constant
guide.

Satan can change himself into an angel of light. / Let
God's curses fall on anyone, including myself, who
preaches any other way to be saved than the one we
told you about; yes, if an angel comes from heaven
and preaches any other message, let him be for ever
cursed.

But as for me, I get as close to him [God] as I can!
I have chosen him and I will tell everyone about the
wonderful ways he rescues me.

*1 Tim. 4:1. Lk. 8:18. Col. 3:16. Eph. 6:16. Ps. 119:165, 103, 104.
Ps. 119:105, 98. 2 Cor. 11:14. Gal. 1:8. Ps. 73:28.*

Loving God means doing what he tells us to do.

It is my Father's will that everyone who sees his Son
and believes on him should have eternal life. / We can
come to the Lord with perfect assurance and trust, and
get whatever we ask for because we are obeying him
and doing the things that please him.

Wear my yoke – for it fits perfectly – and let me
teach you; for I am gentle and humble, and you shall
find rest for your souls; for I give you only light
burdens. / If you love me, obey me. The one who
obeys me is the one who loves me; and because he
loves me, my Father will love him; and I will too, and
I will reveal myself to him.

The man who knows right from wrong and has good
judgment and common sense is happier than the man
who is immensely rich! Wisdom gives a long, good life,
riches, honour, pleasure, peace. / Those who love your
laws have great peace of heart and mind and do not
stumble. / I love to do God's will.

And this is what God says we must do: believe on
the name of his Son Jesus Christ, and love one another. /
Love does no wrong to anyone. That's why it fully
satisfies all of God's requirements. It is the only law
you need.

1 Jn. 5:3. Jn. 6:40. 1 Jn. 3:21, 22. Mt. 11:29, 30. Jn. 14:15, 21.
Prov. 3:13, 17. Ps. 119:165. Rom. 7:22. 1 Jn. 3:23. Rom. 13:10.

Overlook my youthful sins, O Lord!

I've blotted out your sins; they are gone like morning mist at noon! / I, yes, I alone am he who blots away your sins for my own sake and will never think of them again. / 'Come, let's talk this over!' says the Lord; 'no matter how deep the stain of your sins, I can take it out and make you as clean as freshly fallen snow. Even if you are stained as red as crimson, I can make you white as wool!' / I will forgive and forget their sins. / You will tread our sins beneath your feet; you will throw them into the depths of the ocean!

It was good for me to undergo this bitterness, for you have lovingly delivered me from death; you have forgiven all my sins. / Where is another God like you, who pardons the sins of the survivors among his people? You cannot stay angry with your people for you love to be merciful. / All praise to him who always loves us and who set us free from our sins by pouring out his life blood for us. He has gathered us into his kingdom and made us priests of God his Father. Give to him everlasting glory! He rules for ever! Amen.

Ps. 25:6, 7. Is. 44:22. Is. 43:25. Is. 1:18. Jer. 31:34. Mic. 7:19. Is. 38:17. Mic. 7:18. Rev. 1:5, 6.

I continually discipline and punish everyone I love.

My son, don't be angry when the Lord punishes you. Don't be discouraged when he has to show you where you are wrong. For when he punishes you, it proves that he loves you. When he whips you it proves you are really his child. / His punishment is proof of his love. Just as a father punishes a son he delights in to make him better, so the Lord corrects you. / For though he wounds, he binds and heals again. / If you will humble yourselves under the mighty hand of God, in his good time he will lift you up. / I refined you in the furnace of affliction. / I am the Lord your God, who punishes you for your own good and leads you along the paths that you should follow.

He does not enjoy afflicting men and causing sorrow. / He has not punished us as we deserve for all our sins, for his mercy toward those who fear and honour him is as great as the height of the heavens above the earth. He has removed our sins as far away from us as the east is from the west. He is like a father to us, tender and sympathetic to those who reverence him. For he knows we are but dust.

Rev. 3:19. Hebr. 12:5, 6. Prov. 3:12. Job 5:18. 1 Pet. 5:6. Is. 48:10.
Is. 48:17. Lam. 3:33. Ps. 103:10–14.

He is in heaven and you are only here on earth, so let your words be few.

Don't recite the same prayer over and over as the heathen do, who think prayers are answered if they are repeated again and again. Remember, your Father knows exactly what you need even before you ask him!

They called to Baal all morning, shouting, 'O Baal, hear us!'

Two men went to the Temple to pray. One was a proud, self-righteous Pharisee, and the other a cheating tax collector. The proud Pharisee 'prayed' this prayer: 'Thank God, I am not a sinner like everyone else, especially like that tax collector over there! For I never cheat, I don't commit adultery.' But the corrupt tax collector stood at a distance and dared not even lift his eyes to heaven as he prayed, but beat upon his chest in sorrow, exclaiming, 'God, be merciful to me, a sinner.' I tell you, this sinner, not the Pharisee, returned home forgiven! For the proud shall be humbled, but the humble shall be honoured.

We don't even know what we should pray for, nor how to pray as we should. / Lord, teach us.

Eccl. 5:2. Mt. 6:7, 8. 1 Kgs. 18:26. Lk. 18:10, 11, 13, 14. Rom. 8:26. Lk. 11:1.

When the Holy Spirit controls our lives he will produce . . . gentleness.

Follow God's example in everything you do just as a much loved child imitates his father. / Love your *enemies* Pray for those who persecute you! In that way you will be acting as true sons of your Father in heaven. For he gives his sunlight to both the evil and the good, and sends rain on the just and on the unjust too. / Try to show as much compassion as your Father does.

Because of this light within you, you should do only what is good and right and true.

When the time came for the kindness and love of God our Saviour to appear, then he saved us – not because we were good enough to be saved, but because of his kindness and pity – by washing away our sins and giving us the new joy of the indwelling Holy Spirit. He poured him out upon us with wonderful fullness – and all because of what Jesus Christ our Saviour did. / He is good to everyone, and his compassion is intertwined with everything he does. / Since he did not spare even his own Son for us but gave him up for us all, won't he also surely give us everything else?

Gal. 5:22, 23. Eph. 5:1. Mt. 5:44, 45. Lk. 6:36. Eph. 5:9. Tit. 3:4–6. Ps. 145:9. Rom. 8:32.

Ebenezer . . . The Lord has certainly helped us!

I was facing death and then he saved me. Now I can relax. For the Lord has done this wonderful miracle for me. He has saved me from death, my eyes from tears, my feet from stumbling. / Oh, praise the Lord, for he has listened to my pleadings! He is my strength, my shield from every danger. I trusted in him, and he helped me. Joy rises in my heart until I burst out in songs of praise to him. The Lord protects his people.

It is better to trust the Lord than to put confidence in men. It is better to take refuge in him than in the mightiest king! / Happy is the man who has the God of Jacob as his helper, whose hope is in the Lord his God. / He led them straight to safety and a place to live. / Every good thing the Lord had promised them came true.

Don't worry at all about having enough food and clothing . . . your heavenly Father already knows perfectly well that you need them. / How much you have helped me – and how I rejoice through the night beneath the protecting shadow of your wings.

1 Sam. 7:12. Ps. 116:6–8. Ps. 28:6–8. Ps. 118:8–9. Ps. 146:5. Ps. 107:7. Josh. 21:45. Mt. 6:31, 32. Ps. 63:7.

*These are the rules concerning the observance
of the Passover. No foreigners shall eat the lamb.*

We have an altar – the cross where Christ was sacrificed – where those who continue to seek salvation by obeying Jewish laws can never be helped. / Unless you are born again, you can never get into the Kingdom of God. / Remember that in those days you were living utterly apart from Christ; you were enemies of God's children and he had promised you no help. You were lost, without God, without hope. But now you belong to Christ Jesus, and though you once were far away from God, now you have been brought very near to him because of what Jesus Christ has done for you with his blood.

For Christ himself is our way of peace. He has made peace between us Jews and you Gentiles by making us all one family, breaking down the wall of contempt that used to separate us.

Now you are no longer strangers to God and foreigners to heaven, but you are members of God's very own family, citizens of God's country, and you belong in God's household with every other Christian.

If anyone hears me calling him and opens the door, I will come in and enjoy fellowship with him and he with me.

Ex. 12:43. Hebr. 13:10. Jn. 3:3. Eph. 2:12, 13. Eph. 2:14. Eph. 2:19. Rev. 3:20.

[Jesus] went back to prayer the third time.

While Christ was here on earth he pleaded with God, praying with tears and agony of soul to the only one who could save him from [premature] death.

Oh, that we might know the Lord! Let us press on to know him, and he will respond to us as surely as the coming of dawn or the rain of early spring. / Be patient in trouble, and always prayerful. / Pray all the time. Ask God for anything in line with the Holy Spirit's wishes. Plead with him, reminding him of your needs. / Don't worry about anything; instead, pray about everything; tell God your needs and don't forget to thank him for his answers. If you do this you will experience God's peace, which is far more wonderful than the human mind can understand. His peace will keep your thoughts and your hearts quiet and at rest as you trust in Christ Jesus.

I want your will, not mine. / We are sure of this, that he will listen to us whenever we ask him for anything in line with his will. / Be delighted with the Lord. Then he will give you all your heart's desires. Commit everything you do to the Lord. Trust him to help you do it and he will.

Mt. 26:44. Hebr. 5:7. Hos. 6:3. Rom. 12:12. Eph. 6:18. Phil. 4:6, 7. Mt. 26:39. 1 Jn. 5:14. Ps. 37:4, 5.

*Since we are his children, we will share his
treasures – for all God gives to his Son Jesus is now
ours too.*

Now that we are Christ's we are the true descendants
of Abraham, and all of God's promises to him belong
to us.

See how very much our heavenly Father loves us, for
he allows us to be called his children. / Now we are
no longer slaves, but God's own sons. And since we are
his sons, everything he has belongs to us, for that is the
way God planned. / His unchanging plan has always
been to adopt us into his own family by sending Jesus
Christ to die for us. And he did this because he wanted
to!

Father, I want them with me – these you've given
me – so that they can see my glory. You gave me the
glory because you loved me before the world began.

To every one who overcomes – who to the very end
keeps on doing the things that please me – I will give
power over the nations. You will rule them with a rod
of iron just as my Father gave me the authority to rule
them; they will be shattered like a pot of clay that is
broken into tiny pieces. / I will let every one who
conquers sit beside me on my throne, just as I took my
place with my Father on his throne when I had conquered.

*Rom. 8:17. Gal. 3:29. 1 Jn. 3:1. Gal. 4:7. Eph. 1:5. Jn. 17:24. Rev. 2:26, 27.
Rev. 3:21.*

He has chosen a plan despised by the world.

How can this be? . . . These men are all from Galilee, and yet we hear them speaking all the native languages of the lands where we were born!

[Jesus] saw two brothers . . . fishing with a net, for they were fishermen by trade. Jesus called out, 'Come along with me and I will show you how to fish for the souls of men!' / When the council saw the boldness of Peter and John, and could see that they were obviously uneducated working men, they were amazed and realized what being with Jesus had done for them!

My preaching was very plain, not with a lot of oratory and human wisdom, but the Holy Spirit's power was in my words, proving to those who heard them that the message was from God.

You didn't choose me. I chose you. I appointed you to go and produce good fruit always. Whoever lives in me and I in him shall produce a large crop of fruit. For apart from me you can't do a thing. / This precious treasure – this light and power that now shine within us – is held in a perishable container, that is, in our weak bodies. Everyone can see that the glorious power within must be from God and is not our own.

1 Cor. 1:28. Acts 2:7. Mt. 4:18, 19. Acts 4:13. 1 Cor. 2:4. Jn. 15:16, 5. 2 Cor. 4:7.

Sitting next to Jesus.

I will comfort you there as a little one is comforted by
its mother. / Mothers were bringing their children to
Jesus to bless them. He took the children into his arms
and placed his hands on their heads and he blessed
them. / Jesus called his disciples to him and said, 'I
pity these people – they've been here with me for three
days now, and have nothing left to eat; I don't want to
send them away hungry or they will faint along the
road.' Then Jesus told all of the people to sit down on
the ground, and he took the seven loaves and the fish,
and gave thanks to God for them, and divided them
into pieces, and gave them to the disciples who presented them to the crowd. And everyone ate until full. /
This high priest of ours understands our weaknesses. /
In his love and pity he redeemed them.

I will not abandon you or leave you as orphans in
the storm – I will come to you. / Can a mother forget
her little child and not have love for her own son? Yet
even if that should be, I will not forget you.

For the Lamb standing in front of the throne will
feed them and be their shepherd and lead them to the
springs of the water of life. And God will wipe their
tears away.

*Jn. 13:23. Is. 66:13. Mk. 10:13, 16. Mt. 15:32, 35–37. Hebr. 4:15.
Is. 63:9. Jn. 14:18. Is. 49:15. Rev. 7:17.*

*Jesus Christ . . . who pleases God completely . . .
is the forgiveness for our sins.*

Place within the Ark the tablets of stone I shall give
you. And I will meet with you there and talk with you.

Surely his salvation is near to those who reverence
him; our land will be filled with his glory. Mercy and
truth have met together. Grim justice and peace have
kissed!

Lord, if you keep in mind our sins then who can ever
get an answer to his prayers? But you forgive! What
an awesome thing this is! O Israel, hope in the Lord;
for he is loving and kind, and comes to us with arm-
loads of salvation. He himself shall ransom Israel from
her slavery to sin. / Yes, all have sinned; all fall short of
God's glorious ideal; yet now God declares us 'not
guilty' of offending him if we trust in Jesus Christ, who
in his kindness freely takes away our sins. For God sent
Christ Jesus to take the punishment for our sins and
to end all God's anger against us. He used Christ's blood
and our faith as the means of saving us from his wrath.
In this way he was being entirely fair, even though he
did not punish those who sinned in former times. For
he was looking forward to the time when Christ would
come and take away those sins.

1 Jn. 2:1, 2. Ex. 25:21, 22. Ps. 85:9, 10. Ps. 130:3, 4, 7, 8. Rom. 3:23–25.

We know how much God loves us because we have felt his love and because we believe him when he tells us that he loves us dearly.

God is so rich in mercy; he loved us so much that even though we were spiritually dead and doomed by our sins, he gave us back our lives again when he raised Christ from the dead – only by his undeserved favour have we ever been saved – and lifted us up from the grave into glory along with Christ, where we sit with him in the heavenly realms – all because of what Christ Jesus did. And now God can always point to us as examples of how very, very rich his kindness is, as shown in all he has done for us through Jesus Christ.

For God loved the world so much that he gave his only Son so that anyone who believes in him shall not perish but have eternal life. / Since he did not spare even his own Son for us but gave him up for us all, won't he also surely give us everything else? / He is good to everyone, and his compassion is intertwined with everything he does.

Our love for him comes as a result of his loving us first.

You believed that God would do what he said; that is why he has given you this wonderful blessing.

1 Jn. 4:16. Eph. 2:4–7. Jn. 3:16. Rom. 8:32. Ps. 145:9. 1 Jn. 4:19. Lk. 1:45.

Don't try to get into the good books of important people, but enjoy the company of ordinary folk.

How can you claim that you belong to the Lord Jesus Christ, the Lord of glory, if you show favouritism to rich people and look down on poor people? Listen to me, dear brothers: God has chosen poor people to be rich in faith, and the kingdom of heaven is theirs, for that is the gift God has promised to all those who love him.

Don't think only of yourself. Try to think of the other fellow, too, and what is best for him. / We should be well satisfied without money if we have enough food and clothing. People who long to be rich soon begin to do all kinds of wrong things to get money, things that hurt them and make them evil-minded and finally send them to hell itself.

God has deliberately chosen to use ideas the world considers foolish and of little worth in order to shame those people considered by the world as wise and great. He has chosen a plan despised by the world, counted as nothing at all, and used it to bring down to nothing those the world considers great, so that no one anywhere can ever boast in the presence of God.

For it is from God alone that you have your life through Christ Jesus.

Rom. 12:16. Jas. 2:1, 5. 1 Cor. 10:24. 1 Tim. 6:8, 9. 1 Cor. 1:27–29. 1 Cor. 1:30.

Let your conversation be gracious.

Timely advice is as lovely as golden apples in a silver basket. It is a badge of honour to accept valid criticism. / Don't use bad language. Say only what is good and helpful to those you are talking to, and what will give them a blessing. / A good man's speech reveals the rich treasures within him. An evil-hearted man is filled with venom, and his speech reveals it. Your words now reflect your fate then: either you will be justified by them or you will be condemned. / The words of the wise soothe and heal.

Those who feared and loved the Lord spoke often of him to each other. And he had a Book of Remembrance drawn up in which he recorded the names of those who feared him and loved to think about him.

Only if you return to trusting me will I let you continue as my spokesman. You are to influence *them*, not let them influence *you!* / You people there are leaders in so many ways – you have so much faith, so many good preachers, so much learning, so much enthusiasm, so much love for us. Now I want you to be leaders also in the spirit of cheerful giving.

Col. 4:6. Prov. 25:11, 12. Eph. 4:29. Mt. 12:35, 37. Prov. 12:18.
Mal. 3:16. Jer. 15:19. 2 Cor. 8:7.

*I have taken your lovingkindness and your truth
as my ideals.*

Jehovah is kind and merciful, slow to get angry, full of
love. / Your Father in heaven . . . gives his sunlight to
both the evil and the good, and sends rain on the just
and on the unjust too. / Follow God's example in
everything you do just as much loved child imitates
his father. Be full of love for others, following the
example of Christ who loved you and gave himself to
God as a sacrifice to take away your sins. And God
was pleased, for Christ's love for you was like sweet perfume to him. / Be tenderhearted, forgiving one another,
just as God has forgiven you because you belong to
Christ. / Now you can have real love for everyone
because your souls have been cleansed from selfishness
and hatred when you trusted Christ to save you; so
see to it that you really do love each other warmly, with
all your hearts. / Whatever we do, it is certainly not for
our own profit, but because Christ's love controls us
now.

Love your enemies! Do good to them! Lend to them!
And don't be concerned about the fact that they won't
repay. Then your reward from heaven will be very great,
and you will truly be acting as sons of God: for he is
kind to the unthankful and to those who are very
wicked.

*Ps. 26:3. Ps. 145:8. Mt. 5:45. Eph. 5:1, 2. Eph. 4:32. 1 Pet. 1:22.
2 Cor. 5:14. Lk. 6:35.*

*Jesus was led out into the wilderness by the Holy
Spirit, to be tempted there by Satan.*

While Christ was here on earth he pleaded with God,
praying with tears and agony of soul to the only one
who would save him from [premature] death. And God
heard his prayers because of his strong desire to obey
God at all times. Even though Jesus was God's Son,
he had to learn from experience what it was like to obey,
when obeying meant suffering. It was after he had
proved himself perfect in this experience that Jesus
became the giver of eternal salvation to all those who
obey him. / This high priest of ours understands our
weaknesses, since he had the same temptations we have,
though he never once gave way to them and sinned.

The wrong desires that come into your life aren't
anything new and different. Many others have faced
exactly the same problems before you. And no temptation is irresistible. You can trust God to keep the
temptation from becoming so strong that you can't
stand up against it, for he has promised this and will do
what he says. He will show you how to escape temptation's power so that you can bear up patiently against
it. / I am with you; that is all you need. My power
shows up best in weak people.

Mt. 4:1. Hebr. 5:7–9. Hebr. 4:15. 1 Cor. 10:13. 2 Cor. 12:9.

I, the Son of Mankind, did not come to be served, but to serve, and to give my life as a ransom for many.

If under the old system the blood of bulls and goats and the ashes of young cows could cleanse men's bodies from sin, just think how much more surely the blood of Christ will transform our lives and hearts. His sacrifice frees us from the worry of having to obey the old rules, and makes us want to serve the living God.

He was brought as a lamb to the slaughter. / I lay down my life for the sheep. No one can kill me without my consent – I lay down my life voluntarily. For I have the right and power to lay it down when I want to and also the right and power to take it again.

The life of the flesh is in the blood, and I have given you the blood to sprinkle upon the altar as an atonement for your souls; it is the blood that makes atonement, because it is the life. / Without the shedding of blood there is no forgiveness of sins.

God showed his great love for us by sending Christ to die for us while we were still sinners. And since by his blood he did all this for us as sinners, how much more will he do for us now that he has declared us not guilty? Now he will save us from all of God's wrath to come.

Mt. 20:28. Hebr. 9:13, 14. Is. 53:7. Jn. 10:15, 18. Lev. 17:11. Hebr. 9:22. Rom. 5:8, 9.

*If we confess our sins to him, he can be depended
on to forgive us and to cleanse us from every wrong.*

Have pity upon me and take away the awful stain of
my transgressions. Oh, wash me, cleanse me from this
guilt. Let me be pure again. For I admit my shameful
deed – it haunts me day and night. It is against you
and you alone I sinned.

He returned home to his father. And while he was still
a long distance away, his father saw him coming, and
was filled with loving pity and ran and embraced him
and kissed him. / I've blotted out your sins; they are
gone like morning mist at noon! Oh, return to me, for
I have paid the price to set you free. / Your sins have
been forgiven in the name of Jesus our Saviour. / God
has forgiven you because you belong to Christ.

It will be as though I had sprinkled clean water on
you, for you will be clean. And I will give you a new
heart – I will give you new and right desires – and put
a new spirit within you. I will take out your stony
hearts of sin and give you new hearts of love. And I
will put my Spirit within you so that you will obey my
laws and do whatever I command. / They will walk with
me in white, for they are worthy.

*1 Jn. 1:9. Ps. 51:1–4. Lk. 15:20. Is. 44:22. 1 Jn. 2:12. Eph. 4:32.
Ezk. 36:25–27. Rev. 3:4.*

Will you permit a corrupt government to rule under your protection?

You may share the fellowship and the joys we have with the Father and with Jesus Christ his Son. / We are already God's children, right now, and we can't even imagine what it is going to be like later on. But we do know this, that when he comes we will be like him, as a result of seeing him as he really is. And everyone who really believes this will try to stay pure because Christ is pure.

The evil prince of this world approaches. He has no power over me, but I will freely do what the Father requires of me. / He is holy and blameless, unstained by sin, undefiled by sinners.

For we are not fighting against people made of flesh and blood, but against persons without bodies – the evil rulers of the unseen world, those mighty satanic beings and great evil princes of darkness who rule this world; and against huge numbers of wicked spirits in the spirit world. / Satan, the mighty prince of the power of the air.

No one who has become part of God's family makes a practice of sinning, for Christ, God's Son, holds him securely and the Devil cannot get his hands on him.

Ps. 94:20. 1 Jn. 1:3. 1 Jn. 3:2, 3. Jn. 14:30, 31. Hebr. 7:26. Eph. 6:12. Eph. 2:2. 1 Jn. 5:18.

*I have taken away your sins, and now I am
giving you these fine new clothes.*

What happiness for those whose guilt has been forgiven! What joys when sins are covered over! / We
are all infected and impure with sin. / I know I am
rotten through and through so far as my old sinful
nature is concerned. No matter which way I turn I
can't make myself do right. I want to but I can't.

We who have been baptized into union with Christ
are enveloped by him. / Your old life with all its
wickedness . . . is dead and gone. You are living a
brand new kind of life that is continually learning more
and more of what is right, and trying constantly to be
more and more like Christ who created this new life
within you. / No longer counting on being saved by
being good enough or by obeying God's laws, but by
trusting Christ to save me; for God's way of making
us right with himself depends on faith – counting on
Christ alone.

Bring the finest robe in the house and put it on
him. / Let me tell you how happy God has made
me! For he has clothed me with garments of salvation
and draped about me the robe of righteousness. I am
like a bridegroom in his wedding suit or a bride with
her jewels.

*Zech. 3:4. Ps. 32:1. Is. 64:6. Rom. 7:18. Gal. 3:27. Col. 3:9, 10. Phil. 3:9.
Lk. 15:22. Is. 61:10.*

There is going to come a time of testing at Christ's Judgment Day.

Be careful not to jump to conclusions before the Lord returns as to whether someone is a good servant or not. When the Lord comes, he will turn on the light so that everyone can see exactly what each one of us is really like, deep down in our hearts. Then everyone will know why we have been doing the Lord's work. At that time God will give to each one whatever praise is coming to him.

You have no right to criticize your brother or look down on him. Remember, each of us will stand personally before the Judgment Seat of God. Yes, each of us will give an account of himself to God. So don't criticize each other any more.

At God's command Jesus Christ will judge the secret lives of everyone. / The Father leaves all judgment of sin to his Son . . . because he is the Son of Man.

You are loving and kind to thousands, yet children suffer for their fathers' sins; you are the great and mighty God, the Lord of heaven's armies. You have all wisdom and do great and mighty miracles; for your eyes are open to all the ways of men, and you reward everyone according to his life and deeds.

1 Cor. 3:13. 1 Cor. 4:5. Rom. 14:10, 12, 13. Rom. 2:16. Jn. 5:22, 27. Jer. 32:18, 19.

A servant is not above his master.

You call me 'Master' and 'Lord', and you do well to say it, for it is true.

The student shares his teacher's fate. The servant shares his master's. / So since they persecuted me, naturally they will persecute you. And if they had listened to me, they would listen to you. / I have given them your commands. And the world hates them because they don't fit in with it, just as I don't.

If you want to keep from becoming fainthearted and weary, think about his patience as sinful men did such terrible things to him. After all, you have never yet struggled against sin and temptation until you sweat great drops of blood.

Let us run with patience the particular race that God has set before us. Keep your eyes on Jesus, our leader and instructor. He was willing to die a shameful death on the cross because of the joy he knew would be his afterwards; and now he sits in the place of honour by the throne of God. / Since Christ suffered and underwent pain, you must have the same attitude he had; you must be ready to suffer, too.

Mt. 10:24. Jn. 13:13. Mt. 10:25. Jn. 15:20. Jn. 17:14. Hebr. 12:3, 4. Hebr. 12:1, 2. 1 Pet. 4:1.

My son, trust my advice.

Oh, that they would always have such a heart for me, wanting to obey my commandments. Then all would go well with them in the future, and with their children throughout all generations!

Your heart is not right before God. / The old sinful nature within us is against God. It never did obey God's laws and it never will. That's why those who are still under the control of their old sinful selves, bent on following their own evil desires, can never please God.

Their first action was to dedicate themselves to the Lord. / *Above all else, guard your affections.* For they influence everything else in your life.

Work hard and cheerfully at all you do, just as though you were working for the Lord and not merely for your masters. / Don't work hard only when your master is watching and then shirk when he isn't looking; work hard and with gladness all the time, as though working for Christ, doing the will of God with all your hearts.

If you will only help me to want your will, then I will follow your laws even more closely.

Prov. 23:26. Deut. 5:29. Acts 8:21. Rom. 8:7, 8. 2 Cor. 8:5. Prov. 4:23. Col. 3:23. Eph. 6:6, 7. Ps. 119:32.

I am with you to protect and deliver you.

Who can snatch the prey from the hands of a mighty man? Who can demand that a tyrant let his captives go? But the Lord says, 'Even the captives of the most mighty and most terrible shall all be freed; for I will fight those who fight you, and I will save your children. I will feed your enemies with their own flesh and they shall be drunk with rivers of their own blood. All the world shall know that I, the Lord, am your Saviour and Redeemer, the Mighty One of Israel.' / Fear not, for I am with you. Do not be dismayed. I am your God. I will strengthen you; I will help you; I will uphold you with my victorious right hand.

This high priest of ours understands our weaknesses, since he had the same temptations we have, though he never once gave way to them and sinned. / For since he himself has now been through suffering and temptation, he knows what it is like when we suffer and are tempted, and he is wonderfully able to help us. / The steps of good men are directed by the Lord. He delights in each step they take. If they fall it isn't fatal, for the Lord holds them with his hand.

Jer. 15:20. Is. 49:24–26. Is. 41:10. Hebr. 4:15. Hebr. 2:18. Ps. 37:23, 24.

He satisfies the thirsty soul and fills the hungry soul with good.

If you have tasted the Lord's goodness and kindness, cry for more.

O God, my God! How I search for you! How I thirst for you in this parched and weary land where there is no water. How I long to find you! How I wish I could go into your sanctuary to see your strength and glory, for your love and kindness are better to me than life itself. How I praise you! I will bless you as long as I live, lifting up my hands to you in prayer. / I long, yes, faint with longing to be able to enter your courtyard and come near to the Living God. / I long to go and be with Christ.

When I awake in heaven, I will be fully satisfied. / They will never be hungry again, nor thirsty, and they will be fully protected from the scorching noontime heat. For the Lamb standing in front of the throne will feed them and be their shepherd and lead them to the springs of the water of life. And God will wipe their tears away. / You feed them with blessings from your own table and let them drink from your rivers of delight. / I will satisfy my people with my bounty, says the Lord.

Ps. 107:9. 1 Pet. 2:2, 3. Ps. 63:1–4. Ps. 84:2. Phil. 1:23. Ps. 17:15. Rev. 7:16, 17. Ps. 36:8. Jer. 31:14.

I myself will go with you and give you success.

Be strong! Be courageous! Do not be afraid of them. For the Lord your God will be with you. He will neither fail you nor forsake you. Don't be afraid, for the Lord will go before you and will be with you; he will not fail nor forsake you. / Yes, be bold and strong! Banish fear and doubt! For remember, the Lord your God is with you wherever you go. / If you want favour with both God and man, and a reputation for good judgment and common sense, then trust the Lord completely; don't ever trust yourself. In everything you do, put God first, and he will direct you and crown your efforts with success. / The man who knows right from wrong and has good judgment and common sense is happier than the man who is immensely rich! For such wisdom is far more valuable than precious jewels. Nothing else compares with it.

God has said, 'I will never, *never* fail you nor forsake you.' That is why we can say without any doubt or fear, 'The Lord is my helper and I am not afraid of anything that mere man can do to me.' / Our only power and success comes from God.

O Lord, I know it is not within the power of man to map his life and plan his course.

Ex. 33:14. Deut. 31:6, 8. Josh. 1:9. Prov. 3:4–6. Prov. 3:13–15.
Hebr. 13:5, 6. 2 Cor. 3:5. Jer. 10:23.

*Let us outdo each other in being helpful and kind
to each other and in doing good.*

Timely advice is as lovely as golden apples in a
silver basket.

Those who feared and loved the Lord spoke often
of him to each other. And he had a Book of Remembrance drawn up in which he recorded the names of
those who feared him and loved to think about him. /
If two of you agree down here on earth concerning
anything you ask for, my Father in heaven will do it
for you.

The Lord God said, 'It isn't good for man to be
alone.' / Two can accomplish more than twice as
much as one, for the results can be much better. If
one falls, the other pulls him up; but if a man falls
when he is alone, he's in trouble.

Live in such a way that you will never make your
brother stumble by letting him see you doing something he thinks is wrong. If your brother is bothered
by what you eat, you are not acting in love if you go
ahead and eat it. Don't undo the work of God for a
joint of meat. Remember, there is nothing wrong with
the meat, but it is wrong to eat it if it makes another
stumble. / Share each other's troubles and problems,
and so obey our Lord's command.

*Hebr. 10:24. Prov. 25:11. Mal. 3:16. Mt. 18:19. Gen. 2:18. Eccl. 4:9, 10.
Rom. 14:13, 15, 20. Gal. 6:2.*

I am my beloved's and I am the one he desires.

I know the one in whom I trust, and I am sure that
he is able to guard safely all that I have given him
until the day of his return. / For I am convinced that
nothing can ever separate us from his love. Death
can't, and life can't. The angels won't, and all the
powers of hell itself cannot keep God's love away.
Our fears for today, our worries about tomorrow, or
where we are – high above the sky, or in the deepest
ocean – nothing will ever be able to separate us from
the love of God demonstrated by our Lord Jesus
Christ when he died for us. / I have kept safe within
your family all of these you gave me.

For Jehovah enjoys his people. / How happy I was
with what he created. / God is so rich in mercy; he
loved us so much that . . . he gave us back our lives
again. / The greatest love is shown when a person lays
down his life for his friends.

God has bought you with a great price. So use every
part of your body to give glory back to God, because
he owns it. / Living or dying we follow the Lord.
Either way we are his.

*Song 7:10. 2 Tim. 1:12. Rom. 8:38, 39. Jn. 17:12. Ps. 149:4.
Prov. 8:31. Eph. 2:4. Jn. 15:13. 1 Cor. 6:20. Rom. 14:8.*

Search the Book of the Lord.

Keep these commandments carefully in mind. Tie them to your hand to remind you to obey them, and tie them to your forehead between your eyes. / Constantly remind the people about these laws, and you yourself must think about them every day and every night so that you will be sure to obey all of them. For only then will you succeed.

The godly man is a good counsellor. / I have followed your commands and have not gone along with cruel and evil men. / I have thought much about your words, and stored them in my heart so that they would hold me back from sin.

We have seen and proved that what the prophets said came true. You will do well to pay close attention to everything they have written, for, like lights shining into dark corners, their words help us to understand many things that otherwise would be dark and difficult. But when you consider the wonderful truth of the prophets' words, then the light will dawn in your souls and Christ the Morning Star will shine in your hearts. / These things that were written in the Scriptures so long ago are to teach us patience and to encourage us.

Is. 34:16. Deut. 11:18. Josh. 1:8. Ps. 37:30. Ps. 17:4. Ps. 119:11.
2 Pet. 1:19. Rom. 15:4.

A man's heart determines his speech.

Remember what Christ taught and let his words enrich your lives and make you wise. / A good man's speech reveals the rich treasures within him.

Those who love to talk will suffer the consequences. Men have died for saying the wrong thing! / A good man produces good deeds from a good heart. Whatever is in the heart overflows into speech. / The godly man is a good counsellor because he is just and fair and knows right from wrong. / Don't use bad language. Say only what is good and helpful to those you are talking to, and what will give them a blessing.

You must give account on Judgment Day for every idle word you speak. Your words now reflect your fate then: either you will be justified by them or you will be condemned.

If anyone publicly acknowledges me as his friend, I will openly acknowledge him as my friend before my Father in heaven. / Make the most of your chances to tell others the Good News. Be wise in all your contacts with them. Let your conversation be gracious as well as sensible, for then you will have the right answer for everyone.

Mt. 12:34. Col. 3:16. Mt. 12:35. Prov. 18:21. Lk. 6:45. Ps. 37:30, 31. Eph. 4:29. Mt. 12:36–37. Mt. 10:32. Col. 4:5, 6.

I hope to see you soon and then we will have much to talk about together.

Oh, that you would burst forth from the skies and come down! How the mountains would quake in your presence! / As the deer pants for water, so I long for you, O God. I thirst for God, the living God. Where can I find him to come and stand before him? : Come quickly, my beloved, and be like a gazelle or young deer upon the mountains of spices.

Our homeland is in heaven, with our Saviour the Lord Jesus Christ in heaven; and we are looking forward to his return from there. / Looking forward to that time when his glory shall be seen – the glory of our great God and Saviour Jesus Christ. / Jesus Christ our Lord – our only hope. / You love him even though you have never seen him.

He who has said all these things declares; 'Yes, I am coming soon!' Amen! Come, Lord Jesus! / See! He is arriving, surrounded by clouds; and every eye will see him. / In that day the people will proclaim, 'This is our God, in whom we trust, for whom we waited. Now at last he is here.' What a day of rejoicing!

3 Jn. 14. Is. 64:1. Ps. 42:1, 2. Song 8:14. Phil. 3:20. Tit. 2:13. 1 Tim. 1:1. 1 Pet. 1:8. Rev. 22:20. Rev. 1:7. Is. 25:9.

*May your will be done here on earth, just as
it is in heaven.*

Bless the Lord, you mighty angels of his who carry
out his orders, listening for each of his commands.
Yes, bless the Lord, you armies of his angels who
serve him constantly.

I have come here from heaven to do the will of God
who sent me, not to have my own way. / I delight to
do your will, my God, for your law is written upon
my heart! / My Father! If this cup cannot be
removed until I drink it all, your will be done.

Not all who talk like godly people are godly.
They may refer to me as 'Lord', but still won't get
to heaven. For the decisive question is whether they
obey my Father, in heaven. / Now change your mind
and attitude to God and turn to him so that he can
cleanse away your sins and send you wonderful times
of refreshment from the presence of the Lord. / Knowing what is right to do and then not doing it is sin.

Don't copy the behaviour and customs of this world,
but be a new and different person with a freshness in
all you do and think.

*Mt. 6:10. Ps. 103:20, 21. Jn. 6:38. Ps. 40:8. Mt. 26:42. Mt. 7:21.
Acts 3:19. Jas. 4:17. Rom. 12:2.*

We can choose the sounds we want to listen to;
we can choose the taste we want in food.

Dearly loved friends, don't always believe everything you hear just because someone says it is a message from God: test it first to see if it really is. For there are many false teachers around. / You are intelligent people. Look now and see for yourselves whether what I am about to say is true. / Remember what Christ taught and let his words enrich your lives and make you wise.

Let all who can hear, listen to what the Spirit says to the churches. / The spiritual man has insight into everything.

Put into practice what you hear. / I know how many good things you are doing. / You don't tolerate sin among your members, and you have carefully examined the claims of those who say they are apostles but aren't. / Test everything that is said to be sure it is true, and if it is, then accept it.

The sheep hear his voice and come to him; and he calls his own sheep by name and leads them out. He walks ahead of them; and they follow him, for they recognize his voice. They won't follow a stranger but will run from him, for they don't recognize his voice.

Job 34:3. 1 Jn. 4:1. 1 Cor. 10:15. Col. 3:16. Rev. 2:29. 1 Cor. 2:15.
Mk. 4:24. Rev. 2:2. 1 Thess. 5:21. Jn. 10:3–5.

You shall be a kingdom of priests to God, a holy nation.

You were slain, and your blood has bought people from every nation as gifts for God. And you have gathered them into a kingdom and made them priests of our God. / You have been chosen by God himself – you are priests of the King, you are holy and pure, you are God's very own – all this so that you may show to others how God called you out of the darkness into his wonderful light.

You shall be called priests of the Lord, ministers of our God. / Priests of God and of Christ.

Therefore, dear brothers whom God has set apart for himself – you who are chosen for heaven – I want you to think now about this Jesus who is God's messenger and the high priest of our faith. / With Jesus' help we will continually offer our sacrifice of praise to God by telling others of the glory of his name.

It is God himself who has made us what we are and given us new lives from Christ Jesus; and long ages ago he planned that we should spend these lives in helping others. / God's home is holy and clean, and you are that home.

Ex. 19:6. Rev. 5:9, 10. 1 Pet. 2:9. Is. 61:6. Rev. 20:6. Hebr. 3:1. Hebr. 13:15. Eph. 2:10. 1 Cor. 3:17.

We prayed to our God and guarded the city day and night to protect ourselves.

Keep alert and pray. Otherwise temptation will overpower you. / Don't be weary in prayer; keep at it; watch for God's answers and remember to be thankful when they come. / Let him have all your worries and cares, for he is always thinking about you and watching everything that concerns you. Be careful – watch out for attacks by Satan, your great enemy. He prowls around like a hungry, roaring lion, looking for some victim to tear apart. Stand firm when he attacks.

Why do you call me 'Lord' when you won't obey me? : It is a message to obey, not just to listen to.

Then the Lord said to Moses, 'Stop praying and get the people moving. Forward, march!'

Don't worry about anything; instead, pray about everything; tell God your needs and don't forget to thank him for his answers. if you do this you will experience God's peace, which is far more wonderful than the human mind can understand. His peace will keep your thoughts and your hearts quiet and at rest as you trust in Christ Jesus.

Neh. 4:9. Mt. 26:41. Col. 4:2. 1 Pet. 5:7–9. Lk. 6:46. Jas. 1:22. Ex. 14:15. Phil. 4:6, 7.

A gracious God, merciful, slow to get angry, and full of kindness.

Oh, please, show the great power [of your patience] by forgiving our sins and showing us your steadfast love. Forgive us, even though you have said that you don't let sin go unpunished, and that you punish the father's fault in the children to the third and fourth generation.

Oh, do not hold us guilty for our former sins! Let your tenderhearted mercies meet our needs, for we are brought low to the dust. Help us, God of our salvation! Help us for the honour of your name. Oh, save us and forgive our sins. / O Lord, we have sinned against your grievously, yet help us for the sake of your own reputation! O Lord, we confess our wickedness, and that of our fathers too. / Oh, do not be so angry with us, Lord, and do not remember our sins for ever. Oh, look and see that we are all your people.

Lord, if you keep in mind our sins then who can ever get an answer to his prayers? But you forgive! What an awesome thing this is!

Jon. 4:2. Num. 14:17, 18. Ps. 79:8, 9. Jer. 14:7, 20. Is. 64:9. Ps. 130:3, 4.

Cleansing you by the work of the Holy Spirit.

Come, north wind, awake; come, south wind, blow upon my garden and waft its lovely perfume.

Just see how much good this grief from the Lord did for you! You no longer shrugged your shoulders, but became earnest and sincere, and very anxious to get rid of the sin that I wrote to you about. / Because of this light within you, you should do only what is good and right, and true. Learn as you go along what pleases the Lord.

He will give you another Comforter . . . the Holy Spirit. / God loves us, and we feel this warm love everywhere within us because God has given us the Holy Spirit to fill our hearts with his love.

When the Holy Spirit controls our lives he will produce . . . love, joy, peace.

Though they have been going through much trouble and hard times, they have mixed their wonderful joy with their deep poverty, and the result has been an overflow of giving to others.

It is the same and only Holy Spirit who gives all these gifts and powers, deciding which each one of us should have.

2 Thess. 2:13. Song 4:16. 2 Cor. 7:11. Eph. 5:9, 10. Jn. 14:16, 17.
Rom. 5:5. Gal. 5:22. 2 Cor. 8:2. 1 Cor. 12:11.

He calls his own sheep by name and leads
them out.

God's truth stands firm like a great rock, and nothing can shake it. It is a foundation stone with these words written on it: 'The Lord knows those who are really his', and 'A person who calls himself a Christain should not be doing things that are wrong'. / At the Judgment many will tell me, 'Lord, Lord, we told others about you and used your name to cast out demons and to do many other great miracles.' But I will reply, "You have never been mine. Go away, for your deeds are evil.' / For the Lord watches over all the plans and paths of godly men, but the paths of the godless lead to doom.

I have tattooed your name upon my palm. / Seal me in your heart with permanent betrothal, for love is strong as death and jealousy is as cruel as Sheol. / The Lord is good. When trouble comes, he is the place to go! And he knows everyone who trusts in him!

There are many homes up there where my Father lives, and I am going to prepare them for your coming. When everything is ready, then I will come and get you, so that you can always be with me where I am.

Jn. 10:3. 2 Tim. 2:19. Mt. 7:22, 23. Ps. 1:6. Is. 49:16. Song 8:6.
Nah. 1:7. Jn. 14:2, 3.

She has done what she could.

This poor widow has given more than all the rest of them combined. / If anyone so much as gives you a cup of water because you are Christ's – I say this solemnly – he won't lose his reward. / If you are really eager to give, then it isn't important how much you have to give. God wants you to give what you have, not what you haven't.

Let us stop just *saying* we love people; let us *really* love them, and show it by our actions. / If you have a friend who is in need of food and clothing, and you say to him, 'Well, good-bye and God bless you; stay warm and eat up,' and then don't give him clothes or food, what good does that do? / If you give little, you will get little. A farmer who plants just a few seeds will get only a small crop, but if he plants much, he will reap much. Every one must make up his own mind as to how much he should give. Don't force anyone to give more than he really wants to, for cheerful givers are the ones God prizes.

Just so, if you merely obey me, you should not consider yourselves worthy of praise. For you have simply done your duty!

Mk. 14:8. Lk. 21:3. Mk. 9:41. 2 Cor. 8:12. 1 Jn. 3:18. Jas. 2:15, 16. 2 Cor. 9:6, 7. Lk. 17:10.

*He, the mighty Holy One, has done great
things to me.*

Who else is like the Lord among the gods? Who is
glorious in holiness like him? Who is so awesome in
splendour, a wonder-working God? / Where among
the heathen gods is there a god like you? Where are
their miracles? / Who shall not fear, O Lord, and
glorify your Name? For you alone are holy. / We
honour your holy name.

Praise the Lord, the God of Israel, for he has come
to visit his people and has redeemed them.

Who is this who comes from Edom, from the city
of Bozrah, with his magnificent garments of crimson?
Who is this in kingly robes, marching in the greatness
of his strength? 'It is I, the Lord, announcing your
salvation; I, the Lord, the one who is mighty to save!' /
For the Lord your God has arrived to live among you.
He is a mighty Saviour. He will give you victory.

Now glory be to God who by his mighty power at
work within us is able to do far more than we would
ever dare to ask or even dream of — infinitely beyond
our highest prayers, desires, thoughts, or hopes. May
he be given glory for ever and ever.

*Lk. 1:49. Ex. 15:11. Ps. 86:8. Rev. 15:4. Mt. 6:9. Lk. 1:68. Is. 63:1.
Zeph. 3:17. Eph. 3:20, 21.*

The dew on Mount Hermon.

Mount Sirion, or Mount Hermon, as it is sometimes called. / God has pronounced this eternal blessing on Jerusalem, even life for evermore. / I will refresh Israel like the dew from heaven; she will blossom as the lily and root deeply in the soil like cedars in Lebanon.

My words shall fall upon you like the gentle rain and dew, like rain upon the tender grass, like showers on the hillside. / As the rain and snow come down from heaven and stay upon the ground to water the earth, and cause the grain to grow and to produce seed for the farmer and bread for the hungry, so also is my Word. I send it out and it always produces fruit. It shall accomplish all I want it to, and prosper everywhere I send it.

God's Spirit is upon him without measure or limit. / We have all benefited from the rich blessings he brought to us – blessing upon blessing heaped upon us! / As precious as the fragrant anointing oil that was poured over Aaron's head, and ran down onto his beard, and onto the border of his robe.

Ps. 133:3. Deut. 4:48. Ps. 133:3. Hos. 14:5. Deut. 32:2. Is. 55:10, 11. Jn. 3:34. Jn. 1:16. Ps. 133:2.

*They are not part of this world any more
than I am.*

We despised him and rejected him – a man of sorrows, acquainted with bitterest grief. / Here on earth you will have many trials and sorrows; but take courage, I have overcome the world.

He is, therefore, exactly the kind of high priest we need; for he is holy and blameless, unstained by sin, undefiled by sinners, and to him has been given the place of honour in heaven. / That no one can speak a word of blame against you. You are to live clean, innocent lives as children of God in a dark world full of people who are crooked and stubborn.

Jesus of Nazareth . . . went around doing good and healing all who were possessed by demons, for God was with him. / Whenever we can we should always be kind to everyone, and especially to our Christian brothers.

The true Light arrived to shine on everyone coming into the world. / You are the world's light – a city on a hill, glowing in the night for all to see. Let your good deeds glow for all to see, so that they will praise your heavenly Father.

*Jn. 17:16. Is. 53:3. Jn. 16:33. Hebr. 7:26. Phil. 2:15. Acts 10:38.
Gal. 6:10. Jn. 1:9. Mt. 5:14, 16.*

When a man . . . is cheerful, everything
seems right!

The joy of the Lord is your strength. / The important thing for us as Christians is not what we eat or drink but stirring up goodness and peace and joy from the Holy Spirit. / Be filled . . . with the Holy Spirit, and controlled by him. Talk with each other much about the Lord, quoting psalms and hymns and singing sacred songs, making music in your hearts to the Lord. Always give thanks for everything to our God and Father in the name of our Lord Jesus Christ.

With Jesus' help we will continually offer our sacrifice of praise to God by telling others of the glory of his name.

Even though the fig trees are all destroyed, and there is neither blossom left nor fruit, and though the olive crops all fail, and the fields lie barren; even if the flocks die in the fields and the cattle barns are empty, yet I will rejoice in the Lord; I will be happy in the God of my salvation. / Our hearts ache, but at the same time we have the joy of the Lord. / We can rejoice, too, when we run into problems and trials.

Prov. 15:15. Neh. 8:10. Rom. 14:17. Eph. 5:18–20. Hebr. 13:15.
Hab. 3:17, 18. 2 Cor. 6:10. Rom. 5:3.

Is there any value in the Jewish circumcision ceremony?

Yes, being a Jew has many advantages. / Cleanse your minds and hearts, not just your bodies. / When at last their evil hearts are humbled and they accept the punishment I send them for their sins, then I will remember again my promises to Abraham, Isaac, and Jacob, and I will remember the land.

Jesus Christ came to show that God is true to his promises and to help the Jews. / When you came to Christ he set you free from your evil desires, not by a bodily operation of circumscision but by a spiritual operation, the baptism of your souls. / You were dead in sins, and your sinful desires were not yet cut away. Then he gave you a share in the very life of Christ, for he forgave all your sins.

Throw off your old evil nature – the old you that was a partner in your evil ways – rotten through and through, full of lust and sham. Now your attitudes and thoughts must all be constantly changing for the better. Yes, you must be a new and different person, holy and good. Clothe yourself with this new nature.

Rom. 3:1. Rom. 3:2. Jer. 4:4. Lev. 26:41, 42. Rom. 15:8. Col. 2:11.
Col. 2:13. Eph. 4:22–24.

The curtain separating the Holiest Place in the Temple was split apart from top to bottom.

On the night when Judas betrayed him, the Lord Jesus took bread, and when he had given thanks to God for it, he broke it and gave it to his disciples and said, 'Take this and eat it. This is my body, which is given for you. Do this in memory of me." / My flesh is this Bread, given to redeem humanity.

Unless you eat the flesh of the Man of Glory and drink his blood, you cannot have eternal life within you. But anyone who does eat my flesh and drink my blood has eternal life, and I will raise him at the Last Day. Everyone who eats my flesh and drinks my blood is in me, and I in him. I live by the power of the living Father who sent me, and in the same way those who partake of me shall live because of me! Only the Holy Spirit gave eternal life. Those born only once, with physical birth, will never receive this gift. But now I have told you how to get this true spiritual life.

The fresh, new, life-giving way which Christ has opened up for us by tearing the curtain – his human body – to let us into the holy presence of God. Let us go right in, to God himself.

Mt. 27:51. 1 Cor. 11:23, 24. Jn. 6:51, 53, 54, 56, 57, 63. Hebr. 10:20, 22.

*He died once for all to end sin's power, but
now he lives forever in unbroken fellowship
with God.*

He was counted as a sinner. / Christ died only once
as an offering for the sins of many people. / He
personally carried the load of our sins in his own
body when he died on the cross, so that we can be
finished with sin and live a good life from now on. For
his wounds have healed ours! / By that one offering
he made for ever perfect in the sight of God all those
whom he is making holy.

But Jesus lives forever and continues to be a priest
so that no one else is needed. He is able to save completely all who come to God through him. Since he
will live forever, he will always be there to remind God
that he has paid for their sins with his blood. / God
showed his great love for us by sending Christ to die
for us while we were still sinners. And since by his
blood he did all this for us as sinners, how much
more will he do for us now that he has declared us
not guilty?

Since Christ suffered and underwent pain, you must
have the same attitude he had; you must be ready to
suffer, too. For remember, when your body suffers, sin
loses its power, and you won't be spending the rest
of your life chasing after evil desires, but will be
anxious to do the will of God.

*Rom. 6:10. Is. 53:12. Hebr. 9:28. 1 Pet. 2:24. Hebr. 10:14. Hebr. 7:24, 25.
Rom. 5:8, 9. 1 Pet. 4:1, 2.*

*Stay always within the boundaries where
God's love can reach and bless you.*

Take care to live in me, and let me live in you. For a
branch can't produce fruit when severed from the vine.
Nor can you be fruitful apart from me. Yes, I am the
Vine; you are the branches. Whoever lives in me and
I in him shall produce a large crop of fruit. For apart
from me you can't do a thing.

When the Holy Spirit controls our lives he will
produce . . . love.

My true disciples produce bountiful harvests. This
brings great glory to my Father. I have loved you
even as the Father has loved me. Live within my love.
When you obey me you are living in my love, just as I
obey my Father and live in his love. / Those who do
what Christ tells them to will learn to love God more
and more.

I demand that you love each other as much as I
love you. / God showed his great love for us by sending Christ to die for us while we were still sinners. /
We know how much God loves us because we have
felt his love and because we believe in him when he
tells us that he loves us dearly. God is love, and
anyone who lives in love is living with God and God
is living in him.

*Jude 21. Jn. 15:4, 5. Gal. 5:22. Jn. 15:8–10. 1 Jn. 2:5. Jn. 15:12.
Rom. 5:8. 1 Jn. 4:16.*

After that the end will come.

However, no one, not even the angels in heaven, nor I myself, knows the day or hour when these things will happen; only the Father knows. And since you do not know when it will happen, stay·alert. Be on the watch. *Watch for my return* / He isn't really being slow about his promised return, even though it sometimes seems that way. But he is waiting, for the good reason that he is not willing that any should perish, and he is giving more time for sinners to repent. / Yes, be patient. And take courage, for the coming of the Lord is near. The great Judge is coming. he is almost here. / Yes, I am coming soon!

The day of the Lord is surely coming . . . then the heavens will pass away with a terrible noise and the heavenly bodies will disappear in fire, and the earth and everything on it will be burned up. And so since everything around us is going to melt away, what holy, godly lives we should be living.

The end of the world is coming soon. Therefore be earnest, thoughtful men of prayer. / Be prepared – all dressed and ready – for your Lord's return from the wedding feast. Then you will be ready to open the door and let him in the moment he arrives and knocks.

1 Cor. 15:24. Mk. 13:32, 33, 37. 2 Pet. 3:9. Jas. 5:8, 9. Rev. 22:20.
2 Pet. 3:10, 11. 1 Pet. 4:7. Lk. 12:35, 36.

Dear brothers, pray for us.

Is anyone sick? He should call for the elders of the church and they should pray over him and pour a little oil upon him, calling on the Lord to heal him. And their prayer, if offered in faith, will heal him, for the Lord will make him well; and if his sickness was caused by some sin, the Lord will forgive him. The earnest prayer of a righteous man has great power and wonderful results. Elijah was as completely human as we are, and yet when he prayed earnestly that no rain would fall, none fell for the next three and a half years! Then he prayed again, this time that it *would* rain, and down it poured and the grass turned green and the gardens began to grow again.

Pray all the time. Ask God for anything in line with the Holy Spirit's wishes. Plead with him, reminding him of your needs, and keep praying earnestly for all Christians everywhere.

God knows how often I pray for you. Day and night I bring you and your needs in prayer to the one I serve with all my might. / Asking God to make you strong and perfect and to help you know his will in everything you do.

1 Thess. 5:25. Jas. 5:14–18. Eph. 6:18. Rom. 1:9. Col. 4:12.

Be patient in trouble.

It is the Lord's will. Let him do what he thinks best. /
Even if I were sinless I wouldn't say a word. I
would only plead for mercy. / The Lord gave me
everything I had, and they were his to take away.
Blessed be the name of the Lord. / What? Shall we
receive only pleasant things from the hand of God and
never anything unpleasant?

Tears came to Jesus' eyes. / A man of sorrows,
acquainted with bitterest grief. / It was *our* grief he
bore, *our* sorrows that weighed him down.

When he punishes you, it proves that he loves you.
When he whips you it proves you are really his
child. Being punished isn't enjoyable while it is happening – it hurts! But afterwards we can see the result,
a quiet growth in grace and character. So take a new
grip with your tired hands, stand firm on your shaky
legs, and mark out a straight, smooth path for your
feet. / Filled with his mighty, glorious strength so
that you can keep going no matter what happens –
always full of the joy of the Lord. / Here on earth you
will have many trials and sorrows; but take courage,
I have overcome the world.

*Rom. 12:12. 1 Sam. 3:18. Job 9:15. Job 1:21. Job 2:10. Jn. 11:35.
Is. 53:3, 4. Hebr. 12:6, 11–13. Col. 1:11. Jn. 16:33.*

Abraham never doubted. He believed God,
for his faith and trust grew ever stronger.

If you only have faith in God – this is the absolute
truth – you can say to this Mount of Olives, 'Rise up
and fall into the Mediterranean,' and your command
will be obeyed. All that's required is that you really
believe and have no doubt! Listen to me! You can pray
for *anything,* and *if you believe, you have it ;* it's yours! /
You can never please God without faith, without
depending on him. Anyone who wants to come to God
must believe that there is a God and that he rewards
those who sincerely look for him.

Abraham still trusted God and his promises, and so
he offered up his son Isaac, and was ready to slay him
on the altar of sacrifice – yes, to slay even Isaac,
through whom God had promised to give Abraham
a whole nation of descendants! He believed that if
Isaac died God would bring him back to life again. /
He was completely sure that God was well able to do
anything he promised.

Is anything too hard for God? / With God, everything is possible. / We need more faith.

Rom. 4:20. Mk. 11:22–24. Hebr. 11:6. Hebr. 11:17–19. Rom. 4:21.
Gen. 18:14. Mt. 19:26. Lk. 17:5.

*We have been delivered from hell and given
eternal life.*

Anyone who listens to my message and believes in
God who sent me has eternal life, and will never be
damned for his sins, but has already passed out of
death into life. / Whoever has God's Son has life;
whoever does not have his Son, does not have life.

It is this God who has made you and me into faithful Christians and commissioned us apostles to preach
the Good News. He has put his brand upon us – his
mark of ownership – and given us his Holy Spirit in
our hearts as guarantee that we belong to him. / Then
we will know for sure, by our actions, that we are on
God's side, and our consciences will be clear. If our
consciences are clear, we can come to the Lord with
perfect assurance and trust. / We know that we are
children of God.

Once you were under God's curse, doomed forever
for your sins. Even though we were spiritually dead
and doomed by our sins, he gave us back our lives
again when he raised Christ from the dead – only by
his undeserved favour have we ever been saved. / He
has rescued us out of the darkness and gloom of
Satan's kingdom and brought us into the kingdom
of his dear Son.

1 Jn. 3:14. Jn. 5:24. 1 Jn. 5:12. 2 Cor. 1:21, 22. 1 Jn. 3:19, 21.
1 Jn. 5:19. Eph. 2:1, 5. Col. 1:13.

You have let me experience the joys of life.

The Lord says: Take your choice of life or death! / I will continue to teach you those things which are good and right. / I am the Way – yes, and the Truth and the Life. No one can get to the Father except by means of me. / Come . . . with me.

Before every man there lies a wide and pleasant road that seems right but ends in death. / Heaven can be entered only through the narrow gate. The highway to hell is abroad, and its gate is wide enough for all the multitudes who choose its easy way. But the Gateway to Life is small, and the road is narrow, and only a few ever find it.

A main road will go through that once-deserted land; it will be named 'The Holy Highway.' No evil-hearted men may walk upon it. God will walk there with you; even the most stupid cannot miss the way. / Oh, that we might know the Lord! Let us press on to know him.

There are many homes up there where my Father lives, and I am going to prepare them for your coming.

Ps. 16:11. Jer. 21:8. 1 Sam. 12:23. Jn. 14:6. Mt. 4:19. Prov. 14:12. Mt. 7:13, 14. Is. 35:8. Hos. 6:3. Jn. 14:2.

Abraham trusted God, and when God told him to leave home and go far away to another land which he promised to give him, Abraham obeyed.

He . . . will personally select his choicest blessings . . . the very best for those he loves. / God protected them in the howling wilderness as though they were the apple of his eye. He spreads his wings over them, even as an eagle covers her young. She carries them upon her wings – as does the Lord his people! When the Lord alone was leading them, and they lived without foreign gods, God gave them fertile hilltops.

I am the Lord your God, who punishes you for your own good and leads you along the paths that you should follow. / Who is a teacher like him?

We know these things are true by believing, not by seeing. / For this world is not our home; we are looking forward to our everlasting home in heaven. / Dear brothers, you are only visitors here. Since your real home is in heaven I beg you to keep away from the evil pleasures of this world; they are not for you, for they fight against your very souls.

Hebr. 11:8. Ps. 47:4. Deut. 32:10–13. Is. 48:17. Job 36:22. 2 Cor. 5:7. Hebr. 13:14. 1 Pet. 2:11.

*May all who are godly be happy in the Lord
and crown him, our holy God.*

Even the heavens can't be absolutely pure compared
with him! How much less someone like you, who is corrupt and sinful, drinking in sin as a sponge soaks up
water! / Even the moon and stars are less than nothing
as compared to him. How much less is man, who is
but a worm in his sight?

Who else is like the Lord among the gods? Who is
glorious in holiness like him? / Holy, Holy, holy is the
Lord of heaven's armies.

Be holy now in everything you do, just as the Lord
is holy, who invited you to be his child. He himself
has said, 'You must be holy, for I am holy.' / Share
his holiness.

God's home is holy and clean, and you are that
home. / What holy, godly lives we should be living!
Try hard to live without sinning; and be at peace with
everyone so that he will be pleased with you when
he returns.

Don't use bad language. Say only what is good and
helpful to those you are talking to, and what will give
them a blessing. Don't cause the Holy Spirit sorrow
by the way you live. Remember he is the one who
puts a mark on you to keep you for that day when
salvation from sin will be complete.

*Ps. 97:12. Job 15:15, 16. Job 25:5, 6. Ex. 15:11. Is. 6:3. 1 Pet. 1:15, 16.
Hebr. 12:10. 1 Cor. 3:17. 2 Pet. 3:11, 14. Eph. 4:29, 30.*

The glory of Christ, who is God.

The glory of the Lord will be seen by all mankind together. / No one has ever actually seen God, but, of course, his only Son has, for he is the companion of the Father and has told us all about him. And Christ took our human nature and lived here on earth among us and was full of loving forgiveness and truth. And some of us have seen his glory – the glory of the only Son of the heavenly Father. / Anyone who has seen me has seen the Father. / God's Son shines out with God's glory, and all that God's Son is and does marks him as God. / Christ . . . came to earth as a man, was proved spotless and pure in his spirit.

Who bought our freedom with his blood and forgave us all our sins. Christ is the exact likeness of the unseen God. He existed before God made anything at all. / For from the very beginning God decided that those who came to him – and all along he knew who would – should become like his Son, so that his Son would be the firstborn, with many brothers.

Just as each of us now has a body like Adam's, so we shall some day have a body like Christ's.

2 Cor. 4:4. Is. 40:5. Jn. 1:18, 14. Jn. 14:9. Hebr. 1:3. 1 Tim. 3:16.
Col. 1:14, 15. Rom. 8:29. 1 Cor. 15:49.

You have armed me with strong armour for the battle.

When I am weak, then I am strong.

'O Lord,' he cried out to God, 'no one else can help us! Here we are, powerless against this mighty army. Oh, help us, Lord our God! For we trust in you alone to rescue us, and in your name we attack this vast horde. Don't let mere men defeat you!' / Jehoshaphat cried out to the Lord to save him, and the Lord made the charioteers see their mistake and leave him.

It is better to trust the Lord than to put confidence in men. It is better to take refuge in him than in the mightiest king! / The best-equipped army cannot save a king – for great strength is not enough to save anyone. A war horse is a poor risk for winning victories – it is strong but it cannot save.

For we are not fighting against people made of flesh and blood, but against persons without bodies – the evil rulers of the unseen world, those mighty satanic beings and great evil princes of darkness who rule this world; and against huge numbers of wicked spirits in the spirit world.

Ps. 18:39. 2 Cor. 12:10. 2 Chron. 14:11. 2 Chron. 18:31. Ps. 118:8, 9. Ps. 33:16, 17. Eph. 6:12.

Be full of love.

I am giving a new commandment to you now – love each other just as much as I love you. / Show deep love for each other, for love makes up for many of your faults. / Love overlooks insults.

When you are praying, first forgive anyone you are holding a grudge against, so that your Father in heaven will forgive you your sins too. / Love your enemies! Do good to them. Lend to them. And don't be concerned about the fact that they won't repay. / Do not rejoice when your enemy meets trouble. Let there be no gladness when he falls. / Don't repay evil for evil. Don't snap back at those who say unkind things about you. Instead, pray for God's help for them, for we are to be kind to others, and God will bless us for it. Be at peace with everyone, so far as it depends on you. / Be kind to each other, tenderhearted, forgiving one another, just as God has forgiven you because you belong to Christ.

Little children, let us stop just *saying* we love people; let us *really* love them, and show it by our actions. Then we will know for sure, by our actions, that we are on God's side, and our consciences will be clear, even when we stand before the Lord.

Eph. 5:2. Jn. 13:34. 1 Pet. 4:8. Prov. 10:12. Mk. 11:25. Lk. 6:35.
Prov. 24:17. 1 Pet. 3:9. Rom. 12:18. Eph. 4:32. 1 Jn. 3:18, 19.

Pray about everything.

'Father, Father,' he said, 'everything is possible for you. Take away this cup from me. Yet I want your will, not mine.' / I was given a sickness which has been a thorn in my flesh. Three different times I begged God to make me well again. Each time he said, 'No. But I am with you; that is all you need. My power shows up best in weak people.' Now I am glad to boast about how weak I am; I am glad to be a living demonstration of Christ's power.

I implore his mercy, pouring out my troubles before him. / Hannah . . . was in deep anguish and was crying bitterly as she prayed to the Lord. And she made this vow: 'O Lord of heaven, if you will look down upon my sorrow and answer my prayer and give me a son, then I will give him back to you, and he'll be yours for his entire lifetime.' The Lord remembered her petition; in the process of time a baby boy was born to her.

We don't even know what we should pray for, nor how to pray as we should. / He . . . will personally select his choicest blessings . . . the very best for those he loves.

Phil. 4:6. Mk. 14:36. 2 Cor. 12:7–9. Ps. 142:2. 1 Sam. 1:9–11, 20. Rom. 8:26. Ps. 47:4.

*Oh, that you would burst forth from the skies
and come down!*

Come quickly, my beloved, and be like a gazelle or
young deer upon the mountains of spices. / Even we
Christians . . . groan to be released from pain and
suffering. We, too, wait anxiously for that day when
God will give us our full rights as his children, including the new bodies he has promised us – bodies
that will never be sick again and will never die. / Bend
down the heavens, Lord, and come. The mountains
smoke beneath your touch.

Jesus has gone away to heaven, and some day, just as
he went, he will return! / He will come again, but not to
deal again with our sins. This time he will come bringing
salvation to all those who are eagerly and patiently
waiting for him. / In that day the people will proclaim,
'This is our God, in whom we trust, for whom we
waited. Now at last he is here,' What a day of rejoicing!

He who has said all these things declares: 'Yes, I am
coming soon!' Amen! Come, Lord Jesus! / Looking
forward to that time when his glory shall be seen – the
glory of our great God and Saviour Jesus Christ. / Our
homeland is in heaven.

*Is. 64:1. Song 8:14. Rom. 8:23. Ps. 144:5. Acts 1:11. Hebr. 9:28. Is. 25:9.
Rev. 22:20. Tit. 2:13. Phil. 3:20.*

*You have given me the blessings you reserve for
those who reverence your name.*

In that coming day, no weapon turned against you shall
succeed, and you will have justice against every court-
room lie. This is the heritage of the servants of the
Lord. This is the blessing I have given you, says the
Lord. / For the Angel of the Lord guards and rescues
all who reverence him. Oh, put God to the test and see
how kind he is! See for yourself the way his mercies
shower down on all who trust in him. If you belong to
the Lord, reverence him; for everyone who does this
has everything he needs. Even strong young lions sometimes go hungry, but those of us who reverence the Lord
will never lack any good thing. / He sees that I am given
pleasant brooks and meadows as my share! What a
wonderful inheritance!

For you who fear my name, the Sun of Righteousness
will rise with healing in his wings. And you will go free,
leaping with joy like calves let out to pasture. / Since
he did not spare even his own Son for us but gave him
up for us all, won't he also surely give us everything
else?

Ps. 61:5. Is. 54:17. Ps. 34:7–10. Ps. 16:6. Mal. 4:2. Rom. 8:32.

Set your sights on the rich treasures and joys of heaven where he sits beside God in the place of honour and power.

Learn to be wise, and develop good judgment. / Wisdom that comes from heaven. / 'It's not here,' the oceans say; and the seas reply, 'Nor is it here.' / Your old sin-loving nature was buried with him by baptism when he died, and when God the Father, with glorious power, brought him back to life again, you were given his wonderful new life to enjoy. For you have become part of him, and so you died with him, so to speak, when he died; and now you share his new life, and shall rise as he did.

Let us strip off anything that slows us down or holds us back, and especially those sins that wrap themselves so tightly around our feet and trip us up; and let us run with patience the particular race that God has set before us. / But God is so rich in mercy; he loved us so much that even though we were spiritually dead and doomed by our sins, he gave us back our lives again when he raised Christ from the dead – only by his undeserved favour have we ever been saved – and lifted us up from the grave into glory along with Christ, where we sit with him in the heavenly realms – all because of what Christ Jesus did.

Col. 3:1. Prov. 4:5. Jas. 3:17. Job 28:14. Rom. 6:4, 5. Hebr. 12:1. Eph. 2:4–6.

Nicodemus . . . came secretly to interview Jesus.

Peter was following far to the rear. / Even many of the Jewish leaders believed him to be the Messiah but wouldn't admit it to anyone because of their fear that the Pharisees would excommunicate them from the synagogue; for they loved the praise of men more than the praise of God. / Fear of man is a dangerous trap, but to trust in God means safety.

Some will come to me – those the Father has given me – and I will never, never reject them. / He will not break the bruised reed, nor quench the dimly burning flame. / Faith even as small as a tiny mustard seed.

The Holy Spirit, God's gift, does not want you to be afraid of people, but to be wise and strong, and to love them and enjoy being with them. If you stir up this inner power, you will never be afraid to tell others about our Lord. / And now, my little children, stay in happy fellowship with the Lord so that when he comes you will be sure that all is well, and will not have to be ashamed and shrink back from meeting him. / If anyone publicly acknowledges me as his friend, I will openly acknowledge him as my friend before my Father in heaven.

Jn. 7:50. Mt. 26:58. Jn. 12:42, 43. Prov. 29:25. Jn. 6:37. Is. 42:3. Mt. 17:20. 2 Tim. 1:7, 8. 1 Jn. 2:28. Mt. 10:32.

Take your share of suffering as a good soldier of Jesus Christ.

Jesus, our leader and instructor. He was willing to die a shameful death on the cross. / It was right and proper that God, who made everything for his own glory, should allow Jesus to suffer, for in doing this he was bringing vast multitudes of God's people to heaven; for his suffering made Jesus a perfect leader, one fit to bring them into their salvation. / They must enter into the Kingdom of God through many hardships.

For we are not fighting against people made of flesh and blood, but against persons without bodies – the evil rulers of the unseen world, those mighty satanic beings and great evil princes of darkness who rule this world; and against huge numbers of wicked spirits in the spirit world. So use every piece of God's armour. / I don't use human plans and methods to win my battles. I use God's mighty weapons, not those made by men, to knock down the devil's strongholds.

After you have suffered a little while, our God, who is full of kindness through Christ, will give you his eternal glory. He personally will come and pick you up, and set you firmly in place, and make you stronger than ever.

2 Tim. 2:3. Hebr. 12:2. Hebr. 2:10. Acts 14:22. Eph. 6:12, 13. 2 Cor. 10:3, 4. 1 Pet. 5:10.

Be led along together by the Holy Spirit.

We are all parts of one body, we have the same Spirit. /
Now all of us, whether Jews or Gentiles, may come
to God the Father with the Holy Spirit's help because
of what Christ has done for us. Now you are no longer
strangers to God and foreigners to heaven, but you
are members of God's very own family, citizens of
God's country, and you belong in God's household
with every other Christian. What a foundation you
stand on now: the apostles and the prophets; and the
cornerstone of the building is Jesus Christ himself!
We who believe are carefully joined together with
Christ as parts of a beautiful, constantly growing
temple for God. And you also are joined with him and
with each other by the Spirit, and are part of this
dwelling place of God.

How wonderful it is, how pleasant, when brothers
live in harmony! For harmony is as precious as the
fragrant anointing oil that was poured over Aaron's
head.

Now you can have real love for everyone because
your souls have been cleansed from selfishness and
hatred when you trusted Christ to save you; so see to it
that you really do love each other warmly, with all
your hearts.

Eph. 4:3. Eph. 4:4. Eph. 2:18–22. Ps. 133:1, 2. 1 Pet. 1:22.

When the Holy Spirit controls our lives he will produce . . . faithfulness.

Because of his kindness you have been saved through trusting Christ. And even trusting is not of yourselves; it too is a gift from God. / You can never please God without faith, without depending on him. Anyone who wants to come to God must believe that there is a God and that he rewards those who sincerely look for him. / There is no eternal doom awaiting those who trust him to save them. But those who don't trust him have already been tried and condemned for not believing in the only Son of God. / I *do* have faith; oh, help me to have *more!*

Those who do what Christ tells them to will learn to love God more and more. That is the way to know whether or not you are a Christian.

We know these things are true by believing, not by seeing. / I have been crucified with Christ: and I myself no longer live, but Christ lives in me. And the real life I now have within this body is a result of my trusting in the Son of God, who loved me and gave himself for me. / You love him even though you have never seen him; though not seeing him, you trust him; and even now you are happy with the inexpressible joy that comes from heaven itself.

Gal. 5:22. Eph. 2:8. Hebr. 11:6. Jn. 3:18. Mk. 9:24. 1 Jn. 2:5.
2 Cor. 5:7. Gal. 2:20. 1 Pet. 1:8.

The Lord . . . is full of tenderness and mercy.

He is like a father to us, tender and sympathetic to those who reverence him. / Who can forget the wonders he performs – deeds of mercy and of grace? He gives food to those who trust him; he never forgets his promises.

He will never let me stumble, slip or fall. For he is always watching, never sleeping. / He spreads his wings over them, even as an eagle covers her young. She carries them upon her wings – as does the Lord his people!

His compassion never ends. It is only the Lord's mercies that have kept us from complete destruction. Great is his faithfulness; his lovingkindness begins afresh each day.

So when Jesus came out of the wilderness, a vast crowd was waiting for him and he pitied them and healed those of them who were sick. / Jesus Christ is the same yesterday, today and forever.

And the very hairs of your head are all numbered. Not one sparrow – what do they cost – two for a penny? – can fall to the ground without your Father knowing it. So don't worry! You are more valuable to him than many sparrows.

Jas. 5:11. Ps. 103:13. Ps. 111:4,5. Ps. 121:3,4. Deut. 32:11. Lam. 3:22,23. Mt. 14:14. Hebr. 13:8. Mt. 10:30, 29, 31.

*Though you once were far away from God, now
you have been brought very near to him because
of what Jesus Christ has done for you with his blood.*

This animal shall be a year-old male, either a sheep or
a goat, without any defects. On the evening of the
fourteenth day of this month, all these lambs shall be
killed, and their blood shall be placed on the two side-
frames of the door of every home and on the panel
above the door. Use the blood of the lamb eaten in
that home. And when I see the blood I will pass over
you. / Christ, God's lamb, has been slain for us. / God,
following his prearranged plan, let you use the Roman
government to nail him to the cross and murder him. /
That was his plan long before the world began – to
show his love and kindness to us through Christ.

So overflowing is his kindness towards us that he
took away all our sins through the blood of his Son,
by whom we are saved.

Since Christ suffered and underwent pain, you must
have the same attitude he had; you must be ready to
suffer, too. For remember, when your body suffers, sin
loses its power, and you won't be spending the rest of
your life chasing after evil desires, but will be anxious
to do the will of God.

*Eph. 2:13. Ex. 12:5–7, 13. 1 Cor. 5:7. Acts 2:23. 2 Tim. 1:9. Eph. 1:7.
1 Pet. 4:1, 2.*

I have trodden the winepress alone.

Who else is like the Lord among the gods? Who is glorious in holiness like him? Who is so awesome in splendour, a wonder-working God? / He saw no one was helping you, and wondered that no one intervened. Therefore he himself stepped in to save you through his mighty power and justice. / He personally carried the load of our sins in his own body when he died on the cross, so that we can be finished with sin and live a good life from now on. For his wounds have healed ours!

Sing a new song to the Lord telling about his mighty deeds! For he has won a mighty victory by his power and holiness. / God took away Satan's power to accuse you of sin, and God openly displayed to the whole world Christ's triumph at the cross where your sins were all taken away. / And when he sees all that is accomplished by the anguish of his soul, he shall be satisfied; and because of what he has experienced, my righteous Servant shall make many to be counted righteous before God, for he shall bear all their sins.

March on, my soul, with strength! / Overwhelming victory is ours through Christ who loved us enough to die for us.

Is. 63:3. Ex. 15:11. Is. 59:16. 1 Pet. 2:24. Ps. 98:1. Col. 2:15. Is. 53:11. Judg. 5:21. Rom. 8:37.

*His mercy goes on from generation to generation,
to all who reverence him.*

Oh, how great is your goodness to those who publicly declare that you will rescue them. For you have stored up great blessings for those who trust and reverence you. Hide your loved ones in the shelter of your presence, safe beneath your hand, safe from all conspiring men.

And remember that your heavenly Father to whom you pray has no favourites when he judges. He will judge you with perfect justice for everything you do; so act in reverent fear of him from now on until you get to heaven. / He is close to all who call on him sincerely. He fulfils the desires of those who reverence and trust him; he hears their cries for help and rescues them.

Because you were sorry and concerned and humbled yourself before the Lord . . . and because you have torn your clothing and wept before me in contrition, I will listen to your plea. / I will look with pity on the man who has a humble and a contrite heart, who trembles at my word. / The Lord is close to those whose hearts are breaking; he rescues those who are humbly sorry for their sins.

Lk. 1:50. Ps. 31:19, 20. 1 Pet. 1:17. Ps. 145:18, 19. 2 Kgs. 22:18, 19. Is. 66:2. Ps. 34:18.

I will honour only those who honour me, and I will despise those who despise me.

If anyone publicly acknowledges me as his friend, I will openly acknowledge him as my friend before my Father in heaven. / If you love your father and mother more than you love me, you are not worthy of being mine; or if you love your son or daughter more than me, you are not worthy of being mine. If you refuse to take up your cross and follow me, you are not worthy of being mine. If you cling to your life, you will lose it; but if you give it up for me, you will save it.

Happy is the man who doesn't give in and do wrong when he is tempted, for afterwards he will get as his reward the crown of life that God has promised those who love him.

Stop being afraid of what you are about to suffer. Hold fast the faith even when facing death and I will give you the crown of life – an unending, glorious future.

These troubles and sufferings of ours are, after all, quite small and won't last very long. Yet this short time of distress will result in God's richest blessing upon us for ever and ever! / It will bring you much praise and glory and honour on the day of his return.

1 Sam. 2:30. Mt. 10:32. Mt. 10:37–39. Jas. 1:12. Rev. 2:10. 2 Cor. 4:17.
1 Pet. 1:7.

*When Jesus had tasted it, he said, 'It is finished,'
and bowed his head and dismissed his spirit.*

I brought glory to you here on earth by doing everything you told me to. / Under this new plan we have been forgiven and made clean by Christ's dying for us once and for all. Under the old agreement the priests stood before the altar day after day offering sacrifices that could never take away our sins. But Christ gave himself to God for our sins as one sacrifice for all time, and then sat down in the place of highest honour at God's right hand, waiting for his enemies to be laid under his feet. For by that one offering he made for ever perfect in the sight of God all those whom he is making holy. / [God] blotted out the charges proved against you, the list of his commandments which you had not obeyed. He took this list of sins and destroyed it by nailing it to Christ's cross.

The Father loves me because I lay down my life that I may have it back again. No one can kill me without my consent – I lay down my life voluntarily. / The greatest love is shown when a person lays down his life for his friends.

Jn. 19:30. Jn. 17:4. Hebr. 10:10–14. Col. 2:14. Jn. 10:17, 18. Jn. 15:13.

*He reached down from heaven and took me and
drew me out of my great trials.*

He lifted me out of the pit of despair, out from the bog
and the mire, and set my feet on a hard, firm path
and steadied me as I walked along. / Once you were
under God's curse, doomed for ever for your sins. You
went along with the crowd and were just like all the
others, full of sin, obeying Satan, the mighty prince of
the power of the air, who is at work right now in the
hearts of those who are against the Lord.

O God, listen to me! Hear my prayer! For wherever
I am, though far away at the ends of the earth, I will
cry to you for help. When my heart is faint and overwhelmed, lead me to the mighty, towering Rock of
safety. / In my great trouble I cried to the Lord and he
answered me; from the depths of death I called, and
Lord, you heard me! You threw me into the ocean
depths; I sank down into the floods of waters and was
covered by your wild and stormy waves. / You sent
troops to ride across our broken bodies. We went
through fire and flood. But in the end, you brought us
into wealth and great abundance.

When you go through deep waters and great trouble,
I will be with you. When you go through rivers of
difficulty, you will not drown!

*Ps. 18:16. Ps. 40:2. Eph. 2:1, 2. Ps. 61:1, 2. Jon. 2:2, 3. Ps. 66:12.
Is. 43:2.*

You were given his wonderful new life to enjoy.

Just as you used to be slaves to all kinds of sin, so now you must let yourselves be slaves to all that is right and holy. / And so, dear brothers, I plead with you to give your bodies to God. Let them be a living sacrifice, holy – the kind he can accept. When you think of what he has done for you, is this too much to ask? Don't copy the behaviour and customs of this world, but be a new and different person with a freshness in all you do and think. Then you will learn from your own experience how his ways will really satisfy you. / When someone becomes a Christian he becomes a brand new person inside. He is not the same any more. A new life has begun! / It doesn't make any difference now whether we have been circumcised or not; what counts is whether we really have been changed into new and different people. May God's mercy and peace be upon all of you who live by this principle and upon those everywhere who are really God's own.

If you have really heard his voice and learned from him the truths concerning himself . . . you must be a new and different person, holy and good. Clothe yourself with this new nature.

Rom. 6:4. Rom. 6:19. Rom. 12:1, 2. 2 Cor. 5:17. Gal. 6:15, 16. Eph. 4:21, 24.

Your will be done.

O Lord, I know it is not within the power of man to map his life and plan his course. / But I want your will, not mine. / I am quiet before the Lord, just as a child who is weaned from the breast. Yes, my begging has been stilled.

The Holy Spirit helps us with our daily problems and in our praying. For we don't even know what we should pray for, nor how to pray as we should; but the Holy Spirit prays for us with such feeling that it cannot be expressed in words. And the Father who knows all hearts knows, of course, what the Spirit is saying as he pleads for us in harmony with God's own will.

You don't know what you are asking. / So he gave them their demands, but sent them leanness in their souls. / From this lesson we are warned that we must not desire evil things as they did.

In all you do, I want you to be free from worry. / He will keep in perfect peace all those who trust in him, whose thoughts turn often to the Lord!

Mt. 26:42. Jer. 10:23. Mt. 26:39. Ps. 131:2. Rom. 8:26, 27. Mt. 20:22. Ps. 106:15. 1 Cor. 10:6. 1 Cor. 7:32. Is. 26:3.

Just as a father punishes a son he delights in to make him better, so the Lord corrects you.

Don't you see that I alone am God? I kill and make live. I wound and heal – no one delivers from my power. / For I know the plans I have for you, says the Lord. They are plans for good and not for evil, to give you a future and a hope. / This plan of mine is not what you would work out, neither are my thoughts the same as yours!

But I will court her again, and bring her into the wilderness, and speak to her tenderly there. / So you should realize that, as a man punishes his son, the Lord punishes you to help you. / For when he punishes you, it proves that he loves you. When he whips you it proves you are really his child. / Being punished isn't enjoyable while it is happening – it hurts! But afterwards we can see the result, a quiet growth in grace and character. / If you will humble yourselves under the mighty hand of God, in his good time he will lift you up.

I know, O Lord, that your decisions are right and that your punishment was right and did me good.

Prov. 3:12. Deut. 32:39. Jer. 29:11. Is. 55:8. Hos. 2:14. Deut. 8:5. Hebr. 12:6. Hebr. 12:11. 1 Pet. 5:6. Ps. 119:75.

*The earth belongs to God! Everything in all the
world is his!*

She doesn't realize that all she has, has come from me.
It was I who gave her all the gold and silver that she
used in worshipping Baal, her god! But now I will take
back the wine and ripened corn I constantly supplied,
and the clothes I gave her to cover her nakedness – I
will no longer give her rich harvests of grain in its
season, or wine at the time of the grape harvest.

Everything we have has come from you, and we only
give you what is yours already! For we are here for but
a moment, strangers in the land as our fathers were
before us; our days on earth are like a shadow, gone
so soon, without a trace. O Lord our God, all of this
material . . . comes from you! It all belongs to you! /
For everything lives by his power, and everything is for
his glory. To him be glory evermore.

The living God . . . always richly gives us all we
need for our enjoyment.

And it is he who will supply all your needs from
his riches in glory, because of what Christ Jesus has
done for us.

*Ps. 24:1. Hos. 2:8, 9. 1 Chron. 29:14–16. Rom. 11:36. 1 Tim. 6:17.
Phil. 4:19.*

I will ask the Father and he will give you another Comforter, and he will never leave you.

If you only knew what a wonderful gift God has for you, and who I am, you would ask me for some *living* water! / And if even sinful persons like yourselves give children what they need, don't you realize that your heavenly Father will do at least as much, and give the Holy Spirit to those who ask for him? / At that time you won't need to ask me for anything, for you can go directly to the Father and ask him, and he will give you what you ask for because you use my name. / The reason you don't have what you want is that you don't ask God for it.

When the Holy Spirit, who is truth, comes, he shall guide you into all truth, for he will not be presenting his own ideas, but will be passing on to you what he has heard. He will tell you about the future. He shall praise me and bring me great honour by showing you my glory.

I pray . . . that God who gives you hope will keep you happy and full of peace as you believe in him through the Holy Spirit's power within you.

Jn. 14:16. Jn. 4:10. Lk. 11:13. Jn. 16:23. Jas. 4:2. Jn. 16:13, 14. Rom. 15:13.

Do you believe in the Messiah?

Yes, open wide the gates and let the King of Glory in. Who is this King of Glory? The Commander of all of heaven's armies! / On his robe and thigh was written this title: King of Kings and Lord of Lords.

Yes, he is very precious to you who believe; and to those who reject him, well – 'The same Stone that was rejected by the builders has become the cornerstone, the most honoured and important part of the building.' / So when we preach about Christ dying to save them, the Jews are offended and the Gentiles say it's all nonsense. But God has opened the eyes of those called to salvation, both Jews and Gentiles, to see that Christ is the mighty power of God to save them; Christ himself is the centre of God's wise plan for their salvation. / In him lie hidden all the mighty, untapped treasures of wisdom and knowledge.

Yes, everything else is worthless when compared with the priceless gain of knowing Christ Jesus my Lord. I have put aside all else, counting it worth less than nothing, in order that I can have Christ. / Lord, you know my heart.

Jn. 9:35. Ps. 24:9, 10. Rev. 19:16. 1 Pet. 2:7. 1 Cor. 1:23, 24. Col. 2:3. Phil. 3:8. Jn. 21:17.

But the good man walks along in the ever-
brightening light of God's favour; the dawn gives
way to morning splendour.

I don't mean to say I am perfect. I haven't learned all
I should even yet, but I keep working towards that
day when I will finally be all that Christ saved me for
and wants me to be. / Oh, that we might know the
Lord! Let us press on to know him, and he will respond
to us as surely as the coming of dawn or the rain
of early spring.

We Christians have no veil over our faces; we can be
mirrors that brightly reflect the glory of the Lord. And
as the Spirit of the Lord works within us, we become
more and more like him. / We can see and understand
only a little about God now, as if we were peering at
his reflection in a poor mirror; but some day we are
going to see him in his completeness, face to face. Now
all that I know is hazy and blurred, but then I will see
everything clearly, just as clearly as God sees into my
heart right now. / Yes, dear friends, we are already
God's children, right now, and we can't even imagine
what it is going to be like later on. But we do know this,
that when he comes we will be like him, as a result of
seeing him as he really is.

Prov. 4:18. Phil. 3:12. Hos. 6:3. 2 Cor. 3:18. 1 Cor. 13:12. 1 Jn. 3:2.

*Anyone who calls upon the name of the Lord will
be saved.*

But some will come to me – those the Father has given
me – and I will never, never reject them. / 'Jesus, remember me when you come into your Kingdom.' And
Jesus replied, 'Today you will be with me in Paradise.
This is a solemn promise.' / 'What do you want me to
do for you?' 'Sir,' they said, 'we want to be able to see!'
Jesus was moved with pity for them and touched their
eyes. And instantly they could see, and followed him.

And if even sinful persons like yourselves give children what they need, don't you realize that your
heavenly Father will do at least as much, and give the
Holy Spirit to those who ask for him? / And I will put
my Spirit within you. The Lord God says: 'I am ready
to hear Israel's prayers for these blessings, and to grant
them their requests.'

And we are sure of this, that he will listen to us whenever we ask him for anything in line with his will. And
if we really know he is listening when we talk to him
and make our requests, then we can be sure that he will
answer us.

*Rom. 10:13. Jn. 6:37. Lk. 23:42, 43. Mt. 20:32–34. Lk. 11:13.
Ezk. 36:27, 37. 1 Jn. 5:14, 15.*

You are so beautiful, my love.

Oh, my people, haven't you had enough of punishment? Why will you force me to whip you again and again? Must you forever rebel? From head to foot you are sick and weak and faint, covered with bruises and welts and infected wounds, unanointed and unbound. / We are all infected and impure with sin. When we put on our prized robes of righteousness we find they are but filthy rags. / I know I am rotten through and through so far as my old sinful nature is concerned. No matter which way I turn I can't make myself do right. I want to but I can't. / Now your sins are washed away, and you are set apart for God, and he has accepted you because of what the Lord Jesus Christ and the Spirit of our God have done for you.

These are the ones coming out of the great tribulation . . . they washed their robes and made them white by the blood of the Lamb. / A glorious church without a single spot or wrinkle or any other blemish, being holy and without a single fault. / *You have everything when you have Christ.*

Song 4:7. Is. 1:5, 6. Is. 64:6. Rom. 7:18. 1 Cor. 6:11. Rev. 7:14. Eph. 5:27. Col. 2:10.

Broken cisterns that can't hold water!

The people who lived there began to talk about building a great city, with a temple-tower reaching to the skies – a proud, eternal monument to themselves. God scattered them all over the earth; and that ended the building of the city. / I worked hard to be wise instead of foolish – but now I realize that even this was like chasing the wind. For the greater my wisdom, the greater my grief; to increase knowledge only increases distress. / Then I tried to find fulfilment by inaugurating a great public works programme: homes, vineyards, gardens, parks and orchards for myself, and reservoirs to hold the water to irrigate my plantations. I collected silver and gold as taxes from many kings and provinces. But as I looked at everything I had tried, it was all so useless, a chasing of the wind, and there was nothing really worthwhile anywhere.

If anyone is thirsty, let him come to me and drink. / For he satisfies the thirsty soul and fills the hungry soul with good.

Let heaven fill your thoughts; don't spend your time worrying about things down here.

Jer. 2:13. Gen. 11:3, 4, 8. Eccl. 1:17, 18. Eccl. 2:4–6, 8, 11. Jn. 7:37.
Ps. 107:9. Col. 3:2.

I'm not asking you to take them out of the world,
but to keep them safe from Satan's power.

Live clean, innocent lives as children of God in a dark
world full of people who are crooked and stubborn.
Shine out among them like beacon lights. / You are
the world's seasoning . . . you are the world's light. Let
your good deeds glow for all to see, so that they will
praise your heavenly Father.

I held you back from sinning against me. / No temptation is irresistible. You can trust God to keep the
temptation from becoming so strong that you can't
stand up against it, for he has promised this and will
do what he says. He will show you how to escape temptation's power.

The Lord is faithful; he will make you strong and
guard you from satanic attacks of every kind. / He
died for our sins just as God our Father planned, and
rescued us from this evil world in which we live. / And
now – all glory to him who alone is God, who saves us
through Jesus Christ our Lord; yes, splendour and
majesty, all power and authority are his from the beginning; his they are and his they evermore shall be.
And he is able to keep you from slipping and falling
away, and to bring you, sinless and perfect, into his
glorious presence with mighty shouts of everlasting joy.
Amen.

Jn. 17:15. Phil. 2:15. Mt. 5:13, 14, 16. Gen. 20:6. 1 Cor. 10:13.
2 Thess. 3:3. Gal. 1:4. Jude 24, 25.

To trust in God means safety.

The Lord is very great, and lives in heaven. / He is high above the nations; his glory is far greater than the heavens. Far below him are the heavens and the earth; he stoops to look, and lifts the poor from the dirt, and the hungry from the rubbish dump, and sets them among princes!

But God is so rich in mercy; he loved us so much that even though we were spiritually dead and doomed by our sins, he gave us back our lives again when he raised Christ from the dead – only by his undeserved favour have we ever been saved – and lifted us up from the grave into glory along with Christ, where we sit with him in the heavenly realms – all because of what Christ Jesus did.

Since he did not spare even his own Son for us but gave him up for us all, won't he also surely give us everything else? For I am convinced that nothing can ever separate us from his love. Death can't, and life can't. The angels won't, and all the powers of hell itself cannot keep God's love away. Our fears for today, our worries about tomorrow, or where we are – high above the sky, or in the deepest ocean – nothing will ever be able to separate us from the love of God demonstrated by our Lord Jesus Christ when he died for us.

Prov. 29:25. Is. 33:5. Ps. 113:4, 6, 7, 8. Eph. 2:4–6. Rom. 8:32, 38, 39.

*Only as a human being could he die and in dying
break the power of the devil who had the power
of death.*

Our Saviour Jesus Christ . . . broke the power of death
and showed us the way of everlasting life through
trusting him. / He will swallow up death forever. The
Lord God will wipe away all tears and take away forever all insults and mockery against his land and people.
The Lord has spoken – he will surely do it! / When this
happens, then at last this Scripture will come true –
'Death is swallowed up in victory.' O death, where then
your victory? Where then your sting? For sin – the
sting that causes death – will all be gone; and the law,
which reveals our sins, will no longer be our judge.
How we thank God for all of this! It is he who makes
us victorious through Jesus Christ our Lord.

Even when walking through the dark valley of death
I will not be afraid, for you are close beside me,
guarding, guiding all the way. You provide delicious
food for me in the presence of my enemies. You have
welcomed me as your guest; blessings overflow!
Your goodness and unfailing kindness shall be with me
all of my life, and afterwards I will live with you forever in your home.

Hebr. 2:14. 2 Tim. 1:10. Is. 25:8. 1 Cor. 15:54–57. Ps. 23:4–6.

Where does the light come from?

God is Light and in him is no darkness at all. / While I am still here in the world, I give it my light.

If we say we are his friends, but go on living in spiritual darkness and sin, we are lying. But if we are living in the light of God's presence, just as Christ is, then we have wonderful fellowship and joy with each other, and the blood of Jesus his Son cleanses us from every sin. / The Father . . . has made us fit to share all the wonderful things that belong to those who live in the kingdom of light. For he has rescued us out of the darkness and gloom of Satan's kingdom and brought us into the kingdom of his dear Son, who bought our freedom with his blood and forgave us all our sins.

You are all children of the light and the day, and do not belong to darkness and night. / You are the world's light – a city on a hill, glowing in the night for all to see. Let your good deeds glow for all to see, so that they will praise your heavenly Father.

Job 38:19. 1 Jn. 1:5. Jn. 9:5. 1 Jn. 1:6, 7. Col. 1:12–14. 1 Thess. 5:5. Mt. 5:14, 16.

The Lord will not abandon him forever. Although God gives him grief, yet he will show compassion too, according to the greatness of his loving-kindness.

Fear not . . . says the Lord, for I am with you. I will not destroy you. I will punish you, but only enough to correct you. / For a brief moment I abandoned you. But with great compassion I will gather you. In a moment of anger I turned my face a little while; but with everlasting love I will have pity on you, says the Lord, your Redeemer. For the mountains may depart and the hills disappear, but my kindness shall not leave you. My promise of peace for you will never be broken, says the Lord, who has mercy upon you. O my afflicted people, tempest-tossed and troubled, I will rebuild you on a foundation of sapphires and make the walls of your houses from precious jewels.

I will be patient while the Lord punishes me, for I have sinned against him; then he will defend me from my enemies, and punish them for all the evil they have done to me. God will bring me out of my darkness into the light, and I will see his goodness.

Show me the path where I should go, O Lord; point out the right road for me to walk.

Lam. 3:31, 32. Jer. 46:28. Is. 54:7, 8, 10, 11. Mic. 7:9. Ps. 25:4.

*God has deliberately chosen to use ideas the world
considers foolish and of little worth in order to
shame those people considered by the world as wise
and great.*

When they cried to the Lord, he sent them a saviour,
Ehud (son of Gera, a Benjaminite), who was left-
handed. The next judge after Ehud was Shamgar (son
of Anath). He once killed six hundred Philistines with
an ox goad, thereby saving Israel from disaster.

Then the Lord turned to him [Gideon] and said, 'I will
make you strong! Go and save Israel from the
Midianites. I am sending you!' But Gideon replied,
'Sir, how can *I* save Israel? My family is the poorest
in the whole tribe of Manasseh, and I am the least
thought of in the entire family!'

The Lord then said to Gideon, 'There are too many
of you. I can't let all of you fight the Midianites,
for then the people of Israel will boast to me that they
saved themselves by their own strength!'

'Not by might, nor by power, but by my Spirit,' says
the Lord of heaven's armies – 'you will succeed because
of my Spirit, though you are few and weak.' / Your
strength must come from the Lord's mighty power
within you.

1 Cor. 1:27. Judg. 3:15, 31. Judg. 6:14, 15. Judg. 7:2. Zech. 4:6. Eph. 6:10.

He has made a heavenly city for them.

There are many homes up there where my Father lives, and I am going to prepare them for your coming. When everything is ready, then I will come and get you, so that you can always be with me where I am. / The priceless gift of eternal life; it is kept in heaven for you, pure and undefiled, beyond the reach of change and decay. / This world is not our home; we are looking forward to our everlasting home in heaven.

Jesus has gone away to heaven, and some day, just as he went, he will return! / Now as for you, dear brothers who are waiting for the Lord's return, be patient, like a farmer who waits until the autumn for his precious harvest to ripen. Yes, be patient. And take courage, for the coming of the Lord is near. / His coming will not be delayed much longer.

We who are still alive and remain on the earth will be caught up with them in the clouds to meet the Lord in the air and remain with him forever. So comfort and encourage each other with this news.

Hebr. 11:16. Jn. 14:2, 3. 1 Pet. 1:4. Hebr. 13:14. Acts 1:11. Jas. 5:7, 8. Hebr. 10:37. 1 Thess. 4:17, 18.

He has chosen a plan despised by the world.

Don't fool yourselves. Those who live immoral lives, who are idol worshippers, adulterers or homosexuals – will have no share in his kingdom. Neither will thieves or greedy people, drunkards, slanderers, or robbers. There was a time when some of you were just like that, but now your sins are washed away, and you are set apart for God, and he has accepted you because of what the Lord Jesus Christ and the Spirit of our God have done for you.

Once you were under God's curse, doomed forever for your sins. You went along with the crowd and were just like all the others, full of sin, obeying Satan, the mighty prince of the power of the air, who is at work right now in the hearts of those who are against the Lord.

He saved us – not because we were good enough to be saved, but because of his kindness and pity – by washing away our sins and giving us the new joy of the indwelling Holy Spirit. He poured him out upon us with wonderful fullness – and all because of what Jesus Christ our Saviour did.

This plan of mine is not what you would work out, neither are my thoughts the same as yours!

1 Cor. 1:28. 1 Cor. 6:9–11. Eph. 2:1, 2. Tit. 3:5, 6. Is. 55:8.

The joy of the Lord is your strength.

Sing for joy, O heavens; shout, O earth. Break forth
with song, O mountains, for the Lord has comforted
his people, and will have compassion upon them in
their sorrow. / God has come to save me! I will trust
and not be afraid, for the Lord is my strength and song;
he is my salvation. / He is my strength, my shield
from every danger. I trusted in him, and he helped
me. Joy rises in my heart until I burst out in songs of
praise to him.

We rejoice in our wonderful new relationship with
God – all because of what our Lord Jesus Christ has
done in dying for our sins – making us friends of God. /
Even though the fig trees are all destroyed, and there
is neither blossom left nor fruit, and though the olive
crops all fail, and the fields lie barren; even if the
flocks die in the fields and the cattle barns are empty,
yet I will rejoice in the Lord; I will be happy in the
God of my salvation. The Lord God is my Strength,
and he will give me the speed of a deer and bring me
safely over the mountains.

Neh. 8:10. Is. 49:13. Is. 12:2. Ps. 28:7. Rom. 5:11. Hab. 3:17–19.

God has made an everlasting covenant with me;
his agreement is eternal, final, sealed.

I know the one in whom I trust, and I am sure that he is able to guard safely all that I have given him until the day of his return.

How we praise God, the Father of our Lord Jesus Christ, who has blessed us with every blessing in heaven because we belong to Christ. Long ago, even before he made the world, God chose us to be his very own, through what Christ would do for us; he decided then to make us holy in his eyes, without a single fault – we who stand before him covered with his love. His unchanging plan has always been to adopt us into his own family by sending Jesus Christ to die for us. And he did this because he wanted to!

And we know that all that happens to us is working for our good if we love God and are fitting into his plans. For from the very beginning God decided that those who came to him – and all along he knew who would – should become like his Son, so that his Son would be the firstborn, with many brothers. And having chosen us, he called us to come to him; and when we came, he declared us 'not guilty,' filled us with Christ's goodness, gave us a right standing with himself, and promised us his glory.

2 Sam. 23:5. 2 Tim. 1:12. Eph. 1:3–5. Rom. 8:28–30.

The God of peace . . . produce in you through the power of Christ all that is pleasing to him.

Be happy. Grow in Christ. Pay attention to what I have said. Live in harmony and peace.

Because of his kindness you have been saved through trusting Christ. And even trusting is not of yourselves; it too is a gift from God. Salvation is not a reward for the good we have done, so none of us can take any credit for it. / But whatever is good and perfect comes to us from God, the creator of all light, and he shines forever without change or shadow.

Do the good things that result from being saved, obeying God with deep reverence, shrinking back from all that might displease him. For God is at work within you, helping you to want to obey him, and then helping you to do what he wants. / Be a new and different person with a freshness in all you do and think. Then you will learn from your own experience how his ways will really satisfy you. / May you always be doing those good, kind things which show that you are a child of God, for this will bring much praise and glory to the Lord.

Not because we think we can do anything of lasting value by ourselves. Our only power and success comes from God.

Hebr. 13 :20, 21. 2 Cor. 13 :11. Eph. 2 :8, 9. Jas. 1 :17. Phil. 2 :12, 13. Rom. 12 :2. Phil. 1 :11. 2 Cor. 3 :5.

*Leave your bonds and slavery. Put Babylon and
all it represents far behind you.*

The Lord has said, 'Leave them; separate yourselves
from them; don't touch what is unclean, and I will
welcome you, and be a Father to you, and you will be
my sons and daughters.' / Having such great promises
as these, dear friends, let us turn away from everything
wrong, whether of body or spirit, and purify ourselves,
living in the wholesome fear of God, giving ourselves to
him alone.

Jesus suffered and died outside the city, where his
blood washed our sins away. So let us go out to him
beyond the city walls [that is, outside the interests of
this world, being willing to be despised] to suffer with
him there, bearing his shame.

Jesus suggested, 'Let's get away from the crowds
for a while and rest.' / Because the Lord is my
Shepherd, I have everything I need! He lets me rest in
the meadow grass and leads me beside the quiet
streams. He restores my failing health. He helps me do
what honours him the most.

*Is. 52:11. 2 Cor. 6:17, 18. 2 Cor. 7:1. Hebr. 13:12, 13. Mk. 6:31.
Ps. 23:1–3.*

*The Temple of the Lord must be a marvellous
structure, famous and glorious.*

You have become living building-stones for God's
use in building his house. / Don't you realize that all
of you together are the house of God, and that the Spirit
of God lives among you in his house? If anyone
defiles and spoils God's home, God will destroy him.
For God's home is holy and clean, and you are that
home. / Haven't you yet learned that your body is the
home of the Holy Spirit God gave you, and that he lives
within you? Your own body does not belong to you. For
God has brought you with a great price. So use every
part of your body to give glory back to God, because
he owns it. / What union can there be between God's
temple and idols? For you are God's temple, the home
of the living God. / You are members of God's very
own family, citizens of God's country, and you belong
in God's household with every other Christian. What a
foundation you stand on now: the apostles and
prophets; and the cornerstone of the building is Jesus
Christ himself. We who believe are carefully joined together with Christ as parts of a beautiful, constantly
growing temple for God. And you also are joined with
him and with each other by the Spirit, and are part of
this dwelling place of God.

*1 Chron. 22:5. 1 Pet. 2:5. 1 Cor. 3:16, 17. 1 Cor. 6:19, 20. 2 Cor. 6:16.
Eph. 2:19–22.*

He was before all else began.

The faithful and true witness [of all that is or was or evermore shall be], the primeval source of God's creation. / He is the Head of . . . his church – which he began; and he is the leader of all who arise from the dead, so that he is first in everything.

The Lord formed me in the beginning, before he created anything else. From ages past, I am. I existed before the earth began. I was there when he established the heavens and formed the great springs in the depths of the oceans. I was there when he set the limits of the seas and gave them his instructions not to spread beyond their boundaries. I was there when he made the blueprint for the earth and oceans. I was always at his side like a little child. I was his constant delight, laughing and playing in his presence. / From eternity to eternity I am God.

Jesus, our leader and instructor. He was willing to die a shameful death on the cross because of the joy he knew would be his afterwards; and now he sits in the place of honour by the throne of God.

Col. 1:17. Rev. 3:14. Col. 1:18. Prov. 8:22, 23, 27–30. Is. 43:13. Hebr. 12:2.

Admit your faults to one another and pray for each other so that you may be healed.

Abraham spoke again. 'Since I have begun, let me go on and speak further to the Lord, though I am but dust and ashes. *Suppose there are only forty-five?* Will you destroy the city for lack of five?' And God said, 'I will not destroy it if I find forty-five.' / 'Father, forgive these people,' Jesus said, 'for they don't know what they are doing.' / Pray for those who persecute you!

My plea is not for the world but for these you have given me because they belong to you. I am not praying for these alone but also for all future believers who will come to me because of the testimony of these. / Share each other's troubles and problems, and so obey our Lord's command.

The earnest prayer of a righteous man has great power and wonderful results. Elijah was as completely human as we are, and yet when he prayed earnestly that no rain would fall, none fell for the next three and a half years! Then he prayed again, this time that it *would* rain, and down it poured and the grass turned green and the gardens began to grow again.

Jas. 5:16. Gen. 18:27, 28. Lk. 23:34. Mt. 5:44. Jn. 17:9, 20. Gal. 6:2. Jas. 5:16–18.

*Our days are few and brief, like grass, like
flowers, blown by the wind and gone forever.*

Teach us to number our days and recognize how few
they are; help us to spend them as we should. / How does
a man benefit if he gains the whole world and loses
himself in the process?

The grass withers, the flower fades beneath the breath
of God. And so it is with fragile man. The grass
withers, the flowers fade, but the Word of our God
shall stand forever. / This world is fading away, and
these evil, forbidden things will go with it, but whoever
keeps doing the will of God will live forever.

At this moment God is ready to welcome you. Today he is ready to save you. / Those in frequent contact
with the exciting things the world offers should make
good use of their opportunities without stopping to
enjoy them; for the world in its present form will soon
be gone. / Let us outdo each other in being helpful and
kind to each other and in doing good. Let us not neglect
our church duties and meetings, as some people do, but
encourage and warn each other, especially now that the
day of his coming back again is drawing near.

*Ps. 103:15, 16. Ps. 90:12. Mk. 8:36. Is. 40:7, 8. 1 Jn. 2:17. 2 Cor. 6:2.
1 Cor. 7:31. Hebr. 10:24, 25.*

*What God in all of heaven or earth can do what
you have done for us?*

Who in all of heaven can be compared with God?
What mightiest angel is anything like him? O Jehovah,
Commander of the heavenly armies, where is there any
other Mighty One like you? Faithfulness is your very
character. / Where among the heathen gods is there a
god like you? Where are their miracles? / All heaven
shall praise your miracles, O Lord; myriads of angels
will praise you for your faithfulness. / You are doing all
these things just because you promised to and because
you want to. How great you are, Lord God! We have
never heard of any other god like you.

No mere man has ever seen, heard or even imagined
what wonderful things God has ready for those who
love the Lord. But we know about these things because
God has sent his Spirit to tell us, and his Spirit
searches out and shows us all of God's deepest secrets.

Don't you yet understand? Don't you know by now
that the everlasting God, the creator of the farthest parts
of the earth, never grows faint or weary?

*Deut. 3:25. Ps. 89:6, 8. Ps. 86:8. Ps. 89:5. 2 Sam. 7:21, 22. 1 Cor. 2:9, 10.
Is. 40:28.*

If anyone is going to boast, let him boast only of what the Lord has done.

Let the wise man not bask in his wisdom, nor the mighty man in his might, nor the rich man in his riches. Let them boast in this alone: That they truly know me, and understand that I am the Lord.

Everything else is worthless when compared with the priceless gain of knowing Christ Jesus my Lord. I have put aside all else, counting it worth less than nothing, in order that I can have Christ. / He must become greater and greater, and I must become less and less. / I am not ashamed of this Good News about Christ. It is God's powerful method of bringing all who believe it to heaven. This message was preached first to the Jews alone, but now everyone is invited to come to God in this same way.

Whom have I in heaven but you? And I desire no one on earth as much as you! / How I rejoice in the Lord!

Glorify your name, not ours, O Lord! Cause everyone to praise your lovingkindness and your truth.

1 Cor. 1:31. Jer. 9:23, 24. Phil. 3:8. Jn. 3:30. Rom. 1:16. Ps. 73:25.
1 Sam. 2:1. Ps. 115:1.

Be holy now in everything you do, just as the
Lord is holy, who invited you to be his child.

We talked to you as a father to his own children –
don't you remember? – pleading with you, encouraging you and even demanding that your daily lives
should not embarrass God, but bring joy to him who
invited you into his kingdom to share his glory. / That
you may show to others how God called you out of
the darkness into his wonderful light.

For though once your heart was full of darkness,
now it is full of light from the Lord, and your behaviour should show it! Because of this light within you,
you should do only what is good and right and true.
Learn as you go along what pleases the Lord. Take no
part in the worthless pleasures of evil and darkness,
but instead, rebuke and expose them. / May you always
be doing those good, kind things which show that you
are a child of God, for this will bring much praise and
glory to the Lord.

Don't hide your light! Let it shine for all; let your
good deeds glow for all to see, so that they will praise
your heavenly Father. / Do everything for the glory
of God, even your eating and drinking.

1 Pet. 1:15. 1 Thess. 2:11, 12. 1 Pet. 2:9. Eph. 5:8–11. Phil. 1:11.
Mt. 5:15, 16. 1 Cor. 10:31.

*He will listen to us whenever we ask him for
anything in line with his will.*

I will give you a new heart – I will give you new and
right desires – and put a new spirit within you. I will
take out your stony hearts of sin and give you new
hearts of love. And I will put my Spirit within you so that
you will obey my laws and do whatever I command.

If two of you agree down here on earth concerning
anything you ask for, my Father in heaven will do it
for you. For where two or three gather together because
they are mine, I will be there among them.

If our consciences are clear, we can come to the Lord
with perfect assurance and trust, and get whatever we
ask for because we are obeying him and doing the
things that please him. / If you only have faith in God –
this is the absolute truth – you can say to this Mount of
Olives, 'Rise up and fall into the Mediterranean,' and
your command will be obeyed. All that's required is
that you really believe and have no doubt!

1 Jn. 5:14. Ezk. 36:26, 27. Mt. 18:19, 20. 1 Jn. 3:21, 22. Mk. 11:22, 23.

God is not a man that he should lie; he doesn't change his mind like humans do.

God, the creator of all light . . . shines for ever without change or shadow. / Jesus Christ is the same yesterday, today, and forever.

His faithful promises are your armour.

God also bound himself with an oath, so that those he promised to help would be perfectly sure and never need to wonder whether he might change his plans. He has given us both his promise and his oath, two things we can completely count on, for it is impossible for God to tell a lie. Now all those who flee to him to save them can take new courage when they hear such assurances from God; now they can know without doubt that he will give them the salvation he has promised them.

The Lord your God is the faithful God who for a thousand generations keeps his promises and constantly loves those who love him and who obey his commands. / When we obey him, every path he guides us on is fragrant with his lovingkindness and his truth. / Happy is the man who has the God of Jacob as his helper, whose hope is in the Lord his God – the God who made both earth and heaven, the seas and everthing in them. He is the God who keeps every promise.

Num. 23:19. Jas. 1:17. Hebr. 13:8. Ps. 91:4. Hebr. 6:17, 18. Deut. 7:9.
Ps. 25:10. Ps. 146:5, 6.

If even one would show some pity, if even one would comfort me!

You are a poor specimen if you can't stand the pressure of adversity. / He gives power to the tired and worn out, and strength to the weak. / I am with you; that is all you need. My power shows up best in weak people. / When he calls on me I will answer; I will be with him in trouble, and rescue him and honour him. / The eternal God is your Refuge, and underneath are the everlasting arms. He thrusts out your enemies before you; it is he who cries, 'Destroy them!'

The Jewish high priest is merely a man like anyone else, but he is chosen to speak for all other men in their dealings with God. And because he is a man he can deal gently with other men, though they are foolish and ignorant, for he, too, is surrounded with the same temptations and understands their problems very well. And even though Jesus was God's Son, he had to learn from experience what it was like to obey, when obeying meant suffering. It was after he had proved himself perfect in this experience that Jesus became the giver of eternal salvation to all those who obey him. / It was *our* grief he bore, *our* sorrows that weighed him down.

Ps. 69:20. Prov. 24:10. Is. 40:29. 2 Cor. 12:9. Ps. 91:15. Deut. 33:27. Hebr. 5:1–3, 8, 9. Is. 53:4.

Jehovah is mine!

God has already given you everything you need . . .
and you belong to Christ, and Christ is God's. / Jesus
Christ . . . died under God's judgment against our sins,
so that he could rescue us from constant falling into
sin. / God has put all things under his feet and made
him the supreme head of the church. / Christ . . . died
[for the church] so that he could give her to himself
as a glorious church without a single spot or wrinkle
or any other blemish, being holy and without a single
fault.

I will boast of all his kindness to me. / How happy
God has made me! For he has clothed me with garments
of salvation and draped about me the robe of righteousness.

Whom have I in heaven but you? And I desire no
one on earth as much as you! My health fails; my
spirits droop, yet God remains! He is the strength of
my heart; he is mine forever! / I said to him, 'You are
my Lord; I have no other help but yours.' The Lord
himself is my inheritance, my prize. He is my food and
drink, my highest joy! He guards all that is mine. He
sees that I am given pleasant brooks and meadows
as my share! What a wonderful inheritance!

Ps. 119:57. 1 Cor. 3:21, 23. Tit. 2:13, 14. Eph. 1:22. Eph. 5:25, 27.
Ps. 34:2. Is. 61:10. Ps. 73:25, 26. Ps. 16:2, 5, 6.

Before every man there lies a wide and pleasant road that seems right but ends in death.

A man is a fool to trust himself!

Your words are a flashlight to light the path ahead of me, and keep me from stumbling. / I have followed your commands and have not gone along with cruel and evil men.

If there is a prophet among you, or one who claims to foretell the future by dreams, and if his predictions come true but he says, 'Come, let us worship the gods of the other nations,' don't listen to him. For the Lord is testing you to find out whether or not you really love him with all your heart and soul. You must *never* worship any God but Jehovah; obey only his commands and cling to him.

I will instruct you (says the Lord) and guide you along the best pathway for your life; I will advise you and watch your progress. Don't be like a senseless horse or mule that has to have a bit in its mouth to keep it in line! Many sorrows come to the wicked, but abiding love surrounds those who trust in the Lord. So rejoice in him, all those who are his, and shout for joy, all those who try to obey him.

Prov. 14:12. Prov. 28:26. Ps. 119:105. Ps. 17:4. Deut. 13:1–4. Ps. 32:8–11.

We are not our own bosses to live or die as we ourselves might choose.

Living or dying we follow the Lord. Either way we are his. / God has brought you with a great price. So use every part of your body to give glory back to God, because he owns it.

I live in eager expectation that . . . I will always be ready to speak out boldly for Christ while I am going through all these trials here, just as I have in the past; and that I will always be an honour to Christ, whether I live or whether I must die. For to me, living means opportunities for Christ, and dying – well, that's even better! But if living will give me more opportunities to win people to Christ, then I really don't know which is better, to live or die. Sometimes I want to live and at other times I don't, for I long to go and be with Christ.

It was through reading the Scriptures that I came to realize that I could never find God's favour by trying – and failing – to obey the laws. I came to realize that acceptance with God comes by believing in Christ. I have been crucified with Christ: and I myself no longer live, but Christ lives in me. And the real life I now have within this body is a result of my trusting in the Son of God, who loved me and gave himself for me.

Rom. 14:7. Rom. 14:8. 1 Cor. 6:20. Phil. 1:20–23. Gal. 2:19, 20.

God gave Solomon great wisdom and under-standing.

Now a greater than Solomon is here. / The Prince of Peace.

Even if we were good, we really wouldn't expect anyone to die for us, though, of course, that might just be possible. But God showed his great love for us by sending Christ to die for us while we were still sinners. / Jesus Christ, who, though he was God, did not demand and cling to his rights as God, but laid aside his mighty power and glory, taking the disguise of a slave and becoming like men. And he humbled himself even further, going so far as actually to die a criminal's death on a cross. / How long, how wide, how deep, and how high his love really is.

Christ is the mighty power of God to save them; Christ himself is the centre of God's wise plan for their salvation. / In him lie hidden all the mighty, untapped treasures of wisdom and knowledge. / The endless treasures available . . . in Christ. / It is from God alone that you have your life through Christ Jesus. He showed us God's plan of salvation; he was the one who made us acceptable to God; he made us pure and holy and gave himself to purchase our salvation.

*1 Kgs. 4:29. Mt. 12:42. Is. 9:6. Rom. 5:7, 8. Phil. 2:5–8. Eph. 3:19.
1 Cor. 1:24. Col. 2:3. Eph. 3:8. 1 Cor. 1:30.*

I have loved you . . . with an everlasting love;
with lovingkindness I have drawn you to me.

We must for ever give thanks to God for you, our brothers loved by the Lord, because God chose from the very first to give you salvation, cleansing you by the work of the Holy Spirit and by your trusting in the truth. Through us he told you the Good News. Through us he called you to share in the glory of our Lord Jesus Christ. / It is he who saved us and chose us for his holy work, not because we deserved it but because that was his plan long before the world began – to show his love and kindness to us through Christ. / You saw me before I was born and scheduled each day of my life before I began to breathe. Every day was recorded in your Book!

For God loved the world so much that he gave his only Son so that anyone who believes in him shall not perish but have eternal life.

In this act we see what real love is: it is not our love for God, but his love for us when he sent his Son to satisfy God's anger against our sins.

Jer. 31:3. 2 Thess. 2:13, 14. 2 Tim. 1:9. Ps. 139:16. Jn. 3:16. 1 Jn. 4:10.

I made you and I will care for you.

The Lord who created you, O Israel, says, Don't be afraid, for I have ransomed you; I have called you by name; you are mine. When you go through deep waters and great trouble, I will be with you. When you go through rivers of difficulty, you will not drown! When you walk through the fire of oppression you will not be burned up – the flames will not consume you. / I will be your God through all your lifetime, yes, even when your hair is white with age.

He spreads his wings over them, even as an eagle covers her young. She carries them upon her wings – as does the Lord his people! / In his love and pity he redeemed them and lifted them up and carried them through all the years.

Jesus Christ is the same yesterday, today, and forever. / I am convinced that . . . nothing will ever be able to separate us from the love of God demonstrated by our Lord Jesus Christ when he died for us.

Can a mother forget her little child and not have love for her own son? Yet even if that should be, I will not forget you.

Is. 46:4. Is. 43:1, 2. Is. 46:4. Deut. 32:11. Is. 63:9. Hebr. 13:8.
Rom. 8:38, 39. Is. 49:15.

I have seen the deep sorrows of my people.

A man of sorrows, acquainted with bitterest grief. / This high priest of ours understands our weaknesses.

He took our sicknesses and bore our diseases. / Jesus was tired from the long walk in the hot sun and sat wearily beside the well.

When Jesus saw her weeping and the Jewish leaders wailing with her, he was moved with indignation and deeply troubled. Tears came to Jesus' eyes. / For since he himself has now been through suffering and temptation, he knows what it is like when we suffer and are tempted, and he is wonderfully able to help us.

God looked down from his temple in heaven, and heard the groans of his people in slavery – they were children of death – and released them. / He knows every detail of what is happening to me; and when he has examined me, he will pronounce me completely innocent – as pure as solid gold! / I am overwhelmed and desperate, and you alone know which way I ought to turn.

He who harms you sticks his finger in Jehovah's eye! / In all their affliction he was afflicted, and he personally saved them.

Ex. 3:7. Is. 53:3. Hebr. 4:15. Mt. 8:17. Jn. 4:6. Jn. 11:33, 35. Hebr. 2:18. Ps. 102:19, 20. Job 23:10. Ps. 142:3. Zech. 2:8. Is. 63:9.

All of us must quickly carry out the tasks assigned us . . . for there is little time left before the night falls and all work comes to an end.

Lazy people want much but get little, while the diligent are prospering. / The liberal man shall be rich! By watering others, he waters himself.

Jesus explained: 'My nourishment comes from doing the will of God who sent me, and from finishing his work. Do you think the work of harvesting will not begin until the summer ends four months from now? Look around you! Vast fields are ripening all around us, and are ready now for reaping. The reapers will be paid good wages and will be gathering men and women into the granaries of heaven. What joys await the sower and the reaper, both together!'

Preach the Word of God urgently at all times, whenever you get the chance, in season and out, when it is convenient and when it is not.

Whatever I am now it is all because God poured out such kindness and grace upon me – and not without results: for I have worked harder than all the other apostles, yet actually I wasn't doing it, but God working in me, to bless me.

Jn. 9:4. Prov. 13:4. Prov. 11:25. Jn. 4:34–36. 2 Tim. 4:2. 1 Cor. 15:10.

*Consider the quarry from which you were mined,
the rock from which you were cut!*

I was born a sinner, yes, from the moment my mother
conceived me. / No one pitied you or cared for you.
On that day when you were born, you were dumped out
into a field and left to die, unwanted. But I came by
and saw you there, covered with your own blood, and I
said, Live! Thrive like a plant in the field!

He lifted me out of the pit of despair, out from the
bog and the mire, and set my feet on a hard, firm path
and steadied me as I walked along. He has given me a
new song to sing, of praises to our God.

When we were utterly helpless, with no way of escape,
Christ came at just the right time and died for us sinners
who had no use for him. Even if we were good, we
really wouldn't expect anyone to die for us, though, of
course, that might just be possible. But God showed
his great love for us by sending Christ to die for us
while we were still sinners. / God is so rich in mercy; he
loved us so much that even though we were spiritually
dead and doomed by our sins, he gave us back our
lives again when he raised Christ from the dead.

Is. 51:1. Ps. 51:5. Ezk. 16:5, 6. Ps. 40:2, 3. Rom. 5:6–8. Eph. 2:4, 5.

How happy God has made me!

I will praise the Lord no matter what happens. I will
constantly speak of his glories and grace. I will boast
of all his kindness to me. Let all who are discouraged
take heart. Let us praise the Lord together, and exalt
his name. / For Jehovah God is our Light and our
Protector. He gives us grace and glory. No good thing
will he withhold from those who walk along his paths.
O Lord of the armies of heaven, blessed are those who
trust in you. / I bless the holy name of God with all my
heart.

Those who have reason to be thankful should continually be singing praises to the Lord. / Be filled . . .
with the Holy Spirit, and controlled by him. Talk with
each other much about the Lord, quoting psalms and
hymns and singing sacred songs, making music in your
hearts to the Lord. Always give thanks for everything
to our God and Father in the name of our Lord Jesus
Christ. / Singing to the Lord with thankful hearts.

Around midnight . . . Paul and Silas were praying
and singing hymns to the Lord. / Always be full of
joy in the Lord; I say it again, rejoice!

Is. 61:10. Ps. 34:1–3. Ps. 84:11, 12. Ps. 103:1. Jas. 5:13. Eph. 5:18–20.
Col. 3:16. Acts 16:25. Phil. 4:4.

Make a plate of pure gold and engrave on it, just as you would upon a seal, Consecrated to Jehovah.

One who is not holy will not see the Lord. / God is Spirit, and we must have his help to worship as we should. / I will show myself holy among those who approach me, and I will be glorified before all the people. / We are all infected and impure with sin. When we put on our prized robes of righteousness we find they are but filthy rags.

This is the basic law of the Temple: *Holiness!* The entire top of the hill where the Temple is built is *holy.* / Holiness is forever the keynote of your reign.

I consecrate myself to meet their need for growth in truth and holiness. / Jesus the Son of God is our great high priest who has gone to heaven itself to help us. . . . So let us come boldly to the very throne of God and stay there to receive his mercy and to find grace to help us in our times of need. / For it is from God alone that you have your life through Christ Jesus. He showed us God's plan of salvation; he was the one who made us acceptable to God; he made us pure and holy and gave himself to purchase our salvation.

Ex. 28:36. Hebr. 12:14. Jn. 4:24. Lev. 10:3. Is. 64:6. Ezk. 43:12. Ps. 93:5. Jn. 17:19. Hebr. 4:14, 16. 1 Cor. 1:30.

Blessings overflow!

Oh, put God to the test and see how kind he is! See for yourself the way his mercies shower down on all who trust in him. If you belong to the Lord, reverence him; for everyone who does this has everything he needs. Even strong, young lions sometimes go hungry, but those of us who reverence the Lord will never lack any good thing. / *His compassion never ends.* Great is his faithfulness; his lovingkindness begins afresh each day.

The Lord himself is my inheritance, my prize. He is my food and drink, my highest joy! He guards all that is mine. He sees that I am given pleasant brooks and meadows as my share! What a wonderful inheritance! / He has given you the whole world to use, and life and even death are your servants. He has given you all of the present and all of the future. All are yours. / How we praise God, the Father of our Lord Jesus Christ, who has blessed us with every blessing in heaven because we belong to Christ.

I have learned how to get along happily whether I have much or little. / Do you want to be truly rich? You already are if you are happy and good. / God . . . will supply all your needs from his riches in glory, because of what Christ Jesus has done for us.

Ps. 23:5. Ps. 34:8–10. Lam. 3:22, 23. Ps. 16:5, 6. 1 Cor. 3:22. Eph. 1:3. Phil. 4:11. 1 Tim. 6:6. Phil. 4:18, 19.

*Your words are a flashlight to light the path
ahead of me, and keep me from stumbling.*

Every day and all night long their counsel will lead you
and save you from harm; when you wake up in the
morning, let their instructions guide you into the new
day. For their advice is a beam of light directed into
the dark corners of your mind to warn you of danger
and to give you a good life. / And if you leave God's
paths and go astray, you will hear a Voice behind you
say, 'No, this is the way: walk here.'

I am the Light of the world. So if you follow me, you
won't be stumbling through the darkness, for living
light will flood your path. / We have seen and proved
that what the prophets said came true. You will do well
to pay close attention to everything they have written,
for, like lights shining into dark corners, their words
help us to understand many things that otherwise
would be dark and difficult. / We can see and understand only a little about God now, as if we were peering
at his reflection in a poor mirror; but some day we are
going to see him in his completeness, face to face.
Now all that I know is hazy and blurred, but then I will
see everything clearly, just as clearly as God sees into
my heart right now.

Ps. 119:105. Prov. 6:22, 23. Is. 30:21. Jn. 8:12. 2 Pet. 1:19. 1 Cor. 13:12.

*'What do you mean,' he roared, 'sleeping at a
time like this? Get up!'*

This is no more your land and home, for you have
filled it with sin and it will vomit you out. / Let heaven
fill your thoughts; don't spend your time worrying
about things down here. / Don't become rich by extortion and robbery. And don't let the rich men be
proud. / Try with every fibre of your being to obey the
Lord your God.

'Asleep!' he said. 'Get up! Pray God that you will
not fall when you are tempted.' / Watch out! Don't
let my sudden coming catch you unawares; don't let me
find you living in careless ease, carousing and drinking,
and occupied with the problems of this life, like all
the rest of the world.

When the bridegroom was delayed, they lay down to
rest. / His coming will not be delayed much longer. /
You know how late it is; time is running out. Wake
up, for the coming of the Lord is nearer now than
when we first believed. / Keep a sharp lookout! For
you do not know when I will come, at evening, at midnight, early dawn or late daybreak. Don't let me find
you sleeping.

*Jon. 1:6. Mic. 2:10. Col. 3:2. Ps. 62:10, 11. 1 Chron. 22:19. Lk. 22:46.
Lk. 21:34, 35. Mt. 25:5. Hebr. 10:37. Rom. 13:11. Mk. 13:35, 36.*

*The Accuser of our brothers has been thrown
down from heaven on to earth – he accused them
day and night before our God.*

They defeated him by the blood of the Lamb, and by
their testimony. / Who dares accuse us whom God has
chosen for his own? Will God? No! He is the one who
has forgiven us and given us a right standing with
himself. Who then will condemn us? Will Christ? No!
For he is the one who died for us and came back to
life again for us and is sitting at the place of highest
honour next to God, pleading for us there in heaven.

God took away Satan's power to accuse you of sin,
and God openly displayed to the whole world Christ's
triumph at the cross where your sins were all taken
away. / He became flesh and blood too by being born
in human form; for only as a human being could he die
and in dying break the power of the devil who had the
power of death. / Overwhelming victory is ours through
Christ who loved us enough to die for us. / Put on all of
God's armour so that you will be able to stand safe
against the strategies and tricks of Satan. And you will
need the helmet of salvation and the sword of the
Spirit – which is the Word of God. / How we thank God
for all of this! It is he who makes us victorious
through Jesus Christ our Lord!

*Rev. 12:10. Rev. 12:11. Rom. 8:33, 34. Col. 2:15. Hebr. 2:14. Rom. 8:37.
Eph. 6:11, 17. 1 Cor. 15:57.*

The Tree of Life.

What is it that God has said? That he has given us eternal life, and that this life is in his Son. / God loved the world so much that he gave his only Son so that anyone who believes in him shall not perish but have eternal life. / He [Christ] will even raise from the dead anyone he wants to, just as the Father does. The Father has life in himself, and has granted his Son to have life in himself.

To everyone who is victorious, I will give fruit from the tree of life in the Paradise of God. / On each side of the river grew trees of life, bearing twelve crops of fruit, with a fresh crop each month; the leaves were used for medicine to heal the nations.

The man who knows right from wrong and has good judgment and common sense is happier than the man who is immensely rich! Wisdom gives a long, good life, riches, honour, pleasure, peace. Wisdom is a tree of life to those who eat her fruit; happy is the man who keeps on eating it. / God . . . is always ready to give a generous supply of wisdom to all who ask him.

Gen. 2:9. 1 Jn. 5:11. Jn. 3:16. Jn. 5:21, 26. Rev. 2:7. Rev. 22:2.
Prov. 3:13, 16–18. Jas. 1:5.

Happy the man who puts his trust in the Lord.

Abraham never doubted. He believed God, for his faith and trust grew ever stronger, and he praised God for this blessing even before it happened. He was completely sure that God was well able to do anything he promised. / Judah, depending upon the Lord God of their fathers, defeated Israel.

God is our refuge and strength, a tested help in times of trouble. And so we need not fear even if the world blows up, and the mountains crumble into the sea. / It is better to trust the Lord than to put confidence in men. It is better to take refuge in him than in the mightiest king! / The steps of good men are directed by the Lord. He delights in each step they take. If they fall it isn't fatal, for the Lord holds them with his hand.

Oh, put God to the test and see how kind he is! See for yourself the way his mercies shower down on all who trust in him. If you belong to the Lord, reverence him; for everyone who does this has everything he needs.

Prov. 16:20. Rom. 4:20, 21. 2 Chron. 13:18. Ps. 46:1, 2. Ps. 118:8, 9. Ps. 37:23, 24. Ps. 34:8, 9.

*I will lie down in peace and sleep, for though I
am alone, O Lord, you will keep me safe.*

You don't need to be afraid of the dark any more, nor
fear the dangers of the day; nor dread the plagues of
darkness, nor disasters in the morning. He will shield
you with his wings! They will shelter you. His faithful
promises are your armour. / I have wanted to gather
your children together as a hen gathers her chicks beneath her wings. / He will never let me stumble, slip or
fall. For he is always watching, never sleeping. Jehovah
himself is caring for you! He is your defender. He protects you day and night. He keeps you from all evil, and
preserves your life. He keeps his eye upon you as you
come and go, and always guards you.

I shall live forever in your tabernacle; oh, to be safe
beneath the shelter of your wings! / Darkness cannot
hide from God; to you the night shines as bright as
day. Darkness and light are both alike to you.

Since he did not spare even his own Son for us but
gave him up for us all, won't he also surely give us
everything else? / You belong to Christ, and Christ is
God's. / I will trust and not be afraid.

*Ps. 4:8. Ps. 91:5, 6, 4. Mt. 23:37. Ps. 121:3–8. Ps. 61:4. Ps. 139:12.
Rom. 8:32. 1 Cor. 3:23. Is. 12:2.*

*Some will come to me . . . and I will never, never
reject them.*

We know how much God loves us because we have felt
his love and because we believe him when he tells us
that he loves us dearly. God is love, and anyone who
lives in love is living with God and God is living in
him. And as we live with Christ, our love grows more
perfect and complete; so we will not be ashamed and
embarrassed at the day of judgment, but can face him
with confidence and joy, because he loves us and we love
him too. We need have no fear of someone who loves
us perfectly; his perfect love for us eliminates all dread
of what he might do to us. If we are afraid, it is for
fear of what he might do to us, and shows that we are
not fully convinced that he really loves us.

Let us go right in, to God himself, with true hearts
fully trusting him to receive us, because we have been
sprinkled with Christ's blood to make us clean, and
because our bodies have been washed with pure water. /
We can come fearlessly right into God's presence,
assured of his glad welcome when we come with Christ
and trust in him. / So let us come boldly to the very
throne of God and stay there to receive his mercy and to
find grace to help us in our times of need.

Jn. 6:37. 1 Jn. 4:16–18. Hebr. 10:22. Eph. 3:12. Hebr. 4:16.

When the people of Israel saw it they asked each other, 'What is it?'

It is quite true that the way to live a godly life is not an easy matter. But the answer lies in Christ, who came to earth as a man, was proved spotless and pure in his spirit. / The true Bread is a Person – the one sent by God from heaven, and he gives life to the world.

I am that Living Bread that came down out of heaven. Anyone eating this Bread will live forever; my flesh is this bread given to redeem humanity. For my flesh is the true food, and my blood is the true drink.

So the people of Israel went out and gathered it. And when they poured it into a three-litre measure, there was just enough for everyone – three litres apiece; those who gathered a lot had nothing left over and those who gathered little had no lack! Each home had just enough. So they gathered the food morning by morning, each home according to its need.

So don't worry at all about having enough food and clothing. Why be like the heathen? For they take pride in all these things and are deeply concerned about them. But your heavenly Father already knows perfectly well that you need them, and he will give them to you if you give him first place in your life.

Ex. 16:15. 1 Tim. 3:16. Jn. 6:33. Jn. 6:51, 55. Ex. 16:17, 18, 21. Mt. 6:31–33.

Christ freely takes away many sins and gives glorious life.

No matter how deep the stain of your sins, I can take it out and make you as clean as freshly fallen snow. Even if you are stained as red as crimson, I can make you white as wool! / I, yes, I alone am he who blots away your sins for my own sake and will never think of them again. Oh, remind me of this promise of forgiveness, for we must talk about your sins. Plead your case for my forgiving you. / I've blotted out your sins; they are gone like morning mist at noon. Oh, return to me, for I have paid the price to set you free.

For God loved the world so much that he gave his only Son so that anyone who believes in him shall not perish but have eternal life. / What a difference between man's sin and God's forgiveness! For this one man, Adam, brought death to many through his sin. But this one man, Jesus Christ, brought forgiveness to many through God's mercy. / There was a time when some of you were just like that but now your sins are washed away, and you are set apart for God, and he has accepted you because of what the Lord Jesus Christ and the Spirit of our God have done for you.

*Rom. 5:16. Is. 1:18. Is. 43:25, 26. Is. 44:22. Jn. 3:16. Rom. 5:15.
1 Cor. 6:11.*

Commit your work to the Lord, then it will succeed.

My coming can be compared with that of a man who went on a trip to another country. He laid out his employees' work for them to do while he was gone, and told the gatekeeper to watch for his return. / He gave £500 to one, £200 to another, and £100 to the last – dividing it in proportion to their abilities – and then left on his trip.

All of us must quickly carry out the tasks assigned us by the one who sent me, for there is little time left before the night falls and all work comes to an end. / Didn't you realize that I would be here at the Temple, in my Father's House?

Preach the Word of God urgently at all times, whenever you get the chance, in season and out, when it is convenient and when it is not. Correct and rebuke your people when they need it, encourage them to do right, and all the time be feeding them patiently with God's Word. / Everyone's work will be put through the fire so that all can see whether or not it's of lasting value, and what was really accomplished. / So, my dear brothers, since future victory is sure, be strong and steady, always abounding in the Lord's work, nothing you do for the Lord is ever wasted.

Prov. 16:3. Mk. 13:34. Mt. 25:15. Jn. 9:4. Lk. 2:49. 2 Tim. 4:2. 1 Cor. 3:13. 1 Cor. 15:58.

*When the Holy Spirit controls our lives he will
produce . . . gentleness.*

The meek will be filled with fresh joy from the Lord,
and the poor shall exult in the Holy One of Israel.

Unless you turn to God from your sins and become
as little children, you will never get into the Kingdom
of Heaven. Therefore anyone who humbles himself as
this little child, is the greatest in the Kingdom of
Heaven. / Be beautiful inside, in your hearts, with the
lasting charm of a gentle and quiet spirit which is so
precious to God. / Love is very patient and kind, never
jealous or envious, never boastful or proud.

Be patient and gentle. / Wear my yoke – for it fits
perfectly – and let me teach you; for I am gentle and
humble. / He was oppressed and he was afflicted, yet
he never said a word. He was brought as a lamb to the
slaughter; and as a sheep before her shearers is dumb,
so he stood silent before the ones condemning him.

This suffering is all part of the work God has given
you. Christ, who suffered for you, is your example.
Follow in his steps: he never sinned, never told a lie,
never answered back when insulted; when he suffered
he did not threaten to get even; he left his case in the
hands of God who always judges fairly.

*Gal. 5:22, 23. Is. 29:19. Mt. 18:3, 4. 1 Pet. 3:4. 1 Cor. 13:4. 1 Tim. 6:11.
Mt. 11:29. Is. 53:7. 1 Pet. 2:21–23.*

Anyone who wants to follow me must put aside his own desires and conveniences and carry his cross with him every day and keep close to me!

Whether others honour us or despise us, whether they criticize us or commend us. / Suffering will come to all who decide to live godly lives to please Christ Jesus, from those who hate him. / The fact that I am still being persecuted proves that I am still preaching salvation through faith in the cross of Christ alone.

Be happy if you are cursed and insulted for being a Christian, for when that happens the Spirit of God will come upon you with great glory. Don't let me hear of your suffering for murdering or stealing or making trouble or being a busybody and prying into other people's affairs. But it is no shame to suffer for being a Christian. Praise God for the privilege of being in Christ's family and being called by his wonderful name! If you are suffering according to God's will, keep on doing what is right and trust yourself to the God who made you.

For to you has been given the privilege not only of trusting him but also of suffering for him. / And if we think that our present service for him is hard, just remember that some day we are going to sit with him and rule with him.

Lk. 9:23. 2 Cor. 6:8. 2 Tim. 3:12. Gal. 5:11. 1 Pet. 4:14–16, 19. Phil. 1:29. 2 Tim. 2:12.

Don't be impatient. Wait for the Lord, and he will come and save you! Be brave, stout-hearted and courageous.

Don't you yet understand? Don't you know by now that the everlasting God, the Creator of the farthest parts of the earth, never grows faint or weary? He gives power to the tired and worn out, and strength to the weak. / Fear not, for I am with you. Do not be dismayed. I am your God. I will strengthen you; I will help you; I will uphold you with my victorious right hand. / To the poor, O Lord, you are a refuge from the storm, a shadow from the heat, a shelter from merciless men who are like a driving rain that melts down an earthen wall.

When the way is rough, your patience has a chance to grow. So let it grow, and don't try to squirm out of your problems. For when your patience is finally in full bloom, then you will be ready for anything, strong in character, full and complete. / Do not let this happy trust in the Lord die away, no matter what happens. Remember your reward! You need to keep on patiently doing God's will if you want him to do for you all that he has promised. His coming will not be delayed much longer.

Ps. 27:14. Is. 40:28, 29. Is. 41:10. Is. 25:4. Jas. 1:3, 4. Hebr. 10:35–37.

He lets me rest in the meadow grass.

Those who still reject me are like the restless sea, which is never still, but always churns up mire and dirt. There is no peace, says my God, for them!

Come to me and I will give you rest – all of you who work so hard beneath a heavy yoke. / Rest in the Lord. / Christ has already entered there. He is resting from his work, just as God did after the creation.

Do not be attracted by strange, new ideas. Your spiritual strength comes as a gift from God. / Then we will no longer be like children, for ever changing our minds about what we believe because someone has told us something different, or has cleverly lied to us and made the lie sound like the truth. Instead we will lovingly follow the truth at all times – speaking truly, dealing truly, living truly – and so become more and more in every way like Christ who is the head of his body, the church.

I am seated in his much-desired shade and his fruit is lovely to eat. He brings me to the banquet hall and everyone can see how much he loves me.

Ps. 23:2. Is. 57:20, 21. Mt. 11:28. Ps. 37:7. Hebr. 4:10. Hebr. 13:9. Eph. 4:14, 15. Song 2:3, 4.

There must be no yeast in your homes.

If anyone respects and fears God, he will hate evil. / Hate what is wrong. / Keep away from every kind of evil. / Look after each other so that not one of you will fail to find God's best blessings. Watch out that no bitterness takes root among you, for as it springs up it causes deep trouble, hurting many in their spiritual lives.

He would not have listened if I had not confessed my sins.

Don't you realize that if even one person is allowed to go on sinning, soon all will be affected? Remove this evil cancer – this wicked person – from among you, so that you can stay pure. Christ, God's Lamb, has been slain for us. So let us feast upon him and grow strong in the Christian life, leaving entirely behind us the cancerous old life with all its hatreds and wickedness. Let us feast instead upon the pure bread of honour and sincerity and truth. / That is why a man should examine himself carefully before eating the bread and drinking from the cup.

A person who calls himself a Christian should not be doing things that are wrong. / He is, therefore, exactly the kind of high priest we need; for he is holy and blameless, unstained by sin, undefiled by sinners. / There is no sin in him.

Ex. 13:7. Prov. 8:13. Rom. 12:9. 1 Thess. 5:22. Hebr. 12:15. Ps. 66:18. 1 Cor. 5:6–8. 1 Cor. 11:28. 2 Tim. 2:19. Hebr. 7:26. 1 Jn. 3:5.

The serpent hissed. 'You'll not die . . . Your eyes will be opened – you will be able to distinguish good from evil!'

I am frightened, fearing that in some way you will be led away from your pure and simple devotion to our Lord, just as Eve was deceived by Satan in the Garden of Eden.

I want to remind you that your strength must come from the Lord's mighty power within you. Put on all of God's armour so that you will be able to stand safe against the strategies and tricks of Satan. Use every piece of God's armour to resist the enemy whenever he attacks, and when it is all over, you will still be standing up. But to do this, you will need the strong belt of truth and the breastplate of God's approval. Wear shoes that are able to speed you on as you preach the Good News of peace with God. In every battle you will need faith as your shield to stop the fiery arrows aimed at you by Satan. And you will need the helmet of salvation and the sword of the Spirit – which is the Word of God. / Avoid being outwitted by Satan; for we know what he is trying to do.

Simon, Simon, Satan has asked to have you, to sift you like wheat, but I have pleaded in prayer for you that your faith should not completely fail.

Gen. 3:4, 5. 2 Cor. 11:3. Eph. 6:10, 11, 13–17. 2 Cor. 2:11. Lk. 22:31, 32.

Just be patient.

Stop worrying . . . he needn't be frightened. / Stand silent! Know that I am God! / Didn't I tell you that you will see a wonderful miracle from God if you believe? / All the glory of mankind will bow low; the pride of men will lie in the dust, and the Lord alone will be exalted.

Mary sat on the floor, listening to Jesus as he talked. 'There is really only one thing worth being concerned about. Mary has discovered it – and I won't take it away from her.' / Only in returning to me and waiting for me will you be saved; in quietness and confidence is your strength. / Lie quietly upon your bed in silent meditation.

Rest in the Lord; wait patiently for him to act. Don't be envious of evil men who prosper.

He does not fear bad news, nor live in dread of what may happen. For he is settled in his mind that Jehovah will take care of him. That is why he is not afraid, but can calmly face his foes.

He who believes need never run away.

Ruth 3:18. Is. 7:4. Ps. 46:10. Jn. 11:40. Is. 2:17. Lk. 10:39, 42. Is. 30:15. Ps. 4:4. Ps. 37:7. Ps. 112:7, 8. Is. 28:16.

*You don't understand now why I am doing it;
some day you will.*

Do you remember how the Lord led you through the
wilderness for all those forty years, humbling you and
testing you to find out how you would respond, and
whether or not you would really obey him?

I signed a covenant with you, and you became mine. /
When he punishes you, it proves that he loves you.

Dear friends, don't be bewildered or surprised when
you go through the fiery trials ahead, for this is no
strange, unusual thing that is going to happen to you.
Instead, be really glad – because these trials will make
you partners with Christ in his suffering, and afterwards you will have the wonderful joy of sharing his
glory in that coming day when it will be displayed. /
These troubles and sufferings of ours are, after all, quite
small and won't last very long. Yet this short time of
distress will result in God's richest blessing upon us
for ever and ever. So we do not look at what we can
see at this moment, the troubles all around us, but we
look forward to the joys in heaven which we have not
yet seen. The troubles will soon be over, but the joys
to come will last forever.

Jn. 13:7. Deut. 8:2. Ezk. 16:8. Hebr. 12:6. 1 Pet. 4:12, 13. 2 Cor. 4:17, 18.

> *Our bodies have many parts, but the many parts*
> *make up only one body. . . . So it is with the*
> *'body' of Christ.*

He is the Head of the body made up of his people – that
is, his church. / The supreme head of the church –
which is his body, filled with himself, the author and
giver of everything everywhere.

Christ cares for his body the church, of which we are
parts.

You have made ready this body of mine. / You saw
me before I was born and secheduled each day of my
life before I began to breathe. Every day was recorded in your Book!

They were always yours, and you gave them to me. /
Long ago, even before he made the world, God chose
us to be his very own. / For from the very beginning
God decided that those who came to him – and all
along he knew who would – should become like his Son.

Become more and more in every way like Christ who
is the head of his body, the church. Under his direction
the whole body is fitted together perfectly, and each
part in its own special way helps the other parts, so that
the whole body is healthy and growing and full of love.

1 Cor. 12:12. Col. 1:18. Eph. 1:22, 23. Eph. 5:30. Hebr. 10:5. Ps. 139:16.
Jn. 17:6. Eph. 1:4. Rom. 8:29. Eph. 4:15, 16.

The Fountain of Life-giving Water.

How precious is your constant love, O God! All humanity takes refuge in the shadow of your wings. You feed them with blessings from your own table and let them drink from your rivers of delight. For you are the Fountain of life; our light is from your Light.

For my people who have sought me, the plains of Sharon shall again be filled with flocks, and the valley of Achor shall be a place to pasture herds. But because the rest of you have forsaken the Lord . . . the Lord God says, 'You shall starve, but my servants shall eat; you shall be thirsty while they drink; you shall be sad and ashamed, but they shall rejoice.'

'The water I give them,' he said, 'becomes a perpetual spring within them, watering them forever with eternal life.' / (He was speaking of the Holy Spirit, who would be given to everyone believing in him.)

Is anyone thirsty? Come and drink. / The Spirit and the bride say, 'Come.' Let each one who hears them say the same, 'Come.' Let the thirsty one come – anyone who wants to; let him come and drink the water of life without charge.

Jer. 2:13. Ps. 36:7–9. Is. 65:10, 11, 13. Jn. 4:14. Jn. 7:39. Is. 55:1. Rev. 22:17.

Let us lift our hearts and hands to him in heaven.

Who can be compared with God enthroned on high? Far below him are the heavens and the earth; he stoops to look, and lifts the poor from the dirt, and the hungry from the rubbish dump, and sets them among princes! / To you, O Lord, I pray. / I reach out for you. I thirst for you as parched land thirsts for rain. Come quickly, Lord, and answer me, for my depression deepens; don't turn away from me or I shall die. Let me see your kindness to me in the morning, for I am trusting you. Show me where to walk, for my prayer is sincere.

For your love and kindness are better to me than life itself. How I praise you! I will bless you as long as I live, lifting up my hands to you in prayer. / Give me happiness, O Lord, for I worship only you. O Lord, you are so good and kind, so ready to forgive; so full of mercy for all who ask your aid. Listen closely to my prayer, O God. Hear my urgent cry. I will call to you whenever trouble strikes, and you will help me.

If our consciences are clear, we can come to the Lord with perfect assurance and trust, and get whatever we ask for because we are obeying him and doing the things that please him.

Lam. 3:41. Ps. 113:5–8. Ps. 25:1. Ps. 143:6–8. Ps. 63:3, 4. Ps. 86:4–7. 1 Jn. 3:21, 22.

Watchman, what of the night?

Time is running out. Wake up, for the coming of the Lord is nearer now than when we first believed. The night is far gone, the day of his return will soon be here. So discard the evil deeds of darkness and put on the armour of right living, as we who live in the daylight should.

Now learn a lesson from the fig tree. When her branch is tender and the leaves begin to sprout, you know that summer is almost here. Just so, when you see all these things beginning to happen, you can know that my return is near, even at the doors. Heaven and earth will disappear, but my words remain forever.

I wait expectantly, trusting God to help, for he has promised. I long for him more than sentinels long for the dawn.

He who has said all these things declares: 'Yes, I am coming soon!' Amen! Come, Lord Jesus!

So stay awake and be prepared, for you do not know the date or moment of my return.

Is. 21:11. Rom. 13:11, 12. Mt. 24:32, 33, 35. Ps. 130:5, 6. Rev. 22:20. Mt. 25:13.

Be glad for all God is planning for you.

Looking forward to the joys of heaven. / If being a Christian is only of value to us now in this life, we are the most miserable of creatures. / They must enter into the Kingdom of God through many hardships. / No one can be my disciple who does not carry his own cross and follow me. / You know that such troubles are a part of God's plan for us Christians.

Always be full of joy in the Lord; I say it again, rejoice! / I pray . . . that God who gives you hope will keep you happy and full of peace as you believe in him. / All honour to God, the God and Father of our Lord Jesus Christ; for it is his boundless mercy that has given us the privilege of being born again, so that we are now members of God's own family. Now we live in the hope of eternal life because Christ rose again from the dead. / You love him even though you have never seen him; though not seeing him, you trust him; and even now you are happy with the inexpressible joy that comes from heaven itself. / For because of our faith, he has brought us into this place of highest privilege where we now stand, and we confidently and joyfully look forward actually to becoming all that God has had in mind for us to be.

Rom. 12:12. Col. 1:5. 1 Cor. 15:19. Acts 14:22. Lk. 14:27. 1 Thess. 3:3. Phil. 4:4. Rom. 15:13. 1 Pet. 1:3. 1 Pet. 1:8. Rom. 5:2.

*I am poor and needy, yet the Lord is thinking
about me right now!*

'I know the plans I have for you,' says the Lord. 'They
are plans for good and not for evil.' / This plan of mine
is not what you would work out, neither are my
thoughts the same as yours! For just as the heavens
are higher than the earth, so are my ways higher than
yours, and my thoughts than yours.

How precious it is, Lord, to realize that you are
thinking about me constantly! I can't even count how
many times a day your thoughts turn towards me. And
when I wake in the morning, you are still thinking of
me! / O Lord, what miracles you do! And how deep are
your thoughts! / O Lord my God, many and many a
time you have done great miracles for us, and we are
ever in your thoughts.

Few of you who follow Christ have big names or
power or wealth. / God has chosen poor people to be
rich in faith, and the kingdom of heaven is theirs, for
that is the gift God has promised to all those who
love him. / We own nothing, and yet we enjoy everything. / The endless treasures available . . . in Christ.

Ps. 40:17. Jer. 29:11. Is. 55:8, 9. Ps. 139:17, 18. Ps. 92:5. Ps. 40:5.
1 Cor. 1:26. Jas. 2:5. 2 Cor. 6:10. Eph. 3:8.

You have been weighed in God's balances and
have failed the test.

The Lord knows what you have done, and he will
judge your deeds.

Your pretence brings you honour from the people,
but it is an abomination in the sight of God. / Men
judge by outward appearance, but I look at a man's
thoughts and intentions. / Don't be misled; remember
that you can't ignore God and get away with it: a man
will always reap just the kind of crop he sows! If he
sows to please his own wrong desires, he will be
planting seeds of evil and he will surely reap a harvest
of spiritual decay and death; but if he plants the good
things of the Spirit, he will reap the everlasting life
which the Holy Spirit gives him.

What profit is there if you gain the whole world –
and lose eternal life? What can be compared with the
value of eternal life? / All these things that I once
thought very worthwhile – now I've thrown them all
away so that I can put my trust and hope in Christ
alone.

You deserve honesty from the heart; yes, utter sincerity and truthfulness. / You have come even in the
night and found nothing amiss and know that I have
told the truth.

Dan. 5:27. 1 Sam. 2:3. Lk. 16:15. 1 Sam. 16:7. Gal. 6:7, 8. Mt. 16:26.
Phil. 3:7. Ps. 51:6. Ps. 17:3.

Christ rose first.

'I must fall and die like a grain of wheat that falls between the furrows of the earth. Unless I die I will be alone – a single seed. But my death will produce many new wheat grains – a plentiful harvest of new lives.' / Christ actually did rise from the dead, and has become the first of millions who will come back to life again some day. / You have become a part of him, and so you died with him, so to speak, when he died; and now you share his new life, and shall rise as he did. / Our Saviour the Lord Jesus Christ . . . will take these dying bodies of ours and change them into glorious bodies like his own, using the same mighty power that he will use to conquer all else everywhere.

He is the leader of all who arise from the dead, so that he is first in everything. / And if the Spirit of God, who raised up Jesus from the dead, lives in you, he will make your dying bodies live again after you die, by means of this same Holy Spirit living within you.

I am the one who raises the dead and gives them life again. Anyone who believes in me, even though he dies like anyone else, shall live again.

1 Cor. 15:23. Jn. 12:24. 1 Cor. 15:20. Rom. 6:5. Phil. 3:20, 21. Col. 1:18. Rom. 8:11. Jn. 11:25.

*He has satisfied the hungry hearts and sent the rich
away with empty hands.*

You say, 'I am rich, with everything I want; I don't
need a thing!' And you don't realize that spiritually you
are wretched and miserable and poor and blind and
naked. My advice to you is to buy pure gold from me,
gold purified by fire – only then will you truly be rich.
I continually discipline and punish everyone I love; so I
must punish you, unless you turn from your indifference
and become enthusiastic about the things of God.

Happy are those who long for justice for they shall
surely have it. / When the poor and needy seek water
and there is none and their tongues are parched from
thirst, then I will answer when they cry to me. I, Israel's
God, will not ever forsake them. / It was I, Jehovah
your God, who brought you out of the land of Egypt.
Only test me! Open your mouth wide and see if I won't
fill it. You will receive every blessing you can use!

Why spend your money on foodstuffs that don't give
you strength? Why pay for groceries that don't do
you any good? Listen and I'll tell you where to get
good food that fattens up the soul! / I am the Bread
of Life.

Lk. 1:53. Rev. 3:17–19. Mt. 5:6. Is. 41:17. Ps. 81:10. Is. 55:2. Jn. 6:35.

My feet are slipping and I was almost gone.

I screamed, 'I'm slipping, Lord!' and he was kind and saved me. / Simon, Simon, Satan has asked to have you, to sift you like wheat, but I have pleaded in prayer for you that your faith should not completely fail.

Don't you know that this good man, though you trip him up seven times, will each time rise again? / If they fall it isn't fatal, for the Lord holds them with his hand.

Do not rejoice against me, O my enemy, for though I fall, I will rise again! When I sit in darkness, the Lord himself will be my Light.

He will deliver you again and again, so that no evil can touch you.

If you sin, there is someone to plead for you before the Father. His name is Jesus Christ, the one who is all that is good and who pleases God completely. / He is able to save completely all who come to God through him. Since he will live forever, he will always be there to remind God that he has paid for their sins with his blood.

Ps. 73:2. Ps. 94:18. Lk. 22:31, 32. Prov. 24:16. Ps. 37:24. Mic. 7:8. Job 5:19. 1 Jn. 2:1. Hebr. 7:25.

I will give them one heart and mind to worship me forever.

I will give you a new heart – I will give you new and right desires – and put a new spirit within you. I will take out your stony hearts of sin and give you new hearts of love. / The Lord is good and glad to teach the proper path to all who go astray; he will teach the ways that are right and best to those who humbly turn to him. And when we obey him, every path he guides us on is fragrant with his lovingkindness and his truth.

That they will be of one heart and mind, just as you and I are, Father – that just as you are in me and I am in you, so they will be in us, and the world will believe you sent me.

Live and act in a way worthy of those who have been chosen for such wonderful blessings as these. Be humble and gentle. Be patient with each other, making allowance for each other's faults because of your love. Try always to be led along together by the Holy Spirit, and so be at peace with one another. We are all parts of one body, we have the same Spirit, and we have all been called to the same glorious future. For us there is only one Lord, one faith, one baptism, and we all have the same God and Father who is over us all and in us all, and living through every part of us.

Jer. 32:39. Ezk. 36:26. Ps. 25:8–10. Jn. 17:21. Eph. 4:1–6.

They that wait upon the Lord shall renew their strength.

When I am weak, then I am strong. / The Lord . . . has given me the strength to perform this task.

'I am with you; that is all you need. My power shows up best in weak people.' Now I am glad to boast about how weak I am; I am glad to be a living demonstration of Christ's power, instead of showing off my own power and abilities. / Trust in the Lord God always, for in the Lord Jehovah is your everlasting strength.

Give your burdens to the Lord. He will carry them. He will not permit the godly to slip or fall. / Their weapons were shattered by the Mighty One of Jacob, the Shepherd, the Rock of Israel.

I will not let you go until you bless me.

'You come to me with a sword and a spear, but I come to you in the name of the Lord of the armies of heaven and of Israel – the very God whom you have defied.' / I will rejoice in the Lord. He shall rescue me! From the bottom of my heart praise rises to him. Where is his equal in all of heaven and earth? Who else protects the weak and helpless from the strong?

Is. 40:31. 2 Cor. 12:10. Is. 49:5. 2 Cor. 12:9. Is. 26:4. Ps. 55:22. Gen. 49:24. Gen. 32:26. 1 Sam. 17:45. Ps. 35:9, 10.

*Don't copy the behaviour and customs of this
world, but be a new and different person with a
freshness in all you do and think.*

Don't you realize that making friends with God's
enemies – the evil pleasures of this world – makes you
an enemy of God? I say it again, that if your aim is to
enjoy the evil pleasure of the godless world, you cannot
also be a friend of God.

Don't enter into partnership with those who do not
love the Lord, for what do the people of God have in
common with the people of sin? How can light live with
darkness? And what harmony can there be between
Christ and the devil? How can a Christian be a partner
with one who doesn't believe? / Stop loving this evil
world and all that it offers you, for when you love these
things you show that you do not really love God. This
world is fading away, and these evil, forbidden things
will go with it, but whoever keeps doing the will of God
will live for ever.

You went along with the crowd and were just like all
the others, full of sin, obeying Satan, the mighty prince
of the power of the air. / That isn't the way Christ
taught you! If you have really heard his voice and
learned from him the truths concerning himself, then
throw off your old evil nature.

Rom. 12:2. Jas. 4:4. 2 Cor. 6:14, 15. 1 Jn. 2:15, 17. Eph. 2:2. Eph. 4:20–22.

Men go off to work until the evening shadows fall again.

All your life you will sweat to master it, until your dying day. Then you will return to the ground from which you came. / Even while we were still there with you we gave you this rule: He who does not work shall not eat. / This should be your ambition: to live a quiet life, minding your own business and doing your own work.

Whatever you do, do well, for in death, where you are going, there is no working or planning, or knowing, or understanding. / There is little time left before the night falls and all work comes to an end.

And let us not get tired of doing what is right, for after a while we will reap a harvest of blessing if we don't get discouraged and give up. / Always abounding in the Lord's work, for you know that nothing you do for the Lord is ever wasted.

There is a full, complete rest *still waiting* for the people of God. / They could have rest in their own land if they would obey him, if they were kind and good.

Ps. 104:23. Gen. 3:19. 2 Thess. 3:10. 1 Thess. 4:11. Ecc. 9:10. Jn. 9:4. Gal. 6:9. 1 Cor. 15:58. Hebr. 4:9. Is. 28:12.

I have seen what they do, but I will heal them anyway!

I am the Lord who heals you.

O Lord, you have examined my heart and know everything about me. You know when I sit or stand. When far away you know my every thought. You chart the path ahead of me, and tell me where to stop and rest. Every moment, you know where I am. / You spread out our sins before you – our secret sins – and see them all. / He knows about everyone, everywhere. Everything about us is bare and wide open to the all-seeing eyes of our living God; nothing can be hidden from him to whom we must explain all that we have done.

'Come, let's talk this over!' says the Lord; 'no matter how deep the stain of your sins, I can take it out and make you as clean as freshly fallen snow. Even if you are stained as red as crimson, I can make you white as wool!' / He was wounded and bruised for *our* sins. He was chastised that we might have peace; he was lashed – and we were healed! / He has sent me to comfort the broken-hearted. / Your faith has made you well.

Is. 57:18. Ex. 15:26. Ps. 139:1–3. Ps. 90:8. Hebr. 4:13. Is. 1:18. Is. 53:5. Is. 61:1. Mk. 5:34.

The Lord is on my side.

In your day of trouble, may the Lord be with you!
May the God of Jacob keep you from all harm. May
he send you aid from his sanctuary in Zion. May there
be shouts of joy when we hear the news of your victory,
flags flying with praise to God for all that he has done
for you. May he answer all your prayers! Some nations
boast of armies and of weaponry, but our boast is in
the Lord our God. Those nations will collapse and
perish; we will arise to stand firm and sure!

He will come like a flood-tide driven by Jehovah's
breath. / Remember this – the wrong desires that come
into your life aren't anything new and different. Many
others have faced exactly the same problems before you.
And no temptation is irresistible. You can trust God to
keep the temptation from becoming so strong that you
can't stand up against it, for he has promised this and
will do what he says. He will show you how to escape
temptation's power so that you can bear up patiently
against it.

If God is on our side, who can ever be against us? /
He is for me! How can I be afraid? What can mere
man to to me?

Our God is able to deliver us; and he will deliver
us out of your hand.

Ps. 118:7. Ps. 20:1, 2, 5, 7, 8. Is. 59:19. 1 Cor. 10:13. Rom. 8:31.
Ps. 118:6. Dan. 3:17.

If anyone is thirsty, let him come to me and drink.

I long, yes, faint with longing to be able to enter your courtyard and come near to the Living God. / O God, my God! How I search for you! How I thirst for you in this parched and weary land where there is no water. How I long to find you! How I wish I could go into your sanctuary to see your strength and glory.

Is anyone thirsty? Come and drink – even if you have no money! Come, take your choice of wine and milk – it's all free! / The Spirit and the bride say, 'Come.' Let each one who hears them say the same, 'Come.' Let the thirsty one come – anyone who wants to; let him come and drink the water of life without charge. / But the water I give them . . . becomes a perpetual spring within them, watering them forever with eternal life. / I am the A and Z – the Beginning and the End. I will give to the thirsty the springs of the water of life – as a gift. / My blood is the true drink.

Beloved, eat and drink! Yes, drink deeply!

Jn. 7:37. Ps. 84:2. Ps. 63:1, 2. Is. 55:1. Rev. 22:17. Jn. 4:14. Rev. 21:6. Jn. 6:55. Song 5:1.

You are the world's seasoning.

Be beautiful inside, in your hearts, with the lasting charm of a gentle and quiet spirit which is so precious to God. / For you have a new life. It was not passed on to you from your parents, for the life they gave you will fade away. This new one will last forever, for it comes from Christ, God's ever-living message to men. / Anyone who believes in me, even though he dies like anyone else, shall live again. / Sons of God, for they are raised up in new life from the dead. / The glorious, ever-living God.

If anyone doesn't have the Spirit of Christ living in him, he is not a Christian at all. Yet, even though Christ lives within you, your body will die because of sin; but your spirit will live for Christ has pardoned it. And if the Spirit of God, who raised up Jesus from the dead, lives in you, he will make your dying bodies live again after you die, by means of this same Holy Spirit living within you. / Our earthly bodies which die and decay are different from the bodies we shall have when we come back to life again, for they will never die.

Good salt is worthless if it loses its saltiness; it can't season anything. So don't lose your flavour! Live in peace with each other.

Mt. 5:13. 1 Pet. 3:4. 1 Pet. 1:23. Jn. 11:25. Lk. 20:36. Rom. 1:23.
Rom. 8:9–11. 1 Cor. 15:42. Mk. 9:50.

I, even I, am he who comforts you.

What a wonderful God we have – he is the Father of our Lord Jesus Christ, the source of every mercy, and the one who so wonderfully comforts and strengthens us in our hardships and trials. And why does he do this? So that when others are troubled, needing our sympathy and encouragement, we can pass on to them this same help and comfort God has given us. / He is like a father to us, tender and sympathetic to those who reverence him. For he knows we are but dust. / I will comfort you there as a little one is comforted by its mother. / Let him have all your worries and cares, for he is always thinking about you and watching everything that concerns you.

But you are merciful and gentle, Lord, slow in getting angry, full of constant lovingkindness and of truth.

Another Comforter . . . the Holy Spirit, the Spirit who leads into all truth. / The Holy Spirit helps us with our daily problems.

He will wipe away all tears from their eyes, and there shall be no more death, or sorrow, or crying, or pain. All of that has gone forever.

Is. 51:12. 2 Cor. 1:3, 4. Ps. 103:13, 14. Is. 66:13. 1 Pet. 5:7. Ps. 86:15. Jn. 14:16, 17. Rom. 8:26. Rev. 21:4.

God . . . is the one who invited you into this wonderful friendship with his Son, even Christ our Lord.

I was there on the holy mountain when he shone out with honour given him by God his Father; I heard that glorious, majestic voice calling down from heaven, saying, 'This is my much-loved Son; I am well pleased with him.' / How very much our heavenly Father loves us, for he allows us to be called his children.

Follow God's example in everything you do just as a much-loved child imitates his father. / Since we are his children, we will share his treasures – for all God gives to his Son Jesus is now ours too.

God's Son shines out with God's glory, and all that God's Son is and does marks him as God. / Let your good deeds glow for all to see, so that they will praise your heavenly Father.

Keep your eyes on Jesus, our leader and instructor. He was willing to die a shameful death on the cross because of the joy he knew would be his afterwards; and now he sits in the place of honour by the throne of God. / I have told them many things while I was with them so that they would be filled with my joy. / The more we undergo sufferings for Christ, the more he will shower us with his comfort and encouragement.

1 Cor. 1:9. 2 Pet. 1:17, 18. 1 Jn. 3:1. Eph. 5:1. Rom. 8:17. Hebr. 1:3. Mt. 5:16. Hebr. 12:2. Jn. 17:13. 2 Cor. 1:5.

Sin need never again be your master, for now you are no longer tied to the law where sin enslaves you, but you are free under God's favour and mercy.

Does this mean that now we can go ahead and sin and not worry about it? (For our salvation does not depend on keeping the law, but on receiving God's grace.) Of course not! / You 'died', as it were, with Christ on the cross; and since you are 'dead', you are no longer 'married to the law', and it has no more control over you. Then you came back to life again when Christ did, and are a new person. And now you are 'married', so to speak, to the one who rose from the dead, so that you can produce good fruit, that is, good deeds for God. / For sin – the sting that causes death – will all be gone; and the law, which reveals our sins, will no longer be our judge. How we thank God for all of this! It is he who makes us victorious through Jesus Christ our Lord!

The power of the life-giving Spirit – and this power is mine through Christ Jesus – has freed me from the vicious circle of sin and death. / You are slaves to sin, every one of you. So if the Son sets you free, you will indeed be free.

So Christ has made us free. Now make sure that you stay free and don't get tied up again in the chains of slavery.

Rom. 6:14. Rom. 6:15. Rom. 7:4. 1 Cor. 15:56, 57. Rom. 8:2. Jn. 8:34, 36. Gal. 5:1.

A doubtful mind will be unsettled as a wave of the sea that is driven and tossed by the wind.

Anyone who lets himself be distracted from the work I plan for him is not fit for the Kingdom of God.

You can never please God without faith, without depending on him. Anyone who wants to come to God must believe that there is a God and that he rewards those who sincerely look for him. / When you ask him, be sure that you really expect him to tell you. If you don't ask with faith, don't expect the Lord to give you any solid answer. / You can pray for *anything,* and *if you believe, you have it;* it's yours!

We will no longer be like children, for ever changing our minds about what we believe because someone has told us something different, or has cleverly lied to us and made the lie sound like the truth. Instead, we will lovingly follow the truth at all times – speaking . . . in every way like Christ who is the head of his body, the church.

Live in me. / Be strong and steady, always abounding in the Lord's work, for you know that nothing you do for the Lord is ever wasted.

Jas. 1:6. Lk. 9:62. Hebr. 11:6. Jas. 1:6, 7. Mk. 11:24. Eph. 4:14, 15. Jn. 15:4. 1 Cor. 15:58.

God looks at our motives.

The Lord watches over all the plans and paths of godly men, but the paths of the godless lead to doom. / The Lord will show you who are his, and who is holy. / Your Father who knows all secrets will reward you.

Search me, O God, and know my heart; test my thoughts. Point out anything you find in me that makes you sad, and lead me along the paths of everlasting life. / We need have no fear of someone who loves us perfectly; his perfect love for us eliminates all dread of what he might do to us.

Lord, you know how I long for my health once more. You hear my every sigh. / For I am overwhelmed and desperate, and you alone know which way I ought to turn. / The Father who knows all hearts knows, of course, what the Spirit is saying as he pleads for us in harmony with God's own will.

God's truth stands firm like a great rock, and nothing can shake it. It is a foundation stone with these words written on it: 'The Lord knows those who are really his,' and 'A person who calls himself a Christian should not be doing things that are wrong.'

Prov. 21:2. Ps. 1:6. Num. 16:5. Mt. 6:4. Ps. 139:23, 24. 1 Jn. 4:18.
Ps. 38:9. Ps. 142:3. Rom. 8:27. 2 Tim. 2:19.

Weeping may go on all night, but in the morning there is joy.

Troubles are a part of God's plan for us Christians. Even while we were still with you we warned you in advance that suffering would soon come – and it did. / I have told you all this so that you will have peace of heart and mind. Here on earth you will have many trials and sorrows; but take courage, for I have overcome the world.

When I awake in heaven, I will be fully satisfied, for I will see you face to face. / The night is far gone, the day of his return will soon be here. / He shall be as the light of the morning; a cloudless sunrise when the tender grass springs forth upon the earth; as sunshine after rain.

He will swallow up death forever. The Lord God will wipe away all tears. / He will wipe away all tears from their eyes, and there shall be no more death, or sorrow, or crying, or pain. All of that has gone forever. / We who are still alive and remain on the earth will be caught up with them in the clouds to meet the Lord in the air and remain with him forever. So comfort and encourage each other with this news.

Ps. 30:5. 1 Thess. 3:3, 4. Jn. 16:33. Ps. 17:15. Rom. 13:12. 2 Sam. 23:4. Is. 25:8. Rev. 21:4. 1 Thess. 4:17, 18.

He does not crush the weak.

It is a broken spirit you want – remorse and penitence. A broken and a contrite heart, O God, you will not ignore. / He heals the broken-hearted, binding up their wounds. / The high and lofty one who inhabits eternity, the Holy One, says this: I live in that high and holy place where those with contrite, humble spirits dwell; and I refresh the humble and give new courage to those with repentant hearts. For I will not fight against you forever, nor always show my wrath; if I did, all mankind would perish – the very souls that I have made.

I will seek my lost ones, those who strayed away, and bring them safely home again. I will put splints and bandages upon their broken limbs and heal the sick. / When they walk through the Valley of Weeping it will become a place of springs where pools of blessing and refreshment collect after rains! / So take a new grip with your tired hands, stand firm on your shaky legs, and mark out a straight, smooth path for your feet so that those who follow you, though weak and lame, will not fall and hurt themselves, but become strong. / Your God . . . is coming to save you.

Mt. 12:20. Ps. 51:17. Ps. 147:3. Is. 57:15, 16. Ezk. 34:16. Ps. 84:6. Hebr. 12:12, 13. Is. 35:4.

*Oh, put God to the test and see how kind he is! See
for yourself the way his mercies shower down
on all who trust in him.*

When the master of ceremonies tasted the water that
was now wine, not knowing where it had come from,
he called the bridegroom over. 'This is wonderful
stuff!' he said. 'You're different from most. Usually a
host uses the best wine first, and afterwards, when
everyone is full and doesn't care, then he brings out
the cheaper sort. But you have kept the best for the
last!'

We can choose the sounds we want to listen to; we
can choose the taste we want in food. / I believe
and therefore I speak. / I know the one in whom I trust. /
I am seated in his much-desired shade and his fruit is
lovely to eat.

How patient he is. / Since he did not spare even his
own Son for us but gave him up for us all, won't he
also surely give us everything else?

If you have tasted the Lord's goodness and kindness,
cry for more, as a baby cries for his milk.

Make everyone rejoice who puts his trust in you.
Keep them shouting for joy because you are defending
them. Fill all who love you with your happiness.

*Ps. 34:8. Jn. 2:9, 10. Job 34:3. 2 Cor. 4:13. 2 Tim. 1:12. Song 2:3.
Rom. 2:4. Rom. 8:32. 1 Pet. 2:2, 3. Ps. 5:11.*

Open my eyes to see wonderful things in your Word.

He opened their minds to understand at last these many scriptures. / Then he explained to them that only they were permitted to understand about the Kingdom of Heaven, and others were not. / And Jesus prayed this prayer: 'O Father, Lord of heaven and earth, thank you for hiding the truth from those who think themselves so wise, and for revealing it to little children. Yes, Father, for it pleased you to do it this way. / And God has actually given us his Spirit (not the world's spirit) to tell us about the wonderful free gifts of grace and blessing that God has given us. / How precious it is, Lord, to realize that you are thinking about me constantly! I can't even count how many times a day your thoughts turn towards me. And when I wake in the morning, you are still thinking of me! / Oh, what a wonderful God we have! How great are his wisdom and knowledge and riches! How impossible it is for us to understand his decisions and his methods! For who among us can know the mind of the Lord? Who knows enough to be his counsellor and guide? For everything comes from God alone. Everything lives by his power, and everything is for his glory. To him be glory evermore.

Ps. 119:18. Lk. 24:45. Mt. 13:11. Mt. 11:25, 26. 1 Cor. 2:12.
Ps. 139:17, 18. Rom. 11:33, 34, 36.

'The Spring of the Man Who Prayed.'

If you only knew what a wonderful gift God has for you, and who I am, you would ask me for some *living* water! / 'If anyone is thirsty, let him come to me and drink.' He was speaking of the Holy Spirit, who would be given to everyone believing in him.

Bring all the tithes into the storehouse so that there will be food enough in my Temple; if you do, I will open up the windows of heaven for you and pour out a blessing so great you won't have room enough to take it in! Try it! Let me prove it to you! / If even sinful persons like yourselves give children what they need, don't you realize that your heavenly Father will do at least as much, and give the Holy Spirit to those who ask for him? / Keep on asking and you will keep on getting; keep on looking and you will keep on finding.

And because we are his sons God has sent the Spirit of his Son into our hearts, so now we can rightly speak of God as our dear Father. / And so we should not be like cringing, fearful slaves, but we should behave like God's very own children, adopted into the bosom of his family, and calling to him, 'Father, Father.'

Judg. 15:19. Jn. 4:10. Jn. 7:37, 39. Mal. 3:10. Lk. 11:13. Lk. 11:9. Gal. 4:6. Rom. 8:15.

God . . . full of kindness through Christ.

I will make my goodness pass before you, and I will
announce to you the meaning of my name Jehovah, the
Lord. I show kindness and mercy to anyone I want to. /
God pities him and says, 'Set him free. Do not make
him die, for I have found a substitute.' / Yet now
God declares us 'not guilty' of offending him if we trust
in Jesus Christ, who in his kindness freely takes away
our sins. For God sent Christ Jesus to take the punishment for our sins and to end all God's anger against us.
He used Christ's blood and our faith as the means of
saving us from his wrath. In this way he was being
entirely fair, even though he did not punish those who
sinned in former times. For he was looking forward to
the time when Christ would come and take away those
sins. / Jesus Christ brought us loving forgiveness.

   Because of his kindness you have been saved through
trusting Christ. And even trusting is not of yourselves;
it too is a gift from God. / May God our Father and
Jesus Christ our Lord show you his kindness and mercy
and give you great peace of heart and mind. / God has
given each of you some special abilities; be sure to use
them to help each other, passing on to others God's
many kinds of blessings. / He gives us more and more
strength.

1 Pet. 5:10. Ex. 33:19. Job 33:24. Rom. 3:24, 25. Jn. 1:17. Eph. 2:8.
1 Tim. 1:2. 1 Pet. 4:10. Jas. 4:6.

Shall I look to the mountain gods for help? No!
My help is from Jehovah who made the mountains!
And the heavens too!

Just as the mountains surround and protect Jerusalem, so the Lord surrounds and protects his people. / He protects you day and night. He keeps you from all evil, and preserves your life. He keeps his eye upon you as you come and go, and always guards you.

O God enthroned in heaven, I lift my eyes to you. We look to Jehovah our God for his mercy and kindness just as a servant keeps his eyes upon his master or a slave girl watches her mistress for the slightest signal. / How much you have helped me – and how I rejoice through the night beneath the protecting shadow of your wings.

O our God, won't you stop them? We have no way to protect ourselves against this mighty army. We don't know what to do, but we are looking to you. / Oh, help us, Lord our God! For we trust in you alone to rescue us, and in your name we attack this vast horde. / My eyes are ever looking to the Lord for help, for he alone can rescue me. / Our help is from the Lord who made heaven and earth.

Ps. 121:1, 2. Ps. 125:2. Ps. 121:6–8. Ps. 123:1, 2. Ps. 63:7. 2 Chron. 20:12.
2 Chron. 14:11. Ps. 25:15. Ps. 124:8.

*The man who knows right from wrong and has
good judgment and common sense is happier than
the man who is immensely rich!*

Whoever finds me finds life.

The Lord says: Let the wise man not bask in his
wisdom, nor the mighty man in his might, nor the rich
man in his riches. Let them boast in this alone: That
they truly know me, and understand that I am the Lord
of justice and of righteousness whose love is steadfast;
and that I love to be this way. / *The reverence and
fear of God are basic to all wisdom.*

But all these things that I once thought very worthwhile – now I've thrown them all away so that I can put
my trust and hope in Christ alone. Yes, everything else
is worthless when compared with the priceless gain of
knowing Christ Jesus my Lord. I have put aside all else,
counting it worth less than nothing, in order that I can
have Christ. / In him lie hidden all the mighty, untapped treasures of wisdom and knowledge. / I,
Wisdom, give good advice and common sense. Because
of my strength, kings reign in power.

Christ Jesus . . . showed us God's plan of salvation;
he was the one who made us acceptable to God; he made
us pure and holy and gave himself himself to purchase
our salvation.

All who win souls are wise.

*Prov. 3:13. Prov. 8:35. Jer. 9:23, 24. Prov. 9:10. Phil. 3:7, 8. Col. 2:3.
Prov. 8:14. 1 Cor. 1:30. Prov. 11:30.*

We are poor, but we give rich spiritual gifts to others.

You know how full of love and kindness our Lord Jesus was: though he was so very rich, yet to help you he became so very poor, so that by being poor he could make you rich. / We have all benefited from the rich blessings he brought to us – blessing upon blessing heaped upon us. / And it is he who will supply all your needs from his riches in glory, because of what Christ Jesus has done for us. / Giving you everything you need and more, so that there will not only be enough for your own needs, but plenty left over to give joyfully to others.

God has chosen poor people to be rich in faith, and the kingdom of heaven is theirs, for that is the gift God has promised to all those who love him. / Notice among yourselves, dear brothers, that few of you who follow Christ have big names or power or wealth. Instead, God has deliberately chosen to use ideas the world considers foolish and of little worth in order to shame those people considered by the world as wise and great.

But this precious treasure – this light and power that now shine within us – is held in a perishable container, that is, in our weak bodies. Everyone can see that the glorious power within must be from God and is not our own.

2 Cor. 6:10. 2 Cor. 8:9. Jn. 1:16. Phil. 4:19. 2 Cor. 9:8. Jas. 2:5.
1 Cor. 1:26, 27. 2 Cor. 4:7.

We know that all that happens to us is working for our good if we love God and are fitting into his plans.

Man's futile wrath will bring you glory. You will use it as an ornament! / God turned into good what you meant for evil.

God has already given you everything you need. He has given you the whole world to use, and life and even death are your servants. He has given you all of the present and all of the future. All are yours, and you belong to Christ, and Christ is God's. / These sufferings of ours are for your benefit. And the more of you who are won to Christ, the more there are to thank him for his great kindness, and the more the Lord is glorified. That is why we never give up. Though our bodies are dying, our inner strength in the Lord is growing every day. These troubles and sufferings of ours are, after all, quite small and won't last very long. Yet this short time of distress will result in God's richest blessing upon us for ever and ever.

Dear brothers, is your life full of difficulties and temptations? Then be happy, for when the way is rough, your patience has a chance to grow. So let it grow, and don't try to squirm out of your problems. For when your patience is finally in full bloom, then you will be ready for anything, strong in character, full and complete.

Rom. 8:28. Ps. 76:10. Gen. 50:20. 1 Cor. 3:21–23. 2 Cor. 4:15–17. Jas. 1:2–4.

May God's love and the Holy Spirit's friendship be yours.

I will ask the Father and he will give you another Comforter, and he will never leave you. He is the Holy Spirit, the Spirit who leads into all truth. The world at large cannot receive him, for it isn't looking for him and doesn't recognize him. But you do, for he lives with you now and some day shall be in you. / He will not be presenting his own ideas, but will be passing on to you what he has heard. He shall praise me and bring me great honour by showing you my glory.

We know how dearly God loves us, and we feel this warm love everywhere within us because God has given us the Holy Spirit to fill our hearts with his love.

If you give yourself to the Lord, you and Christ are joined together as one person. Haven't you yet learned that your body is the home of the Holy Spirit God gave you, and that he lives within you? Your own body does not belong to you.

Don't cause the Holy Spirit sorrow by the way you live. Remember, he is the one who puts a mark on you to keep you for that day when salvation from sin will be complete. / And in the same way – by our faith – the Holy Spirit helps us with our daily problems and in our praying.

2 Cor. 13:14. Jn. 14:16, 17. Jn. 16:13, 14. Rom. 5:5. 1 Cor. 6:17, 19. Eph. 4:30. Rom. 8:26.

May he be pleased by all these thoughts about him, for he is the source of all my joy.

My lover is an apple tree, the finest in the orchard as compared with any of the other youths. I am seated in his much-desired shade and his fruit is lovely to eat. / For who in all of heaven can be compared with God? What mightiest angel is anything like him?

My beloved one is tanned and handsome, better than ten thousand others! / A pearl of great value. / He is far greater than any king in all the earth.

His head is purest gold, and he has wavy, raven hair. / God has put all things under his feet and made him the supreme head of the church. / He is the head of the body made up of his people – that is, his church.

His cheeks are like sweetly scented beds of spices. / He . . . tried to keep it a secret that he was there, but couldn't.

His lips are perfumed lilies, his breath like myrrh. / He says such wonderful things!

His legs are as pillars of marble set in sockets of finest gold, like cedars of Lebanon; none can rival him. / Let your favour shine again upon your servant. / Many say that God will never help us. Prove them wrong, O Lord.

Ps. 104:34. Song 2:3. Ps. 89:6. Song 5:10. Mt. 13:46. Rev. 1:5. Song 5:11. Eph. 1:22. Col. 1:18. Song 5:13. Mk. 7:24. Song 5:13. Jn. 7:46. Song 5:15. Ps. 31:16. Ps. 4:6.

My Father! If it is possible, let this cup be taken away from me. But I want your will, not mine.

Now my soul is deeply troubled. Shall I pray, 'Father, save me from what lies ahead'? But that is the very reason why I came.

I have come here from heaven to do the will of God who sent me, not to have my own way. / He humbled himself even further, going so far as actually to die a criminal's death on a cross. / Yet while Christ was here on earth he pleaded with God, praying with tears and agony of soul to the only one who could save him from [premature] death. And God heard his prayers because of his strong desire to obey God at all times. Even though Jesus was God's Son, he had to learn from experience what it was like to obey, when obeying meant suffering.

Don't you realize that I could ask my Father for thousands of angels to protect us, and he would send them instantly? / Yes, it was written long ago that the Messiah must suffer and die and rise again from the dead on the third day; and that this message of salvation should be taken from Jerusalem to all the nations: *There is forgiveness of sins for all who turn to me.*

Mt. 26:39. Jn. 12:27. Jn. 6:38. Phil. 2:8. Hebr. 5:7, 8. Mt. 26:53. Lk. 24:46, 47.

You did not abandon us.

Dear friends, don't be bewildered or surpised when you go through the fiery trials ahead, for this is no strange, unusual thing that is going to happen to you. / Let God train you, for he is doing what any loving father does for his children. Whoever heard of a son who was never corrected? If God doesn't punish you when you need it, as other fathers punish their sons, then it means that you aren't really God's son at all – that you don't really belong in his family.

The Lord is testing you to find out whether or not you really love him with all your heart and soul.

The Lord will not abandon his chosen people, for that would dishonour his great name. He made you a special nation for himself – just because he wanted to! / Can a mother forget her little child and not have love for her own son? Yet even if that should be, I will not forget you. / Happy is the man who has the God of Jacob as his helper, whose hope is in the Lord his God.

Don't you think that God will surely give justice to his people who plead with him day and night? Yes, he will answer them quickly!

Ezra 9:9. 1 Pet. 4:12. Hebr. 12:7, 8. Deut. 13:3. 1 Sam. 12:22. Is. 49:15. Ps. 146:5. Lk. 18:7, 8.

*Everyone who conquers will inherit all these
blessings.*

If being a Christian is only of value to us now in this
life, we are the most miserable of creatures. / They
were living for heaven. And now God is not ashamed to
be called their God, for he has made a heavenly city
for them. / And God has reserved for his children the
priceless gift of eternal life; it is kept in heaven for you,
pure and undefiled, beyond the reach of change and
decay.

God has already given you everything you need. He
has given you the whole world to use, and life and even
death are your servants. He has given you all of the
present and all of the future. All are yours. / No mere
man has ever seen, heard or even imagined what
wonderful things God has ready for those who love the
Lord. But we know about these things because God
has sent his Spirit to tell us, and his Spirit searches out
and shows us all of God's deepest secrets.

Beware of . . . losing the prize that you and I have
been working so hard to get. See to it that you win
your full reward from the Lord. / Let us strip off anything that slows us down or holds us back, and especially
those sins that wrap themselves so tightly around our
feet and trip us up; and let us run with patience the
particular race that God has set before us.

*Rev. 21:7. 1 Cor. 15:19. Hebr. 11:16. 1 Pet. 1:4. 1 Cor. 3:21, 22.
1 Cor. 2:9, 10. 2 Jn. 8. Hebr. 12:1.*

But as for me, I get as close to him as I can

Lord, I love your home, this shrine where the brilliant, dazzling splendour of your presence lives. / A single day spent in your Temple is better than a thousand anywhere else! I would rather be a doorman of the Temple of my God than live in palaces of wickedness. / How greatly to be envied are those you have chosen to come and live with you within the holy tabernacle courts! What joys await us among all the good things there.

The Lord is wonderfully good to those who wait for him, to those who seek for him. / Yet the Lord still waits for you to come to him, so he can show you his love; he will conquer you to bless you, just as he said. For the Lord is faithful to his promises.

And so, dear brothers, now we may walk right into the very Holy of Holies where God is, because of the blood of Jesus. This is the fresh, new, life-giving way which Christ has opened up for us by tearing the curtain – his human body – to let us into the holy presence of God . . . let us go right in, to God himself, with true hearts fully trusting him to receive us, because we have been sprinkled with Christ's blood to make us clean, and because our bodies have been washed with pure water.

Ps. 73:28. Ps. 26:8. Ps. 84:10. Ps. 65:4. Lam. 3:25. Is. 30:18. Hebr. 10:19, 20, 22.

You know how full of love and kindness our Lord Jesus was.

Christ took our human nature and lived here on earth among us and was full of loving forgiveness and truth. And some of us have seen his glory – the glory of the only Son of the heavenly Father! / You are the fairest of all; your words are filled with grace. / All who were there spoke well of him and were amazed by the beautiful words that fell from his lips.

Long to grow up into the fullness of your salvation; cry for this as a baby cries for his milk. / All who believe this know in their hearts that it is true. / I am telling you what I know and have seen.

Oh, put God to the test and see how kind he is! See for yourself the way his mercies shower down on all who trust in him. / I am seated in his much-desired shade and his fruit is lovely to eat.

I am with you; that is all you need. My power shows up best in weak people. / Christ has given each of us special abilities – whatever he wants us to have out of his rich storehouse of gifts. / Be sure to use them to help each other, passing on to others God's many kinds of blessings.

2 Cor. 8:9. Jn. 1:14. Ps. 45:2. Lk. 4:22. 1 Pet. 2:3. 1 Jn. 5:10. Jn. 3:11. Ps. 34:8. Song 2:3. 2 Cor. 12:9. Eph. 4:7. 1 Pet. 4:10.

*When your patience is finally in full bloom, then
you will be ready for anything, strong in character,
full and complete.*

There is wonderful joy ahead, even though the going is
rough for a while down here. These trials are only to
test your faith, to see whether or not it is strong and
pure. It is being tested as fire tests gold and purifies
it – and your faith is far more precious to God than
mere gold. So if your faith remains strong after being
tried in the test tube of fiery trials, it will bring you
much praise and glory and honour on the day of his
return. / We can rejoice, too, when we run into problems
and trials for we know that they are good for us – they
help us learn to be patient. And patience develops
strength of character in us and helps us trust God
more each time we use it until finally our hope and
faith are strong and steady.

It is good both to hope and wait quietly for the salvation of the Lord. / You were actually joyful when
all you owned was taken from you, knowing that
better things were awaiting you in heaven, things that
would be yours forever. Do not let this happy trust in
the Lord die away, no matter what happens. Remember
your reward! You need to keep on patiently doing
God's will if you want him to do for you all that he
has promised.

Jas. 1:4. 1 Pet. 1:6, 7. Rom. 5:3, 4. Lam. 3:26. Hebr. 10:34–36.

At God's command Jesus Christ will judge the secret lives of everyone.

Be careful not to jump to conclusions before the Lord returns as to whether someone is a good servant or not. When the Lord comes, he will turn on the light so that everyone can see exactly what each one of us is really like, deep down in our hearts. Then everyone will know why we have been doing the Lord's work. At that time God will give to each one whatever praise is coming to him. / The Father leaves all judgment of sin to his Son . . . because he is the Son of Man. / The Son of God, whose eyes penetrate like flames of fire.

Does God realize what is going on? / I remained silent – you thought I didn't care – but now your time of punishment has come, and I list all the above charges against you. / Hypocrisy cannot be hidden forever. It will become as evident as yeast in dough.

Lord . . . you hear my every sigh. / Dismiss all the charges against me, Lord, for I have tried to keep your laws and have trusted you without wavering. Cross-examine me, O Lord, and see that this is so; test my motives and affections too.

Rom. 2:16. 1 Cor. 4:5. Jn. 5:22, 27. Rev. 2:18. Ps. 73:11. Ps. 50:21. Lk. 12:1, 2. Ps. 38:9. Ps. 26:1, 2.

*He is the Rock. His work is perfect. Everything
he does is just and fair. He is faithful, without sin.*

God, who always judges fairly. / We must all stand
before Christ to be judged and have our lives laid
bare before him. Each of us will receive whatever he
deserves for the good or bad things he has done in his
earthly body. / Yes, each of us will give an account of
himself to God. / It is for a man's own sins that he will
die.

Awake, O sword, against my Shepherd, the man who
is my associate and equal, says the Lord of heaven's
armies. Strike down the Shepherd. / God laid on *him*
the guilt and sins of every one of us. / Mercy and truth
have met together. Grim justice and peace have
kissed! / God's mercy towards you will outweigh his
judgment against you. / The wages of sin is death, but
the free gift of God is eternal life through Jesus Christ
our Lord.

There is no other God but me – a just God and a
Saviour – no, not one! / In these days also he can receive
sinners . . . because Jesus took away their sins. He does
it on the basis of their trust in Jesus. / God declares
us 'not guilty' of offending him if we trust in Jesus
Christ, who in his kindness freely takes away our sins.

*Deut. 32:4. 1 Pet. 2:23. 2 Cor. 5:10. Rom. 14:12. Ezk. 18:4. Zech. 13:7.
Is. 53:6. Ps. 85:10. Jas. 2:13. Rom. 6:23. Is. 45:21. Rom. 3:26.
Rom. 3:24.*

Death is swallowed up in victory.

How we thank God for all of this! It is he who makes us victorious through Jesus Christ our Lord!

Since we, God's children, are human beings – made of flesh and blood – he became flesh and blood too by being born in human form; for only as a human being could he die and in dying break the power of the devil who had the power of death. Only in that way could he deliver those who through fear of death have been living all their lives as slaves to constant dread.

And since your old sin-loving nature 'died' with Christ, we know that you will share his new life. Christ rose from the dead and will never die again. Death no longer has any power over him. He died once for all to end sin's power, but now he lives forever in unbroken fellowship with God. So look upon your old sinful nature as dead and unresponsive to sin, and instead be alive to God, alert to him, through Jesus Christ our Lord.

Despite all this, overwhelming victory is ours through Christ who loved us enough to die for us.

1 Cor. 15:54. 1 Cor. 15:57. Hebr. 2:14, 15. Rom. 6:8–11. Rom. 8:37.

The serpent came to the woman. 'Really?' he asked. 'None of the fruit in the garden?'

Satan tempted him to get food by changing stones into loaves of bread. 'It will prove you are the Son of God,' he said. But Jesus told him, 'No! For the Scriptures tell us that bread won't feed men's souls: obedience to every word of God is what we need. It also tells us not to put the Lord God to a foolish test! The Scriptures say, "Worship only the Lord God. Obey only him."

'I am not allowed to eat anything or to drink any water at Bethel. The Lord strictly warned me against it.' But the old man said, 'I am a prophet too, just as you are; and an angel gave me a message from the Lord. I am to take you home with me and give you food and water.' But the old man was lying to him. So they went back together, and the prophet ate some food and drank some water at the old man's home. The prophet started off again. But as he was travelling along, a lion came out and killed him. The prophet . . . disobeyed the Lord's command; the Lord fulfilled his warning. / Let God's curses fall on anyone . . . who preaches any other way to be saved than the one we told you about; yes, if an angel comes from heaven and preaches any other message, let him be forever cursed. / I have thought much about your words, and stored them in my heart so that they would hold me back from sin.

Gen. 3:1. Mt. 4:3, 4, 7, 10, 11. 1 Kgs. 13:16–19, 24, 26. Gal. 1:8. Ps. 119:11.

*If you will humble yourselves under the mighty
hand of God, in his good time he will lift you up.*

Pride disgusts the Lord. Take my word for it – *proud
men shall be punished.*

And yet, O Lord, you are our Father. We are the
clay and you are the Potter. We are all formed by your
hand. Oh, do not be so angry with us, Lord, and do
not remember our sins for ever. Oh, look and see that
we are all your people. / You have punished me
greatly; but I needed it all, as a calf must be trained
for the yoke. Turn me again to you and restore me,
for you alone are the Lord, my God. I turned away
from God but I was sorry afterwards. I kicked myself
for my stupidity. I was thoroughly ashamed of all I did
in younger days. / It is good for a young man to be
under discipline, for it casues him to sit apart in silence
beneath the Lord's demands, to lie face downward in
the dust; then at last there is hope for him.

Misery comes upon them to punish them for sowing
seeds of sin. Mankind heads for sin and misery as
predictably as flames shoot upwards from a fire. /
Although God gives him grief, yet he will show compassion too, according to the greatness of his lovingkindness. For he does not enjoy afflicting men and
causing sorrow.

*1 Pet. 5:6. Prov. 16:5. Is. 64:8, 9. Jer. 31:18, 19. Lam. 3:27–29.
Job 5:6, 7. Lam. 3:32, 33.*

Aaron and his sons shall call down my blessings upon the people of Israel; and I myself will personally bless them.

O Lord our God, once we worshipped other gods; but now we worship you alone. / O God, why do you treat us as though we weren't your people, as though we were a heathen nation that never called you 'Lord?'

All the nations in the world shall see that you belong to the Lord, and they will stand in awe. / The Lord will not abandon his chosen people, for that would dishonour his great name. He made you a special nation for himself – just because he wanted to!

'O Lord, hear; O Lord, forgive. O Lord, listen to me and act! Don't delay – for your own sake, O my God, because your people and your city bear your name.' / Help us, God of our salvation! Help us for the honour of your name. Oh, save us and forgive our sins. Why should the heathen nations be allowed to scoff, 'Where is their God?' / The Lord is a strong fortress. The good men run to him and are safe. / The Lord saves the godly! He is their salvation and their refuge when trouble comes. Because they trust in him, he helps them and delivers them from the plots of evil men.

Num. 6:27. Is. 26:13. Is. 63:19. Deut. 28:10. 1 Sam. 12:22. Dan. 9:19. Ps. 79:9, 10. Prov. 18:10. Ps. 37:39, 40.

The heavens are telling the glory of God; they are a marvellous display of his craftsmanship.

Since earliest times men have seen the earth and sky and all God made, and have known of his existence and great eternal power. / He never left himself without a witness. / Day and night they keep on telling about God. Without a sound or word, silent in the skies, their message reaches out to all the world.

When I look up into the night skies and see the work of your fingers – the moon and the stars you have made – I cannot understand how you can bother with mere puny man, to pay any attention to him!

The sun has one kind of glory while the moon and stars have another kind. And the stars differ from each other in their beauty and brightness. In the same way, our earthly bodies which die and decay are different from the bodies we shall have when we come back to life again, for they will never die. / And those who are wise – the people of God – shall shine as brightly as the sun's brilliance, and those who turn many to righteousness will glitter like stars forever.

Ps. 19:1. Rom. 1:20. Acts 14:17. Ps. 19:2, 3. Ps. 8:3, 4. 1 Cor. 15:41, 42. Dan. 12:3.

We know what real love is from Christ's example in dying for us.

God's marvellous love . . . so great that you will never see the end of it or fully know or understand it. / The greatest love is shown when a person lays down his life for his friends. / You know how full of love and kindness our Lord Jesus was: though he was so very rich, yet to help you he became so very poor, so that by being poor he could make you rich. / Since God loved us as much as that, we surely ought to love each other too. / Be kind to each other, tenderhearted, forgiving one another, just as God has forgiven you because you belong to Christ. / Be gentle and ready to forgive; never hold grudges. Remember, the Lord forgave you, so you must forgive others. / For even I, the Man from Heaven, am not here to be served, but to help others, and to give my life as a ransom for many. / Christ, who suffered for you, is your example. Follow in his steps.

You ought to wash each other's feet. I have given you an example to follow: do as I have done to you. / We . . . ought to lay down our lives for our Christian brothers.

1 Jn. 3:16. Eph. 3:17, 19. Jn. 15:13. 2 Cor. 8:9. 1 Jn. 4:11. Eph. 4:32. Col. 3:13. Mk. 10:45. 1 Pet. 2:21. Jn. 13:14, 15. 1 Jn. 3:16.

*The Son can do nothing by himself. He does only
what he sees the Father doing, and in the same way.*

The Lord grants wisdom! His every word is a treasure
of knowledge and understanding. He grants good sense
to the godly – his saints. He is their shield, protecting
them and guarding their pathway. / I will give you the
right words and such logic that none of your opponents
will be able to reply.

Wait for the Lord, and he will come and save you!
Be brave, stouthearted and courageous. Yes, wait and
he will help you. / I am with you; that is all you
need. My power shows up best in weak people.

God the Father has chosen you and Jesus Christ
has kept you safe. / We who have been made holy by
Jesus, now have the same Father as he has. That is why
Jesus is not ashamed to call us his brothers.

Am I not everywhere in all of heaven and earth? /
His body, filled with himself, the author and giver of
everything everywhere.

I am the Lord, and there is no other Saviour. /
He is indeed the Saviour of the world.

May God the Father and Christ Jesus our Saviour
give you his blessings and his peace.

*Jn. 5:19. Prov. 2:6–8. Lk. 21:15. Ps. 27:14. 2 Cor. 12:9. Jude 1.
Hebr. 2:11. Jer. 23:24. Eph. 1:23. Is. 43:11. Jn. 4:42. Tit. 1:4.*

He knows every detail of what is happening to me; and when he has examined me, he will pronounce me completely innocent – as pure as solid gold!

He knows we are but dust. / He does not enjoy afflicting men and causing sorrow.

God's truth stands firm like a great rock, and nothing can shake it. It is a foundation stone with these words written on it: 'The Lord knows those who are really his,' and 'A person who calls himself a Christian should not be doing things that are wrong.' In a wealthy home there are dishes made of gold and silver as well as some made from wood and clay. The expensive dishes are used for guests, and the cheap ones are used in the kitchen or to put rubbish in. If you stay away from sin you will be like one of these dishes made of purest gold – the very best in the house – so that Christ himself can use you for his highest purposes.

Like a refiner of silver he will sit and closely watch as the dross is burned away. / I will bring the third that remain through the fire and make them pure, as gold and silver are refined and purified by fire. They will call upon my name and I will hear them; I will say, 'These are my people,' and they will say, 'The Lord is our God.'

Job 23:10. Ps. 103:14. Lam. 3:33. 2 Tim. 2:19–21. Mal. 3:3. Zech. 13:9.

*Show me the path where I should go, O Lord;
point out the right road for me to walk.*

Moses talked there with the Lord and said to him . . .
'You say you are my friend, and that I have found
favour before you; please, if this is really so, guide me
clearly along the way you want me to travel so that I
will understand you and walk acceptably before you.'
And the Lord replied, 'I myself will go with you and
give you success.' / He revealed his will and nature to
Moses and the people of Israel.

He will teach the ways that are right and best to those
who humbly turn to him. Where is the man who fears
the Lord? God will teach him how to choose the best. /
Trust the Lord completely; don't ever trust yourself.
In everything you do, put God first, and he will direct
you and crown your efforts with success.

You have let me experience the joys of life and the
exquisite pleasures of your own eternal presence. / I will
instruct you (says the Lord) and guide you along the
best pathway for your life; I will advise you and watch
your progress. / The good man walks along in the ever-
brightening light of God's favour; the dawn gives way
to morning splendour.

*Ps. 25:4. Ex. 33:12–14. Ps. 103:7. Ps. 25:9, 12. Prov. 3:5, 6. Ps. 16:11.
Ps. 32:8. Prov. 4:18.*

When the Holy Spirit controls our lives he will produce . . . self-control.

To win the contest you must deny yourselves many things that would keep you from doing your best. An athlete goes to all this trouble just to win a ribbon or a silver cup, but we do it for a heavenly reward that never disappears. So I run straight to the goal with purpose in every step. I fight to win. I'm not just shadow-boxing or playing around. Like an athlete I punish my body, treating it roughly, training it to do what it should, not what it wants to. Otherwise I fear that after enlisting others for the race, I myself might be declared unfit and ordered to stand aside.

Don't drink too much wine, for many evils lie along that path; be filled instead with the Holy Spirit, and controlled by him.

If anyone wants to be a follower of mine, let him deny himself and take up his cross and follow me.

Be on your guard, not asleep like the others. Watch for his return and stay sober. Night is the time for sleep and the time when people get drunk. But let us who live in the light keep sober. / God wants us to turn from godless living and sinful pleasures and to live good, God-fearing lives day after day.

Gal. 5:22, 23. 1 Cor. 9:25–27. Eph. 5:18. Mt. 16:24. 1 Thess. 5:6–8. Tit. 2:12.

*Become more and more in every way like Christ
who is the head of his body, the church.*

First a leaf-blade pushed through, and later the wheat-
heads formed and finally the grain ripened. / Until
finally we all believe alike about our salvation and
about our Saviour, God's Son, and all become full-
grown in the Lord – yes, to the point of being filled
full with Christ.

They are only comparing themselves with each other,
and measuring themselves against their own little ideas.
What stupidity! If anyone is going to boast, let him
boast about what the Lord has done and not about
himself. When someone boasts about himself and how
well he has done, it doesn't count for much. But when
the Lord commends him, that's different!

Shadows of the real thing – of Christ himself. Don't
let anyone declare you lost when you refuse to worship
angels, as they say you must. These proud men have a
very clever imagination. But they are not connected to
Christ, the head to which all of us who are his body
are joined; for we are joined together by his strong
sinews and we grow only as we get our nourishment
and strength from him.

Grow in spiritual strength and become better acquainted with our Lord and Saviour Jesus Christ.
*Eph. 4:15. Mk. 4:28. Eph. 4:13. 2 Cor. 10:12, 17, 18. Col. 2:17–19.
2 Pet. 3:18.*

The goat shall carry all the sins of the people into a land where no one lives, and the man shall let it loose in the wilderness.

He has removed our sins as far away from us as the east is from the west. / 'In those days,' says the Lord, 'no sin shall be found in Israel or in Judah, for I will pardon the remnant I preserve.' / I, yes, I alone am he who blots away your sins for my own sake and will never think of them again.

You will tread our sins beneath your feet; you will throw them into the depths of the ocean! Where is another God like you, who pardons the sins of the survivors among his people?

We are the ones who strayed away like sheep! *We,* who left God's paths to follow our own. Yet God laid on *him* the guilt and sins of every one of us! / He shall bear all their sins. Therefore I will give him the honours of one who is mighty and great, because he has poured out his soul unto death. He was counted as a sinner, and he bore the sins of many, and he pleaded with God for sinners. / The Lamb of God who takes away the world's sins! / In this man Jesus, there is forgiveness for your sins! Everyone who trusts in him is freed from all guilt and declared righteous.

Lev. 16:22. Ps. 103:12. Jer. 50:20. Is. 43:25. Mic. 7:19, 18. Is. 53:6. Is. 53:11, 12. Jn. 1:29. Acts 13:38, 39.

*What are you so puffed up about? What do you
have that God hasn't given you?*

Whatever I am now it is all because God poured out
such kindness and grace upon me. / It was a happy day
for him when he gave us our new lives, through the
truth of his word. / God's blessings are not given just
because someone decides to have them or works hard
to get them. / Then what can we boast about doing, to
earn our salvation? Nothing at all. / For it is from
God alone that you have your life through Christ Jesus.
If anyone is going to boast, let him boast only of what
the Lord has done.

Once you were under God's curse, doomed for ever
for your sins. You went along with the crowd and were
just like all the others, full of sin, obeying Satan, the
mighty prince of the power of the air, who is at work right
now in the hearts of those who are against the Lord.
All of us used to be just as they are, our lives expressing the evil within us, doing every wicked thing
that our passions or our evil thoughts might lead us
into. We started out bad, being born with evil natures,
and were under God's anger just like everyone else. /
Now your sins are washed away, and you are set apart
for God, and he has accepted you because of what the
Lord Jesus Christ and the Spirit of our God have done
for you.

*1 Cor. 4:7. 1 Cor. 15:10. Jas. 1:18. Rom. 9:16. Rom. 3:27. 1 Cor. 1:30, 31.
Eph. 2:1–3. 1 Cor. 6:11.*

All praise to him who always loves us and who set us free from our sins by pouring out his lifeblood for us.

Many waters cannot quench the flame of love, neither can the floods drown it. Love is strong as death. / The greatest love is shown when a person lays down his life for his friends.

He personally carried the load of our sins in his own body when he died on the cross, so that we can be finished with sin and live a good life from now on. For his wounds have healed ours! / So overflowing is his kindness towards us that he took away all our sins through the blood of his Son, by whom we are saved.

Your sins are washed away, and you are set apart for God, and he has accepted you because of what the Lord Jesus Christ and the Spirit of our God have done for you. / You have been chosen by God himself – you are priests of the King, you are holy and pure, you are God's very own – all this so that you may show to others how God called you out of the darkness into his wonderful light. / I plead with you to give your bodies to God. Let them be a living sacrifice, holy – the kind he can accept. When you think of what he has done for you, is this too much to ask?

Rev. 1:5. Song 8:7, 6. Jn. 15:13. 1 Pet. 2:24. Eph. 1:7. 1 Cor. 6:11.
1 Pet. 2:9. Rom. 12:1.

There are different kinds of service to God, but it is the same Lord we are serving.

Azmaveth (son of Adi-el) was the chief financial officer in charge of the palace treasuries, and Jonathan (son of Uzziah) was chief of the regional treasuries throughout the cities, villages, and fortresses of Israel. Ezri (son of Chelub) was manager of the labourers of the king's estates. And Shime-i from Ramath had the supervision of the king's vineyards; and Zabdi from Shiphma was responsible for his wine production and storage. These men were King David's overseers.

Here is a list of some of the parts he has placed in his church, which is his body: apostles, prophets – those who preach God's Word with inspiration, teachers, those who do miracles, those who have the gift of healing, those who can help others, those who can get others to work together, those who speak in languages they have never learned.

God has given each of you some special abilities; be sure to use them to help each other, passing on to others God's many kinds of blessings. Are you called to preach? Then preach as though God himself were speaking through you. Are you called to help others? Do it with all the strength and energy that God supplies, so that God will be glorified through Jesus Christ – to him be glory and power for ever and ever. Amen.

1 Cor. 12:5. 1 Chron. 27:25–27, 31. 1 Cor. 12:28. 1 Pet. 4:10, 11.

Moses didn't realize as he came back down the mountain with the tablets that his face glowed from being in the presence of God.

Glorify your name, not ours, O Lord! Cause everyone to praise your lovingkindness and your truth. / Sir, when did we ever see you hungry and feed you? Or thirsty and give you anything to drink? / When you did it to these my brothers you were doing it to me! / Be humble, thinking of others as better than yourself. / Serve each other with humble spirits.

His [Jesus'] appearance changed so that his face shone like the sun and his clothing became dazzling white. / Everyone in the Council Chamber saw Stephen's face become as radiant as an angel's! / I have given them the glory you gave me. / We Christians have no veil over our faces; we can be mirrors that brightly reflect the glory of the Lord. And as the Spirit of the Lord works within us, we become more and more like him.

You are the world's light – a city on a hill, glowing in the night for all to see. Don't hide your light! / Shine out among them like beacon lights, holding out to them the Word of Life.

Ex. 34:29. Ps. 115:1. Mt. 25:37. Mt. 25:40. Phil. 2:3. 1 Pet. 5:5.
Mt. 17:2. Acts 6:15. Jn. 17:22. 2 Cor. 3:18. Mt. 5:14, 15. Phil. 2:15,16.

*There are many ways in which God works in our
lives, but it is the same God who does the work
in and through all of us who are his.*

Some men from Manesseh deserted the Israeli army
and joined David. They were brave and able warriors,
and they assisted David when he fought against the
Amalek raiders at Ziklag. / The Holy Spirit displays
God's power through each of us as a means of helping
the entire church.

From the tribe of Issachar there were 200 leaders of
the tribe with their relatives – all men who understood
the mood of the times and knew the best course for
Israel to take. / To one person the Spirit gives the
ability to give wise advice; to another is given the
ability to speak with knowledge, and this comes from
the same Spirit.

From the tribe of Zebulun there were 50,000 trained
warriors; they were fully armed and totally loyal to
David. / I delight to do your will, my God, for your
law is written upon my heart!

God . . . has made many parts for our bodies and has
put each part just where he wants it. If one part suffers,
all parts suffer with it, and if one part is honoured,
all the parts are glad.

One Lord, one faith, one baptism.

*1 Cor. 12:6. 1 Chron. 12:19, 21. 1 Cor. 12:7. 1 Chron. 12:32. 1 Cor. 12:8.
1 Chron. 12:33. Ps. 40:8. 1 Cor. 12:18, 26. Eph. 4:5.*

I want you to trust me in your times of trouble,
so I can rescue you, and you can give me glory.

But O my soul, don't be discouraged. Don't be upset.
Expect God to act! For I know that I shall again have
plenty of reason to praise him for all that he will do.
He is my help! He is my God! / Lord, you know the
hopes of humble people. Surely you will hear their cries
and comfort their hearts by helping them. / O Lord,
you are so good and kind, so ready to forgive; so full
of mercy for all who ask your aid.

Jacob instructed all those in his household . . . to
wash themselves and to put on fresh clothing. 'For we
are going to Bethel,' he told them, 'and I will build an
altar there to the God who answered my prayers in
the day of my distress, and was with me on my
journey.' / I will bless the Lord and not forget the
glorious things he does for me.

I love the Lord because he hears my prayers and
answers them. Because he bends down and listens, I
will pray as long as I breathe! Death stared me in the
face – I was frightened and sad. Then I cried, 'Lord,
save me!'

Ps. 50:15. Ps. 42:11. Ps. 10:17. Ps. 86:5. Gen. 35:2, 3. Ps. 103:2.
Ps. 116:1–4.

His coming will not be delayed much longer.

Write my answer on a billboard, large and clear, so that anyone can read it at a glance and rush to tell the others. But these things I plan won't happen right away. Slowly, steadily, surely, the time approaches when the vision will be fulfilled. If it seems slow, do not despair, for these things will surely come to pass. Just be patient! They will not be overdue a single day!

But don't forget this, dear friends, that a day or a thousand years from now is like tomorrow to the Lord. He isn't really being slow about his promised return, even though it sometimes seems that way. But he is waiting, for the good reason that he is not willing that any should perish, and he is giving more time for sinners to repent. / But you are merciful and gentle, Lord, slow in getting angry, full of constant lovingkindness and of truth. / Oh, that you would burst forth from the skies and come down! How the mountains would quake in your presence! For since the world began no one has seen or heard of such a God as ours, who works for those who wait for him!

Hebr. 10:37. Hab. 2:2, 3. 2 Pet. 3:8, 9. Ps. 86:15. Is. 64:1, 4.

The Lord our God, the Almighty, reigns.

I know that you can do anything. / God can do what
men can't. / He does whatever he thinks best among
the company of heaven, as well as here among the inhabitants of earth. No one can stop him or challenge
him, saying, 'What do you mean by doing these
things?' / From eternity to eternity I am God. No one
can oppose what I do. / Father, Father . . . everything
is possible for you.

'Do you believe I can make you see?' 'Yes, Lord,'
they told him, 'we do.' Then he touched their eyes
and said, 'Because of your faith it will happen.' / *'If
you want to, you can heal me.' Jesus touches the man.
'I want to,' he says; 'be healed.'* / The Mighty God. /
I have been given all authority in heaven and earth.

Some nations boast of armies and of weaponry, but
our boast is in the Lord our God. / Be strong, be
brave, and do not be afraid . . . for there is someone
with us who is far greater than he is!

*Rev. 19:6. Job 42:2. Lk. 18:27. Dan. 4:35. Is. 43:13. Mk. 14:36.
Mt. 9:28, 29. Mt. 8:2, 3. Is. 9:6. Mt. 28:18. Ps. 20:7. 2 Chron. 32:7.*

What did the Lord say to you?

He has told you what he wants, and this is all it is: *to be
fair and just and merciful, and to walk humbly with your
God.* / To listen carefully to all he says to you, and to
obey for your own good the commandments I am giving
you today, and to love him, and to worship him with
all your hearts and souls.

Those who depend on the Jewish laws to save them
are under God's curse, for the Scriptures point out very
clearly, 'Cursed is everyone who at any time breaks a
single one of these laws that are written in God's Book
of the Law.' Consequently, it is clear that no one can
ever win God's favour by trying to keep the Jewish
laws, because God has said that the only way we can be
right in his sight is by faith. As the prophet Habakkuk
puts it, 'The man who finds life will find it through
trusting God.' Well then, why were the laws given?
They were added after the promise was given, to show
men how guilty they are of breaking God's laws. But this
system of law was to last only until the coming of Christ.

Long ago God spoke in many different ways to our
fathers through the prophets [in visions, dreams, and
even face to face] telling them little by little about his
plans. But now in these days he has spoken to us
through his Son.

Yes, Lord, I'm listening.

*1 Sam. 3:17. Mic. 6:8. Deut. 10:13. Gal. 3:10, 11, 19. Hebr. 1:1, 2.
1 Sam. 3:9.*

He will teach the ways that are right and best to those who humbly turn to him.

The meek and lowly are fortunate!

Again I looked throughout the earth and saw that the swiftest person does not always win the race, nor the strongest man the battle, and that wise men are often poor, and skilful men are not necessarily famous. / We should make plans – counting on God to direct us.

O God enthroned in heaven, I lift my eyes to you. We look to Jehovah our God for his mercy and kindness just as a servant keeps his eyes upon his master or a slave girl watches her mistress for the slightest signal. / Show me where to walk, for my prayer is sincere.

O our God, won't you stop them? We have no way to protect ourselves against this mighty army. We don't know what to do, but we are looking to you.

If you want to know what God wants you to do, ask him, and he will gladly tell you, for he is always ready to give a generous supply of wisdom to all who ask him; he will not resent it.

When the Holy Spirit, who is truth, comes, he will guide you into all truth.

Ps. 25:9. Mt. 5:5. Eccl. 9:11. Prov. 16:9. Ps. 123:1, 2. Ps. 143:8.
2 Chron. 20:12. Jas. 1:5. Jn. 16:13.

Bless me and my family forever! . . . for you,
Lord God, have promised it.

When you grant a blessing, Lord it is an eternal blessing! / The Lord's blessing is our greatest wealth. All our work adds nothing to it!

I remembered the words of the Lord Jesus, 'It is more blessed to give than to receive.' / When you give a dinner . . . invite the poor, the crippled, the lame, and the blind. Then at the resurrection of the godly, God will reward you for inviting those who can't repay you. / Come, blessed of my Father, into the Kingdom prepared for you from the founding of the world. For I was hungry and you fed me; I was thirsty and you gave me water; I was a stranger and you invited me into your homes; naked and you clothed me; sick and in prison, and you visited me.

Feed the hungry! Help those in trouble! Then your light will shine out from the darkness, and the darkness around you shall be as bright as day. And the Lord will guide you continually, and satisfy you with all good things.

For Jehovah God is our Light and our Protector.

2 Sam. 7:29. 1 Chron. 17:27. Prov. 10:22. Acts 20:35. Lk. 14:12–14. Mt. 25:34–36. Is. 58:10, 11. Ps. 84:11.

I am not afraid of anything that mere man can do to me.

Who then can ever keep Christ's love from us? When we have trouble or calamity, when we are hunted down or destroyed, is it because he doesn't love us any more? And if we are hungry, or penniless, or in danger, or threatened with death, has God deserted us? Despite all this, overwhelming victory is ours through Christ who loved us enough to die for us.

Don't be afraid of these who want to murder you. They can only kill the body; they have no power over your souls. But I'll tell you whom to fear – fear God who has the power to kill and then cast into hell.

Happy are those who are persecuted because they are good, for the Kingdom of Heaven is theirs. When you are reviled and persecuted and lied about because you are my followers – wonderful! Be *happy* about it! Be *very glad.* For a *tremendous reward* awaits you up in heaven. / But life is worth nothing unless I use it for doing the work assigned me by the Lord Jesus – the work of telling others the Good News about God's mighty kindness and love. / I will speak to kings . . . and they will listen with interest and respect.

Hebr. 13:6. Rom. 8:35, 37. Lk. 12:4, 5. Mt. 5:10–12. Acts 20:24. Ps. 119:46.

He . . . set my feet on a hard, firm path.

Christ . . . a mighty Rock of spiritual refreshment. /
Simon Peter answered, 'The Christ, the Messiah, the
Son of the living God.' Upon this rock I will build
my church; and all the powers of hell shall not prevail
against it. / There is salvation in no one else! Under
all heaven there is no other name for men to call upon
to save them.

Fully trusting him. No longer any room for doubt. /
A doubtful mind will be as unsettled as a wave of the
sea that is driven and tossed by the wind.

Who then can ever keep Christ's love from us? When
we have trouble or calamity, when we are hunted down
or destroyed, is it because he doesn't love us any
more? And if we are hungry, or penniless, or in
danger, or threatened with death, has God deserted us?
Despite all this, overwhelming victory is ours through
Christ who loved us enough to die for us. I am convinced that . . . nothing will ever be able to separate us
from the love of God demonstrated by our Lord Jesus
Christ when he died for us.

*Ps. 40:2. 1 Cor. 10:4. Mt. 16:16, 18. Acts 4:12. Hebr. 10:22, 23.
Jas. 1:6. Rom. 8:35, 37–39.*

You are a God of forgiveness, always ready to pardon, gracious and merciful.

He isn't really being slow about his promised return, even though it sometimes seems that way. But he is waiting, for the good reason that he is not willing that any should perish, and he is giving more time for sinners to repent. / He is giving us time to get his message of salvation out to others.

God had mercy on me so that Christ Jesus could use me as an example to show everyone how patient he is with even the worst sinners, so that others will realize that they, too, can have everlasting life. / These things that were written in the Scriptures so long ago are to teach us patience and to encourage us, so that we will look forward expectantly to the time when God will conquer sin and death.

Don't you realize how patient he is being with you? Or don't you care? Can't you see that he has been waiting all this time without punishing you, to give you time to turn from your sin? His kindness is meant to lead you to repentance. / Let your remorse tear at your hearts and not your garments. Return to the Lord your God, for he is gracious and merciful. He is not easily angered; he is full of kindness, and anxious not to punish you.

Neh. 9:17. 2 Pet. 3:9. 2 Pet. 3:15. 1 Tim. 1:16. Rom. 15:4. Rom. 2:4. Joel 2:13.

*The Lord's promise is sure. He speaks no
careless word; all he says is purest truth.*

I have thoroughly tested your promises and that is
why I love them so much. / God's laws are perfect.
They protect us, make us wise, and give us joy and
light. / Every word of God proves true. He defends
all who come to him for protection. Do not add to his
words, in case he rebuke you, and you be found a liar.

I have thought much about your words, and stored
them in my heart so that they would hold me back
from sin. I will meditate upon them and give them my
full respect. / God's laws are pure, eternal, just. They
are more desirable than gold. They are sweeter than
honey dripping from a honeycomb. / Fix your thoughts
on what is true and good and right. Think about things
that are pure and lovely, and dwell on the fine, good
things in others. Think about all you can praise God for
and be glad about. / If you have tasted the Lord's
goodness and kindness, cry for more as a baby cries
for his milk.

What a God he is! How perfect in every way! All
his promises prove true. He is a shield for everyone
who hides behind him. For who is God except our Lord?
Who but he is as a rock?

*Ps. 12:6. Ps. 119:140. Ps. 19:7, 8. Prov. 30:5, 6. Ps. 119:11, 15.
Ps. 19:9, 10. Phil. 4:8. 1 Pet. 2:3. Ps. 18:30, 31.*

The great family of God – some of them already in heaven and some down here on earth.

We all have the same God and Father who is over us all and in us all, and living through every part of us. / We are all children of God through faith in Jesus Christ. / When the time is ripe he will gather us all together from wherever we are – in heaven or on earth – to be with him in Christ, for ever.

Jesus is not ashamed to call us his brothers. / 'These are my mother and brothers. Anyone who obeys my Father in heaven is my brother, sister and mother!' / 'Go and find my brothers and tell them that I ascend to my Father and your Father, my God and your God.'

I saw an altar, and undernearth it all the souls of those who had been martyred for preaching the Word of God and for being faithful in their witnessing. They called loudly to the Lord and said, 'O Sovereign Lord, holy and true, how long will it be before you judge the people of the earth for what they've done to us? When will you avenge our blood against those living on the earth?' White robes were given to each of them, and they were told to rest a little longer until their other brothers, fellow servants of Jesus, had been martyred on the earth and joined them. / For God wanted them to wait and share the even better rewards that were prepared for us.

Eph. 3:15. Eph. 4:6. Gal. 3:26. Eph. 1:10. Hebr. 2:11. Mt. 12:49, 50. Jn. 20:17. Rev. 6:9–11. Hebr. 11:40.

Pray along these lines: Our Father in heaven.

Jesus . . . looked up to heaven and said, 'Father.' / My Father and your Father.

We are all children of God through faith in Jesus Christ. / And so we should not be like cringing, fearful slaves, but we should behave like God's very own children, adopted into the bosom of his family, and calling to him, 'Father, Father.' For his Holy Spirit speaks to us deep in our hearts, and tells us that we really are God's children.

And because we are his sons God has sent the Spirit of his Son into our hearts, so now we can rightly speak of God as our dear Father. Now we are no longer slaves, but God's own sons.

You won't need to ask me for anything, for you can go directly to the Father and ask him, and he will give you what you ask for because you use my name. You haven't tried this before, [but begin now]. Ask, using my name, and you will receive, and your cup of joy will overflow.

I will welcome you, and be a Father to you, and you will be my sons and daughters.

Mt. 6:9. Jn. 17:1. Jn. 20:17. Gal. 3:26. Rom. 8:15, 16. Gal. 4:6, 7. Jn. 16:23, 24. 2 Cor. 6:17, 18.

Don't leave me now, for trouble is near.

How long will you forget me, Lord? Forever? How long will you look the other way when I am in need? How long must I be hiding daily anguish in my heart? / Oh, do not hide yourself when I am trying to find you. Do not angrily reject your servant. You have been my help in all my trials before; don't leave me now. Don't forsake me, O God of my salvation.

When he calls on me I will answer; I will be with him in trouble, and rescue him and honour him. / He is close to all who call on him sincerely. He fulfils the desires of those who reverence and trust him; he hears their cries for help and rescues them.

I will not abandon you or leave you as orphans – I will come to you. / I am with you always, even to the end of the world.

God is our refuge and strength, a tested help in times of trouble. / I stand silently before the Lord, waiting for him to rescue me. For salvation comes from him alone. Yes, he alone is my Rock, my rescuer, defence and fortress – why then should I be tense with fear when troubles come?

Ps. 22:11. Ps. 13:1, 2. Ps. 27:9. Ps. 91:15. Ps. 145:18, 19. Jn. 14:18. Mt. 28:20. Ps. 46:1. Ps. 62:5, 6.

We honour your holy name.

You must worship no other gods, but only Jehovah, for he is a God who claims absolute loyalty and exclusive devotion.

Who else is like the Lord among the gods? Who is glorious in holiness like him? Who is so awesome in splendour, a wonder-working God? / Holy, holy, holy, Lord God Almighty.

Worship the Lord when clothed with holiness. / I saw the Lord! He was sitting on a lofty throne, and the Temple was filled with his glory. Hovering about him were mighty, six-winged seraphs. They sang to each other 'Holy, holy, holy is the Lord of heaven's armies, the whole earth is filled with his glory.' My doom is sealed, for I am a foul-mouthed sinner, a member of a sinful, foul-mouthed race. / I had heard about you before, but now I have seen you, and I loathe myself and repent in dust and ashes.

The blood of Jesus his Son cleanses us from every sin. / That we may share his holiness. / Now we may walk right into the very Holy of Holies where God is, because of the blood of Jesus. This is the fresh, new, life-giving way which Christ has opened up for us by tearing the curtain – his human body to let us into the holy presence of God.

Mt. 6:9. Ex. 34:14. Ex. 15:11. Rev. 4:8. 1 Chron. 16:29. Is. 6:1–3, 5. Job 42:5, 6. 1 Jn. 1:7. Hebr. 12:10. Hebr. 10:19, 20.

God was in Christ, restoring the world to himself,
no longer counting men's sins against them but
blotting them out.

God wanted all of himself to be in his Son. It was through
what his Son did that God cleared a path for everything
to come to him – all things in heaven and on earth – for
Christ's death on the cross has made peace with God for
all by his blood. / Mercy and truth have met together. Grim justice and peace have kissed!

I know the plans I have for you, says the Lord. They
are plans for good and not for evil, to give you a future and
a hope. / Come, let's talk this over! says the Lord; no
matter how deep the stain of your sins, I can take it out and
make you as clean as freshly fallen snow. Even if you are
stained as red as crimson, I can make you white as wool!

Where is another God like you, who pardons the sins
of the survivors among his people?

Stop quarrelling with God! Agree with him and you
will have peace at last! His favour will surround you if
you will only admit that you were wrong. / Do the good
things that result from being saved, obeying God with
deep reverence, shrinking back from all that might
displease him. For God is at work within you, helping
you to want to obey him, and then helping you to do
what he wants. / Lord, grant us peace; for all we have
and are has come from you.

2 Cor. 5:19. Col. 1:19, 20. Ps. 85:10. Jer. 29:11. Is. 1:18. Mic. 7:18.
Job 22:21. Phil. 2:12, 13. Is. 26:12.

We ask that your kingdom will come soon.

During the reigns of those kings, the God of heaven will set up a kingdom that will never be destroyed; no one will ever conquer it. It will shatter all these kingdoms into nothingness, but it shall stand forever, indestructible. / A Rock was cut from the mountainside by supernatural means. / 'Not by might, nor by power, but by my Spirit,' says the Lord of heaven's armies. / The Kingdom of God isn't ushered in with visible signs. You won't be able to say, 'It has begun here in this place or there in that part of the country.' For the Kingdom of God is within you.

You are permitted to know some truths about the Kingdom of God. Here is another story illustrating what the Kingdom of God is like: A farmer sowed his field, and went away, and as the days went by, the seeds grew and grew without his help. Then the farmer came at once with his sickle and harvested it.

You can avoid trouble by always being ready for my unannounced return.

The Spirit and the bride say, 'Come.' Let each one who hears them say the same, 'Come.'

Mt. 6 :10. Dan. 2 :44. Dan. 2 :34. Zech. 4 :6. Lk. 17 :20, 21. Mk. 4 :11, 26, 27, 29. Mt. 24 :44. Rev. 22 :17.

Your request has been heard in heaven and was answered the very first day you began to fast before the Lord and pray for understanding.

The high and lofty one who inhabits eternity, the Holy One, says this: 'I live in that high and holy place where those with contrite, humble spirits dwell; and I refresh the humble and give new courage to those with repentant hearts.' / It is a broken spirit you want – remorse and penitence. A broken and a contrite heart, O God, you will not ignore. / Yet though he is so great, he respects the humble, but proud men must keep their distance. / If you will humble yourselves under the mighty hand of God, in his good time he will lift you up. / God gives strength to the humble, but sets himself against the proud and haughty. So give yourselves humbly to God. / He has told you what he wants, and this is all it is: *to be fair and just and merciful, and to walk humbly with your God.*

O Lord, you are so good and kind, so ready to forgive; so full of mercy for all who ask your aid. Listen closely to my prayer, O God. Hear my urgent cry. I will call to you whenever trouble strikes, and you will help me.

Dan. 10:12. Is. 57:15. Ps. 51:17. Ps. 138:6. 1 Pet. 5:6. Jas. 4:6, 7. Mic. 6:8. Ps. 86:5–7.

May your will be done here on earth, just as it is in heaven.

Try to find out and do whatever the Lord wants you to.

It is not my Father's will that even one of these little ones should perish.

God wants you to be holy and pure. / You won't be spending the rest of your life chasing after evil desires, but will be anxious to do the will of God. / It was a happy day for him when he gave us our new lives, through the truth of his word. So get rid of all that is wrong in your life, both inside and outside.

You must be holy, for I am holy. / [Jesus] said, 'These are my mother and brothers! Anyone who does God's will is my brother, and my sister, and my mother.' / All who listen to my instructions and follow them are wise, like a man who builds his house on solid rock. Though the rain comes in torrents, and the floods rise and the storm winds beat against his house, it won't collapse, for it is built on rock. / This world is fading away, and these evil, forbidden things will go with it, but whoever keeps doing the will of God will live for ever.

Mt. 6:10. Eph. 5:17. Mt. 18:14. 1 Thess. 4:3. 1 Pet. 4:2. Jas. 1:18, 21. 1 Pet. 1:16. Mk. 3:34, 35. Mt. 7:24, 25. 1 Jn. 2:17.

Christ died and rose again for this very purpose, so that he can be our Lord both while we live and when we die.

It was the Lord's good plan to bruise him and fill him with grief. But when his soul has been made an offering for sin, then he shall have a multitude of children, many heirs. He shall live again and God's programme shall prosper in his hands. And when he sees all that is accomplished by the anguish of his soul, he shall be satisfied; and because of what he has experienced, my righteous Servant shall make many to be counted righteous before God, for he shall bear all their sins. / Wasn't it clearly predicted by the prophets that the Messiah would have to suffer all these things before entering his time of glory? / Since we believe that Christ died for all of us, we should also believe that we have died to the old life we used to live. He died for all so that all who live – having received eternal life from him – might live no longer for themselves, to please themselves, but to spend their lives pleasing Christ who died and rose again for them.

I clearly state to everyone in Israel that God has made this Jesus you crucified to be the Lord, the Messiah! / God chose him for this purpose long before the world began.

Rom. 14:9. Is. 53:10, 11. Lk. 24:26. 2 Cor. 5:14, 15. Acts 2:36. 1 Pet. 1:20.

Give us our food again today, as usual.

I have been young and now I am old. And in all my years I have never seen the Lord forsake a man who loves him; nor have I seen the children of the godly go hungry. / Food will be supplied to them and they will have all the water they need. / The ravens brought him bread and meat each morning and evening, and he drank from the brook.

It is he who will supply all your needs from his riches in glory, because of what Christ Jesus has done for us. / Be satisfied with what you have. For God has said, 'I will never, *never* fail you nor forsake you.'

Yes, he humbled you by letting you go hungry and then feeding you with manna . . . He did it to help you realize that food isn't everything, and that real life comes by obeying every command of God. / Jesus said, 'Moses didn't give it to them. My Father did. And now he offers you true Bread from heaven. The true Bread is a Person – the one sent by God from heaven, and he gives life to the world.' 'Sir,' they said, 'give us that bread every day of our lives!'

Mt. 6:11. Ps. 37:25. Is. 33:16. 1 Kgs. 17:6. Phil. 4:19. Hebr. 13:5. Deut. 8:3. Jn. 6:32–34.

You are my place of safety.

Jehovah is my rock, my fortress and my Saviour. I will hide in God, who is my rock and my refuge. He is my shield and my salvation, my refuge and high tower. / He is my strength, my shield from every danger. I trusted in him, and he helped me. Joy rises in my heart until I burst out in songs of praise to him.

They will reverence and glorify the name of God from west to east. For he will come like a flood-tide driven by Jehovah's breath. / That is why we can say without any doubt or fear, 'The Lord is my Helper and I am not afraid of anything that mere man can do to me.'

The Lord is my light and my salvation; whom shall I fear? / When I sit in darkness, the Lord himself will be my Light.

Just as the mountains surround and protect Jerusalem, so the Lord surrounds and protects his people. / How I rejoice through the night beneath the protecting shadow of your wings.

Honour your name by leading me. / Be our strength each day and our salvation in the time of trouble.

Ps. 59:9. 2 Sam. 22:2, 3. Ps. 28:7. Is. 59:19. Hebr. 13:6. Ps. 27:1. Mic. 7:8. Ps. 125:2. Ps. 63:7. Ps. 31:3. Is. 33:2.

Forgive us our sins, just as we have forgiven those who have sinned against us.

'How often should I forgive a brother who sins against me? Seven times?' 'No!' Jesus replied, 'seventy times seven!'

'You evil-hearted wretch! Here I forgave you all that tremendous debt, just because you asked me to – shouldn't you have mercy on others, just as I had mercy on you?' Then the angry king sent the man to the torture chamber until he had paid every last penny due. So shall my heavenly Father do to you if you refuse truly to forgive your brothers. / Be kind to each other, tender-hearted, forgiving one another, just as God has forgiven you because you belong to Christ. / When you are praying, first forgive anyone you are holding a grudge against, so that your Father in heaven will forgive you your sins too. / He gave you a share in the very life of Christ, for he forgave all your sins, and blotted out the charges proved against you, the list of his commandments which you had not obeyed. He took this list of sins and destroyed it by nailing it to Christ's cross.

Remember, the Lord forgave you, so you must forgive others.

Mt. 6:12. Mt. 18:21, 22, 32–35. Eph. 4:32. Mk. 11:25. Col. 2:13, 14. Col. 3:13.

Never be lazy in your work but serve the Lord enthusiastically.

Whatever you do, do well, for in death, where you are going, there is no working or planning, or knowing, or understanding. / Work hard and cheerfully at all you do, just as though you were working for the Lord and not merely for your masters, remembering that it is the Lord Christ who is going to pay you, giving you your full portion of all he owns. He is the one you are really working for. / Remember, the Lord will pay you for each good thing you do.

All of us must quickly carry out the tasks assigned us by the one who sent me, for there is little time left before the night falls and all work comes to an end.

So, dear brothers, work hard to prove that you really are among those God has called and chosen, and then you will never stumble or fall away. / And we are anxious that you keep on loving others as long as life lasts, so that you will get your full reward. Then, knowing what lies ahead for you, you won't become bored with being a Christian, nor become spiritually dull and indifferent, but you will be anxious to follow the example of those who receive all that God has promised them because of their strong faith and patience. / So run your race to win.

Rom. 12:11. Eccl. 9:10. Col. 3:23, 24. Eph. 6:8. Jn. 9:4. 2 Pet. 1:10. Hebr. 6:11, 12. 1 Cor. 9:24.

*Don't bring us into temptation, but deliver us
from the Evil One.*

A man is a fool to trust himself! But those who use
God's wisdom are safe.

When someone wants to do wrong it is never God
who is tempting him, for God never wants to do wrong
and never tempts anyone else to do it. Temptation
is the pull of man's own evil thoughts and wishes. /
Leave them; separate yourselves from them; don't
touch what is unclean, and I will welcome you.

Lot took a long look at the fertile plains of the river
Jordan, well watered everywhere . . . the whole section
was like the Garden of Eden, or like the beautiful
countryside around Zoar in Egypt. So that is what Lot
chose – the Jordan valley to the east of them. The men
of this area were unusually wicked, and sinned greatly
against Jehovah. / But at the same time the Lord rescued
Lot out of Sodom because he was a good man, sick of
the terrible wickedness he saw everywhere around
him day after day. So also the Lord can rescue you
and me from the temptations that surround us. / Let
him tell them whether they are right or wrong. And
God is able to make them do as they should.

*Mt. 6:13. Prov. 28:26. Jas. 1:13, 14. 2 Cor. 6:17. Gen. 13:10, 11, 13.
2 Pet. 2:7, 9. Rom. 14:4.*

*They rejoice all day long in your wonderful
reputation and in your perfect righteousness.*

'In Jehovah is all my righteousness and strength,' the
people shall declare. And all who were angry with him
shall come to him and be ashamed. In Jehovah all the
generations of Israel shall be justified, triumphant. /
So rejoice in him, all those who are his, and shout
for joy, all those who try to obey him.

But now God has shown us a different way to
heaven – not by 'being good enough' and trying to keep
his laws, but by a new way (though not new, really,
for the Scriptures told about it long ago). Now God
says he will accept and acquit us – declare us 'not
guilty' – if we trust Jesus Christ to take away our sins.
And we all can be saved in this same way, by coming
to Christ, no matter who we are or what we have been
like. And now in these days also he can receive sinners
in this same way, because Jesus took away their sins.
But isn't this unfair for God to let criminals go free,
and say that they are innocent? No, for he does it on the
basis of their trust in Jesus.

Always be full of joy in the Lord; I say it again,
rejoice! / You love him even though you have never
seen him; though not seeing him, you trust him; and
even now you are happy with the inexpressible joy
that comes from heaven itself.

*Ps. 89:16. Is. 45:24, 25. Ps. 32:11. Rom. 3:21, 22, 26. Phil. 4:4.
1 Pet. 1:8.*

Amen.

Amen! Praise God! / And yet, the days will come when all who invoke a blessing or take an oath shall swear by the God of Truth.

For instance, there was God's promise to Abraham: God took an oath in his own name, since there was no one greater to swear by. When a man takes an oath, he is calling upon someone greater than himself to force him to do what he has promised, or to punish him if he later refuses to do it; the oath ends all argument about it. God also bound himself with an oath, so that those he promised to help would be perfectly sure and never need to wonder whether he might change his plans. He has given us both his promise and his oath, two things we can completely count on, for it is impossible for God to tell a lie. Now all those who flee to him to save them can take new courage when they hear such assurances from God; now they can know without doubt that he will give them the salvation he has promised them.

This message is from the one who stands firm, the faithful and true witness. / He carries out and fulfils all of God's promises, no matter how many of them there are; and we have told everyone how faithful he is, giving glory to his name.

Mt. 6:13. 1 Kgs. 1:36. Is. 65:16. Hebr. 6:13, 16–18. Rev. 3:14. 2 Cor. 1:20.

*One of the soldiers pierced his side with a spear,
and blood and water flowed out.*

This blood confirms and seals the covenant the Lord
has made with you. / For the life of the flesh is in the
blood, and I have given you the blood to sprinkle
upon the altar as an atonement for your souls; it is the
blood that makes atonement, because it is the life. / It is
not possible for the blood of bulls and goats really to
take away sins.

And he said to them, 'This is my blood, poured
out for many.' / He took his own blood, and with it he,
by himself, made sure of our eternal salvation. / Peace
with God for all by his blood.

The ransom he paid was not mere gold or silver, as
you very well know. But with the precious lifeblood
of Christ . . . brought into public view, in these last
days, as a blessing to you.

Then it will be as though I had sprinkled clean
water on you, for you will be clean – your filthiness
will be washed away, your idol worship gone. / Let us
go right in, to God himself, with true hearts fully
trusting him to receive us, because we have been
sprinkled with Christ's blood to make us clean, and
because our bodies have been washed with pure water.

Jn. 19:34. Ex. 24:8. Lev. 17:11. Hebr. 10:4. Mk. 14:24. Hebr. 9:12.
Col. 1:20. 1 Pet. 1:18–20. Ezk. 36:25. Hebr. 10:22.

I am the First and Last, the living one who died, who is now alive for evermore.

Jehovah is King! He is robed in majesty and strength. The world is his throne. O Lord, you have reigned from prehistoric times, from the everlasting past.

His power is incredible. / If God is on our side, who can ever be against us? / Our God is able to deliver us; and he will deliver us out of your hand. / My Father has given them to me, and he is more powerful than anyone else, so no one can kidnap them from me. / You belong to God and have already won your fight with those who are against Christ, because there is someone in your hearts who is stronger than any evil teacher in this wicked world.

Glorify your name, not ours, O Lord! / Yours is the mighty power and glory and victory and majesty. Everything in the heavens and earth is yours, O Lord, and this is your kingdom. We adore you as being in control of everything. O our God, we thank you and praise your glorious name, but who am I and who are my people that we should be permitted to give anything to you? Everything we have has come from you, and we only give you what is yours already!

Rev. 1:18. Ps. 93:1, 2. Nah. 1:3. Rom. 8:31. Dan. 3:17. Jn. 10:29. 1 Jn. 4:4. Ps. 115:1. 1 Chron. 29:11, 13, 14.

The Lord is with you; he protects you.

Man's futile wrath will bring you glory. You will use it as an ornament! / Just as water is turned into irrigation ditches, so the Lord directs the king's thoughts. He turns them wherever he wants to. / When a man is trying to please God, God makes even his worst enemies to be at peace with him.

I wait expectantly trusting God to help, for he has promised. I long for him more than sentinels long for the dawn. / I cried to him and he answered me! He freed me from all my fears.

The eternal God is your Refuge, and underneath are the everlasting arms. He thrusts out your enemies before you; it is he who cries, 'Destroy them!' / Blessed is the man who trusts in the Lord and has made the Lord his hope and confidence. He is like a tree planted along a riverbank, with its roots reaching deep into the water – a tree not bothered by the heat nor worried by long months of drought. Its leaves stay green and it goes right on producing all its luscious fruit.

What can we ever say to such wonderful things as these? If God is on our side, who can ever be against us?

Prov. 3:26. Ps. 76:10. Prov. 21:1. Prov. 16:7. Ps. 130:5, 6. Ps. 34:4. Deut. 33:27. Jer. 17:7, 8. Rom. 8:31.

Christians cheering each other up . . . brothers in the Lord, sharing the same Spirit.

How frail is man, how few his days, how full of trouble! He blossoms for a moment like a flower – and withers; as the shadow of a passing cloud, he quickly disappears. / My health fails; my spirits droop, yet God remains! He is the strength of my heart; he is mine forever!

The Father . . . will give you another Comforter, and he will never leave you. The Father sends the Comforter to represent me – and by the Comforter I mean the Holy Spirit – he will teach you much. / What a wonderful God we have – he is the Father of our Lord Jesus Christ, the source of every mercy, and the one who so wonderfully comforts and strengthens us in our hardships and trials. And why does he do this? So that when others are troubled, needing our sympathy and encouragement, we can pass on to them this same help and comfort God has given us.

For since we believe that Jesus died and then came back to life again, we can also believe that when Jesus returns, God will bring back with him all the Christians who have died. Then we who are still alive and remain on the earth will be caught up with them in the clouds to meet the Lord in the air and remain with him forever. So comfort and encourage each other with this news.

Phil. 2:1. Job 14:1, 2. Ps. 73:26. Jn. 14:16, 26. 2 Cor. 1:3, 4.
1 Thess. 4:14, 17, 18.

I love to do God's will so far as my new nature is concerned.

Your words. Oh, how I love them. I think about them all day long. / Your words are what sustain me; they are food to my hungry soul. They bring joy to my sorrowing heart and delight me. / I am seated in his much-desired shade and his fruit is lovely to eat. / I have not refused his commandments but have enjoyed them more than my daily food.

I delight to do your will, my God, for your law is written upon my heart! / My nourishment comes from doing the will of God who sent me, and from finishing his work.

God's laws are perfect. They protect us, make us wise, and give us joy and light. They are more desirable than gold. They are sweeter than honey dripping from a honeycomb. / And remember, it is a message to obey, not just to listen to. So don't fool yourselves. For if a person just listens and doesn't obey, he is like a man looking at his face in a mirror. As soon as he walks away, he can't see himself any more or remember what he looks like.

Rom. 7:22. Ps. 119:96, 97. Jer. 15:16. Song 2:3. Job 23:12. Ps. 40:8. Jn. 4:34. Ps. 19:7, 8, 10. Jas. 1:22–24.

May the Lord God accept your sacrifice.

'How can we make up to you for what we've done?'
you ask. 'Shall we bow before the Lord with offerings
of yearling calves?' Oh, no! For if you offered him
thousands of rams and ten thousands of rivers of olive
oil – would that please him? Would he be satisfied? If
you sacrificed your oldest child, would that make him
glad? Then would he forgive your sins? Of course not!
No, he has told you what he wants, and this is all it is:
*to be fair and just and merciful, and to walk humbly with
your God.*

We are all infected and impure with sin. When we put
on our prized robes of righteousness we find they are
but filthy rags. / No one is good – no one in all the
world is innocent. Yes, all have sinned; all fall short
of God's glorious ideal; yet now God declares us 'not
guilty' of offending him if we trust in Jesus Christ, who
in his kindness freely takes away our sins. For God sent
Christ Jesus to take the punishment for our sins and to
end all God's anger against us. He used Christ's blood
and our faith as the means of saving us from his wrath.

We belong to his dearly loved Son. / You have
everything when you have Christ.

2 Sam. 24:23. Mic. 6:6–8. Is. 64:6. Rom. 3:10, 23–25. Eph. 1:6. Col. 2:10.

We have all benefited from the rich blessings he brought to us – blessing upon blessing heaped upon us.

This is my beloved Son, and I am wonderfully pleased with him. / How very much our heavenly Father loves us, for he allows us to be called his children – think of it – and we really *are!*

His Son to whom he has given everything. / And since we are his children, we will share his treasures – for all God gives to his Son Jesus is now ours too. But if we are to share his glory, we must also share his suffering. / And if we think that our present service for him is hard, just remember that some day we are going to sit with him and rule with him.

I and the Father are one. The Father is in me, and I in the Father. / My Father and your Father, my God and your God. / I in them and you in me, all being perfected into one.

The church – which is his body, filled with himself, the author and giver of everything everywhere.

Having such great promises as these, dear friends, let us turn away from everything wrong, whether of body or spirit, and purify ourselves, living in the wholesome fear of God, giving ourselves to him alone.

Jn. 1:16. Mt. 17:5. 1 Jn. 3:1. Hebr. 1:2. Rom. 8:17. 2 Tim. 2:12.
Jn. 10:30, 38. Jn. 20:17. Jn. 17:23. Eph. 1:22, 23. 2 Cor. 7:1.

*A servant is not greater than his master. Nor is
the messenger more important than the one who
sends him. You know these things – now do them.
That is the path of blessing.*

They began to argue among themselves as to who
would have the highest rank [in the coming Kingdom].
Jesus told them, 'In this world the kings and great
men order their slaves around, and the slaves have
no choice but to like it! But among you, the one who
serves you best will be your leader. Out in the world the
master sits at the table and is served by his servants.
But not here! For I am your servant.' / Your care for
others is the measure of your greatness. / Anyone
wanting to be a leader among you must be your servant.
And if you want to be right at the top, you must serve
like a slave. Your attitude must be like my own, for
I, the Son of Mankind, did not come to be served, but
to serve, and to give my life as a ransom for many.

He [Jesus] got up from the upper table, took off his
robe, wrapped a towel around his loins, poured water
into a basin, and began to wash the disciples' feet and
to wipe them with the towel he had around him.

Lead them by your good example.

*Jn. 13:16, 17. Lk. 22:24–27. Lk. 9:48. Mt. 20:26–28. Jn. 13:4–5.
1 Pet. 5:3.*

O God, my heart is ready to praise you!

The Lord is my light and my salvation; whom shall I fear?

He will keep in perfect peace all those who trust in him, whose thoughts turn often to the Lord! For good men the path is not uphill and rough. God does not give them a rough and treacherous path, but smooths the road before them. / He does not fear bad news, nor live in dread of what may happen. For he is settled in his mind that Jehovah will take care of him. That is why he is not afraid, but can calmly face his foes.

But when I am afraid, I will put my confidence in you. Yes, I will trust the promises of God. / There I'll be when troubles come. He will hide me. He will set me on a high rock out of reach of all my enemies. Then I will bring him sacrifices and sing his praises with much joy.

After you have suffered a little while, our God, who is full of kindness through Christ, will give you his eternal glory. He personally will come and pick you up, and set you firmly in place, and make you stronger than ever. To him be all power over all things, for ever and ever. Amen.

Ps. 108:1. Ps. 27:1. Is. 26:3, 7. Ps. 112:7, 8. Ps. 56:3. Ps. 27:5, 6. 1 Pet. 5:10, 11.

The Lord has made the heavens his throne; from there he rules over everything there is.

We toss the coin, but it is the Lord who controls its decision. / The alarm has sounded – listen and fear! For I, the Lord, am sending disaster into your land.

I am Jehovah; there is no other God. I will strengthen you and send you out to victory even though you don't know me, and all the world from east to west will know there is no other God. I am Jehovah and there is no one else. I alone am God. I form the light and make the dark. I send good times and bad. I, Jehovah, am he who does these things.

He does whatever he thinks best among the company of heaven, as well as here among the inhabitants of earth. No one can stop him or challenge him, saying, 'What do you mean by doing these things?' / If God is on our side, who can ever be against us?

For Christ will be King until he has defeated all his enemies. / So don't be afraid, little flock. For it gives your Father great happiness to give you the Kingdom.

Ps. 103:19. Prov. 16:33. Amos 3:6. Is. 45:5–7. Dan. 4:35. Rom. 8:31. 1 Cor. 15:25. Lk. 12:32.

Don't always be wishing for what you don't have.

It is better to have little and be godly than to own an evil man's wealth. / Better a little with reverence for God, than great treasure and trouble with it. / Do you want to be truly rich? You already are if you are happy and good. We should be well satisfied without money if we have enough food and clothing.

Give me neither poverty nor riches! Give me just enough to satisfy my needs! For if I grow rich, I may become content without God. And if I am too poor, I may steal, and thus insult God's holy name. / Give us our food again today, as usual.

Don't worry about *things* – food, drink, money and clothes. For you already have life and a body – and they are far more important than what to eat and wear. / 'When I sent you out to preach the Good News and you were without money, bag, or extra clothing, how did you get along?' 'All right,' they replied. / Stay away from the love of money; be satisfied with what you have. For God has said, 'I will never, *never* fail you nor forsake you.'

Lk. 12:15. Ps. 37:16. Prov. 15:16. 1 Tim. 6:6, 8. Prov. 30:8, 9. Mt. 6:11. Mt. 6:25. Lk. 22:35. Hebr. 13:5.

Only the Holy Spirit gives eternal life.

The Scriptures tell us that the first man, Adam, was given a natural, human body but Christ is more than that, for he was life-giving Spirit. / Men can only reproduce human life, but the Holy Spirit gives new life from heaven. / He saved us – not because we were good enough to be saved, but because of his kindness and pity – by washing away our sins and giving us the new joy of the indwelling Holy Spirit.

You are controlled by your new nature if you have the Spirit of God living in you. Yet, even though Christ lives within you, your body will die because of sin; but your spirit will live, for Christ has pardoned it. And if the Spirit of God, who raised up Jesus from the dead, lives in you, he will make your dying bodies live again after you die, by means of this same Holy Spirit living within you.

I have been crucified with Christ: and I myself no longer live, but Christ lives in me. And the real life I now have within this body is a result of my trusting in the Son of God, who loved me and gave himself for me. / So look upon your old sinful nature as dead and unresponsive to sin, and instead be alive to God, alert to him, through Jesus Christ our Lord.

Jn. 6:63. 1 Cor. 15:45. Jn. 3:6. Tit. 3:5. Rom. 8:9–11. Gal. 2:20. Rom. 6:11.

O Lord, you have rejected me and cast me away.
How shall I ever again see your holy Temple?

Yet they say, 'My Lord deserted us; he has forgotten us.' Never! Can a mother forget her little child and not have love for her own son? Yet even if that should be, I will not forget you.

O Lord, all peace and all prosperity have long since gone, for you have taken them away. I have forgotten what enjoyment is. All hope is gone; my strength has turned to water, for the Lord has left me. / Wake up! Rouse yourself! Don't sleep, O Lord! Are we cast off forever? / O Jacob, O Israel, how can you say that the Lord doesn't see your troubles and isn't being fair? / 'In a moment of anger I turned my face a little while; but with everlasting love I will have pity on you,' says the Lord, your Redeemer.

O my soul, why be so gloomy and discouraged? Trust in God! I shall again praise him for his wonderful help; he will make me smile again, *for he is my God!* / We are pressed on every side by troubles, but not crushed and broken. We are perplexed because we don't know why things happen as they do, but we don't give up. We are hunted down, but God never abandons us. We get knocked down, but we get up again and keep going.

Jon. 2:4. Is. 49:14, 15. Lam. 3:17, 18. Ps. 44:23. Is. 40:27. Is. 54:8.
Ps. 43:5. 2 Cor. 4:8, 9.

*When the poor and needy seek water and there is
none and their tongues are parched from thirst, then
I will answer when they cry to me. I, Israel's God,
will not ever forsake them.*

Many say that God will never help us. / So I turned
in despair from hard work as the answer to my search
for satisfaction. For though I spend my life searching
for wisdom, knowledge, and skill, I must leave all of it
to someone who hasn't done a day's work in his life; he
inherits all my efforts, free of charge. This is not only
foolish, but unfair. So what does a man get for all his
hard work? Days full of sorrow and grief, and restless,
bitter nights. It is all utterly ridiculous. So now I hate
life because it is all so irrational; all is foolishness,
chasing the wind. / They have forsaken me, the Fountain of Life-giving Water; and they have built for themselves broken cisterns that can't hold water!

Some will come to me . . . and I will never, never
reject them. / I will give you abundant water for your
thirst. / Happy are those who long for justice for they
shall surely have it.

O God, my God! How I search for you! How I thirst
for you in this parched and weary land where there is
no water. How I long to find you!

*Is. 41:17. Ps. 4:6. Eccl. 2:20–23, 17. Jer. 2:13. Jn. 6:37. Is. 44:3.
Mt. 5:6. Ps. 63:1.*

I am with you always, even to the end of the world.

If two of you agree down here on earth concerning anything you ask for, my Father in heaven will do it for you. For where two or three gather together because they are mine, I will be there among them. / I have been standing at the door and I am constantly knocking. If anyone hears me calling him and opens the door, I will come in and enjoy fellowship with him and he with me. / The one who obeys me is the one who loves me; and because he loves me, my Father will love him; and I will too, and I will reveal myself to him.

'Sir, why are you going to reveal yourself only to us disciples and not to the world at large?' Jesus replied, 'Because I will only reveal myself to those who love me and obey me. The Father will love them too, and we will come to them and live with them.' / Keep on believing what you have been taught from the beginning. If you do, you will always be in close fellowship with both God the Father and his Son.

He is able to keep you from slipping and falling away, and to bring you, sinless and perfect, into his glorious presence with mighty shouts of everlasting joy. Amen.

Mt. 28:20. Mt. 18:19, 20. Rev. 3:20. Jn. 14:21. Jn. 14:22, 23. 1 Jn. 2:24. Jude 25.

The end of the world is coming soon.

I saw a great white throne and the one who sat upon it, from whose face the earth and sky fled away, but they found no place to hide. / God has commanded that the earth and the heavens be stored away for a great bonfire at the judgment day, when all ungodly men will perish.

God is our refuge and strength, a tested help in times of trouble. And so we need not fear even if the world blows up, and the mountains crumble into the sea. Let the oceans roar and foam; let the mountains tremble! / When you hear of wars beginning, this does not signal my return; these must come, but the end is not yet.

We will have wonderful new bodies in heaven, homes that will be ours for evermore, made for us by God himself, and not by human hands. / We are looking forward to God's promise of new heavens and a new earth afterwards, where there will be only goodness. Dear friends, while you are waiting for these things to happen and for him to come, try hard to live without sinning; and be at peace with everyone so that he will be pleased with you when he returns.

1 Pet. 4:7. Rev. 20:11. 2 Pet. 3:7. Ps. 46:1–3. Mt. 24:6. 2 Cor. 5:1. 2 Pet. 3:13, 14.

Jehovah is King!

Have you no respect at all for me? the Lord God asks.
How can it be that you don't even tremble in my
presence? I set the shorelines of the world by perpetual
decrees, so that the oceans, though they toss and roar,
can never pass those bounds. Isn't such a God to be
feared and worshipped? / For promotion and power
come from nowhere on earth, but only from God. He
promotes one and deposes another.

World events are under his control. He removes
kings and sets others on their thrones. He gives wise
men their wisdom, and scholars their intelligence. /
When you hear of wars beginning, this does not signal
my return; these must come, but the end is not yet.

If God is on our side, who can ever be against
us? / Not one sparrow – what do they cost? Two for a
penny? – can fall to the ground without your Father
knowing it. And the very hairs of your head are all
numbered. So don't worry? You are more valuable to
him than many sparrows.

*Ps. 99:1. Jer. 5:22. Ps. 75:6, 7. Dan. 2:21. Mt. 24:6. Rom. 8:31.
Mt. 10:29–31.*

He made no distinction between them and us, for he cleansed their lives through faith, just as he did ours.

'Master, we saw someone using your name to cast out demons. And we told him not to. After all, he isn't in our group.' But Jesus said, 'You shouldn't have done that. For anyone who is not against you is for you.'

The people of the village refused to have anything to do with them. James and John said to Jesus, 'Master, shall we order fire down from heaven to burn them up?' But Jesus turned and rebuked them, and they went on to another village.

Two of the seventy – Eldad and Medad . . . prophesied. Joshua (the son of Nun), one of Moses' personally chosen assistants, protested, 'Sir, make them stop!' But Moses replied, 'Are you jealous for my sake? I only wish that all of the Lord's people were prophets, and that the Lord would put his Spirit upon them all!'

But when the Holy Spirit controls our lives he will produce this kind of fruit in us: love, joy, peace, patience, kindness, goodness, faithfulness, gentleness and self-control. Those who belong to Christ have nailed their natural evil desires to his cross and crucified them there. If we are living now by the Holy Spirit's power, let us follow the Holy Spirit's leading in every part of our lives.

Acts 15:9. Lk. 9:49, 50. Lk. 9:53–56. Num. 11:26–29. Gal. 5:22–25.

He took our sicknesses and bore our diseases.

He shall require two living birds of a kind permitted for food, and shall take some cedar wood, a scarlet string, and some hyssop branches, to be used for the purification ceremony of the one who is healed. The priest shall then order one of the birds to be killed in an earthenware pot held above running water. The other bird, still living, shall be dipped in the blood, along with the cedar wood, the scarlet thread, and the hyssop branch. Then the priest shall sprinkle the blood seven times upon the man cured of his leprosy, and the priest shall pronounce him cured, and shall let the living bird fly into the open field.

One day in a certain village he was visiting, there was a man with an advanced case of leprosy. When he saw Jesus he fell to the ground before him, face downward in the dust, begging to be healed. 'Sir,' he said, 'if you only will, you can clear me of every trace of my disease.' / And Jesus, moved with pity, touched him and said, 'I want to. Be healed!' Immediately the leprosy was gone – the man was healed!

Mt. 8:17. Lev. 14:4–7. Lk. 5:12. Mk. 1:41, 42.

I know what fantastic blessings fall on those whom you bless.

'Humble men are very fortunate!' he told them, 'for the Kingdom of Heaven is given to them.'

Those who mourn are fortunate! For they shall be comforted. The meek and lowly are fortunate! For the whole wide world belongs to them. Happy are those who long for justice for they shall surely have it. Happy are the kind and merciful, for they shall be shown mercy. Happy are those whose hearts are pure, for they shall see God. Happy are those who strive for peace – they shall be called the sons of God. Happy are those who are persecuted because they are good, for the Kingdom of Heaven is theirs. When you are reviled and persecuted and lied about because you are my followers – wonderful! Be *happy* about it! Be *very glad* – for a *tremendous reward* awaits you up in heaven. / Blessed are all who hear the Word of God and put it into practice.

Blessed for ever are all who are washing their robes, to have the right to enter in through the gates of the city, and to eat the fruit from the tree of life.

Num. 22:6. Mt. 5:3–12. Lk. 11:28. Rev. 22:14.

*He saw no one was helping you, and wondered
that no one intervened. Therefore he himself
stepped in to save you through his mighty power
and justice.*

It isn't sacrifices and offerings which you really want
from your people. Burnt animals bring no special joy
to your heart. But you have accepted the offer of my
lifelong service. Then I said, 'See, I have come, just as
all the prophets foretold. And I delight to do your will,
my God, for your law is written upon my heart!' / I
lay down my life that I may have it back again. No one
can kill me without my consent – I lay down my life
voluntarily. For I have the right and power to lay it
down when I want to and also the right and power to
take it again. For the Father has given me this right.

There is no other God but me – a just God and a
Saviour – no, not one! Let all the world look to me for
salvation! For I am God; there is no other. / There is
salvation in no one else! Under all heaven there is
no other name for men to call upon to save them.

You know how full of love and kindness our Lord
Jesus was: though he was so very rich, yet to help you
he became so very poor, so that by being poor he
could make you rich.

Is. 59:16. Ps. 40:6–8. Jn. 10:17, 18. Is. 45:21, 22. Acts 4:12. 2 Cor. 8:9.

The Enemy.

Be careful – watch out for attacks from Satan, your great enemy. He prowls around like a hungry, roaring lion, looking for some victim to tear apart. / Resist the devil and he will flee from you.

Put on all of God's armour so that you will be able to stand safe against the strategies and tricks of Satan. For we are not fighting against people made of flesh and blood, but against persons without bodies – the evil rulers of the unseen world, those mighty satanic beings and great evil princes of darkness who rule this world; and against huge numbers of wicked spirits in the spirit world. So use every piece of God's armour to resist the enemy whenever he attacks, and when it is all over, you will still be standing up. But to do this, you will need the strong belt of truth and the breastplate of God's approval. Wear shoes that are able to speed you on as you preach the Good News of peace with God. In every battle you will need faith as your shield to stop the fiery arrows aimed at you by Satan.

Do not rejoice against me, O my enemy, for though I fall, I will rise again!

Lk. 10:19. 1 Pet. 5:8. Jas. 4:7. Eph. 6:11–16. Mic. 7:8.

My beloved.

May he be pleased by all these thoughts about him, for he is the source of all my joy. / My beloved . . . better than ten thousand others! / Christ . . . the carefully chosen, precious cornerstone of my church, and I will never disappoint those who trust in him. / You are the fairest of all; your words are filled with grace; God himself is blessing you forever. / God raised him up to the heights of heaven and gave him a name which is above every other name. / For God wanted all of himself to be in his Son.

You love him even though you have never seen him; though not seeing him, you trust him; and even now you are happy with the inexpressible joy that comes from heaven itself.

Everything else is worthless when compared with the priceless gain of knowing Christ Jesus my Lord. I have put aside all else, counting it worth less than nothing, in order that I can have Christ, and become one with him, no longer counting on being saved by being good enough or by obeying God's laws, but by trusting Christ to save me; for God's way of making us right with himself depends on faith – counting on Christ alone.

Song 2:2. Ps. 104:34. Song 5:10. 1 Pet. 2:6. Ps. 45:2. Phil. 2:9. Col. 1:19. 1 Pet. 1:8. Phil. 3:8, 9.

David took strength from the Lord.

Master, to whom shall we go? You alone have the words that give eternal life. / I know the one in whom I trust, and I am sure that he is able to guard safely all that I have given him until the day of his return.

In my distress I screamed to the Lord for his help. And he heard me from heaven; my cry reached his ears. On the day when I was weakest, they attacked. But the Lord held me steady. He led me to a place of safety, for he delights in me. He reached down from heaven and took me and drew me out of my great trials. He rescued me from deep waters. He delivered me from my strong enemy, from those who hated me – I who was helpless in their hands.

I will praise the Lord no matter what happens. I will constantly speak of his glories and grace. I will boast of all his kindness to me. Let all who are discouraged take heart. Let us praise the Lord together, and exalt his name. For I cried to him and he answered me! He freed me from all my fears. Oh, put God to the test and see how kind he is! See for yourself the way his mercies shower down on all who trust in him.

1 Sam. 30:6. Jn. 6:68. 2 Tim. 1:12. Ps. 18:6, 18, 19. 16, 17. Ps. 34:1-4, 8.

It is good both to hope and wait quietly for the salvation of the Lord.

Has he forgotten to be kind to one so undeserving? Has he slammed the door in anger on his love? / I spoke too hastily when I said, 'The Lord has deserted me,' for you listened to my plea and answered me. Oh, love the Lord, all of you who are his people; for the Lord protects those who are loyal to him, but harshly punishes all who haughtily reject him. So cheer up! Take courage if you are depending on the Lord.

Don't you think that God will surely give justice to his people who plead with him day and night? Yes! He will answer them quickly! / Wait for the Lord to handle the matter. / Rest in the Lord; wait patiently for him to act. Don't be envious of evil men who prosper.

You will not need to fight! Take your places; stand quietly and see the incredible rescue operation God will perform for you.

Let us not get tired of doing what is right, for after a while we will reap a harvest of blessing if we don't get discouraged and give up. / Be patient, like a farmer who waits until the autumn for his precious harvest to ripen.

Lam. 3:26. Ps. 77:9. Ps. 31:22–24. Lk. 18:7, 8. Prov. 20:22. Ps. 37:7. 2 Chron. 20:17. Gal. 6:9. Jas. 5:7.

The little foxes are ruining the vineyards.

How can I ever know what sins are lurking in my heart? Cleanse me from these hidden faults. / Look after each other so that not one of you will fail to find God's best blessings. Watch out that no bitterness takes root among you, for as it springs up it causes deep trouble, hurting many in their spiritual lives.

God who began the good work within you will keep right on helping you grow in his grace until his task within you is finally finished on that day when Jesus Christ returns. Remember always to live as Christians should. / So also the tongue is a small thing, but what enormous damage it can do. A great forest can be set on fire by one tiny spark. And the tongue is a flame of fire. It is full of wickedness, and poisons every part of the body. And the tongue is set on fire by hell itself, and can turn our whole lives into a blazing flame of destruction and disaster. No human being can tame the tongue. It is always ready to pour out its deadly poison. / Let your conversation be gracious as well as sensible.

Song 2:15. Ps. 19:12. Hebr. 12:15. Phil. 1:6, 27. Jas. 3:5, 6, 8. Col. 4:6.

> *Not by might, nor by power, but by my Spirit,*
> *says the Lord of heaven's armies.*

Who can advise the Spirit of the Lord or be his teacher
or give him counsel?

God has deliberately chosen to use ideas the world
considers foolish and of little worth in order to shame
those people considered by the world as wise and great.
He has chosen a plan despised by the world, counted
as nothing at all, and used it to bring down to nothing
those the world considers great, so that no one anywhere can ever boast in the presence of God.

Just as you can hear the wind but can't tell where it
comes from or where it will go next, so it is with the
Spirit. We do not know on whom he will next bestow
this life from heaven. / Reborn – not a physical rebirth
resulting from human passion or plan, but from the will
of God.

I promised . . . that my Spirit would remain among
you; so don't be afraid. / The battle is not yours,
but God's!

The Lord does not depend on weapons to fulfil
his plans – he works without regard to human means.

Zech. 4:6. Is. 40:13. 1 Cor. 1:27–29. Jn. 3:8. Jn. 1:13. Hag. 2:5.
2 Chron. 20:15. 1 Sam. 17:47.

Do as you have promised.

Reassure me that your promises are for me, for I trust and revere you. Then I will have an answer for those who taunt me, for I trust your promises. Never forget your promises to me your servant, for they are my only hope. For these laws of yours have been my source of joy and singing through all these years of my earthly pilgrimage. They are more valuable to me than millions in silver and gold! Forever, O Lord, your Word stands firm in heaven. Your faithfulness extends to every generation.

God also bound himself with an oath, so that those he promised to help would be perfectly sure and never need to wonder whether he might change his plans. He has given us both his promise and his oath, two things we can completely count on, for it is impossible for God to tell a lie. Now all those who flee to him to save them can take new courage when they hear such assurances from God; now they can know without doubt that he will give them the salvation he has promised them. This certain hope of being saved is a strong and trustworthy anchor for our souls.

Rich and wonderful blessings he promised.

2 Sam. 7:25. Ps. 119:38, 42, 49, 54, 72, 89, 90. Hebr. 6:17–19. 2 Pet. 1:4.

*Happy is the man who is so anxious to be with me
that he watches for me daily at my gates, or
waits for me outside my home!*

We look to Jehovah our God for his mercy and kindness just as a servant keeps his eyes upon his master
or a slave girl watches her mistress for the slightest
signal.

This shall be a perpetual daily offering at the door of
the Tabernacle before the Lord, where I will meet with
you and speak with you. / Build altars only where I
tell you to, and I will come and bless you there.

Where two or three gather together because they are
mine, I will be there among them.

The time is coming . . . when we will no longer be
concerned about whether to worship the Father here
or in Jerusalem. For it's not *where* we worship that
counts, but *how* we worship – is our worship spiritual
and real? For God is Spirit, and we must have his help
to worship as we should. The Father wants this kind
of worship from us.

Pray all the time. Ask God for anything in line with
the Holy Spirit's wishes. / Always keep on praying.

Prov. 8:34. Ps. 123:2. Ex. 29:42. Ex. 20:24. Mt. 18:20. Jn. 4:21–24.
Eph. 6:18. 1 Thess. 5:17.

Counsellor.

And the Spirit of the Lord shall rest upon him, the Spirit of wisdom, understanding, counsel and might; the Spirit of knowledge and of the fear of the Lord. His delight will be obedience to the Lord.

Can't you hear the voice of wisdom? She is standing at the city gates and at every fork in the road, and at the door of every house. 'Listen, men!' she calls. 'How foolish and naive you are! Let me give you understanding. O foolish ones, let me show you common sense! Listen to me! For I have important information for you. Everything I say is right and true. I, Wisdom, give good advice and common sense. Because of my strength, kings reign in power.'

The Lord of heaven's armies is a wonderful teacher and gives the farmer wisdom. / If you want to know what God wants you to do, ask him, and he will gladly tell you, for he is always ready to give a generous supply of wisdom to all who ask him; he will not resent it. / Trust the Lord completely; don't ever trust yourself. In everything you do, put God first, and he will direct you and crown your efforts with success.

Is. 9:6. Is. 11:2, 3. Prov. 8:1–7, 14. Is. 28:29. Jas. 1:5. Prov. 3:5, 6.

Always try to do good.

This suffering is all part of the work God has given you. Christ, who suffered for you, is your example. Follow in his steps: he never sinned, never told a lie, never answered back when insulted; when he suffered he did not threaten to get even; he left his case in the hands of God who always judges fairly. / If you want to keep from becoming fainthearted and weary, think about his patience as sinful men did such terrible things to him.

Let us strip off anything that slows us down or holds us back, and especially those sins that wrap themselves so tightly around our feet and trip us up; and let us run with patience the particular race that God has set before us. Keep your eyes on Jesus, our leader and instructor. He was willing to die a shameful death on the cross because of the joy he knew would be his afterwards; and now he sits in the place of honour by the throne of God.

Let me say this one more thing: fix your thoughts on what is true and good and right. Think about things that are pure and lovely, and dwell on the fine, good things in others. Think about all you can praise God for and be glad about.

1 Thess. 5:15. 1 Pet. 2:21–23. Hebr. 12:3. Hebr. 12:1, 2. Phil. 4:8.

The Mighty God.

You are the fairest of all; your words are filled with grace; God himself is blessing you forever. Arm yourself, O Mighty One, so glorious, so majestic! And in your majesty go on to victory, defending truth, humility and justice. Go forth to awe-inspiring deeds! Your throne, O God, endures forever. Justice is your royal sceptre. / Who is this . . . with his magnificent garments of crimson? Who is this in kingly robes, marching in the greatness of his strength? 'It is I, the Lord, announcing your salvation; I, the Lord, the one who is mighty to save!'

See, God has come to save me! I will trust and not be afraid, for the Lord is my strength and song; he is my salvation. / But thanks be to God! For through what Christ has done, he has triumphed over us.

God's Son shines out with God's glory, and all that God's Son is and does marks him as God. He is the one who died to cleanse us and clear our record of all sin, and then sat down in highest honour beside the great God of heaven. / He is able to keep you from slipping and falling away, and to bring you, sinless and perfect, into his glorious presence with mighty shouts of everlasting joy. Amen.

Is. 9:6. Ps. 45:2–4, 6. Is. 63:1. Is. 12:2. 2 Cor. 2:14. Hebr. 1:3. Jude 25.

The paths of the Lord are true and right, and good men walk along them. But sinners trying it will fail.

He is very precious to you who believe; and to those who reject him . . . he is the Stone that some will stumble over, and the Rock that will make them fall. They will stumble because they will not listen to God's Word, nor obey it, and so this punishment must follow – that they will fall. / God protects the upright but destroys the wicked.

If ever you were willing to listen, listen now! / Listen, if you are wise, to what I am saying. Think about the lovingkindness of the Lord! / If your eye is pure, there will be sunshine in your soul. / If any of you really determines to do God's will, then you will certainly know whether my teaching is from God or is merely my own. / For to him who has will more be given . . . and he will have great plenty.

Anyone whose Father is God listens gladly to the words of God. Since you don't, it proves you aren't his children. / You won't come to me so that I can give you this life eternal. / My sheep recognize my voice, and I know them, and they follow me.

Hos. 14:9. 1 Pet. 2:7, 8. Prov. 10:29. Mt. 11:15. Ps. 107:43. Mt. 6:22. Jn. 7:17. Mt. 13:12. Jn. 8:47. Jn. 5:40. Jn. 10:27.

The Everlasting Father.

O Israel, listen: Jehovah is our God, Jehovah alone.

I and the Father are one. The Father is in me, and I in the Father. / You don't know who I am, so you don't know who my Father is. If you knew me, then you would know him too. / Philip said, 'Sir, show us the Father and we will be satisfied.' Jesus replied, 'Don't you even yet know who I am, Philip, even after all this time I have been with you? Anyone who has seen me has seen the Father! So why are you asking to see him?' / Here am I and the children God gave me. / When he sees all that is accomplished by the anguish of his soul, he shall be satisfied. / 'I am the A and Z, the beginning and the ending of all things,' says God, who is the Lord, the all powerful one who is, and was, and is coming again! / I was in existence before Abraham was ever born! / The Sovereign God . . . I Am has sent me!

Of his Son he says, 'Your kingdom, O God, will last for ever and ever.' / He was before all else began and it is his power that holds everything together. / In Christ there is the perfection of God in a human body.

Is. 9:6. Deut. 6:4; Jn. 10:30, 38. Jn. 8:19. Jn. 14:8, 9. Hebr. 2:13.
Is. 53:11. Rev. 1:8. Jn. 8:58. Ex. 3:14. Hebr. 1:8. Col. 1:17. Col. 2:9.

*There is wonderful joy ahead, even though the
going is rough for a while down here.*

Dear friends, don't be bewildered or surprised when
you go through the fiery trials ahead. Instead, be
really glad – because these trials will make you partners
with Christ in his suffering, and afterwards you will
have the wonderful joy of sharing his glory. / Have you
quite forgotten the encouraging words God spoke to
you, his child? He said, 'My son, don't be angry when
the Lord punishes you. Don't be discouraged when he
has to show you where you are wrong.' / Being
punished isn't enjoyable while it is happening – it
hurts! But afterwards we can see the result, a quiet
growth in grace and character.

  This high priest of ours understands our weaknesses, since he had the same temptations we have,
though he never once gave way to them and sinned. /
For since he himself has now been through suffering
and temptation, he knows what it is like when we suffer
and are tempted, and he is wonderfully able to help
us. / No temptation is irresistible. You can trust God
to keep the temptation from becoming so strong that
you can't stand up against it, for he has promised this
and will do what he says. He will show you how to
escape temptation's power so that you can bear up
patiently against it.

*1 Pet. 1:6. 1 Pet. 4:12, 13. Hebr. 12:5. Hebr. 12:11. Hebr. 4:15.
Hebr. 2:18. 1 Cor. 10:13.*

The Prince of Peace.

Help him to give justice to your people, even to the poor. May the mountains and hills flourish in prosperity because of his good reign. Help him to defend the poor and needy and to crush their oppressors. May the poor and needy revere you constantly, as long as sun and moon continue in the skies! Yes, forever! / Glory to God . . . and peace on earth for all those pleasing him.

Because the mercy of our God is very tender . . . heaven's dawn is about to break upon us, to give light to those who sit in darkness and death's shadow, and to guide us to the path of peace. / Peace with God through Jesus, the Messiah, who is Lord of all creation.

I have told you all this so that you will have peace of heart and mind. Here on earth you will have many trials and sorrows; but take courage, I have overcome the world. / I am leaving you with a gift – peace of mind and heart. And the peace I give isn't fragile like the peace the world gives. So don't be troubled or afraid. / God's peace . . . far more wonderful than the human mind can understand. His peace will keep your thoughts and your hearts quiet and at rest as you trust in Christ Jesus.

Is. 9:6. Ps. 72:2–5. Lk. 2:14. Lk. 1:78, 79. Acts 10:36. Jn. 16:33. Jn. 14:27. Phil. 4:7.

*Collect the choicest of spices . . . compound
all this into a holy anointing oil.*

It must never be poured upon an ordinary person,
and you shall never make any of it yourselves, for it is
holy, and it shall be treated by you as holy. / God gives
us many kinds of special abilities, but it is the same
Holy Spirit who is the source of them all.

God, your God, has given you more gladness than
anyone else. / Jesus of Nazareth was anointed by God
with the Holy Spirit and with power. / God's Spirit
is upon him without measure or limit.

We have all benefited from the rich blessings he
brought to us – blessing upon blessing heaped upon
us. / You have received the Holy Spirit and he lives
within you, in your hearts, so that you don't need
anyone to teach you what is right. / It is this God who
has made you and me into faithful Christians and commissioned us apostles to preach the Good News. He
has put his brand upon us – his mark of ownership –
and given us his Holy Spirit in our hearts as guarantee
that we belong to him.

When the Holy Spirit controls our lives he will
produce this kind of fruit in us: love, joy, peace,
patience, kindness, goodness, faithfulness, gentleness
and self-control.

*Ex. 30:22, 25. Ex. 30:32. 1 Cor. 12:4. Ps. 45:7. Acts 10:38. Jn. 3:34.
Jn. 1:16. 1 Jn. 2:27. 2 Cor. 1:21, 22. Gal. 5:22, 23.*

The world in its present form will soon be gone.

A Christian who doesn't amount to much in this world should be glad, for he is great in the Lord's sight. But a rich man should be glad that his riches mean nothing to the Lord, for he will soon be gone, like a flower that has lost its beauty and fades away, withered – killed by the scorching summer sun. So it is with rich men. They will soon die and leave behind all their busy activities. / How do you know what is going to happen tomorrow? For the length of your lives is as uncertain as the morning mist – now you see it; soon it is gone. / This world is fading away, and these evil, forbidden things will go with it, but whoever keeps doing the will of God will live for ever.

Lord, help me to realize how brief my time on earth will be. Help me to know that I am here for but a moment more. / When people are saying, 'All is well, everything is quiet and peaceful' – then, all of a sudden, disaster will fall upon them as suddenly as a woman's birth pains begin when her child is born. And these people will not be able to get away anywhere – there will be no place to hide.

1 Cor. 7:31. Jas. 1:9–11. Jas. 4:14. 1 Jn. 2:17. Ps. 39:4. 1 Thess. 5:3.

*When Christ who is our real life comes back again,
you will shine with him and share in all his glories.*

I am the one who raises the dead and gives them life
again. Anyone who believes in me, even though he dies
like anyone else, shall live again. / And what is it that
God has said? That he has given us eternal life, and
that this life is in his Son. So whoever has God's
Son has life; whoever does not have his Son, does not
have life.

The Lord himself will come down from heaven with
a mighty shout and with the soul-stirring cry of the
archangel and the great trumpet-call of God. And the
Christians who are dead will be the first to rise to meet
the Lord. Then we who are still alive and remain on
the earth will be caught up with them in the clouds
to meet the Lord in the air and remain with him forever. So comfort and encourage each other with this
news. / When he comes we will be like him, as a result
of seeing him as he really is. / The bodies we have now
embarrass us for they become sick and die; but they will
be full of glory when we come back to life again. Yes,
they are weak, dying bodies now, but when we live again
they will be full of strength.

There are many homes up there where my Father
lives, and I am going to prepare them for your coming.
Col. 3:4. Jn. 11:25. 1 Jn. 5:11, 12. 1 Thess. 4:16–18. 1 Jn. 3:2. 1 Cor. 15:43.
Jn. 14:2.

Lead me; teach me.

When the Holy Spirit, who is truth, comes, he will guide you into all truth, for he will not be presenting his own ideas, but will be passing on to you what he has heard. / The Holy Spirit has come upon you, and you know the truth.

Check these witches' words against the Word of God! If their messages are different from mine, it is because I have not sent them; for they have no light or truth in them. / Every Scripture was given to us by inspiration from God and is invaluable to teach us what is true and to make us realize what is wrong in our lives; it straightens us out and helps us do what is right. It is God's way of making us well – prepared at every point, fully equipped to do good to everyone.

I will instruct you (says the Lord) and guide you along the best pathway for your life; I will advise you and watch your progress. / If your eye is pure, there will be sunshine in your soul. / If any of you really determines to do God's will, then he will certainly know whether my teaching is from God or is merely my own. / God will walk there with you; even the most stupid cannot miss the way.

Ps. 25:5. Jn. 16:13. 1 Jn. 2:20. Is. 8:20. 2 Tim. 3:16, 17. Ps. 32:8. Mt. 6:22. Jn. 7:17. Is. 35:8.

*Oh, that these men would praise the Lord for his
lovingkindness, and for all of his wonderful deeds!*

Oh, put God to the test and see how kind he is! See for
yourself the way his mercies shower down on all who
trust in him. / Oh, how great is your goodness to those
who publicly declare that you will rescue them. For you
have stored up great blessings for those who trust and
reverence you.

His unchanging plan has always been to adopt us into
his own family by sending Jesus Christ to die for us.
And he did this because he wanted to! Now all praise
to God for his wonderful kindness to us and his favour
that he has poured out upon us, because we belong to
his dearly loved Son.

How wonderful and beautiful all shall be! The abundance of grain and wine will make the young men and
girls flourish, they will be radiant with health and
happiness. / He is good to everyone, and his compassion is intertwined with everything he does. All
living things shall thank you, Lord, and your people
will bless you. They will talk together about the glory
of your kingdom and mention examples of your power.
They will tell about your miracles and about the
majesty and glory of your reign.

Ps. 107:8. Ps. 34:8. Ps. 31:19. Eph. 1:5, 6. Zech. 9:17. Ps. 145:9–12.

We know how happy they are now because they stayed true.

We can rejoice, too, when we run into problems and trials for we know that they are good for us – they help us learn to be patient. And patience develops strength of character in us and helps us trust God more each time we use it until finally our hope and faith are strong and steady. Then, when that happens, we are able to hold our heads high no matter what happens and know that all is well, for we know how dearly God loves us.

Being punished isn't enjoyable while it is happening – it hurts! But afterwards we can see the result, a quiet growth in grace and character. / When your patience is finally in full bloom, then you will be ready for anything, strong in character, full and complete.

I am glad to boast about how weak I am; I am glad to be a living demonstration of Christ's power, instead of showing off my own power and abilities. Since I know it is all for Christ's good, I am quite happy about 'the thorn,' and about insults and hardships, persecutions and difficulties; for when I am weak, then I am strong – the less I have, the more I depend on him.

Jas. 5:11. Rom. 5:3–5. Hebr. 12:11. Jas. 1:4. 2 Cor. 12:9, 10.

Let us who live in the light keep sober, protected
by the armour of faith and love, and wearing as
our helmet the happy hope of salvation.

You can look foward soberly and intelligently to more
of God's kindness to you when Jesus Christ returns. /
You will need the strong belt of truth and the breast-
plate of God's approval. In every battle you will need
faith as your shield to stop the fiery arrows aimed at
you by Satan. And you will need the helmet of salvation
and the sword of the Spirit – which is the Word of God.

He will swallow up death forever. The Lord God will
wipe away all tears and take away forever all insults
and mockery against his land and people. The Lord has
spoken – he will surely do it! In that day the people
will proclaim, 'This is our God, in whom we trust, for
whom we waited. Now at last he is here.' What a day
of rejoicing!

What is faith? It is the confident assurance that
something we want is going to happen. It is the certainty
that what we hope for is waiting for us, even though
we cannot see it ahead.

1 Thess. 5:8. 1 Pet. 1:13. Eph. 6:14, 16, 17. Is. 25:8, 9. Hebr. 11:1.

*The Israeli army looked like two little flocks of
baby goats in comparison with the vast Syrian
forces that filled the countryside!*

Then a prophet went to the king of Israel with this
message from the Lord: Because the Syrians have declared, 'The Lord is a God of the hills and not of the
plains,' I will help you defeat this vast army, and you
shall know that I am indeed the Lord. The two armies
camped opposite each other for seven days, and on the
seventh day the battle began. And the Israelis killed
100,000 Syrian infantrymen that first day. / You belong
to God and have already won your fight with those who
are against Christ, because there is someone in your
hearts who is stronger than any evil teacher in this
wicked world. / If anyone comes to teach you, and he
doesn't believe what Christ taught, don't even invite
him into your home. Don't encourage him in any way. /
For we are not fighting against people made of flesh
and blood, but against . . . mighty satanic beings.

Here on earth you will have many trials and sorrows;
but take courage, I have overcome the world. / Fear
not, for I am with you. Do not be dismayed. I am
your God. I will strengthen you . . . with my victorious
right hand.

'They will try, but they will fail. For I am with you,'
says the Lord. 'I will deliver you.'

*1 Kgs. 20:27. 1 Kgs. 20:28, 29. 1 Jn. 4:4. 2 Jn. 10. Eph. 6:12. Jn. 16:33.
Is. 41:10. Jer. 1:19.*

This is my beloved Son, and I am wonderfully pleased with him.

I am the Lord, and there is no other Saviour. / God is on one side and all the people on the other side, and Christ Jesus, himself man, is between them to bring them together. / There is salvation in no one else! Under all heaven there is no other name for men to call upon to save them.

The Mighty God. / Jesus Christ, who, though he was God . . . laid aside his mighty power and glory, taking the disguise of a slave and becoming like men. And he humbled himself even further, going so far as actually to die a criminal's death on a cross. Yet it was because of this that God raised him up to the heights of heaven and gave him a name which is above every other name. / We do see Jesus – who for a while was a little lower than the angels – crowned now by God with glory and honour because he suffered death for us. Yes, because of God's great kindness, Jesus tasted death for everyone in all the world. / Since we, God's children, are human beings – made of flesh and blood – he became flesh and blood too by being born in human form; for only as a human being could he die and in dying break the power of the devil who had the power of death.

Mt. 3:17. Is. 43:11. 1 Tim. 2:5. Acts 4:12. Is. 9:6. Phil. 2:5–9. Hebr. 2:9. Hebr. 2:14.

*Gather together my own people who by their
sacrifice upon my altar have promised to obey me.*

Christ died only once as an offering for the sins of
many people; and he will come again, but not to deal
again with our sins. This time he will come bringing
salvation to all those who are eagerly and patiently
waiting for him. / Christ came with this new agreement
so that all who are invited may come and have forever
all the wonders God has promised them. For Christ
died to rescue them from the penalty of the sins they
had committed.

Father, I want them with me – these you've given
me. / I will send out the angels to gather together
my chosen ones from all over the world – from the
farthest bounds of earth and heaven. / Though you are
at the ends of the earth, he will go and find you and
bring you back again.

The Christians who are dead will be the first to rise
to meet the Lord. Then we who are still alive and
remain on the earth will be caught up with them in the
clouds to meet the Lord in the air and remain with
him forever.

*Ps. 50:5. Hebr. 9:28. Hebr. 9:15. Jn. 17:24. Mk. 13:27. Deut. 30:4.
1 Thess. 4:16, 17.*

Always please the Lord and honour him, so that you will always be doing good, kind things for others, all the time learning to know God better and better.

Dear brothers, I plead with you to give your bodies to God. Let them be a living sacrifice, holy – the kind he can accept. When you think of what he has done for you, is this too much to ask? Don't copy the behaviour and customs of this world, but be a new and different person with a freshness in all you do and think. Then you will learn from your own experience how his ways will really satisfy you. / Just as you used to be slaves to all kinds of sin, so now you must let yourselves be slaves to all that is right and holy. / It doesn't make any difference now whether we have been circumcised or not; what counts is whether we really have been changed into new and different people. May God's mercy and peace be upon all of you who live by this principle and upon those everywhere who are really God's own.

My true disciples produce bountiful harvests. This brings great glory to my Father. / You didn't choose me. I chose you. I appointed you to go and produce good fruit always, so that no matter what you ask for from the Father, using my name, he will give it to you.

Col. 1:10. Rom. 12:1, 2. Rom. 6:19. Gal. 6:15, 16. Jn. 15:8. Jn. 15:16.

I got up to look for him but couldn't find him.

Return to the Lord, your God, for you have been crushed by your sins. Bring your petition. Come to the Lord and say, 'O Lord, take away our sins; be gracious to us and receive us, and we will offer you the sacrifice of praise.'

Remember, when someone wants to do wrong it is never God who is tempting him, for God never wants to do wrong and never tempts anyone else to do it. Temptation is the pull of man's own evil thoughts and wishes. These evil thoughts lead to evil actions and afterwards to the death penalty from God. So don't be misled, dear brothers. But whatever is good and perfect comes to us from God, the creator of all light, and he shines for ever without change or shadow.

Don't be impatient. Wait for the Lord, and he will come and save you! Be brave, stouthearted and courageous. Yes, wait and he will help you. / It is good both to hope and wait quietly for the salvation of the Lord. / Don't you think that God will surely give justice to his people who plead with him day and night?

I stand silently before the Lord, waiting for him to rescue me. For salvation comes from him alone.

Song 3:1. Hos. 14:1, 2. Jas. 1:13–17. Ps. 27:14. Lam. 3:26. Lk. 18:7. Ps. 62:1.

He kept them safe.

My paths are those of justice and right. Those who love and follow me are indeed wealthy. I fill their treasuries.

I am sending an Angel before you to lead you safely to the land I have prepared for you. / In all their affliction he was afflicted, and he personally saved them. In his love and pity he redeemed them and lifted them up and carried them through all the years.

They did not conquer by their own strength and skill, but by your mighty power and because you smiled upon them and favoured them. / Like fine stallions racing through the desert, they never stumbled. Like cattle grazing in the valleys, so the Spirit of the Lord gave them rest.

Lord, lead me as you promised me you would; otherwise my enemies will conquer me. Tell me clearly what to do, which way to turn. / Oh, send out your light and your truth – let them lead me. Let them lead me to your Temple on your holy mountain, Zion. There I will go to the altar of God my exceeding joy, and praise him with my harp. O God – my God!

Ps. 78:53. Prov. 8:20, 21. Ex. 23:20. Is. 63:9. Ps. 44:3. Is. 63:13, 14. Ps. 5:8. Ps. 43:3, 4.

Your sins are washed away, and you are set apart for God, and he has accepted you.

The blood of Jesus his Son cleanses us from every sin. / He was chastised that we might have peace; he was lashed – and we were healed!

The . . . love . . . Christ showed to the church when he died for her, to make her holy and clean, washed by baptism and God's word; so that he could give her to himself as a glorious church without a single spot or wrinkle or any other blemish, being holy and without a single fault. / She is permitted to wear the cleanest and whitest and finest of linens. (Fine linen represents the good deeds done by the people of God.) / Let us go right in, to God himself, with true hearts fully trusting him to receive us, because we have been sprinkled with Christ's blood to make us clean, and because our bodies have been washed with pure water.

Who dares accuse us whom God has chosen for his own? Will God? No! He is the one who has forgiven us and given us a right standing with himself. / What happiness for those whose guilt has been forgiven! What joys when sins are covered over! What relief for those who have confessed their sins and God has cleared their record.

1 Cor. 6:11. 1 Jn. 1:7. Is. 53:5. Eph. 5:25–27. Rev. 19:8. Hebr. 10:22. Rom. 8:33. Ps. 32:1, 2.

*God sometimes uses sorrow in our lives to help
us turn away from sin and seek eternal life.*

Peter remembered what Jesus had said, 'Before the
cock crows, you will deny me three times.' And he went
away, crying bitterly. / If we confess our sins to him,
he can be depended on to forgive us and to cleanse us
from every wrong. / The blood of Jesus his Son
cleanses us from every sin.

I perish, for problems far too big for me to solve are
piled higher than my head. Meanwhile my sins, too
many to count, have all caught up with me and I am
ashamed to look up. My heart quails within me. Please,
Lord, rescue me! Quick! Come and help me!

You have been crushed by your sins. / Come back
to God. Live by the principles of love and justice, and
always be expecting much from him, your God. / Rest
in the Lord; wait patiently for him to act.

It is a broken spirit you want – remorse and penitence. A broken and a contrite heart, O God, you
will not ignore. / He heals the broken-hearted,
binding up their wounds. / He has told you what he
wants, and this is all it is: *to be fair and just and
merciful, and to walk humbly with your God.*

2 Cor. 7:10. Mt. 26:75. 1 Jn. 1:9. 1 Jn. 1:7. Ps. 40:12, 13. Hos. 14:1.
Hos. 12:6. Ps 37:7. Ps. 51:17. Ps. 147:3. Mic. 6:8.

There is wonderful joy ahead, even though the going is rough for a while down here.

The world ignores us, but we are known to God; we live close to death, but here we are, still very much alive. We have been injured but kept from death. Our hearts ache, but at the same time we have the joy of the Lord. We are poor, but we give rich spiritual gifts to others. We own nothing, and yet we enjoy everything.

We are pressed on every side by troubles, but not crushed and broken. We are perplexed because we don't know why things happen as they do, but we don't give up. We are hunted down, but God never abandons us. We get knocked down, but we get up again and keep going.

Though our bodies are dying, our inner strength in the Lord is growing every day. These troubles and sufferings of ours are, after all, quite small and won't last very long. Yet this short time of distress will result in God's richest blessing upon us for ever and ever.

So we do not look at what we can see at this moment, the troubles all around us, but we look forward to the joys in heaven which we have not yet seen. The troubles will soon be over, but the joys to come will last for ever.

1 Pet. 1:6. 2 Cor. 6:9, 10. 2 Cor. 4:8, 9, 16–18.

Love each other as much as I love you.

Be full of love for others, following the example of
Christ who loved you and gave himself to God as a
sacrifice to take away your sins. And God was pleased,
for Christ's love for you was like sweet perfume to
him. / The message to us from the beginning has been
that we should love one another. / As far as God is
concerned there is a sweet, wholesome fragrance in our
lives. It is the fragrance of Christ within us.

   You have a new life. It was not passed on to you
from your parents, for the life they gave you will fade
away. This new one will last forever, for it comes from
Christ, God's ever-living message to man. / Make them
pure and holy through teaching them your words of
truth. / Unless one is born of water and the Spirit, he
cannot enter the Kingdom of God. / He saved us – not
because we were good enough to be saved, but because
of his kindness and pity – by washing away our sins
and giving us the new joy of the indwelling Holy
Spirit. / Your promises . . . refresh and revive me!

   May God who gives patience, steadiness, and encouragement help you to live in complete harmony
with each other – each with the attitude of Christ
towards the other.

Jn. 15:12. Eph. 5:2. 1 Jn. 3:11. 2 Cor. 2:15. 1 Pet. 1:23. Jn. 17:17.
Jn. 3:5. Tit. 3:5. Ps. 119:49, 50. Rom. 15:5.

*All of us . . . may come to God the Father with
the Holy Spirit's help because of what Christ has
done for us.*

I in them and you in me, all being perfected into one.
You can ask him for anything, using my name, and I
will do it, for this will bring praise to the Father because
of what I, the Son, will do for you. Yes, ask anything,
using my name, and I will do it! I will ask the Father
and he will give you another Comforter, and he will
never leave you. He is the Holy Spirit, the Spirit who
leads into all truth. The world at large cannot receive
him, for it isn't looking for him and doesn't recognize
him. But you do, for he lives with you now and some
day shall be in you. / We are all parts of one body,
we have the same Spirit, and we have all been called
to the same glorious future. For us there is only one
Lord, one faith, one baptism, and we all have the same
God and Father who is over us all and in us all, and
living through every part of us. / This is the prayer he
taught them: Father, may your name be honoured.
    Now we may walk right into the very Holy of Holies
where God is, because of the blood of Jesus. This is
the fresh, new, life-giving way which Christ has opened
up for us . . . to let us into the holy presence of God.

*Eph. 2:18. Jn. 17:23. Jn. 14:13, 14, 16, 17. Eph. 4:4–6. Lk. 11:2.
Hebr. 10:19, 20.*

*O my God, you are my helper. You are my
Saviour; come quickly, and save me. Please don't
delay!*

The steps of good men are directed by the Lord. He
delights in each step they take. If they fall it isn't fatal,
for the Lord holds them with his hand. / Reverence
for God gives a man deep strength; his children have
a place of refuge and security. / What right have you to
fear mere mortal men, who wither like the grass and
disappear? And yet you have no fear of God, your
Maker – you have forgotten him, the one who spread
the stars throughout the skies and made the earth.

I, the Lord, will be with you and see you through. /
Be strong! Be courageous! Do not be afraid of them!
For the Lord your God will be with you. He will neither
fail you nor forsake you.

I will sing each morning about your power and
mercy. For you have been my high tower of refuge, a
place of safety in the day of my distress. / You are
my hiding place from every storm of life; you even
keep me from getting into trouble! You surround me
with songs of victory.

*Ps. 40:17. Ps. 37:23, 24. Prov. 14:26. Is. 51:12, 13. Jer. 1:8. Deut. 31:6.
Ps. 59:16. Ps. 32:7.*

*I am the Lord, who opens a way through the
waters, making a path right through the sea.*

It was the harvest season and the Jordan was overflowing all its banks but as the people set out to cross
the river and as the feet of the priests who were carrying
the Ark touched the water at the river's edge, suddenly,
far up the river . . . the water began piling up as though
against a dam! The priests who were carrying the Ark
stood on dry ground in the middle of the Jordan and
waited as all the people passed by.

We do see Jesus – who for a while was a little lower
than the angels – crowned now by God with glory and
honour because he suffered death for us. Yes, because
of God's great kindness, Jesus tasted death for everyone in all the world.

Even when walking through the dark valley of death
I will not be afraid, for you are close beside me,
guarding, guiding all the way. / When you go through
deep waters and great trouble, I will be with you.
When you go through rivers of difficulty, you will not
drown!

Don't be afraid! I am the First and Last, the living
one who died, who is now alive for evermore, who
has the keys of hell and death.

Is. 43:16. Josh. 13:14–17. Hebr. 2:9. Ps. 23:4. Is. 43:2. Rev. 1:17, 18.

God . . . always does just what he says, and he is the one who invited you into this wonderful friendship with his Son, even Christ our Lord.

We can look forward to the salvation God has promised us. There is no longer any room for doubt, and we can tell others that salvation is ours, for there is no question that he will do what he says. / You are God's temple, the home of the living God, and God has said of you, 'I will live in them and walk among them, and I will be their God and they shall be my people.' / Share the fellowship and the joys we have with the Father and with Jesus Christ his Son. / Be really glad – because these trials will make you partners with Christ in his suffering, and afterwards you will have the wonderful joy of sharing his glory in that coming day when it will be displayed.

I pray that Christ will be more and more at home in your hearts, living within you as you trust in him. May your roots go down deep into the soil of God's marvellous love; and may you be able to feel and understand, as all God's children should, how long, how wide, how deep, and how high his love really is; and to experience this love for yourselves, though it is so great that you will never see the end of it or fully know or understand it. And so at last you will be filled up with God himself.

1 Cor. 1:9. Hebr. 10:23. 2 Cor. 6:16. 1 Jn. 1:3. 1 Pet. 4:13. Eph. 3:17–19.

It is God himself who has made us what we are.

The stonecutters quarried and shaped huge blocks of stone – a very expensive job – for the foundation of the Temple. / The stones used in the construction of the Temple were prefinished at the quarry, so the entire structure was built without the sound of hammer, axe, or any other tool at the building site.

And now you have become living building-stones for God's use in building his house. / What a foundation you stand on now: the apostles and the prophets; and the cornerstone of the building is Jesus Christ himself! We who believe are carefully joined together with Christ as parts of a beautiful, constantly growing temple for God. And you also are joined with him and with each other by the Spirit, and are part of this dwelling place of God. / Once you were less than nothing; now you are God's own.

You are *God's* building. / When someone becomes a Christian he becomes a brand new person inside. He is not the same any more. A new life has begun! / This is what God has prepared for us and, as a guarantee, he has given us his Holy Spirit.

Eph. 2:10. 1 Kgs. 5:17. 1 Kgs. 6:7. 1 Pet. 2:5. Eph. 2:20–22. 1 Pet. 2:10. 1 Cor. 3:9. 2 Cor. 5:17. 2 Cor. 5:5.

Make them pure and holy through teaching them your words of truth.

He has already tended you by pruning you back for greater strength and usefulness by means of the commands I gave you. / Remember what Christ taught and let his words enrich your lives and make you wise.

How can a young man stay pure? By reading your Word and following its rules. I have tried my best to find you – don't let me wander off from your instructions.

For wisdom and truth will enter the very centre of your being, filling your life with joy. You will be given the sense to stay away from evil men.

I have stayed in God's paths, following his steps. I have not turned aside. I have not refused his commandments but have enjoyed them more than my daily food. / Nothing is perfect except your words. Oh, how I love them. I think about them all day long. They make me wiser than my enemies, because they are my constant guide. Yes, wiser than my teachers, for I am ever thinking of your rules. / You are truly my disciples if you live as I tell you to, and you will know the truth, and the truth will set you free.

Jn. 17:17. Jn. 15:3. Col. 3:16. Ps. 119:9, 10. Prov. 2:10, 11. Job 23:11, 12. Ps. 119:96–99. Jn. 8:31, 32.

Citizens of God's country, and you belong in God's household with every other Christian.

You have come right up to Mount Zion, to the city of the living God, the heavenly Jerusalem, and to the gathering of countless happy angels; and to the church, composed of all those registered in heaven; and to God who is Judge of all; and to the spirits of the redeemed in heaven, already made perfect.

Men of faith . . . . died without ever receiving all that God had promised them; but they saw it all awaiting them ahead and were glad, for they agreed that this earth was not their real home but that they were just strangers visiting down here. / But our homeland is in heaven, where our Saviour the Lord Jesus Christ is; and we are looking forward to his return from there. When he comes back he will take these dying bodies of ours and change them into glorious bodies like his own, using the same mighty power that he will use to conquer all else everywhere. / Always thankful to the Father who has made us fit to share all the wonderful things that belong to those who live in the kingdom of light. For he has rescued us out of the darkness and gloom of Satan's kingdom and brought us into the kingdom of his dear Son.

Eph. 2:19. Hebr. 12:22, 23. Hebr. 11:13. Phil. 3:20, 21. Col. 1:12, 13.

How deep are your thoughts!

We have kept on praying and asking God to help you understand what he wants you to do, and to make you wise about spiritual things. / And I pray that Christ will be more and more at home in your hearts, living within you as you trust in him. May your roots go down deep into the soil of God's marvellous love; and may you be able to feel and understand, as all God's children should, how long, how wide, how deep, and how high his love really is; and to experience this love for yourselves, though it is so great that you will never see the end of it or fully know or understand it. And so at last you will be filled up with God himself.

How great are his wisdom and knowledge and riches! How impossible it is for us to understand his decisions and his methods! / This plan of mine is not what you would work out, neither are my thoughts the same as yours! For just as the heavens are higher than the earth, so are my ways higher than yours, and my thoughts than yours. / O Lord my God, many and many a time you have done great miracles for us, and we are ever in your thoughts. Who else can do such glorious things? No one else can be compared with you.

Ps. 92:5. Col. 1:9. Eph. 3:17–19. Rom. 11:33. Is. 55:8, 9. Ps. 40:5.

A man will always reap just the kind of crop he sows!

Experience teaches that it is those who sow sin and trouble who harvest the same. / They have sown the wind and they will reap the whirlwind. / If he sows to please his own wrong desires, he will be planting seeds of evil and he will surely reap a harvest of spiritual decay and death.

The good man's reward lasts forever. / If he plants the good things of the Spirit, he will reap the everlasting life which the Holy Spirit gives him. And let us not get tired of doing what is right, for after a while we will reap a harvest of blessing if we don't get discouraged and give up. That's why whenever we can we should always be kind to everyone, and especially to our Christian brothers.

It is possible to give away and become richer! It is also possible to hold on too tightly and lose everything. Yes, the liberal man shall be rich! By watering others, he waters himself. / If you give little, you will get little. A farmer who plants just a few seeds will get only a small crop, but if he plants much, he will reap much.

Gal. 6:7. Job 4:8. Hos. 8:7. Gal. 6:8. Prov. 11:18. Gal. 6:8–10. Prov. 11:24, 25. 2 Cor. 9:6.

*He has punished Israel but a little, exiling her far
from her own land as though blown away in a
storm from the east.*

It is better to fall into the hand of the Lord (for his
mercy is great) than into the hands of men. / 'I am with
you and I will save you,' says the Lord '. . . I will not
exterminate you; I will punish you, yes – you will not
go unpunished.' / He never bears a grudge, nor remains
angry forever. He has not punished us as we deserve for
all our sins. For he knows we are but dust. / I will
spare them as a man spares an obedient and dutiful son.

No temptation is irresistible. You can trust God to
keep the temptation from becoming so strong that you
can't stand up against it, for he has promised this and
will do what he says. He will show you how to escape
temptation's power so that you can bear up patiently
against it. / Satan has asked to have you, to sift you like
wheat, but I have pleaded in prayer for you that your
faith should not completely fail.

To the poor, O Lord, you are a refuge from the
storm, a shadow from the heat, a shelter from merciless
men who are like a driving rain that melts down an
earthen wall.

*Is. 27:8. 2 Sam. 24:14. Jer. 30:11. Ps. 103:9, 10, 14. Mal. 3:17.
1 Cor. 10:13. Lk. 22:31, 32. Is. 25:4.*

*The half had not been told me! Your wisdom and
prosperity are far greater than anything I've ever
heard of!*

The Queen of Sheba . . . came from a distant land to
hear the wisdom of Solomon; and now a greater than
Solomon is here – and you refuse to believe him. / Full
of loving forgiveness and truth. Some of us have seen
his glory – the glory of the only Son of the heavenly
Father!

My preaching was very plain, not with a lot of oratory
and human wisdom, but the Holy Spirit's power was
in my words, proving to those who heard them that the
message was from God. I did this because I wanted
your faith to stand firmly upon God, not on some man's
great ideas. No mere man has ever seen, heard or even
imagined what wonderful things God has ready for
those who love the Lord. But we know about these
things because God has sent his Spirit to tell us, and
his Spirit searches out and shows us all of God's
deepest secrets.

Your eyes will see the King in his beauty. / We will
be like him, as a result of seeing him as he really is. /
This body shall see God! / I will be fully satisfied.

1 Kgs. 10:7. Mt. 12:42. Jn. 1:14. 1 Cor. 2:4, 5, 9, 10. Is. 33:17.
1 Jn. 3:2. Job. 19:26. Ps. 17:15.

The way to identify a tree or a person is by the kind of fruit produced.

Oh, dear children, don't let anyone deceive you about this: if you are constantly doing what is good, it is because you *are* good, even as he is. / Does a spring of water bubble out first with fresh water and then with bitter water? Can you pick olives from a fig tree, or figs from a grape vine? No, and you can't draw fresh water from a salty pool. If you are wise, live a life of steady goodness, so that only good deeds will pour forth. And if you don't brag about them, then you will be truly wise! / Be careful how you behave among your unbelieving neighbours; for then, even if they are suspicious of you and talk against you, they will end up praising God for your good works when Christ returns.

A tree is identified by its fruit. A tree from a select variety produces good fruit; poor varieties don't. / A good man's speech reveals the rich treasures within him. An evil-hearted man is filled with venom, and his speech reveals it.

What more could I have done? Why did my vineyard give me wild grapes instead of sweet?

Mt. 7:20. 1 Jn. 3:7. Jas. 3:11–13. 1 Pet. 2:12. Mt. 12:33. Mt. 12:35. Is. 5:4.

My Temple will be glorious.

Heaven is my throne and the earth is my footstool: what Temple can you build for me as good as that?

Will God really live upon the earth with men? Why, even the heaven and the heaven of heavens cannot contain you – how much less this Temple which I have built!

For the Lord of heaven's armies says, 'In just a little while I will begin to shake the heavens and earth – and the oceans, too, and the dry land – I will shake all nations, and the Desire of All Nations shall come to this Temple, and I will fill this place with my glory,' says the Lord of heaven's armies. 'The future splendour of this Temple will be greater than the splendour of the first one!'

Then I saw a new earth (with no oceans) and a new sky, for the present earth and sky had disappeared. I heard a loud shout from the throne saying, 'Look, the home of God is now among men, and he will live with them and they will be his people; yes, God himself will be among them.'

Is. 60:13. Is. 66:1. 2 Chron. 6:18. Hag. 2:6–8. Rev. 21:1, 3.

When I sit in darkness, the Lord himself will be my Light.

When you go through deep waters and great trouble, I will be with you. When you go through rivers of difficulty, you will not drown! When you walk through the fire of oppression, you will not be burned up – the flames will not consume you. For I am the Lord your God, your Saviour, the Holy One of Israel. / He will bring blind Israel along a path they have not seen before. He will make the darkness bright before them and smooth and straighten out the road ahead. He will not forsake them. / Who among you fears the Lord and obeys his Servant? If such men walk in darkness, without one ray of light, let them trust the Lord, let them rely upon their God.

Even when walking through the dark valley of death I will not be afraid, for you are close beside me, guarding, guiding all the way. / When I am afraid, I will put my confidence in you. Yes, I will trust the promises of God. And since I am trusting him, what can mere man do to me? / The Lord is my light and my salvation; whom shall I fear?

Mic. 7:8. Is. 43:2, 3. Is. 42:16. Is. 50:10. Ps. 23:4. Ps. 56:3, 4. Ps. 27:1.

*God is one one side and all the people on the other
side, and Christ Jesus, himself man, is between
them to bring them together.*

O Israel, listen: Jehovah is our God, Jehovah alone.

Both we and our fathers have sinned so much. They
weren't impressed by the wonder of your miracles in
Egypt, and soon forgot your many acts of kindness to
them. So the Lord declared he would destroy them.
But Moses, his chosen one, stepped into the breach
between the people and their God and begged him to
turn from his wrath, and not destroy them.

Therefore, dear brothers whom God has set apart
for himself – you who are chosen for heaven – I want
you to think now about this Jesus who is God's
messenger and the high priest of our faith. For Jesus
was faithful to God who appointed him high priest,
just as Moses also faithfully served in God's house. But
Jesus has far more glory than Moses, just as a man who
builds a fine house gets more praise than his house
does.

Christ, as a minister in heaven, has been rewarded
with a far more important work than those who serve
under the old laws, because the new agreement which
he passes on to us from God contains far more wonderful promises. 'And I will be merciful to them in their
wrongdoings, and I will remember their sins no more.'

1 Tim. 2:5. Deut. 6:4. Ps. 106:6, 7, 23. Hebr. 3:1–3. Hebr. 8:6, 12.

> *Some will come to me – those the Father has given me – and I will never, never reject them.*

If . . . he cries to me for help, I will hear and be very gracious to him . . . for I am very compassionate. / Despite all they have done, I will not utterly destroy them and my covenant with them, for I am Jehovah their God. / I will keep the pledge I made to you when you were young. I will establish an everlasting covenant with you forever.

'Come, let's talk this over,' says the Lord; 'no matter how deep the stain of your sins, I can take it out and make you as clean as freshly fallen snow. Even if you are stained as red as crimson, I can make you white as wool!' / Let men cast off their wicked deeds; let them banish from their minds the very thought of doing wrong! Let them turn to the Lord that he may have mercy upon them, and to our God, for he will abundantly pardon! / 'Jesus, remember me when you come into your kingdom.' And Jesus replied, 'Today you will be with me in Paradise.'

He will not break the bruised reed, nor quench the dimly burning flame.

Jn. 6:37. Ex. 22:27. Lev. 26:44. Ezk. 16:60. Is. 1:18. Is. 55:7. Lk. 23:42,43. Is. 42:3.

His dear Son.

A voice from heaven said, 'This is my beloved Son, and I am wonderfully pleased with him.' / See my Servant, whom I uphold; my Chosen One, in whom I delight. / His only Son . . . the companion of the Father.

God showed how much he loved us by sending his only Son into this wicked world to bring to us eternal life through his death. In this act we see what real love is: it is not our love for God, but his love for us when he sent his Son to satisfy God's anger against our sins. We know how much God loves us because we have felt his love and because we believe him when he tells us that he loves us dearly. God is love, and anyone who lives in love is living with God and God is living in him.

I have given them the glory you gave me – the glorious unity of being one, as we are – I in them and you in me, all being perfected into one – so that the world will know you sent me and will understand that you love them as much as you love me.

How very much our heavenly Father loves us, for he allows us to be called his children.

Col 1:13. Mt. 3:17. Is. 42:1. Jn. 1:18. 1 Jn. 4:9, 10, 16. Jn. 17:22, 23.
1 Jn. 3:1.

Learning to pray in the power and strength of the Holy Spirit.

God is Spirit, and we must have his help to worship as we should. / All of us, whether Jews or Gentiles, may come to God the Father with the Holy Spirit's help because of what Christ has done for us.

My Father! If it is possible, let this cup be taken away from me. But I want your will, not mine.

The Holy Spirit helps us with our daily problems and in our praying. For we don't even know what we should pray for, nor how to pray as we should; but the Holy Spirit prays for us with such feeling that it cannot be expressed in words. And the Father who knows all hearts knows, of course, what the Spirit is saying as he pleads for us in harmony with God's own will. / And we are sure of this, that he will listen to us whenever we ask him for anything in line with his will. / When the Holy Spirit, who is truth, comes, he shall guide you into all truth.

Pray all the time. Ask God for anything in line with the Holy Spirit's wishes. Plead with him, reminding him of your needs, and keep praying earnestly for all Christians everywhere.

Jude 20. Jn. 4:24. Eph. 2:18. Mt. 26:39. Rom. 8:26, 27. 1 Jn. 5:14. Jn. 16:13. Eph. 6:18.

There is hope for a tree – if it's cut down it sprouts again, and grows tender, new branches.

He will not break the bruised reed. / He restores my failing health.

God sometimes uses sorrow in our lives to help us turn away from sin and seek eternal life. We should never regret his sending it. But the sorrow of the man who is not a Christian is not the sorrow of true repentance and does not prevent eternal death. / Being punished isn't enjoyable while it is happening – it hurts! But afterwards we can see the result, a quiet growth in grace and character.

I used to wander off until you punished me; now I closely follow all you say.

Do not rejoice against me, O my enemy, for though I fall, I will rise again! When I sit in darkness, the Lord himself will be my Light. I will be patient while the Lord punishes me, for I have sinned against him; then he will defend me from my enemies, and punish them for all the evil they have done to me. God will bring me out of my darkness into the light, and I will see his goodness.

Job 14:7. Is. 42:3. Ps. 23:3. 2 Cor. 7:10. Hebr. 12:11. Ps. 119:67. Mic. 7:8, 9.

*All who listen to me shall live in peace and safety,
unafraid.*

Lord, through all the generations you have been our
home! / We live within the shadow of the Almighty,
sheltered by the God who is above all gods. / His
faithful promises are your armour.

Your real life is in heaven with Christ and God. / He
who harms you sticks his finger in Jehovah's eye! /
Don't be afraid. Just stand where you are and watch,
and you will see the wonderful way the Lord will rescue
you today. The Lord will fight for you, and you won't
need to lift a finger! / God is our refuge and strength,
a tested help in times of trouble. And so we need not
fear even if the world blows up, and the mountains
crumble into the sea.

Jesus immediately spoke to them, reassuring them.
'Don't be afraid!' he said. / 'Why are you frightened?'
he asked. 'Why do you doubt that it is really I? Look
at my hands! Look at my feet! Touch me and make
sure that I am not a ghost! For ghosts don't have
bodies, as you see that I do!' / I know the one in whom
I trust, and I am sure that he is able to guard safely
all that I have given him until the day of his return.

*Prov. 1:33. Ps. 90:1. Ps. 91:1. Ps. 91:4. Col. 3:3. Zech. 2:8. Ex. 14:13, 14.
Ps. 46:1. Mt. 14:27. Lk. 24:38, 39. 2 Tim. 1:12.*

My Kingdom is not of the world.

Christ gave himself to God for our sins as one sacrifice for all time, and then sat down in the place of highest honour at God's right hand, waiting for his enemies to be laid under his feet. / In the future you will see me, the Son of Mankind, sitting at the right hand of God and returning on the clouds of heaven.

Christ will be King until he has defeated all his enemies.

We thank God for all of this! It is he who makes us victorious through Jesus Christ our Lord! / It is that same mighty power that raised Christ from the dead and seated him in the place of honour at God's right hand in heaven, far, far above any other king or ruler or dictator or leader. Yes, his honour is far more glorious than that of anyone else either in this world or in the world to come. And God has put all things under his feet and made him the supreme head of the church – which is his body, filled with himself, the author and giver of everything everywhere. / For in due season Christ will be revealed from heaven by the blessed and only Almighty God, the King of kings and Lord of lords.

Jn. 18:36. Hebr. 10:12, 13. Mt. 26:64. 1 Cor. 15:25. 1 Cor. 15:57. Eph. 1:19–23. 1 Tim. 6:15.

*My mother and my brothers are all those who
hear the message of God and obey it.*

We who have been made holy by Jesus, now have the
same Father as he has. This is why Jesus is not ashamed
to call us his brothers. For he says in the book of
Psalms, 'I will talk to my brothers about God my
Father, and together we will sing his praises.' / We to
whom Christ has given eternal life don't need to worry
about whether we have been circumcised or not, or
whether we are obeying the Jewish ceremonies or not;
for all we need is faith working through love. / You
are my friends if you obey me. / Blessed are all who
hear the Word of God and put it into practice.

Not all who talk like godly people are godly. They
may refer to me as 'Lord', but still won't get to heaven.
For the decisive question is whether they obey my
Father in heaven. / My nourishment comes from doing
the will of God who sent me, and from finishing his
work.

If we say we are his friends, but go on living in
spiritual darkness and sin, we are lying. / Those who do
what Christ tells them to will learn to love God more
and more. That is the way to know whether or not you
are a Christian.

*Lk. 8:21. Hebr. 2:11, 12. Gal. 5:6. Jn. 15:14. Lk. 11:28. Mt. 7:21.
Jn. 4:34. 1 Jn. 1:6. 1 Jn. 2:5.*

What are you doing here, Elijah?

He knows every detail of what is happening to me. / O Lord, you have examined my heart and know everything about me. You know when I sit or stand. When far away you know my every thought. You chart the path ahead of me, and tell me where to stop and rest. Every moment, you know where I am. I can *never* be lost to your Spirit! I can *never* get away from my God! If I ride the morning winds to the farthest oceans, even there your hand will guide me, your strength will support me.

Elijah was as completely human as we are. / Fear of man is a dangerous trap, but to trust in God means safety. / If they fall it isn't fatal, for the Lord holds them with his hand. / Don't you know that this good man, though you trip him up seven times, will each time rise again?

Let us not get tired of doing what is right, for after a while we will reap a harvest of blessing if we don't get discouraged and give up. / The spirit indeed is willing, but how weak the body is. / He is like a father to us, tender and sympathetic to those who reverence him. For he knows we are but dust.

1 Kgs. 19:9. Job 23:10. Ps. 139:1–3, 7, 9, 10. Jas. 5:17. Prov. 29:25. Ps. 37:24. Prov. 24:16. Gal. 6:9. Mt. 26:41. Ps. 103:13, 14.

*Now you are free from your old master, sin; and
you have become slaves to your new master,
righteousness.*

You cannot serve two masters: God and money. /
When you were slaves of sin you didn't bother much
with goodness. And what was the result? Evidently
not good, since you are ashamed now even to think
about those things you used to do, for all of them end
in eternal doom. But now you are free from the power
of sin and are slaves of God, and his benefits to you
include holiness and everlasting life.

Christ gives to those who trust in him everything
they are trying to get by keeping his laws.

If these Greeks want to be my disciples, tell them to
come and follow me, for my servants must be where I
am. And if they follow me, the Father will honour
them. / Wear my yoke – for it fits perfectly – and let
me teach you; for I am gentle and humble, and you shall
find rest for your souls; for I give you only light burdens.

O Lord our God, once we worshipped other gods;
but now we worship you alone. / If you will only
help me to want your will, then I will follow your
laws even more closely.

*Rom. 6:18. Mt. 6:24. Rom. 6:20–22. Rom. 10:4. Jn. 12:16. Mt. 11:29, 30.
Is. 26:13. Ps. 119:32.*

*Anyone who asks for mercy from the Lord shall
have it and shall be saved.*

Manasseh . . . rebuilt the hilltop shrines which his
father Hezekiah had destroyed. He built altars for
Baal and made a shameful Asherah idol, just as Ahab
the king of Israel had done. Heathen altars to the sun
god, moon god, and the gods of the stars were placed
even in the Temple of the Lord – in the very city and
building which the Lord had selected to honour his
own name. And he sacrificed one of his sons as a burnt
offering on a heathen altar. He practised black magic
and used fortune-telling, and patronized mediums and
wizards. So the Lord was very angry, for Manasseh
was an evil man, in God's opinion. / Then at last he
came to his senses and cried out humbly to God for
help. And the Lord listened, and answered his plea by
returning him to Jerusalem and to his kingdom! At
that point Manasseh finally realized that the Lord was
really God!

Come, let's talk this over, says the Lord; no matter
how deep the stain of your sins, I can take it out and
make you as clean as freshly fallen snow. Even if you
are stained as red as crimson, I can make you white
as wool! / He is not willing that any should perish.

Acts 2:21. 2 Kgs. 21:1, 3–6. 2 Chron. 33:12, 13. Is. 1:18. 2 Pet. 3:9.

The Lord delights in you.

The Lord who created you, O Israel, says, Don't be afraid, for I have ransomed you; I have called you by name; you are mine. / Can a mother forget her little child and not have love for her own son? Yet even if that should be, I will not forget you. See, I have tattooed your name upon my palm and ever before me is a picture of Jerusalem's walls in ruin.

The steps of good men are directed by the Lord. He delights in each step they take. / How happy I was with what he created – his wide world and all his family of mankind! / His joy is in those who reverence him, those who expect him to be loving and kind. / 'They shall be mine,' says the Lord of heaven's armies, 'in that day when I make up my jewels. And I will spare them as a man spares an obedient and dutiful son.'

You were his enemies and hated him and were separated from him by your evil thoughts and actions, yet now he has brought you back as his friends. He has done this through the death on the cross of his own human body, and now as a result Christ has brought you into the very presence of God, and you are standing there before him with nothing left against you – nothing left that he could even chide you for.

Is. 62:4. Is. 43:1. Is. 49:15, 16. Ps. 37:23. Prov. 8:31. Ps. 147:11. Mal. 3:17. Col. 1:21, 22.

*The sorrow of the man who is not a Christian is
not the sorrow of true repentance and does not
prevent eternal death.*

Ahithophel – publicly disgraced when Absalom refused his advice – saddled his donkey, went to his home
town, set his affairs in order, and hanged himself;
so he died. / When courage dies, what hope is left?

I weep for the hurt of my people; I stand amazed,
silent, dumb with grief. / The Spirit of the Lord God
is upon me, because the Lord has anointed me to bring
good news to the suffering and afflicted. He has sent
me to comfort the brokenhearted, to announce liberty
to captives and to open the eyes of the blind. He has
sent me to tell those who mourn that the time of God's
favour to them has come, and the day of his wrath
to their enemies. To all who mourn in Israel he will
give: beauty for ashes; joy instead of mourning;
praise instead of heaviness. For God has planted them
like strong and graceful oaks for his own glory. / Come
to me and I will give you rest – all of you who work so
hard beneath a heavy yoke. Wear my yoke – for it fits
perfectly – and let me teach you; for I am gentle and
humble, and you shall find rest for your souls; for I
give you only light burdens. / He heals the broken-
hearted, binding up their wounds.

*2 Cor. 7:10. 2 Sam. 17:23. Prov. 18:14. Jer. 8:21. Is. 61:1–3. Mt. 11:28–30.
Ps. 147:3.*

I have given them the glory you gave me.

I saw the Lord! He was sitting on a lofty throne, and the Temple was filled with his glory. Hovering about him were mighty, six-winged seraphs. With two of their wings they covered their faces; with two others they covered their feet, and with two they flew. They sang to each other, 'Holy, holy, holy is the Lord of heaven's armies; the whole earth is filled with his glory.' / Isaiah was referring to Jesus . . . for he had seen a vision of the Messiah's glory. / High in the sky above them was what looked like a throne . . . upon it sat someone who appeared to be a Man. There was a glowing halo like a rainbow all around him. That was the way the glory of the Lord appeared to me.

Moses asked to see God's glory. The Lord replied . . . 'You may not see the glory of my face, for man may not see me and live.' / No man has ever actually seen God, but, of course, his only Son has, for he is the companion of the Father and has told us all about him. / God, who said, 'Let there be light in the darkness,' has made us understand that it is the brightness of his glory that is seen in the face of Jesus Christ.

Jn. 17:22. Is. 6:1–3. Jn. 12:41. Ezk. 1:26, 28. Ex. 33:18–20. Jn. 1:18. 2 Cor. 4:6.

*If young toughs tell you, 'Come and join us' –
turn your back on them!*

The woman was convinced . . . It would make her so
wise! So she ate some of the fruit and gave some to
her husband, and he ate it too. / Don't you remember
that when Achan, the son of Zerah, sinned against the
Lord, the entire nation was punished in addition to
the one man who had sinned?

Don't join mobs intent on evil.

Heaven can be entered only through the narrow
gate. The highway to hell is broad, and its gate is wide
enough for all the multitudes who choose its easy way.

We are not our own bosses to live or die as we ourselves might choose. / Dear brothers, you have been
given freedom: not freedom to do wrong, but freedom
to love and serve each other. / Be careful in using your
freedom that you don't . . . cause some Christian
brother to sin whose conscience is weaker than yours.
And it is a sin against Christ to sin against your
brother by encouraging him to do something he thinks
is wrong.

We are the ones who strayed away like sheep! *We*,
who left God's paths to follow our own. Yet God laid
on *him* the guilt and sins of every one of us.

*Prov. 1:10. Gen. 3:6. Josh. 22:20. Ex. 23:2. Mt. 7:13. Rom. 14:7.
Gal. 5:13. 1 Cor. 8:9, 12. Is. 53:6.*

*Just as the body is dead when there is no spirit in
it, so faith is dead if it is not the kind that
results in good deeds.*

Not all who talk like godly people are godly. They
may refer to me as 'Lord', but still won't get to heaven.
For the decisive question is whether they obey my
Father in heaven.

Seek to live a clean and holy life, for one who is not
holy will not see the Lord. / You need more than faith;
you must also work hard to be good, and even that is
not enough. For then you must learn to know God
better and discover what he wants you to do. Next,
learn to put aside your own desires so that you will
become patient and godly, gladly letting God have his
way with you. This will make possible the next step,
which is for you to enjoy other people and to like them,
and finally you will grow to love them deeply. The
more you go on in this way, the more you will grow
strong spiritually and become fruitful and useful to our
Lord Jesus Christ. But anyone who fails to go after
these additions to faith is blind indeed, or at least
very shortsighted, and has forgotten that God delivered
him from the old life of sin so that now he can live a
strong, good life for the Lord.

Salvation is not a reward for the good we have done,
so none of us can take any credit for it.

Jas. 2:26. Mt. 7:21. Hebr. 12:14. 2 Pet. 1:5–10. Eph. 2:9.

*Since we, God's children, are human beings –
made of flesh and blood – he became flesh and
blood too by being born in human form; for only as
a human being could he die and in dying break the
power of the devil who had the power of death.*

O death, where then your victory? Where then your
sting? How we thank God. It is he who makes us victorious through Jesus Christ our Lord! / That is why
we never give up. Though our bodies are dying, our
inner strength in the Lord is growing every day.

We know that when this tent we live in now is taken
down – when we die and leave these bodies – we will
have wonderful new bodies in heaven, homes that will
be ours for evermore, made for us by God himself,
and not by human hands. Now we look forward with
confidence to our heavenly bodies, realizing that every
moment we spend in these earthly bodies is time spent
away from our eternal home in heaven with Jesus. We
know these things are true by believing, not be seeing.
And we are not afraid, but are quite content to die,
for then we will be at home with the Lord.

Let not your heart be troubled. You are trusting
God, now trust in me. There are many homes up there
where my Father lives, and I am going to prepare them
for your coming.

Hebr. 2:14. 1 Cor. 15:55, 57. 2 Cor. 4:16. 2 Cor. 5:1, 6–8. Jn. 14:1, 2.

*How greatly to be envied are those you have
chosen to come and live with you within the holy
tabernacle courts! What joys await us among all
the good things there.*

The one thing I want from God, the thing I seek most
of all, is the privilege of meditating in his Temple,
living in his presence every day of my life, delighting
in his incomparable perfections and glory.

Happy are those who long for justice for they shall
surely have it. / He has satisfied the hungry hearts and
sent the rich away with empty hands.

He satisfies the thirsty soul and fills the hungry soul
with good. / I am the Bread of Life. No one coming
to me will ever be hungry again. Those believing in me
will never thirst.

How precious is your constant love, O God! All
humanity takes refuge in the shadow of your wings.
You feed them with blessings from your own table and
let them drink from your rivers of delight. For you are
the Fountain of life; our light is from your light.

Ps. 65:4. Ps. 27:4. Mt. 5:6. Lk. 1:53. Ps. 107:9. Jn. 6:35. Ps. 36:7–9.

Do you finally believe this?

What's the use of saying that you have faith and are Christians if you aren't proving it by helping others? Will *that* kind of faith save anyone? It isn't enough just to have faith. You must also do good to prove that you have it. Faith that doesn't show itself by good works is no faith at all – it is dead and useless.

While God was testing him, Abraham still trusted in God and his promises, and so he offered up his son Isaac, and was ready to slay him on the altar of sacrifice; yes, to slay even Isaac, through whom God has promised to give Abraham a whole nation of descendants! He believed that if Isaac died God would bring him back to life again. / Our father Abraham was declared good because of what he *did*, when he was willing to obey God, even if it meant offering his son Isaac to die on the altar. So you see, a man is saved by what he does, as well as by what he believes.

The way to identify a tree or a person is by the kind of fruit produced. Not all who talk like godly people are godly. They may refer to me as 'Lord', but still won't get to heaven. For the decisive question is whether they obey my Father in heaven. / You know these things – now do them. That is the path of blessing.

Jn. 16:31. Jas. 2:14, 17. Hebr. 11:17–19. Jas. 2:21, 24. Mt. 7:20, 21. Jn. 13:17.

May the Lord of peace himself give you his peace no matter what happens. The Lord be with you all.

May you have grace and peace from God who is, and was, and is to come! / God's peace . . . far more wonderful than the human mind can understand. His peace will keep your thoughts and your hearts quiet and at rest as you trust in Christ Jesus.

Jesus himself was suddenly standing there among them, and greeted them. / I am leaving you with a gift – peace of mind and heart. And the peace I give isn't fragile like the peace the world gives. So don't be troubled or afraid.

The Comforter – the Holy Spirit, the source of all truth. / When the Holy Spirit controls our lives he will produce this kind of fruit in us: love, joy, peace. / His Holy Spirit speaks to us deep in our hearts, and tells us that we really are God's children.

'I myself will go with you and give you success.' For Moses had said, 'If you aren't going with us, don't let us move a step from this place. If you don't go with us, who will ever know that I and my people have found favour with you?'

2 Thess. 3:16. Rev. 1:4. Phil. 4:7. Lk. 24:36. Jn. 14:27. Jn. 15:26. Gal. 5:22. Rom. 8:16. Ex. 33:14–16.

*We can rejoice, too, when we run into problems
and trials for we know that they are good for us.*

If being a Christian is only of value to us now in this
life, we are the most miserable of creatures.

Dear friends, don't be bewildered or surprised when
you go through the fiery trials ahead, for this is no
strange, unusual thing that is going to happen to you.
Instead, be really glad – because these trials will make
you partners with Christ in his suffering, and afterwards
you will have the wonderful joy of sharing his glory in
that coming day wnen it will be displayed. / Our hearts
ache, but at the same time we have the joy of the Lord.

Always be full of joy in the Lord; I say it again,
rejoice! / They left the Council Chamber rejoicing that
God had counted them worthy to suffer dishonour for
his name.

I pray . . . that God who gives you hope will keep you
happy and full of peace as you believe in him.

Even though the fig trees are all destroyed, and there
is neither blossom left nor fruit, and though the olive
crops all fail, and the fields lie barren; even if the
flocks die in the fields and the cattle barns are empty,
yet I will rejoice in the Lord; I will be happy in the
God of my salvation.

*Rom. 5:3. 1 Cor. 15:19. 1 Pet. 4:12, 13. 2 Cor. 6:10. Phil. 4:4. Acts 5:41.
Rom. 15:13. Hab. 3:17, 18.*

He will shelter Israel from the storm and wind. He
will refresh her as a river in the desert and as
the cooling shadow of a mighty rock within a
hot and weary land.

Since we, God's children, are human beings – made
of flesh and blood – he became flesh and blood too by
being born in human form. / 'The man who is my
associate and equal,' says the Lord of heaven's
armies. / I and the Father are one.

We live within the shadow of the Almighty, sheltered
by the God who is above all gods. / Protecting . . .
from daytime heat and from rains and storms. /
Jehovah himself is caring for you! He is your defender.
He protects you day and night.

When my heart is faint and overwhelmed, lead me
to the mighty, towering Rock of safety. / You are my
hiding place from every storm of life; you even keep
me from getting into trouble! / To the poor, O Lord,
you are a refuge from the storm, a shadow from the
heat, a shelter from merciless men who are like a driving
rain that melts down an earthen wall. / He gives power
to the tired and worn out, and strength to the weak.

Is. 32:2. Hebr. 2:14. Zech. 13:7. Jn. 10:30. Ps. 91:1. Is. 4:6. Ps. 121:5, 6.
Ps. 61:2. Ps. 32:7. Is. 25:4. Is. 40:29.

I am creating new heavens and a new earth.

As surely as my new heavens and earth shall remain, so surely shall you always be my people, with a name that shall never disappear.

We are looking forward to God's promise of new heavens and a new earth afterwards, where there will be only goodness.

Then I saw a new earth (with no oceans) and a new sky, for the present earth and sky had disappeared. And I, John, saw the Holy City, the new Jerusalem, coming down from God out of heaven. It was a glorious sight, beautiful as a bride at her wedding.

I heard a loud shout from the throne, saying, 'Look, the home of God is now among men, and he will live with them and they will be his people; yes, God himself will be among them. He will wipe away all tears from their eyes, and there shall be no more death, or sorrow, or crying, or pain. All of that has gone for ever.'

And the one sitting on the throne said, 'See, I am making all things new! I will give to the thirsty the springs of the water of life – as a gift. Everyone who conquers will inherit all these blessings, and I will be his God and he will be my son.'

Is. 65:17. Is. 66:22. 2 Pet. 3:13. Rev. 21:1–7.

The Holy Spirit has come upon you, and you know the truth.

Jesus of Nazareth was anointed by God with the Holy Spirit and with power. / God wanted all of himself to be in his Son. / We have all benefited from the rich blessings he brought to us – blessing upon blessing heaped upon us.

Blessings overflow! / You have received the Holy Spirit and he lives within you, in your hearts, so that you don't need anyone to teach you what is right. For he teaches you all things, and he is the truth, and no liar; and so, just as he has said, you must live in Christ, never to depart from him.

When the Father sends the Comforter to represent me – and by the Comforter I mean the Holy Spirit – he will teach you much, as well as remind you of everything I myself have told you.

The Holy Spirit helps us with our daily problems and in our praying. For we don't even know what we should pray for, nor how to pray as we should; but the Holy Spirit prays for us with such feeling that it cannot be expressed in words.

1 Jn. 2:20. Acts 10:38. Col. 1:19. Jn. 1:16. Ps. 23:5. 1 Jn. 2:27. Jn. 14:26. Rom. 8:26.

*With true hearts fully trusting him to receive us,
because we have been sprinkled with Christ's blood
to make us clean.*

And if under the old system the blood of bulls and
goats and the ashes of young cows could cleanse men's
bodies from sin, just think how much more surely the
blood of Christ will transform our lives and hearts. His
sacrifice frees us from the worry of having to obey the
old rules, and makes us want to serve the living God. /
The sprinkled blood which graciously forgives instead
of crying out for vengeance as the blood of Abel did.

So overflowing is his kindness towards us that he
took away all our sins through the blood of his Son,
by whom we are saved.

After Moses had given the people all of God's laws,
he took the blood of calves and goats, along with water,
and sprinkled the blood over the book of God's laws
and over all the people, using branches of hyssop
bushes and scarlet wool to sprinkle with. And in the
same way he sprinkled blood on the sacred tent and
on whatever instruments were used for worship. In fact
we can say that under the old agreement almost everything was cleansed by sprinkling it with blood, and
without the shedding of blood there is no forgiveness
of sins.

Hebr. 10:22. Hebr. 9:13, 14. Hebr. 12:24. Eph. 1:7. Hebr. 9:19, 21, 22.

My eyes are ever looking to the Lord for help.

Is anything too hard for God? / Commit everything
you do to the Lord. Trust him to help you do it and
he will. / Don't worry about anything; instead, pray
about everything; tell God your needs and don't forget
to thank him for his answers. / Let him have all your
worries and cares, for he is always thinking about
you and watching everything that concerns you. / Be
delighted with the Lord. Then he will give you all your
heart's desires.

When Moses and Aaron and Samuel, his prophets,
cried to him for help, he answered them. He spoke to
them from the pillar of cloud and they followed his
instructions.

I will answer them before they even call to me. While
they are still talking to me about their needs, I will go
ahead and answer their prayers! / The earnest prayer
of a righteous man has great power and wonderful
results.

I love the Lord because he hears my prayers and
answers them. Because he bends down and listens, I will
pray as long as I breathe!

*Ps. 25:15. Gen. 18:14. Ps. 37:5. Phil. 4:6. 1 Pet. 5:7. Ps. 37:4.
Ps. 99:6, 7. Is. 65:24. Jas. 5:16. Ps. 116:1, 2.*

Our bodies have been washed with pure water.

Make a bronze basin with a bronze pedestal. Put it between the Tabernacle and the altar, and fill it with water. Aaron and his sons shall wash their hands and feet there, when they go into the Tabernacle to appear before the Lord, or when they approach the altar to burn offerings to the Lord. They must always wash before doing so, or they will die. These are instructions to Aaron and his sons from generation to generation. / Haven't you yet learned that your body is the home of the Holy Spirit God gave you, and that he lives within you? / If anyone defiles and spoils God's home, God will destroy him. For God's home is holy and clean, and you are that home.

And I know that after this body has decayed, this body shall see God! Then he will be on *my* side! Yes, I shall see him, not as a stranger, but as a friend! What a glorious hope! / Nothing evil will be permitted in it – no one immoral or dishonest. / I plead with you to give your bodies to God. Let them be a living sacrifice, holy – the kind he can accept. When you think of what he has done for you, is this too much to ask?

Hebr. 10:22. Ex. 30:18–21. 1 Cor. 6:19. 1 Cor. 3:17. Job 19:26,27.
Rev. 21:27. Rom. 12:1.

They don't know where to find wisdom.

If you want to know what God wants you to do, ask him, and he will gladly tell you, for he is always ready to give a generous supply of wisdom to all who ask him; he will not resent it. But when you ask him, be sure that you really expect him to tell you, for a doubtful mind will be as unsettled as a wave of the sea that is driven and tossed by the wind. / Trust the Lord completely; don't ever trust yourself. In everything you do, put God first, and he will direct you and crown your efforts with success. / He alone is God, and full of wisdom. / Don't be conceited, sure of your own wisdom.

'O Lord God,' I said, 'I can't do that! I'm far too young! I'm only a youth!' 'Don't say that,' he replied, 'for you will go wherever I send you and speak whatever I tell you to. And don't be afraid of the people, for I, the Lord, will be with you and see you through.'

Go directly to the Father and ask him, and he will give you what you ask for because you use my name. You haven't tried this before, [but begin now]. Ask, using my name, and you will receive, and your cup of joy will overflow. / You can get anything – *anything* you ask for in prayer – if you believe.

Job 28:12. Jas. 1:5, 6. Prov. 3:5, 6. 1 Tim. 1:17. Prov. 3:7. Jer. 1:6–8. Jn. 16:23, 24. Mt. 21:22.

Let me alone for these few remaining days.

Oh, for wings like a dove, to fly away and rest! I would flee to some refuge from all this storm.

How weary we grow of our present bodies. That is why we look forward eagerly to the day when we shall have heavenly bodies which we shall put on like new clothes. These earthly bodies make us groan and sigh. / Sometimes I want to live and at other times I don't, for I long to go and be with Christ. How much happier for *me* than being here!

Let us strip off anything that slows us down or holds us back, and especially those sins that wrap themselves so tightly around our feet and trip us up; and let us run with patience the particular race that God has set before us. Keep your eyes on Jesus, our leader and instructor. He was willing to die a shameful death on the cross because of the joy he knew would be his afterwards; and now he sits in the place of honour by the throne of God.

I am leaving you with a gift – peace of mind and heart. So don't be troubled or afraid.

Job 7:16. Ps. 55:6, 8. 2 Cor. 5:2, 4. Phil, 1:23. Hebr. 12:1, 2. Jn. 14:27.

*The punishment you gave me was the best thing
that could have happened to me, for it taught me
to pay attention to your laws.*

Even though Jesus was God's Son, he had to learn
from experience what it was like to obey, when obeying
meant suffering. / If we are to share his glory, we must
also share his suffering. Yet what we suffer now is
nothing compared to the glory he will give us later. / Is
your life full of difficulties and temptations? Then be
happy, for when the way is rough, your patience has
a chance to grow. So let it grow, and don't try to
squirm out of your problems.

He knows every detail of what is happening to me;
and when he has examined me, he will pronounce me
completely innocent – as pure as solid gold! I have
stayed in God's paths, following his steps. I have not
turned aside.

Do you remember how the Lord led you through
the wilderness for all those forty years, humbling
you and testing you to find out how you would
respond, and whether or not you would really obey
him? So you should realize that, as a man punishes
his son, the Lord punishes you to help you. Obey the
laws of the Lord your God. Walk in his ways and
fear him.

*Ps. 119:71. Hebr. 5:8. Rom. 8:17, 18. Jas. 1:2–4. Job 23:10, 11.
Deut. 8:2, 5, 6.*

No one shall succeed by strength alone.

David shouted in reply, 'You come to me with a sword and a spear, but I come to you in the name of the Lord of the armies of heaven and of Israel – the very God whom you have defied.' David . . . reaching into his shepherd's bag, took out a stone, hurled it from his sling, and hit the Philistine in the forehead. The stone sank in, and the man fell on his face to the ground. So David conquered the Philistine giant with a sling and a stone.

The best-equipped army cannot save a king – for great strength is not enough to save anyone. But the eyes of the Lord are watching over those who fear him, who rely upon his steady love. / Riches and honour come from you alone, and you are the Ruler of all mankind; your hand controls power and might, and it is at your discretion that men are made great and given strength.

I am glad to boast about how weak I am; I am glad to be a living demonstration of Christ's power, instead of showing off my own power and abilities. For when I am weak, then I am strong – the less I have, the more I depend on him.

1 Sam. 2:9. 1 Sam. 17:45, 49, 50. Ps. 33:16, 18. 1 Chron. 29:12.
2 Cor. 12:9, 10.

God is at work within you.

Not because we think we can do anything of lasting value by ourselves. Our only power and success comes from God. / God in heaven appoints each man's work. / No one can come to me unless the Father who sent me draws him to me, and at the Last Day I will bring all such back to life. / And I will give them one heart and mind to worship me forever.

Don't be misled, dear brothers. But whatever is good and perfect comes to us from God, the creator of all light, and he shines for ever without change or shadow. And it was a happy day for him when he gave us our new lives, through the truth of his word, and we became, as it were, the first children in his new family.

It is God himself who has made us what we are and given us new lives from Christ Jesus; and long ages ago he planned that we should spend these lives in helping others.

Lord, grant us peace; for all we have and are has come from you.

Phil. 2:13. 2 Cor. 3:5. Jn. 3:27. Jn. 6:44. Jer. 32:39. Jas. 1:16–18. Eph. 2:10. Is. 26:12.

The spirit indeed is willing, but how weak the body is.

O Lord, we love to do your will! Our hearts' desire is to glorify your name. All night long I search for you; earnestly I seek for God.

I know I am rotten through and through so far as my old sinful nature is concerned. No matter which way I turn I can't make myself do right. I want to but I can't. I love to do God's will so far as my new nature is concerned; but there is something else deep within me, in my lower nature, that is at war with my mind and wins the fight and makes me a slave to the sin that is still within me. / For we naturally love to do evil things that are just the opposite of the things that the Holy Spirit tells us to do; and the good things we want to do when the Spirit has his way with us are just the opposite of our natural desires. These two forces within us are constantly fighting each other to win control over us, and our wishes are never free from their pressures.

I can do everything God asks me to with the help of Christ who gives me the strength and power. / Our only power and success comes from God. / I am with you; that is all you need.

Mt. 26:41. Is. 26:8, 9. Rom. 7:18, 22, 23. Gal. 5:17. Phil. 4:13. 2 Cor. 3:5. 2 Cor. 12:9.

*God took the sinless Christ and poured into him
our sins. Then, in exchange, he poured God's
goodness into us!*

God laid on *him* the guilt and sins of every one of us. /
He personally carried the load of our sins in his own
body when he died on the cross, so that we can be
finished with sin and live a good life from now on. For
his wounds have healed ours! / Adam caused many to
be sinners because he disobeyed God, and Christ caused
many to be made acceptable to God because he obeyed.

When the time came for the kindness and love of
God our Saviour to appear, then he saved us – not
because we were good enough to be saved, but because
of his kindness and pity – by washing away our sins
and giving us the new joy of the indwelling Holy
Spirit. He poured him out upon us with wonderful
fullness – and all because of what Jesus Christ our
Saviour did so that he could declare us good in God's
eyes – all because of his great kindness; and now we
can share in the wealth of the eternal life he gives us,
and we are eagerly looking forward to receiving it. /
So there is now no condemnation awaiting those who
belong to Christ Jesus.

The Lord Our Righteousness.

2 Cor. 5:21. Is. 53:6. 1 Pet. 2:24. Rom. 5:19. Tit. 3:4–7. Rom. 8:1.
Jer. 23:6.

I will refresh Israel like the dew from heaven.

My Chosen One, in whom I delight. He will be gentle.
He will not break the bruised reed, nor quench the
dimly burning flame.

'The Spirit of the Lord is upon me; he has appointed me to preach Good News to the poor; he has
sent me to announce that captives shall be released
and the blind shall see, that the down-trodden shall be
freed from their oppressors, and that God is ready to
give blessings to all who come to him.' He closed the
book and handed it back to the attendant. Then he
[Jesus] added, 'These Scriptures came true today!' All
who were there spoke well of him and were amazed by
the beautiful words that fell from his lips.

At that moment Jesus turned and looked at Peter.
Then Peter remembered what he had said – 'Before
the rooster crows tomorrow morning, you will deny
me three times.' And Peter walked out of the courtyard, weeping bitterly. / Lord, you know my heart.

He will feed his flock like a shepherd; he will carry
the lambs in his arms and gently lead the ewes with
young.

Hos. 14:5. Is. 42:1-3. Lk. 4:18, 19, 21, 22. Lk. 22:61, 62. Jn. 21:17.
Is. 40:11.

Love and serve each other.

Dear brothers, if a Christian is overcome by some sin, you who are godly should gently and humbly help him back on to the right path, remembering that next time it might be one of you who is in the wrong. Share each other's troubles and problems, and so obey our Lord's command.

Dear brothers, if anyone has slipped away from God and no longer trusts the Lord, and someone helps him understand the Truth again, that person who brings him back to God will have saved a wandering soul from death, bringing about the forgiveness of his many sins. / Now you can have real love for everyone because your souls have been cleansed from selfishness and hatred when you trusted Christ to save you; so see to it that you really do love each other warmly, with all your hearts. / Pay all your debts except the debt of love for others – never finish paying that! For if you love them, you will be obeying all of God's laws, fulfilling all his requirements. / Love each other with brotherly affection and take delight in honouring each other. / All of you serve each other with humble spirits, for God gives special blessings to those who are humble, but sets himself against those who are proud.

Gal. 5:13. Gal. 6:1, 2. Jas. 5:19, 20. 1 Pet. 1:22. Rom. 13:8. Rom. 12:10. 1 Pet. 5:5.

The dust returns to the earth as it was.

Our earthly bodies . . . die and decay. The bodies we have now embarrass us for they become sick and die. Yes, they are weak, dying bodies . . . human bodies. / Adam was made from the dust of the earth.

You were made from the ground, and to the ground you will return. / He destroys those who are healthy, wealthy, fat, and prosperous; God also destroys those in deep and grinding poverty who have never known anything good. Both alike are buried in the same dust, both eaten by the same worms.

Heart, body and soul are filled with joy. / I know that after this body has decayed, this body shall see God! / The Lord Jesus Christ . . . will take these dying bodies of ours and change them into glorious bodies like his own, using the same mighty power that he will use to conquer all else everywhere.

Lord, help me to realize how brief my time on earth will be. Help me to know that I am here for but a moment more. / Teach us to number our days and recognize how few they are; help us to spend them as we should.

Eccl. 12:7. 1 Cor. 15:42–44. 1 Cor. 15:47. Gen. 3:19. Job 21:23–26. Ps. 16:9. Job 19:26. Phil. 3:20, 21. Ps. 39:4. Ps. 90:12.

*God is more pleased when we are just and fair
than when we give him gifts.*

He has told you what he wants, and this is all it is: *to
be fair and just and merciful, and to walk humbly with
your God.* / Has the Lord as much pleasure in your
burnt offerings and sacrifices as in your obedience?
Obedience is far better than sacrifice. He is much more
interested in your listening to him than in your offering
the fat of rams to him. / It is far more important to
love him with all my heart and understanding and
strength, and to love others as myself, than to offer all
kinds of sacrifices on the altar of the Temple.

Oh, come back to God. Live by the principles of
love and justice, and always be expecting much from
him, your God. / Mary sat on the floor, listening
to Jesus as he talked. 'There is really only one thing
worth being concerned about. Mary has discovered
it – and I won't take it away from her.'

God is at work within you, helping you want to obey
him, and then helping you to do what he wants. /
May he produce in you through the power of Christ all
that is pleasing to him. To him be glory for ever and
ever. Amen.

*Prov. 21:3. Mic. 6:8. 1 Sam. 15:22. Mk.12:33. Hos. 12:6. Lk. 10:39, 42.
Phil. 2:13. Hebr. 13:21.*

The spirit returns to God who gave it.

The Lord God formed a man's body from the dust of the ground and breathed into it the breath of life. And man became a living person. / It is not mere age that makes men wise. Rather, it is the spirit in a man, the breath of the Almighty which makes him intelligent.

We look forward with confidence to our heavenly bodies, realizing that every moment we spend in these earthly bodies is time spent away from our eternal home in heaven with Jesus. / I long to go and be with Christ. How much happier for *me* than being here! / And now, dear brothers, I want you to know what happens to a Christian when he dies so that when it happens, you will not be full of sorrow, as those are who have no hope. For since we believe that Jesus died and then came back to life again, we can also believe that when Jesus returns, God will bring back with him all the Christians who have died.

There are many homes up there where my Father lives, and I am going to prepare them for your coming. When everything is ready, then I will come and get you, so that you can always be with me where I am.

Eccl. 12:7. Gen. 2:7. Job 32:8, 9. 2 Cor. 5:6. Phil 1:23. 1 Thess. 4:13, 14. Jn. 14:2, 3.

No one çan kidnap them from me.

I know the one in whom I trust, and I am sure that he
is able to guard safely all that I have given him until
the day of his return. / The Lord will always deliver me
from all evil and will bring me into his heavenly kingdom. / Overwhelming victory is ours through Christ
who loved us enough to die for us. For I am convinced
that nothing can ever separate us from his love. Death
can't, and life can't. The angels won't, and all the
powers of hell itself cannot keep God's love away. Our
fears for today, our worries about tomorrow, or where
we are – high above the sky, or in the deepest ocean –
nothing will ever be able to separate us from the love
of God demonstrated by our Lord Jesus Christ when
he died for us. / Your real life is in heaven with Christ
and God.

God has chosen poor people to be rich in faith, and
the kingdom of heaven is theirs, for that is the gift God
has promised to all those who love him.

May our Lord Jesus Christ himself and God our
Father, who has loved us and given us everlasting
comfort and hope which we don't deserve, comfort
your hearts with all comfort, and help you in every
good thing you say and do.

Jn. 10:29. 2 Tim. 1:12. 2 Tim. 4:18. Rom. 8:37–39. Col. 3:3. Jas. 2:5.
2 Thess. 2:16, 17.

Looking steadily into God's law.

'You will know the truth, and the truth will set you free.' 'But we are descendants of Abraham,' they said, 'and have never been slaves to any man on earth! What do you mean, "set free"?' Jesus replied, 'You are slaves to sin, every one of you. So if the Son sets you free, you will indeed be free.'

So Christ has made us free. Now make sure that you stay free and don't get tied up again in the chains of slavery. For, dear brothers, you have been given freedom: not freedom to do wrong, but freedom to love and serve each other. For the whole Law can be summed up in this one command: 'Love others as you love yourself.' / Now you are free from your old master, sin; and you have become slaves to your new master, righteousness. / Let me illustrate: when a woman marries, the law binds her to her husband as long as he is alive. But if he dies, she is no longer bound to him; the laws of marriage no longer apply to her.

For the power of the life-giving Spirit – and this power is mine through Christ Jesus – has freed me from the vicious circle of sin and death. / I will keep on obeying you forever and forever, free within the limits of your laws.

Jas. 1:25. Jn. 8:32–34, 36. Gal. 5:1, 13, 14. Rom. 6:18. Rom. 7:2. Rom. 8:2. Ps. 119:45.

Don't do anything that will cause criticism against yourself even though you know that what you do is right.

Keep away from every kind of evil. / God knows we are honest, but I want everyone else to know it too. / It is God's will that your good lives should silence those who foolishly condemn the Gospel without knowing what it can do for them, having never experienced its power.

Don't let me hear of your suffering for murdering or stealing or making trouble or being a busy-body and prying into other people's affairs. But it is no shame to suffer for being a Christian. Praise God for the privilege of being in Christ's family and being called by his wonderful name!

For, dear brothers, you have been given freedom: not freedom to do wrong, but freedom to love and serve each other. / The important thing for us as Christians is not what we eat or drink but stirring up goodness and peace and joy from the Holy Spirit. / But be careful . . . that you don't cause some Christian brother to sin whose conscience is weaker than yours. / But if any of you causes one of these little ones who trust in me to lose his faith, it would be better for you to have a rock tied to your neck and be thrown into the sea. / When you refused to help the least of these my brothers you were refusing help to me.

Rom. 14:16. 1Thess. 5:22. 2 Cor. 8:21. 1 Pet. 2:15. 1 Pet. 4:15, 16. Gal. 5:13. Rom. 14:17. 1 Cor. 8:9. Mt. 18:6. Mt. 25:45.

Awake, O sleeper, and rise up from the dead;
and Christ shall give you light.

Wake up, for the coming of the Lord is nearer now
than when we first believed. / So be on your guard,
not asleep like the others. Watch for his return and stay
sober. Night is the time for sleep and the time when
people get drunk. But let us who live in the light
keep sober, protected by the armour of faith and love,
and wearing as our helmet the happy hope of salvation.

Let your light shine for all the nations to see. For the
glory of the Lord is streaming from you. Darkness as
black as night shall cover all the peoples of the earth,
but the glory of the Lord will shine from you.

You can look forward soberly and intelligently to
more of God's kindness to you when Jesus Christ
returns. / Be prepared – all dressed and ready – for
your Lord's return from the wedding feast. Then you
will be ready to open the door and let him in the
moment he arrives and knocks. / God will shed his own
glorious light upon you. He will heal you; your god-
liness will lead you forward, and goodness will be a
shield before you, and the glory of the Lord will protect
you from behind.

Eph. 5:14. Rom. 13:11. 1 Thess. 5:6–8. Is. 60:1, 2. 1 Pet. 1:13.
Lk. 12:35, 36. Is. 58:8.

The Lord himself . . . will live among you!

Fear not, for I am with you. Do not be dismayed. I am your God. I will strengthen you; I will help you; I will uphold you with my victorious right hand. / With this news bring cheer to all discouraged ones. Encourage those who are afraid. Tell them, 'Be strong, fear not, for your God is coming to destroy your enemies. He is coming to save you.' / For the Lord your God has arrived to live among you. He is a mighty Saviour. He will give you victory. He will rejoice over you in great gladness; he will love you and not accuse you. Is that a joyous choir I hear? No, it is the Lord himself exulting over you in happy song. / Don't be impatient. Wait for the Lord, and he will come and save you! Be brave, stout-hearted and courageous. Yes, wait and he will help you.

I heard a loud shout from the throne saying, 'Look, the home of God is now among men, and he will live with them and they will be his people; yes, God himself will be among them. He will wipe away all tears from their eyes, and there shall be no more death, or sorrow, or crying, or pain. All of that has gone forever.'

Zeph. 3:15. Is. 41:10. Is. 35:3, 4. Zeph. 3:17. Ps. 27:14. Rev. 21:3, 4.

Stop praying and get the people moving! Forward, march!

Be courageous and let us act like men to save our people and the cities of our God. And may the Lord do what is best. / We prayed to our God and guarded the city day and night to protect ourselves.

Not all who talk like godly people are godly. They may refer to me as 'Lord', but still won't get to heaven. For the decisive question is whether they obey my Father in heaven. / If any of you really determines to do God's will, then you will certainly know whether my teaching is from God or is merely my own. / Oh, that we might know the Lord! Let us press on to know him, and he will respond to us as surely as the coming of dawn or the rain of early spring.

Keep alert and pray. Otherwise temptation will over-power you. / Keep your eyes open for spiritual danger; stand true to the Lord; act like men; be strong. / Never be lazy in your work but serve the Lord enthusiastically.

With this news bring cheer to all discouraged ones. Encourage those who are afraid. Tell them, 'Be strong, fear not, for your God is coming to destroy your enemies. He is coming to save you.'

Ex. 14:15. 1 Chron. 19:13. Neh. 4:9. Mt. 7:21. Jn. 7:17. Hos. 6:3. Mt. 26:41. 1 Cor. 16:13. Rom. 12:11. Is. 35:3, 4.

Be strong with the strength Christ Jesus gives you.

Filled with his mighty, glorious strength so that you can keep going no matter what happens – always full of the joy of the Lord. / Just as you trusted Christ to save you, trust him, too, for each day's problems; live in vital union with him. Let your roots grow down into him and draw up nourishment from him. See that you go on growing in the Lord, and become strong and vigorous in the truth. Let your lives overflow with joy and thanksgiving for all he has done. / God has planted them like strong and graceful oaks for his own glory. / What a foundation you stand on now: the apostles and the prophets; and the cornerstone of the building is Jesus Christ himself!

And now I entrust you to God and his care and to his wonderful words which are able to build your faith and give you all the inheritance of those who are set apart for himself. / May you always be doing those good, kind things which show that you are a child of God, for this will bring much praise and glory to the Lord.

Fight on for God. / Fearlessly, no matter what your enemies may do.

2 Tim. 2:1. Col. 1:11. Col. 2:6, 7. Is. 61:3. Eph. 2:20. Acts 20:32. Phil. 1:11. 1 Tim. 6:12. Phil. 1:28.

He rewards each one of us according to the work we do for him.

No one can ever lay any other real foundation than that one we already have – Jesus Christ. Every workman who has built on the foundation with the right materials, and whose work still stands, will get his pay. But if the house he has built burns, it will be a great loss to him. He himself will be saved, but like a man escaping through a wall of flames. / We must all stand before Christ to be judged and have our lives laid bare before him. Each of us will receive whatever he deserves for the good or bad things he has done in his earthly body.

When you do a kindness to someone, do it secretly – don't tell your left hand what your right hand is doing. And your Father who knows all secrets will reward you. / There will be glory and honour and peace from God for all who obey him.

Not because . . . . we can do anything of lasting value by ourselves. Our only power and success comes from God. / Lord, grant us peace; for all we have and are has come from you.

Ps. 62:12. 1 Cor. 3:11, 14, 15. 2 Cor. 5:10. Mt. 6:3, 4. Rom. 2:10.
2 Cor. 3:5. Is. 26:12.

Sing of his glorious name! Tell the world how wonderful he is.

I have made Israel for myself, and these my people will some day honour me before the world. / And I will cleanse away all their sins against me, and pardon them. Then this city will be an honour to me, and it will give me joy and be a source of praise and glory to me before all the nations of the earth! The people of the world will see the good I do for my people and will tremble with awe! / With Jesus' help we will continually offer our sacrifice of praise to God by telling others of the glory of his name.

With all my heart I will praise you. I will give glory to your name forever, for you love me so much! You are constantly so kind! You have rescued me from deepest hell. / Who else is like the Lord among the gods? Who is glorious in holiness like him? Who is so awesome in splendour, a wonder-working God? / I will praise God with my singing! My thanks will be his praise. / They were singing the song of Moses, the servant of God, and the song of the Lamb: Great and marvellous are your doings, Lord God Almighty.

Ps. 66:2. Is. 43:21. Jer. 33:8, 9. Hebr. 13:15. Ps. 86:12, 13. Ex. 15:11. Ps 69:30. Rev. 15:3.

*All of us used to be just as they are, our lives
expressing the evil within us.*

Once we, too, were foolish and disobedient; we were
misled by others and became slaves to many evil
pleasures and wicked desires. Our lives were full of
resentment and envy. We hated others and they hated
us. / Don't be surprised at my statement that you must
be born again.

Job replied to God: 'I am nothing – how could I
ever find the answers? I lay my hand upon my mouth in
silence.' / Then the Lord asked Satan, 'Have you
noticed my servant Job? He is the finest man in all the
earth – a good man who fears God and will have
nothing to do with evil.'

I was born a sinner, yes, from the moment my mother
conceived me. / God said, 'David (son of Jesse) is a man
after my own heart, for he will obey me.'

I used to scoff at the name of Christ. I hunted down
his people, harming them in every way I could. But
God had mercy on me.

Men can only reproduce human life, but the Holy
Spirit gives new life from heaven.

*Eph. 2:3. Tit. 3:3. Jn. 3:7. Job 40:3, 4. Job 1:8. Ps. 51:5. Acts 13:22.
1 Tim. 1:13. Jn. 3:6.*

Share each other's troubles and problems, and so obey our Lord's command.

Don't just think about your own affairs, but be interested in others, too, and in what they are doing. Your attitude should be the kind that was shown us by Jesus Christ, who . . . laid aside his mighty power and glory, taking the disguise of a slave. / Even I, the Man from Heaven, am not here to be served, but to help others, and to give my life as a ransom for many. / He died for all so that all who live – having received eternal life from him – might live no longer for themselves, to please themselves, but to spend their lives pleasing Christ who died and rose again for them.

When Jesus saw her weeping and the Jewish leaders wailing with her, he was moved with indignation and deeply troubled. Tears came to Jesus' eyes. / When others are happy, be happy with them. If they are sad, share their sorrow.

You should be like one big happy family, full of sympathy toward each other, loving one another with tender hearts and humble minds.

Gal. 6:2. Phil. 2:4, 5, 7. Mk. 10:45. 2 Cor. 5:15. Jn. 11:33, 35. Rom. 12:15. 1 Pet. 3:8.

*Try hard to live without sinning; and be at peace
with everyone so that he will be pleased with you
when he returns.*

Now we are no longer slaves, but God's own sons.
And since we are his sons, everything he has belongs
to us, for that is the way God planned.

So look upon your old sinful nature as dead and unresponsive to sin, and instead be alive to God, alert to
him, through Jesus Christ our Lord. Do not let sin
control your puny body any longer; do not give in to its
sinful desires. Do not let any part of your bodies
become tools of wickedness, to be used for sinning;
but give yourself completely to God – every part of
you – for you are back from death and you want to be
tools in the hands of God, to be used for his good purposes. / Obey God because you are his children; don't
slip back into your old ways – doing evil because you
knew no better. But be holy now in everything you do,
just as the Lord is holy, who invited you to be his
child. / If you stay away from sin you will be like . . .
purest gold . . . Christ himself can use you for his
highest purposes.

So, my dear brothers, since future victory is sure, be
strong and steady, always abounding in the Lord's
work, for you know that nothing you do for the Lord
is ever wasted.

2 Pet. 3:14. Gal. 4:7. Rom. 6:11–13. 1 Pet. 1:14, 15. 2 Tim. 2:21.
1 Cor. 15:58.

How he loved his disciples!

My plea is not for the world but for those you have
given me because they belong to you. And all of them,
since they are mine, belong to you; and you have given
them back to me with everything else of yours, and
so they are my glory. I'm not asking you to take them
out of the world, but to keep them safe from Satan's
power. They are not part of this world any more than
I am.

I have loved you even as the Father has loved me.
Live within my love. / The greatest love is shown when
a person lays down his life for his friends; and you
are my friends if you obey me. / And so I am giving
a new commandment to you now – love each other
just as much as I love you.

God who began the good work within you will keep
right on helping you grow in his grace until his task
within you is finally finished on that day when Jesus
Christ returns. / The same kind of love . . . as Christ
showed to the church when he died for her, to make her
holy and clean, washed by baptism and God's Word.

Jn. 13:1. Jn. 17:9, 10, 15, 16. Jn. 15:9. Jn. 15:13, 14. Jn. 13:34.
Phil. 1:6. Eph. 5:25, 26.

God's deepest secrets.

I no longer call you slaves, for a master doesn't confide in his slaves; now you are my friends, proved by the fact that I have told you everything the Father told me.

And God has actually given us his Spirit (not the world's spirit) to tell us about the wonderful free gifts of grace and blessing that God has given us.

When I think of the wisdom and scope of his plan I fall down on my knees and pray to the Father of all the great family of God – some of them already in heaven and some down here on earth – that out of his glorious, unlimited resources he will give you the mighty inner strengthening of his Holy Spirit. And I pray that Christ will be more and more at home in your hearts, living within you as you trust in him. May your roots go down deep into the soil of God's marvellous love; and may you be able to feel and understand, as all God's children should, how long, how wide, how deep, and how high his love really is; and to experience this love for yourselves, though it is so great that you will never see the end of it or fully know or understand it. And so at last you will be filled up with God himself.

1 Cor. 2:10. Jn. 15:15. 1 Cor. 2:12. Eph. 3:14–19.

Revive us to trust in you.

Only the Holy Spirit gives eternal life. / And in the same way – by our faith – the Holy Spirit helps us with our daily problems and in our praying. For we don't even know what we should pray for, nor how to pray as we should; but the Holy Spirit prays for us with such feeling that it cannot be expressed in words. And the Father who knows all hearts knows, of course, what the Spirit is saying as he pleads for us in harmony with God's own will. / Pray all the time. Ask God for anything in line with the Holy Spirit's wishes. Plead with him, reminding him of your needs.

I will never lay aside your laws, for you have used them to restore my joy and health. / I have told you how to get this true spiritual life. / The old way, trying to be saved by keeping the Ten Commandments, ends in death; in the new way, the Holy Spirit gives them life. / But if you stay in me and obey my commands, you may ask any request you like, and it will be granted. / And we are sure of this, that he will listen to us whenever we ask him for anything in line with his will.

Ps. 80:18. Jn. 6:63. Rom. 8:26, 27. Eph. 6:18. Ps. 119:93. Jn. 6:63. 2 Cor. 3:6. Jn. 15:7. 1 Jn. 5:14.

*Take no part in the worthless pleasures of evil
and darkness, but instead, rebuke and expose them.*

What a terrible thing it is that you are boasting about
your purity, and yet you let this sort of thing go on.
Don't you realize that if even one person is allowed
to go on sinning, soon all will be affected? Remove
this evil cancer – this wicked person – from among
you, so that you can stay pure. Christ, God's Lamb,
has been slain for us. When I wrote to you before I
told you not to mix with evil people. But when I said
that I wasn't talking about unbelievers who live in
sexual sin, or are greedy cheats and thieves and idol
worshippers. For you can't live in this world without
being with people like that. What I meant was that you
are not to keep company with anyone who claims to
be a brother Christian but indulges in sexual sins, or is
greedy, or is a swindler, or worships idols, or is a
drunkard, or abusive. Don't even eat a meal with such
a person.

   That no one can speak a word of blame against you.
You are to live clean, innocent lives as children of
God in a dark world full of people who are crooked
and stubborn. Shine out among them like beacon
lights.

Eph. 5:11. 1 Cor. 5:6, 7, 9–11. Phil. 2:15.

*Let us come boldly to the very throne of God and
stay there to receive his mercy and to find grace
to help us in our times of need.*

Don't worry about anything; instead, pray about
everything; tell God your needs and don't forget to
thank him for his answers. If you do this you will
experience God's peace, which is far more wonderful
than the human mind can understand. His peace will
keep your thoughts and your hearts quiet and at rest
as you trust in Christ Jesus. / And so we should not
be like cringing, fearful slaves, but we should behave
like God's very own children, adopted into the bosom
of his family, and calling to him, 'Father, Father.'

You can ask him for anything, using my name, and
I will do it. / And so, dear brothers, now we may walk
right into the very Holy of Holies where God is, because
of the blood of Jesus. Let us go right in, to God himself, with true hearts fully trusting him to receive us,
because we have been sprinkled with Christ's blood to
make us clean, and because our bodies have been
washed with pure water. / That is why we can say without any doubt or fear, 'The Lord is my helper and
I am not afraid of anything that mere man can do to
me.'

Hebr. 4:16. Phil. 4:6, 7. Rom. 8:15. Jn. 14:14. Hebr. 10:19, 22. Hebr. 13:6.

You will know the truth, and the truth will set you free.

The Lord is the Spirit who gives them life, and where he is there is freedom. / For the power of the life-giving Spirit – and this power is mine through Christ Jesus – has freed me from the vicious circle of sin and death. / So if the Son sets you free, you will indeed be free.

Dear brothers, we are not slave children, under obligation to the Jewish laws, but children of the free woman, acceptable to God because of our faith. / And yet we Jewish Christians know very well that we cannot become right with God by obeying our Jewish laws, but only by faith in Jesus Christ to take away our sins. And so we, too, have trusted Jesus Christ, that we might be accepted by God because of faith – and not because we have obeyed the Jewish laws. For no one will ever be saved by obeying them.

But if anyone keeps looking steadily into God's law for free men, he will not only remember it but he will do what it says, and God will greatly bless him in every-thing he does. / So Christ has made us free. Now make sure that you stay free and don't get tied up again in the chains of slavery.

Jn. 8:32. 2 Cor. 3:17. Rom. 8:2. Jn. 8:36. Gal. 4:31. Gal. 2:16. Jas. 1:25. Gal. 5:1.

When darkness overtakes him, light will come bursting in.

Who among you fears the Lord and obeys his Servant? If such men walk in darkness, without one ray of light, let them trust the Lord, let them rely upon their God. / If they fall it isn't fatal, for the Lord holds them with his hand. / Their advice is a beam of light directed into the dark corners of your mind to warn you of danger and give you a good life.

Do not rejoice against me, O my enemy, for though I fall, I will rise again! When I sit in darkness, the Lord himself will be my Light. I will be patient while the Lord punishes me, for I have sinned against him; then he will defend me from my enemies, and punish them for all the evil they have done to me. God will bring me out of my darkness into the light, and I will see his goodness.

If your eye is pure, there will be sunshine in your soul. But if your eye is clouded with evil thoughts and desires, you are in deep spiritual darkness. And oh, how deep that darkness can be!

Ps. 112:4. Is. 50:10. Ps. 37:24. Prov. 6:23. Mic. 7:8, 9. Mt. 6:22, 23.

He will feed his flock like a shepherd; he will carry the lambs in his arms and gently lead the ewes with young.

Then Jesus called his disciples to him and said, 'I pity these people – they've been here with me for three days now, and have nothing left to eat; I don't want to send them away hungry or they will faint along the road.' / This high priest of ours understands our weaknesses.

Once when some mothers were bringing their children to Jesus . . . he took the children into his arms and placed his hands on their heads and he blessed them.

I have wandered away like a lost sheep; come and find me. / I, the Son of Mankind, have come to search for and to save such people. / Like sheep you wandered away from God, but now you have returned to your Shepherd, the Guardian of your souls who keeps you safe from all attacks.

Don't be afraid, little flock. For it gives your Father great happiness to give you the Kingdom. / I myself will be the Shepherd of my sheep, and cause them to lie down in peace, the Lord God says.

Is. 40:11. Mt. 15:32. Hebr. 4:15. Mk. 10:13, 16. Ps. 119:176. Lk. 19:10.
1 Pet. 2:25. Lk. 12:32. Ezk. 34:15.

Long ago, even before he made the world, God chose us to be his very own.

He decided then to make us holy in his eyes, without a single fault – we who stand before him covered with his love.

God chose from the very first to give you salvation, cleansing you by the work of the Holy Spirit and by your trusting in the truth. Through us he told you the Good News. Through us he called you to share in the glory of our Lord Jesus Christ. / For from the very beginning God decided that those who came to him – and all along he knew who would – should become like his Son, so that his Son would be the firstborn, with many brothers. And having chosen us, he called us to come to him; and when we came, he declared us 'not guilty,' filled us with Christ's goodness, gave us a right standing with himself, and promised us his glory. / God the Father chose you long ago and knew you would become his children. And the Holy Spirit has been at work in your hearts, cleansing you with the blood of Jesus Christ and enabling you to please him.

And I will give you a new heart – I will give you new and right desires – and put a new spirit within you. I will take out your stony hearts of sin and give you new hearts of love.

Eph. 1:4. Eph. 1:4. 2 Thess. 2:13, 14. Rom. 8:29, 30. 1 Pet. 1:2. Ezk. 36:26.

That couldn't happen if the Lord made windows in the sky!

Have faith in God. / You can never please God without faith. / With God, everything is possible.

Was I too weak to save you? Is that why the house is silent and empty when I come home? Have I no longer power to deliver?

This plan of mine is not what you would work out, neither are my thoughts the same as yours! For just as the heavens are higher than the earth, so are my ways higher than yours, and my thoughts than yours. / I will open up the windows of heaven for you and pour out a blessing so great you won't have room enough to take it in!

The Lord isn't too weak to save you. And he isn't getting deaf! He can hear you when you call! / 'O Lord,' he cried out to God, 'no one else can help us! Here we are, powerless against this mighty army. Oh, help us, Lord our God! For we trust in you alone to rescue us.'

We felt we were doomed to die and saw how powerless we were to help ourselves; but that was good, for then we put everything into the hands of God, who alone could save us, for he can even raise the dead.

2 Kgs. 7:2. Mk. 11:22. Hebr. 11:6. Mt. 19:26. Is. 50:2. Is. 55:8, 9. Mal. 3:10. Is. 59:1. 2 Chron. 14:11. 2 Cor. 1:9.

Your days of mourning all will end.

Here on earth you will have many trials and sorrows. /
For we know that even the things of nature, like
animals and plants, suffer in sickness and death as they
await this great event. And even we Christians, although we have the Holy Spirit within us as a foretaste
of future glory, also groan to be released from pain
and suffering. We, too, wait anxiously for that day
when God will give us our full rights as his children,
including the new bodies he has promised us – bodies
that will never be sick and will never die. / These
earthly bodies make us groan and sigh.

'These are the ones coming out of the great tribulation,' he said; 'they washed their robes and whitened
them by the blood of the Lamb. That is why they are
here before the throne of God, serving him day and
night in his temple. The one sitting on the throne will
shelter them; they will never be hungry again, nor
thirsty, and they will be fully protected from the
scorching noontime heat. For the Lamb standing in
front of the throne will feed them and be their Shepherd
and lead them to the springs of the water of life. And
God will wipe their tears away.'

Is. 60:20. Jn. 16:33. Rom. 8:22, 23. 2 Cor. 5:4. Rev. 7:14–17.

*Master, don't you even care that we are all about
to drown?*

He is good to everyone, and his compassion is intertwined with everything he does.

'All wild animals and birds and fish will be afraid of
you,' God told him; 'for I have placed them in your
power, and they are yours to use for food, in addition
to grain and vegetables.' / As long as the earth remains,
there will be spring-time and harvest, cold and heat,
winter and summer, day and night.

The Lord is good. When trouble comes, he is the
place to go! And he knows everyone who trusts in
him! / Then God answered the lad's cries, and the
Angel of God called to Hagar from the sky, 'Hagar,
what's wrong? Don't be afraid! For God has heard
the lad's cries as he is lying there.' Then God opened
her eyes and she saw a well; so she refilled the container
and gave the lad a drink.

So don't worry at all about having enough food and
clothing. Why be like the heathen? For they take pride
in all these things and are deeply concerned about them.
But your heavenly Father already knows perfectly well
that you need them. / Trust . . . in the living God who
always richly gives us all we need for our enjoyment.

*Mk. 4:38. Ps. 145:9. Gen. 9:2, 3. Gen. 8:22. Nah. 1:7. Gen. 21:17, 19.
Mt. 6:31, 32. 1 Tim. 6:17.*

Your strong faith.

This is the will of God, that you believe in the one he has sent.

Faith that doesn't show itself by good works is no faith at all – it is dead and useless. / All we need is faith working through love. / If he sows to please his own wrong desires, he will be planting seeds of evil and he will surely reap a harvest of spiritual decay and death; but if he plants the good things of the Spirit, he will reap the everlasting life which the Holy Spirit gives him. / It is God himself who has made us what we are and given us new lives from Christ Jesus; and long ages ago he planned that we should spend these lives in helping others. / He died under God's judgment against our sins, so that he could rescue us from constant falling into sin and make us his very own people, with cleansed hearts and real enthusiasm for doing kind things for others.

God will make you the kind of children he wants to have – will make you as good as you wish you could be! – rewarding your faith with his power. / God is at work within you, helping you to want to obey him, and then helping you to do what he wants.

1 Thess. 1:3. Jn. 6:29. Jas. 2:17. Gal. 5:6. Gal. 6:8. Eph. 2:10. Tit. 2:14. 2 Thess. 1:11. Phil. 2:13.

Jesus promised to come back, did he? Then where is he?

See, the Lord is coming with millions of his holy ones. He will bring the people of the world before him in judgment, to receive just punishment . . . revealing all they have said against him. / See! He is arriving, surrounded by clouds; and every eye will see him – yes, and those who pierced him. And the nations will weep in sorrow and in terror when he comes.

For the Lord himself will come down from heaven with a mighty shout and with the soul-stirring cry of the archangel and the great trumpet-call of God. And the Christians who are dead will be the first to rise to meet the Lord. Then we who are still alive and remain on the earth will be caught up with them in the clouds to meet the Lord in the air and remain with him for-ever.

For the free gift of eternal salvation is now being offered to everyone; and along with this gift comes the realization that God wants us to turn from godless living and sinful pleasures and to live good, God-fearing lives day after day, looking forward to that time when his glory shall be seen – the glory of our great God and Saviour Jesus Christ.

2 Pet. 3:4. Jude 14, 15. Rev. 1:7. 1 Thess. 4:16, 17. Tit. 2:11–13.

Surrender and beg for peace and my protection.

I know the plans I have for you, says the Lord. They are plans for good and not for evil. / There is no peace, says the Lord, for the wicked.

Now you belong to Christ Jesus, and though you once were far away from God, now you have been brought very near to him because of what Jesus Christ has done for you with his blood. For Christ himself is our way of peace.

God wanted all of himself to be in his Son. It was through what his Son did that God cleared a path for everything to come to him – all things in heaven and on earth – for Christ's death on the cross has made peace with God for all by his blood. / God sent Christ Jesus to take the punishment for our sins and to end all God's anger against us. He used Christ's blood and our faith as the means of saving us from his wrath. / If we confess our sins to him, he can be depended on to forgive us and to cleanse us from every wrong.

Trust in the Lord God always, for in the Lord Jehovah is your everlasting strength.

Is. 27:5. Jer. 29:11. Is. 48:22. Eph. 2:13, 14. Col. 1:19, 20. Rom. 3:25, 26. 1 Jn. 1:9. Is. 26:4.

What is it that God has said? That he has given us eternal life, and that this life is in his Son.

The Father has life in himself, and has granted his Son to have life in himself. He will even raise from the dead anyone he wants to, just as the Father does.

I am the one who raises the dead and gives them life again. Anyone who believes in me, even though he dies like anyone else, shall live again. He is given eternal life for believing in me and shall never perish. / I am the Good Shepherd. The Good Shepherd lays down his life for the sheep. The Father loves me because I lay down my life that I may have it back again. No one can kill me without my consent – I lay down my life voluntarily. For I have the right and power to lay it down when I want to and also the right and power to take it again. For the Father has given me this right. / I am the Way – yes, and the Truth and the Life. No one can get to the Father except by means of me. / So whoever has God's Son has life; whoever does not have his Son, does not have life. / You should have as little real desire for this world as a dead person does. Your real life is in heaven with Christ and God. And when Christ who is our real life comes back again, you will shine with him and share in all his glories.

1 Jn. 5:11. Jn. 5:26, 21. Jn. 11:25, 26. Jn. 10:11, 17, 18. Jn. 14:6. 1 Jn. 5:12. Col. 3:3, 4.

*Your old sinful nature . . . if you keep on following
it you are lost and will perish, but if through the
power of the Holy Spirit you crush it and its evil
deeds, you shall live.*

When you follow your own wrong inclinations your
lives will produce these evil results: impure thoughts,
eagerness for lustful pleasure, idolatry, spiritism . . .
hatred and fighting, jealousy and anger . . . and all that
sort of thing. Let me tell you again as I have before,
that anyone living that sort of life will not inherit the
kingdom of God. But when the Holy Spirit controls
our lives he will produce this kind of fruit in us: love,
joy, peace, patience, kindness, goodness, faithfulness,
gentleness, and self-control. Those who belong to
Christ have nailed their natural evil desires to his cross
and crucified them there.

The free gift of eternal salvation is now being offered
to everyone; and along with this gift comes the realization that God wants us to turn from godless living
and sinful pleasures and to live good, God-fearing lives
day after day, looking forward to that time when his
glory shall be seen – the glory of our great God and
Saviour Jesus Christ.

Rom. 8:12, 13. Gal. 5:19–24. Tit. 2:11–13.

The Philistine commanders demanded, 'What are these Israelis doing here?'

Be happy if you are cursed and insulted for being a Christian, for when that happens the Spirit of God will come upon you with great glory.

Don't do anything that will cause criticism against yourself even though you know that what you do is right. / Be careful how you behave among your unbelieving neighbours; for then, even if they are suspicious of you and talk against you, they will end up praising God for your good works when Christ returns.

Don't enter into partnership with those who do not love the Lord, for what do the people of God have in common with the people of sin? How can light live with darkness? And what union can there be between God's temple and idols? For you are God's temple, the home of the living God, and God has said of you, 'I will live in them and walk among them, and I will be their God and they shall be my people.'

You have been chosen by God himself . . . that you may show to others how God called you out of the darkness into his wonderful light.

1 Sam. 29:3. 1 Pet. 4:14. Rom. 14:16. 1 Pet. 2:12. 2 Cor. 6:14, 16. 1 Pet. 2:9.

*The time came for the kindness and love of God
our Saviour to appear.*

I have loved you, O my people, with an everlasting
love.

God showed how much he loved us by sending his
only Son into this wicked world to bring to us eternal
life through his death. In this act we see what real
love is: it is not our love for God, but his love for us
when he sent his Son to satisfy God's anger against
our sins.

But when the right time came, the time God decided
on, he sent his Son, born of a woman, born as a Jew,
to buy freedom for us who were slaves to the law so
that he could adopt us as his very own sons. / And
Christ took our human nature and lived here on earth
among us and was full of loving forgiveness and truth.
And some of us have seen his glory – the glory of the
only Son of the heavenly Father! / It is quite true that
the way to live a godly life is not an easy matter. But
the answer lies in Christ, who came to earth as a man,
was proved spotless and pure in his spirit.

Since we, God's children, are human beings – made
of flesh and blood – he became flesh and blood too by
being born in human form; for only as a human being
could he die and in dying break the power of the devil
who had the power of death.

*Tit. 3:4. Jer. 31:3. 1 Jn. 4:9, 10. Gal. 4:4, 5. Jn. 1:14. 1 Tim. 3:16.
Hebr. 2:14.*

Thank God for his Son – his gift too wonderful for words.

Shout with joy before the Lord, O earth! Obey him gladly; come before him, singing with joy. Go through his open gates with great thanksgiving; enter his courts with praise. Give thanks to him and bless his name. / For unto us a Child is born; unto us a Son is given; and the government shall be upon his shoulder. These will be his royal titles: Wonderful, Counsellor, The Mighty God, The Everlasting Father, The Prince of Peace.

God loved the world so much. / He did not spare even his own Son for us but gave him up for us all. / There was only one left – his only son. He finally sent him. / Anyone who believes in him shall . . . have eternal life. / He has given you the whole world to use, and life and even death are your servants. He has given you all of the present and all of the future. All are yours, and you belong to Christ, and Christ is God's.

Oh, that these men would praise the Lord for his lovingkindness and for all of his wonderful deeds! / I bless the holy name of God with all my heart.

Oh, how I praise the Lord. How I rejoice in God my Saviour!

2 Cor. 9:15. Ps. 100:1, 2, 4. Is. 9:6. Jn. 3:16. Rom. 8:32. Mk. 12:6. Jn. 3:16. 1 Cor. 3:22, 23. Ps. 107:21. Ps. 103:1. Lk. 1:46, 47.

*Be strong and steady, always abounding in the
Lord's work.*

You know that nothing you do for the Lord is ever
wasted. / Just as you trusted Christ to save you, trust
him, too, for each day's problems; live in vital union
with him. Let your roots grow down into him and draw
up nourishment from him. See that you go on growing
in the Lord, and become strong and vigorous in the
truth you were taught. Let your lives overflow with joy
and thanksgiving for all he has done. / Those enduring
to the end shall be saved.

Your faith . . . it is strong.

All of us must quickly carry out the tasks assigned
us by the one who sent me, for there is little time left
before the night falls and all work comes to an end.

If he sows to please his own wrong desires, he will be
planting seeds of evil and he will surely reap a harvest
of spiritual decay and death; but if he plants the good
things of the Spirit, he will reap the everlasting life
which the Holy Spirit gives him. And let us not get tired
of doing what is right, for after a while we will reap a
harvest of blessing if we don't get discouraged and give
up.

*1 Cor. 15 :58. 1 Cor. 15:58. Col. 2:6, 7. Mt. 24:13. 2 Cor. 1:24.
Jn. 9:4. Gal. 6:8, 9.*

He is able to save completely all who come to God through him.

I am the Way – yes, and the Truth and the Life. No one can get to the Father except by means of me. / There is salvation in no one else! Under all heaven there is no other name for men to call upon to save them.

My sheep recognize my voice, and I know them, and they follow me. I give them eternal life and they shall never perish. No one shall snatch them away from me, for my Father has given them to me, and he is more powerful than anyone else, so no one can kidnap them from me. / God who began the good work within you will keep right on helping you grow in his grace until his task within you is finally finished on that day when Jesus Christ returns. / Is anything too hard for God?

And now – all glory to him who alone is God, who saves us through Jesus Christ our Lord; yes, splendour and majesty, all power and authority are his from the beginning; his they are and his they evermore shall be. And he is able to keep you from slipping and falling away, and to bring you, sinless and perfect, into his glorious presence with mighty shouts of everlasting joy. Amen.

Hebr. 7:25. Jn. 14:6. Acts 4:12. Jn. 10:27, 28. Phil. 1:6. Gen. 18:14. Jude 24, 25.

*We do not look at what we can see at this moment,
the troubles all around us.*

But we look forward to the joys in heaven which we
have not yet seen. The troubles will soon be over, but
the joys to come will last for ever. / This world is not
our home. / Better things . . . awaiting you in heaven,
things that would be yours forever.

Don't be afraid, little flock. For it gives your Father
great happiness to give you the Kingdom.

There is wonderful joy ahead, even though the going
is rough for a while down here. / No mere man has
ever seen, heard or even imagined what wonderful
things God has ready for those who love the Lord.

These earthly bodies make us groan and sigh. / He
will wipe away all tears from their eyes, and there shall
be no more death, or sorrow, or crying, or pain. All of
that has gone for ever.

What we suffer now is nothing compared to the glory
he will give us later. / These troubles and sufferings
of ours are, after all, quite small and won't last
very long. Yet this short time of distress will result
in God's richest blessing upon us for ever and ever!

*2 Cor. 4:18. Hebr. 13:14. Hebr. 10:34. Lk. 12:32. 1 Pet. 1:6. 1 Cor. 2:9.
2 Cor. 5:4. Rev. 21:4. Rom. 8:18. 2 Cor. 4:17.*

Christ himself is our way of peace.

For God was in Christ, restoring the world to himself,
no longer counting men's sins against them but blotting
them out. This is the wonderful message he has given
us to tell others. For God took the sinless Christ and
poured into him our sins. Then, in exchange, he poured
God's goodness into us! / It was through what his Son
did that God cleared a path for everything to come to
him – all things in heaven and on earth – for Christ's
death on the cross has made peace with God for all by
his blood. And now as a result Christ has brought you
into the very presence of God, and you are standing
there before him with nothing left against you –
nothing left that he could even chide you for. / He forgave all your sins, and blotted out the charges proved
against you, the list of his commandments which you
had not obeyed. He took this list of sins and destroyed
it by nailing it to Christ's cross.

I am leaving you with a gift – peace of mind and
heart! And the peace I give isn't fragile like the peace
the world gives. So don't be troubled or afraid.

Eph. 2:14. 2 Cor. 5:19, 21. Col. 1:20, 22. Col. 2:13, 14. Jn. 14:27.

Your sins are forgiven!

I will forgive and forget their sins. / Only God can forgive sins.

I, yes, I alone am he who blots away your sins for my own sake and will never think of them again. / What happiness for those whose guilt has been forgiven! What joys when sins are covered over! What relief for those who have confessed their sins and God has cleared their record. / Where is another God like you, who pardons the sins of the survivors among his people?

God has forgiven you because you belong to Christ. / The blood of Jesus his Son cleanses us from every sin. If we say that we have no sin, we are only fooling ourselves, and refusing to accept the truth. But if we confess ours sins to him, he can be depended on to forgive us and to cleanse us from every wrong.

He has removed our sins as far away from us as the east is from the west. / Sin need never again be your master, for now you are no longer tied to the law where sin enslaves you, but you are free under God's favour and mercy.

Mk. 2:5. Jer. 31:34. Mk. 2:7. Is. 43:25. Ps. 32:1, 2. Mic. 7:18. Eph. 4:32. 1 Jn. 1:7–9. Ps. 103:12. Rom. 6:14.

We want to meet Jesus.

O Lord, we love to do your will! Our hearts' desire is to glorify your name.

He is close to all who call on him sincerely.

For where two or three gather together because they are mine, I will be there among them. / I will not abandon you or leave you as orphans – I will come to you. / I am with you always, even to the end of the world.

Let us run with patience the particular race that God has set before us. Keep your eyes on Jesus, our leader and instructor.

We can see and understand only a little about God now, as if we were peering at his reflection in a poor mirror; but some day we are going to see him in his completeness, face to face. / I long to go and be with Christ. How much happier for *me* than being here!

Yes, dear friends, we are already God's children, right now, and we can't even imagine what it is going to be like later on. But we do know this, that when he comes we will be like him, as a result of seeing him as he really is.

Jn. 12:21. Is. 26:8. Ps. 145:18. Mt. 18:20. Jn. 14:18. Mt. 28:20.
Hebr. 12:1, 2. 1 Cor. 13:12. Phil. 1:23. 1 Jn. 3:2, 3.

Try to find out and do whatever the Lord wants you to.

God wants you to be holy and pure. / Stop quarrelling with God! Agree with him and you will have peace at last! His favour will surround you if you will only admit that you were wrong. / And this is the way to have eternal life – by knowing you, the only true God, and Jesus Christ, the one you sent to earth. / And we know that Christ, God's Son, has come to help us understand and find the true God. And now we are in God because we are in Jesus Christ his Son, who is the only true God; and he is eternal life.

Ever since we first heard about you we have kept on praying and asking God to help you understand what he wants you to do; asking him to make you wise about spiritual things. / God, the glorious Father of our Lord Jesus Christ . . . give you wisdom to see clearly and really understand who Christ is and all that he has done for you. I pray that your hearts will be flooded with light so that you can see something of the future he has called you to share. I want you to realize that God has been made rich because we who are Christ's have been given to him! I pray that you will begin to understand how incredibly great his power is to help those who believe him.

Eph. 5:17. 1 Thess. 4:3. Job 22:21. Jn. 17:3. 1 Jn. 5:20. Col. 1:9. Eph. 1:17–19.

When you draw close to God, God will draw close to you.

Enoch . . . lived . . . in fellowship with God. / How can we walk together with your sins between us? / But as for me, I get as close to him as I can! I have chosen him and I will tell everyone about the wonderful ways he rescues me.

The Lord will stay with you as long as you stay with him! Whenever you look for him, you will find him. But if you forsake him, he will forsake you. Whenever they have turned again to the Lord God of Israel in their distress, and searched for him, he has helped them.

I know the plans I have for you, says the Lord. They are plans for good and not for evil, to give you a future and a hope. In those days when you pray, I will listen. You will find me when you seek me, if you look for me in earnest.

Now we may walk right into the very Holy of Holies where God is, because of the blood of Jesus. This is the fresh, new, life-giving way which Christ has opened up for us by tearing the curtain – his human body – to let us into the holy presence of God. And since this great high priest of ours rules over God's household, let us go right in, to God himself, with true hearts fully trusting him to receive us.

Jas. 4:8. Gen. 5:24. Amos 3:3. Ps. 73:28. 2 Chron. 15:2, 4. Jer. 29:11–13. Hebr. 10:19–22.

Free from all sin and guilt on that day when he returns.

You who were once so far away from God . . . were his enemies and hated him and were separated from him by your evil thoughts and actions, yet now he has brought you back as his friends. He has done this through the death on the cross of his own human body, and now as a result Christ has brought you into the very presence of God, and you are standing there before him with nothing left against you – nothing left that he could even chide you for. The only condition is that you fully believe the Truth, standing in it steadfast and firm, strong in the Lord, convinced of the Good News that Jesus died for you, and never shifting from trusting him to save you. / Live clean, innocent lives as children of God in a dark world full of people who are crooked and stubborn. Shine out among them like beacon lights.

And now – all glory to him who alone is God, who saves us through Jesus Christ our Lord; yes, splendour and majesty, all power and authority are his from the beginning; his they are and his they evermore shall be. And he is able to keep you from slipping and falling away, and to bring you, sinless and perfect, into his glorious presence with mighty shouts of everlasting joy. Amen.

1 Cor. 1:8. Col. 1:21–23. Phil. 2:15. Jude 24, 25.

He will protect his godly ones.

If we say we are his friends, but go on living in spiritual darkness and sin, we are lying. But if we are living in the light of God's presence, just as Christ is, then we have wonderful fellowship and joy with each other, and the blood of Jesus his Son cleanses us from every sin. / Let us strip off anything that slows us down or holds us back, and especially those sins that wrap themselves so tightly around our feet and trip us up.

I would have you learn this great fact: that a life of doing right is the wisest life there is. If you live that kind of life, you'll not limp or stumble as you run. Don't do as the wicked do. Avoid their haunts – turn away, go somewhere else. Look straight ahead; don't even turn your head to look. Watch your step. Stick to the path and be safe. Don't sidetrack; pull back your foot from danger.

The Lord will always deliver me from all evil and will bring me into his heavenly kingdom. To God be the glory for ever and ever. Amen.

1 Sam. 2:9. 1 Jn. 1:6, 7. Hebr. 12:1. Prov. 4:11, 12, 14, 15, 25–27. 2 Tim. 4:18.

You know how he has cared for you again and again here in the wilderness, just as a father cares for his child!

I brought you to myself as though on eagle's wings. / In his love and pity he redeemed them and lifted them up and carried them through all the years. / He spreads his wings over them, even as an eagle covers her young. She carries them upon her wings – as does the Lord his people!

I will be your God through all your lifetime, yes, even when your hair is white with age. I made you and I will care for you. I will carry you along and be your Saviour. / For this great God is our God forever and ever. He will be our guide until we die. / I have been young and now I am old. And in all my years I have never seen the Lord forsake a man who loves him; nor have I seen the children of the godly go hungry.

Give your burdens to the Lord. He will carry them. He will not permit the godly to slip or fall. / Don't worry about *things* – food, drink, money, and clothes. Your heavenly Father already knows perfectly well that you need them.

The Lord has certainly helped us!

Deut. 1:31. Ex. 19:4. Is. 63:9. Deut. 32:11, 12. Is. 46:4. Ps. 48:14. Ps. 37:25. Ps. 55:22. Mt. 6:25, 32. 1 Sam. 7:12.

There are still many nations to be conquered.

I haven't learned all I should even yet, but I keep working towards that day when I will finally be all that Christ saved me for and wants me to be.

You are to be perfect, even as your Father in heaven is perfect. / You need more than faith; you must also work hard to be good, and even that is not enough. For then you must learn to know God better and discover what he wants you to do. Next, learn to put aside your own desires so that you will become patient and godly, gladly letting God have his way with you. This will make possible the next step, which is for you to enjoy other people and to like them, and finally you will grow to love them deeply.

My prayer for you is that you will overflow more and more with love for others, and at the same time keep on growing in spiritual knowledge and insight.

No mere man has ever seen, heard or even imagined what wonderful things God has ready for those who love the Lord.

There is a full complete rest *still waiting* for the people of God. / Your eyes will see the King in his beauty, and the highlands of heaven far away.

Josh. 13:1. Phil. 3:12. Mt. 5:48. 2 Pet. 1:5–7. Phil. 1:9. 1 Cor. 2:9. Hebr. 4:9. Is. 33:17.